From Plan to Market

Transitions: Asia and Asian America

Series Editor, *Mark Selden*

From Plan to Market

The Economic Transition in Vietnam

Adam Fforde and
Stefan de Vylder

WestviewPress

A Division of HarperCollins*Publishers*

Transitions: Asia and Asian America

Copyright © 1996 by Westview Press, Inc., A Division of HarperCollins Publishers, Inc.

Published in 1996 in the United States of America by Westview Press, Inc., 5500 Central Avenue,
Boulder, Colorado 80301-2877, and in the United Kingdom by Westview Press, 12 Hid's Copse
Road, Cumnor Hill, Oxford OX2 9JJ

A CIP catalog record for this book is available from the Library of Congress.
ISBN 0-8133-2684-2 (HC) — 0-8133-2683-4 (PB)

The paper used in this publication meets the requirements of the American National Standard for
Permanence of Paper for Printed Library Materials Z39.48-1984.

10   9   8   7   6   5   4   3   2   1

Contents

Preface

Vietnamese history since national reunification in 1975-1976 has an air of high drama, and deservedly so, in our opinion. After decades of war and struggle, Vietnam set off along a path that was to encompass neo-Stalinism and economic failure. This failure meant that Vietnam "lost" some fifteen years in its attempt to catch up with the rapidly growing countries of East Asia. The relatively egalitarian income distribution and rather advanced welfare services of the traditional development model mitigated, but could not compensate for, the lack of dynamic accumulation. Widespread hunger and poverty therefore continued. During these years, the Vietnamese people also endured the social consequences of neo-Stalinism, through which they were isolated from the outside world and had their freedoms greatly curtailed. During the decade after 1975, Vietnam thus endured a second tragedy to follow the sorrows of war. For this, the political leadership, as in any country, must bear much of the blame, and in this regard reference will inevitably be made to the wartime party leader, Le Duan, who remained in power until he died in 1986.

Yet if this was Act One, then Act Two was rather different. There was little apparent conscious intent to reform the system into extinction, when change started in the very late 1970s, and it created a sufficient head of political and economic steam for national political leaders in 1985-86 to herald the introduction of *doi moi*, the Vietnamese slogan for "reform." By 1989, we argue, Vietnam possessed the essential characteristics of a market economy, and by 1994-95 sharp increases in savings supported by large inflows of FDI (foreign direct investment) were financing GDP (gross domestic product) growth rates near 8-10 percent annually. The chronic hunger that had faced the Vietnamese living in the high population density regions of the North and North-center had eased and seemed set to ease further. However, wide income gaps, corruption, and "social ills" also accompanied the shift to a market economy. Under Party General Secretary Nguyen Van Linh (1986-1992), Vietnam enjoyed de-Stalinization, followed by a partial reversal as the party rejected political pluralism. However, by the mid-1990s the high level of tension that had marked

Vietnamese society until around 1992-93 had disappeared, and families appeared to feel that on the whole they faced a positive future. This was Act Two of the postwar history of Vietnam. The Communist Party remained in power, and as in many countries, the government gained credit from the social and economic successes. Time will tell, as always, what Act Three is to bring.

This book is an economic analysis of the transition from plan to market in Vietnam and it draws upon a number of different sources. It is a substantial rewrite of an earlier work (de Vylder and Fforde 1988), which was based on fieldwork in 1987 and on a program of research dating back to the middle of the 1970s (Fforde 1982, 1983, 1989a; Fforde and Paine 1987). Between 1988 and 1995, both authors have regularly visited Vietnam and have been involved in policy discussions with Vietnamese researchers and government officials. One of the authors (Fforde) was resident in the country during most of the period 1988-92. The other (de Vylder) possesses enormous comparative experience of the problems facing Third World countries that attempt to build what they understand to be socialist societies. These experiences provide a basis for attempting to analyze the 1979-94 period in the Socialist Republic of Vietnam. The authors have stressed from very early on in their work the largely spontaneous and "bottom-up" nature of social and economic change in Vietnam, thus taking a revisionist position compared with some other writers.[1]

Writing in the early 1990s about such a recent historical period is risky. Many of the events we look at will be studied in greater detail both by ourselves and others, and errors will no doubt be found. We therefore stress the analytical aspects of this study: the attempt to lay out a framework for examining the transition, its internal logic, and the essential nature of "policy," the perennial focus of social science. We see official policy, however, not as the main active factor in the equation but more as a passive respondent to changes effected by other elements in Vietnam. To support this view, we present a quasi-theoretical analysis of Vietnamese reality. Our analysis has a strongly economic character, for we believe that the social changes that took place in Vietnam over the period predominantly had to do with the economic aspects of the society.

Through 1990-92 we were at times visiting fellows at the Stockholm School of Economics (de Vylder, 1989-93, and Fforde, 1991) and the Australian National University (Fforde, 1990 and 1993 to the present). This exposed us to the New Institutional school of thinking and also permitted a rethinking of the political economy of reform. Early results can be found in Fforde (1990b, 1992, 1993). In general, we base our work on a combination of a wide range of contacts with Vietnamese at many levels and the use of officially available texts. However, the macro evidence available is rather limited. We hope this will change as more research is done.

This study was finished in early 1994, with final editing in early 1995. At the beginning of 1994 Fforde started work with David Marr and Melanie Beresford on an Australian Research Council Project called the Australian Vietnam Research Project, formally titled "Economic Development and Institutional Change in Contemporary Vietnam." The project addresses issues covered in this book, though in far greater empirical and theoretical depth than found herein. This study should thus be seen as an attempt to define a structure for researchers looking at contemporary Vietnam (including ourselves), by advancing a particular view of how Vietnam had arrived at a situation in the mid-1990s in which national economic and political norms had radically changed from those of the immediate post-reunification period.

Finally, it will be noticed by many readers that this book contains little about the war and its importance in explaining what happened in Vietnam during peacetime. Justification for the pre-1975 economic system and the way it operated in the DRV (Democratic Republic of Vietnam) is often given both outside and within Vietnam along the lines that it was "necessary" for prosecution of the armed struggle. A common retort in Vietnam is that it had not been necessary during the earlier and also successful struggle to remove the French. Such debate is, we feel, best left to others. However, we wish to remind readers that the DRV model (by which we mean the outcome of the implementation of neo-Stalinist thinking in Vietnam) was set in concrete by 1963-64, before the start of U.S. bombing raids. It is also striking that very little of the internal Vietnamese debate in the late 1970s and 1980s took this line of "necessity"; proponents and oppponents alike preferred instead to argue their case on the peacetime merits of the various options. In this study, we choose to ignore the war-- partly because we are economists, but also because others have. We do not forget it.

Adam Fforde and Stefan de Vylder

Notes

1. We can be seen as being in some ways in agreement with part of a certain reformist school in Vietnam, of which Dao Xuan Sam (1986, 1989) is but one example.

Acknowledgments

The authors would like to thank the many people who assisted them with this work. In particular, for their help with the original study: the Central Institute for Economic Management Research (CIEM), the Vietnamese Chamber of Commerce, the Development Cooperation Office of the Swedish International Development Authority (Swedish Embassy, Hanoi), and the General Statistical Office.

Both the earlier and the later work have benefited greatly from comments and suggestions from a number of individuals. In particular, we would like to mention: Dao The Tuan, Le Dang Doanh, Dang Phong, Tran Viet Phuong, Dao Xuan Sam, Lu Phuong, David Marr, Melanie Beresford, Borje Ljunggren, Nguyen Van Bich, Le Trang, Nguyen Tri, Nguyen Phap, Phan Van Tiem and Phan Quang Tue. We also owe much to farmers, managers, and workers who were interviewed. Fforde would like to thank the National Center for Development Studies, Australian National University, for having him as a visiting scholar for three months in 1990; the Department of International Economics and Geography, Stockholm School of Economics, for a welcoming environment when he visited there in 1991; and the Department of Economics, Research School of Pacific and Asian Studies, Australian National University, as well as the Australian Research Council via the Australian Vietnam Research Project, for funds for a Visiting Fellowship to finish the text in 1993-95. Lena Ekroth of the Swedish International Development Authority (SIDA) was instrumental in getting the original study off the ground (and back to earth again safely); Milla Johansson provided typing assistance, and Nguyen Manh Hai of the Institute of Prices and Markets, Hanoi, and Wollongong University provided research assistance. Final thanks are expressed to Suki Allen and Gillian Robson of ADUKI Pty Ltd for valuable text editing. We would like to express our thanks to SIDA for its assistance in many ways and in particular for financial assistance toward copyediting and for subsidizing the price of the paperback edition.

We, of course, remain responsible for the shortcomings that inevitably remain.

A.F. and S. de V.

Introduction

Vietnam is a country that evokes strong images; for many people those images are of war and a gray communist conformity. However, such views are now being challenged by the evidence of change of a substantial pace and nature. Between the late 1970s, when communism "pure and hard" was the touchstone, and the early 1990s, Vietnam changed its economic and social system. The norms of Soviet central planning were replaced by a Vietnamese variant of the market mechanism that helped lift the East Asian NICs (newly industrilized countries) out of underdevelopment during the decades after the World War II. Rapid export growth, social differentiation, widening regional gaps, urban congestion, and corruption came to Vietnam, as they had to other countries.1. This book presents a socio-economic history of this transition from plan to market and attempts to throw light on how this fundamental shift occured. How did the Vietnamese communist leadership, and many Vietnamese, come to abandon the fierce ideals of socialism that had combined with an ardent nationalism to create the unified and independent Vietnam of 1975 and replace these ideals with the economic pragmatism of a conflicting ideology?

The reader is taken through a series of topics within which the theoretical and the empirical are mixed. Key ideas are presented in this introduction to provide the background necessary to the following chapters. In particular, we emphasize the following notions:

- "Reform" in Vietnam was largely a bottom-up process; in the strict sense, therefore, the changes that took place in Vietnam during the 1980s and early 1990s should perhaps not be called reform at all.
- "Policy" was, therefore, responsive, rather than proactive; it should be seen as an endogenous element of the transition process rather than as something outside it.

- "The facts" that describe this process of transition were necessarily created by it. Their nature changed qualitatively over time, since Vietnamese knowledge and understanding were not fixed.
- The "historical starting-point," as the transition commenced, was largely bound up with Vietnam's relatively abundant human and natural resources and with what had actually happened in north and south Vietnam prior to 1975.

Two important elements of the analysis are two "models"--the so-called DRV[2] and transitional models. We view these as historically specific socioeconomic systems. However, they embody various ideas and policies, more or less clearly defined in policy documents and legislation, whose implementation became a major issue. The interaction between these ideas and "reality" (loosely understood to mean what people actually did) tells much of the story of the transition. If the readers can assume that the issue of policy implementability was contentious unless otherwise stated, then they will be on the way toward understanding much about Vietnam in general and the transition in particular.

This introduction concludes with an overview of the stages of the transition, noting the distinction between the "hard reform" socialism of the period 1980-85 that was followed by the "soft reform" socialism from 1986 through the early 1990s (these terms are discussed further later in this chapter). The similarities and differences between the systemic change undergone by Vietnam and the experiences of some other developing countries in the 1980s are also discussed.

Theoretical Preliminaries

One element that runs through Vietnamese sources and memories of the 1980s is that of tension between the norms and ways of the socialist, or "planned," parts of the economy and other activities. This tension pervaded economic decisionmaking at all levels. Closely related to this, indeed logically related, is the most striking feature of the Vietnamese transition--its largely spontaneous character. As shall be seen, this means that our notion of the transition from plan to market in Vietnam essentially concerns that of historical process rather than government program. Official policies at times sought to oppose the transition. However, policy implementation frequently had the opposite effect to that intended, strengthening rather than weakening the forces pushing for further moves along the transition path.

If that historical process is to be understood, it is useful to attempt to analyze it rigorously-- to try to set out the underlying structure of the systemic shifts and the relations between the subsystems of the whole. The basic dualism of the system ocurred in the interaction between plan and market. It is therefore important to start off in a way that avoids the confusion that easily follows if transition is equated with reform.

Reform as Process, or as Government Program?

The above is a crucial question, with wide-ranging implications. If the term "reform" is to be understood in a limited way, as policy within a broader notion of transition, then government actions have to be understood within that wider process. This means that ideas of political economy have to be used in order to better understand the influences upon government policy. There also has to be a discussion of the role of Vietnamese economic thinking and perceptions as they evolved.

We consider that any discussion of Vietnamese reality that is based upon a reasonably close appreciation of what people, families, cooperatives, and state enterprises were actually doing must recognize the importance of the plan-market duality.[3] In the Vietnamese vernacular this was expressed as "inside" and "outside" (*noi-ngoai*), and led to the pungent phrase, "the outside foot is longer than the inside foot" (*chan ngoai dai hon chan trong*).[4] This expression implied that activities subject to categorization as planned were usually of lower value to the immediate producer or consumer than those deemed to be marketable.[5] Considerable pressure for change arose as a result of this. However, identifying the boundaries between these two areas as being set by policy does not grasp essential aspects of Vietnamese reality and also cannot explain important elements of the transition process.[6] In this study we therefore use the term "reform" simply to refer to official policy, and as such, reform makes up part of the historical process of transition.

As mentioned above, the transition is seen as involving two government programs associated with two socioeconomic orders analyzed as models.[7] In our terminology, "models" and "programs" are quite different things. This distinction is related to the issues of policy implementability and the adaptation of the neo-Stalinist formula when it was applied under Vietnamese conditions. We label the two most important models the DRV model and the transitional model.[8] The division of Vietnam at the 17th parallel at the 1954 Geneva Conference meant that the post-1975 government had only had experience of socialist construction in the North--in the Democratic Republic of Vietnam (DRV). The program that this government sought to impose upon the united country after 1976 was thus derived from the North. We therefore refer to it as the DRV program. This is partly done in order to distinguish it from its origins in the neo-Stalinist system advocated throughout the communist world in the 1950s.

The attempt to apply the DRV program to a reunited Vietnam lasted only until around 1980, when important changes took place. These included, among other things, passage of legislation[9] that helped to define a hybrid system within which unplanned "outside" activities had more opportunity to operate than before. This we call the transitional model. In 1988-89 the defining elements of this model were formally abandoned, ushering in a new stage, when there was in fact no clear program to specify a Vietnamese variant of market economy. No ideological alternative was found to replace the DRV program, and no clear set of policy debates could be identified similar to those that accompanied the transitional model during its decade of existence (1979-89).

For some Vietnamese communists, it was already clear in the early 1960s (before the onset of U.S. bombing) that the DRV model was ineffective. It could not attain the goals set for it--rapid urban industrialization based upon Soviet central-planning techniques and institutions. Furthermore, it was inefficient to the extent that national economic development would have been better achieved had another model been used. As a result, in the period when the model had an effect on the economy, resources in Vietnam were underutilized. There was considerable economic slack as higher output would have been possible through a more efficient use of existing resources without additional inputs.

Neo-Stalinism, as practiced, and its Vietnamese expression--the DRV model--created many problems and the legacy was long-lasting. In particular, it has been argued that in response to the growth of a wide differential between state and free market prices, the institutional forms of neo-Stalinism were systematically endogenized and adapted to Vietnamese conditions (Fforde and Paine 1987). This can be summed up in the notion that the DRV was a "weak state," unable to prevent the rise of internal threats to its existence and in particular unable to resist the emergence of the transitional model in the late 1970s.

In the 1980s, experience with the transitional model showed that other forms of economic organization were able to take up economic slack. At little cost in terms of additional resource needs, substantial short-term output gains were experienced in response to such organizational changes. However, the ineffectiveness of the DRV model and its lingering effects meant that the authorities, governing through a weak state, started the 1980s without a firm basis for implementing any top-down program of reforms. Central political authority was lacking. The country did not possess, for example, such basic institutional foundations as an effectively functioning legal system, national implementation of central policies, or an adequate statistical basis for economic planning.

As a result, the picture, for analysts and contemporary policymakers alike, was often confused. This confusion did, however, have its positive aspects. It seems certain that material considerations were important in supporting both policy changes and the equally important turning of a blind eye. Spontaneous bottom-up processes could therefore tap relatively easily into the economic rents created by the slack inherent in the DRV model. These rents could--and, we argue, did--produce commercial capital for accumulation as well as emergent interests that would operate politically. In this way, too, the political economy of the transition is an important element of its history.

We therefore posit an interaction between short-run shifts in output drawing upon spontaneous efficiency-raising organizational changes and the resulting creation of economic and social forces that operate politically while accumulating capital. These occur within a growing economy, where technical change, population growth, and other factors all operate.

Thus, it is necessary to identify three areas:

- First, those where short-run resource utilization remained poor and economic rents remained high. Systematic price distortion was an intrinsic part of the DRV model.
- Second, those where systemic shifts had already occurred.
- Third, structural factors constraining socioeconomic development in the longer term.

Prior to 1979-80, the DRV model had certainly helped create prerequisites for such a growth pattern. Severe macroeconomic distortions had become structurally rooted. They resulted from policies of excess investment in state industry, the precocious overdevelopment of nonproductive state employment, and the systematic use of state monopolies so extreme that comparisons of economic costs and benefits became very distant from economic fundamentals.[10] Essential to the neo-Stalinist program was the creation of a highly distorted economy. However, planners were not the only ones able to access the resulting economic rents.[11]

Throughout this period the social costs of systemic reforms as well as macrostabilization policies appeared to policymakers to be great: State workers in protected state-owned enterprises (SOEs) could lose their jobs if the system were dismantled, and spending cuts to balance the budget would threaten the welfare benefits enjoyed by all state employees. However, we argue that the large improvements in resource utilization from further liberalization (whether spontaneous via "fence-breaking" or policy-induced) were usually likely to generate large output gains. It was therefore often easier than expected to generate major improvements in the foreign and fiscal deficits while also seeing real incomes rise. Conversely, attempts at macro stabilization that did not take advantage of the capacity to mobilize economic slack and instead tried to support the planned sectors through administrative measures usually failed to take into account the extent and nature of interactions between the planned and unplanned sectors of the economy. This drove down economic activity and real incomes in both sectors. Surprises for policymakers, both pleasant (as in 1980 and 1989) and unpleasant (as in 1985), were therefore an essential element of what happened.

"Reform as Process": Implications for the 1979-89 Transition

In our analysis, the Vietnamese transition from central planning to a market economy should thus appear as an example of a historical shift in social organization. It is also the outcome of the activities of a variety of interests (predominantly but not solely economic) and of the changing view taken by the political leadership. It was conditioned by the nature of what preceded it. Because of the predominantly economic nature of the proclaimed goals of competing social models and the importance of economic interests, an economic perspective should be able to say interesting and relevant things about the transition. To do this, it is necessary to analyze the economic implications of the different models and what happened to them in Vietnam. It is also necesary to explore the economic impact of aspects of the transition upon production, consumption, distribution, and exchange. To understand this impact it is not sufficient simply to assert the economic inefficiency of various forms of production and exchange. In order to illuminate the political pressures acting upon policymakers and the nature of the surprises mentioned above, we will have to discuss in some detail the nature of plan-market interactions. It is important to keep an open mind. Note the following statement in a discussion of reform in Vietnam and Laos: "For a market economy to work, first of all, a country must have economic stability," (Perkins, in Ljunggren 1993b:6).

Dwight Perkins argues that macroeconomic stabilization should be the most important single goal of policymakers in a transitional economy. World Bank advice tends to follow the same line. However, it is not true that market economies require stability to function (or what should we call, for example, Latin American economies suffering from hyperinflation?). The point is that such economies tend to function differently--arguably better--under such conditions. However, a transitional economy is *not* a market economy and under certain conditions economic instability may actually assist the transition. It is most interestingl that this may occur through maintenance of a high differential between the values of products and factors of production in planned and unplanned activities through inflation, which restores such differentials after misguided price reforms. This is what occurred in Vietnam, and it is arguable that under such circumstances, macroeconomic stabilization would have had a negative effect.[12] Such issues are only brought out when the interactions between various subsystems are integrated into the analysis and not discarded in favor of a view that rests upon the (fallacious) assumption that one is actually dealing with a market economy. Thus one important theoretical implication of the attempt to analyze Vietnamese experience is that transitional economies require a different analytical perspective from either market or centrally planned economies. This allows us to take account of the interactions between the "plan" and "market" (legally sanctioned) elements that they contain, which is what makes them different.

A second point is that the Vietnamese experience supports the argument that transitional models that combine plan and market may in this way contain powerful forces for further systemic change. In other words, such models are in essence transitional and cannot without considerable effort last long. This suggests the analytical need for a stress upon mechanisms that speed up or slow down the process.

Finally, perhaps most interesting of all is the political and human side. The various entities that the world has known as "communisms" are as much ideas as they are social systems. It is striking how Vietnamese views of the situation changed and how very important the subjective element was. The national political and intellectual leadership seems to have changed its sense of what could and should happen to the economy, shifting from hard-line support for the DRV model to an acceptance of a Vietnamese version of market-oriented development. At the same time, popular perceptions of what socialism meant also shifted. In terms of historical exegesis, this suggests that there is an interesting series of stories to be told related to the debates and discussions that occurred, not only during the transition period but also prior to it.[13] It is wrong simply to dismiss as conservative those who resisted the processes of transition. Tran Phuong, for example, was a deputy prime minister and as such was one of the most senior government officials in charge of economic management during the period of hard reform socialism of the early 1980s. At this time, in the logic of hard reform socialism, the authorities tried to rein in and control markets and so defend the basic institutions of the DRV.[14] Tran Phuong was sacked in the aftermath of the failed and nominally antimarket price-wage-money reforms of 1985. He was, however, reportedly the author of the telling phrase "buying like stealing, selling like giving" (*mua nhu cuop, ban nhu cho*), a polemic *against* the realities of state procurement and supply in the Vietnamese economy.[15]

Materials and Evidence

Neither of us is a professional historian. We have based this study on a variety of sources, including interviews in Vietnam, written Vietnamese materials, and various statistical sources. The nature of the sources available itself says something about the transition. Generally, it is true that the most revealing and reliable data was local and informal, whereas data on macro aggregates, such as the Soviet equivalent of gross domestic product (GDP) - produced national income (PNI) - did not show important trends.

Prior to the early 1990s, the DRV and its post-1976 successor, the Socialist Republic of Vietnam, used statistical methodology different from the orthodox national income accounting system. They both used the so-called net material product (NMP) system, which was used in the Soviet Union and other members of the Councilof Mutual Economic Assistance) CMEA. Although this does not prevent analysis, it does mean that international comparisons are unreliable. Superficially similar terminology,for example, national income, hides different ways of defining and measuring economic activity.

During the transition, the data problem became particularly severe as quasi-legal market-oriented activity emerged and developed. This was especially true when such activities were, as was often the case, *within* the planned economy itself. Official statistics were unreliable and subject to considerable political influence and revision. However, more fundamentally, because the DRV model had been abandoned, the socioeconomic assumptions behind the statistical system were no longer valid (if in fact they ever had been).[16] Under transitional conditions, unplanned activities, both within and outside the state and collective sectors, were officially encourged--but within limits.. The statistical system's stress upon quantity indicators was therefore a major difficulty. As a result, much of the data that could be expressed in value terms, especially on aggregate income flows, was not collected. At a time when official wages were usually insufficient for people to live on, requiring extensive moonlighting and reliance upon gray markets, this was a major omission. There are therefore no accurate measures of unplanned economic activity for the transitional period, although there are indirect pointers and surveys that illuminate the picture. Revisions to official data were commonly made by government officials.[17]

Other examples are easy to cite. The secrecy of the authorities should not be denied, nor should the pressure for data to reflect the official line. But for the outside analyst working with hindsight, the problem is not so much that there was a deliberate effort to conceal or hide the truth--one had only to read the official press to see the way in which many difficulties were openly discussed[18]--it is more that the statistical collection services in Vietnam did not have the resources, or the technical reserves, needed to supply statistics of the required quality. Furthermore, at a time when state finances were under considerable pressure, resources were not available to finance improvements in the quality of the statistical base.

This suggests that any detailed "blueprint for reform" would have been of little value since the parameters behind it would not have been based upon any reliable quantitative knowledge. Although the authorities certainly knew far more than they made public about what was happening, knowledge was inadequate to cope with a fully articulated top-down reform, even if the government and party had possessed both the power and the desire to take that route. This information and knowledge gap was an important element in determining the pace of the transition, which was mirrored by the pace at which information could be created at the micro level to provide a basis for stable commodity relations. Whether things would have been different if political conservatives had had the benefit of foresight is another matter.[19]

Micro Evidence[20]

Whereas the orthodox macro data is of limited value, the same cannot be said of microlevel information. The media produced many reports about economic activities both legal and illegal. These covered state enterprises, cooperatives, farming families, urban workers, consumers, and many others. Although the media tended to have a surface bias in favor of the status quo, they reveal in great clarity the "realities of life" (*cuoc song*). There is also considerable evidence that the political and technocratic leadership was very well informed about local realities. Internal party surveys covered such topics as land abandonment by collectivized peasants (Fforde 1989a:79 referring to Dinh Thu Cuc 1977). It was the custom for central level cadres to carry out extensive programs of visits, which at the least challenged conservative thinking with the intemperate climate of the streets and at the most led to creative rethinking. This rethinking not only focused criticisms of central planning but also, even more creatively, led to development of an acute indigenous understanding of the logic of the transitional model. This can be observeved in the enormous volume of writings in the official press and journals of the period, such as *Ke hoach hoa* (Planning), and *Nghien cuu kinh te* (Economic research). However, arriving at a sense of the macro "laws of motion" of the whole system as opposed to the rather easy-to- perceive logic at the micro level, is particularly difficult to achieve, and such insights were extremely rare.[21]

The use made of such material here is largely impressionistic. With the resources available and with the confidence that we are correct in pointing to the main themes in the overall structure of events, we feel our impression is correct for the time being. However, if the heavy weight of change in families, factories, and villages is not fully brought out to the satisfaction of those who lived through it, then we can only reply that we have tried to strike a balance between the two poles of "policy" and "life," in order to analyze and explain just how the transition from plan to market took place.

The Givens

Vietnam: A Rich Country with a Poor People

During the 1980s Vietnam's gross national output (GNP) per capita of some US$150-200[22] made it one of the poorest countries in the world. Other measures of material welfare--daily calorie intake per head, access to consumer goods, consumption of electricity, and so on--confirm the picture of a country with a people in deep poverty. However, the latent potential for growth was large, as was revealed in 1989-90.

Poverty was fairly evenly distributed, and various indicators reveal that the social welfare system was well developed, given the low per capita income. Vietnamese life expectancy was, for example, higher than in countries such as Peru, Brazil, Iran, and Algeria, all of which had a per capita income more than ten times that of Vietnam.

Such low per capita income did not do justice to Vietnam's vast development potential. The fertile Mekong Delta alone, if double cropping had expanded and yields per hectare had reached levels equivalent to those in neighboring countries, could have supplied the nation with food.[23] Other natural resources, such as minerals, energy--Vietnam possesses rich coal and oil deposits, in addition to its hydroelectric potential--forests, and waters rich in marine products, were there to lay the foundation for a well-diversified development.

Since the removal of the colonial power in 1954 (if not before), the major resource of the country has been its people. Compared to populations in other countries with low per capita income, the Vietnamese population had appreciably better educational levels. Most people in the North had completed eight years of schooling, and the rate of literacy was better than in many Third World countries with far higher average incomes. The Vietnamese people also have a profound sense of history and national identity, forged by, among other things, prolonged struggles for national independence throughout the history of the nation. Most Vietnamese speak the same language and share a common cultural heritage, a factor that had proved a valuable asset in many battles in the past and should have facilitated the struggle for economic and social development. Rapid population growth was one factor that posed difficulties. During the 1980s, the population rose from 53.6 million in 1980 to 64.4 million in 1990--a rise of 20.1 percent. With a continuation of this trend in the rate of increase, the population was predicted to double within less than forty years. In many parts of the country, high population pressure was also giving rise to rapid environmental degradation. During the 1980s, the margins between Vietnam's physical carrying capacity and its population were narrowing. Unemployment had become an increasingly serious problem; of the more than 1 million new entrants into the labor force each year, only around one in ten was able to secure a job within the state sector, as shown in Table 3.7. Neither agriculture nor the urban private sector in services and small-scale industry could absorb all the job-seeking youths.

During most of the 1980s Vietnam had an essentially introspective economy that stressed the development of the domestic market. Involvement with CMEA did not change this fundamentally. After the loss of Soviet bloc aid in 1988-90 and drawing upon the opening up to foreign investment initiated by the Foreign Investment Law of 1988, Vietnam started to become increasingly integrated into the international economy. Vietnam's proximity to the Pacific market made it a natural trading partner for the rapidly growing economies of the region. By the end of the decade, however, its comparative advantages--natural resources and a hard-working, educated, and disciplined labor force with real wages below the Asian average[24]--had still only been very marginally exploited. Despite impressive growth in exports in 1989 and 1990, in 1991 Vietnamese hard currency export earnings still amounted to little more than US$20 per capita.

North Vietnam, the DRV Model, and the Transition

The essential premise of the DRV model was Soviet-style central planning aimed at rapid industrialization with collectivization of agriculture and strong central control of the economy. As in other centrally planned economies (CPEs), this created, compared with market economies, a situation of low agricultural prices and high profit rates in state industry. Price policy, suppression of markets, and the pattern of state investment (priority to state industry) created resources that the authorities could use to finance high rates of accumulation. These "economic rents" relied upon relative prices set at levels that required the use of administrative powers and rationing to secure a coherent outcome. These relative prices were different both from those that would have existed had the system relied upon markets and from those on parallel, or black, markets. The state sector, fueled by subsidized inputs and subject to planning orders from the authorities, was the "engine of growth." There was virtually no room for small-scale private production. The system required strong state monopoly in the allocation of resources to both industry and agriculture, and industrial enterprises and agricultural cooperatives were given quantitative targets for their compulsory deliveries to the state.

In North Vietnam, this attempt to implement neo-Stalinism was soon characterized by increasing sectoral imbalances and micro inefficiency. By 1961-62 this had led to inflation on parallel markets (Fforde and Paine 1987). *The DRV model emerged as a de facto compromise, and the nature of this is what distinguishes the Vietnamese experience from that of other CPEs.*[25] Various debates in the closing years of the First (1961-65) Five Year Plan (FYP) were resolved in favor of continuing with assertions of the rectitude of neo-Stalinist orthodoxy. The first post-reunification Party Congress (the Fourth, in 1976) again asserted the correctness of these ideas and policies and their applicability to the entire country (CPV 1978; Fforde 1989a). However, the contradictions expressed in the DRV model, and its basic problems, were not solved by national reunification. Indeed, they deteriorated (Beresford 1989).

The model came under increasing strain during the late 1970s, when bad harvests, in combination with the military intervention in Cambodia and the political and economic isolation of Vietnam from most of the outside world, triggered a systemic crisis as the state's ability to supply inputs to the planned economy, and food to people, broke down. The planning system's failure in 1978-79 to maintain control over resources forced economic agents--individuals as well as agricultural cooperatives and state enterprises--to engage in a process of "reform from below."[26] "Fence-breaking" (*pha rao*), to use a translation of a Vietnamese expression describing this phenomenon,[27] became increasingly common, and the authorities had to admit tacitly that the DRV model had (perhaps temporarily) become unsustainable. Spontaneous processes were then accompanied by piecemeal economic reforms from above, starting with the Sixth Plenum of the Central Committee in 1979. Retail trade was liberalized (but then frowned upon), and the introduction in 1981 of the so-called output contract system in agriculture and the Three Plan system in industry (similar to the Chinese dual-pricing system) can be interpreted as the beginning of the official process of reform and the legal basis for the transitional model (see Chapters 4 and 5).

The Transition: An Overview

Hard Reform Socialism and Reaction, 1980-85

These policy changes in the very early 1980s were also tactical retreats to preserve basic tenets of the DRV program through concessions to spontaneous processes that could not be controlled. This interpretation can be supported by the fact that the authorities, when the economic situation had improved after the crisis of 1979-80, broke off economic liberalization in an attempt at recentralization. This was shown by, among other things, the clampdown on the free market in Ho Chi Minh City (formerly Saigon) and by the campaign to resuscitate agricultural collectivization in the Mekong Delta in the South. The 1982 Fifth Party Congress expressed and drove home the hard reform position, which is discussed in greater detail in Chapter 4. The congress accepted that economic policy had failed to create economic development, but although it accepted that criticism, it did not reject the essence of the DRV program.

Irrespective of the motives behind the policies of the early 1980s, the combination of fence-breaking and policy concessions had terminated the hegemony of the DRV program. The plan now had to coexist with the world of autonomous transactions in the hybrid transitional model.[28] Prices, costs, and markets began to play a larger role, and economic agents became used to thinking in more market-oriented terms. Independent commercial capital emerged and grew in significance.

The reactionary attitude of the authorities meant that the rules of the game were extremely unclear, but people's perceptions of what was possible were changing. As markets emerged and developed and local leaders adopted different positions, the rules of the game varied from place to place.[29] If the basis for action in the 1970s had been that everything that was not explicitly permitted was forbidden, from the early 1980s on people could often assume that even a wide range of forbidden activities would in actual practice be tolerated, and sometimes even encouraged, by some authorities. This continuing decentralization of political power was one important social aspect of the transition from plan to market. Furthermore, the process of transition itself started to be seen as possessing a momentum of its own. It was seen by some as operating according to "laws of nature" (*quy luat*). People started to sense the inevitability of some sort of market economy, and they often took appropriate action.

The transitional system, with its accompanying growth in independent capital, gradually helped to create a political basis for active and concerted state measures to introduce a market economy. After the failure of the 1985 price-wage-money reforms to reimpose state control over the economy and the resulting fall of Deputy Premier Tran Phuong and Politburo member To Huu from power, the way was open for a change in overall policy. After the death of Party General Secretary Le Duan in 1986, the Sixth Party Congress of that year saw the party approve soft reform socialism which sanctioned development of the nonsocialist sectors and private capital accumulation while opening the road to a market economy. It set in motion the opening up of the Vietnamese economy to foreign direct investment (FDI), which reached flood proportions by the mid-1990s. It also allowed an expansion of trade with world markets, which would commence with notable force in the early 1990s.

Soft Reform Socialism and the Road to a Market Economy, 1986-89

The policy changes of 1986-89 had their origins in this early period, and it is thus useful to stress the continuity in the transition process. Developments after 1986 retained many spontaneous elements, but a major difference compared with the first phase was open recognition of the shortcomings of the old development model, leading to a desire for its abolition rather than its reform. Official confirmation of the Vietnamese leaders' commitment to abandoning neo-Stalinism and the DRV program can be dated to December 1986, when accelerated economic reform--now identified by ideologists and party propagandists as *doi moi*, or renovation--was approved by the Sixth Party Congress. From then on, policy changes were not regarded as tactical retreats in the face of difficult but temporary circumstances, but as fundamentally new strategic concepts. Naturally, however, there still existed different opinions within the leadership about the desirable pace of change. Also, whereas ideological abandonment of the DRV program led to an acceptance of the positive role of the private sector, the position of the state sector remained extremely hard to resolve (see Chapter 7).

The transition process accelerated--somewhat unexpectedly--during 1989. Soviet aid was declining rapidly and was expected to fall still further. The year witnessed a forceful attack upon the remaining vestiges of central planning, including price reform (more accurately, a reform of state sector distributional relations), which put an end to the former two-price system by allowing virtually all prices to be market determined. In this sense, by 1989 Vietnam had progressed much farther along the road to economic reform than, say, the contemporary Union of Soviet Socialist Republics (USSR) or China.[30]

It should be noted, however, that the Vietnamese transition, although certainly strongly influenced by such external factors as the aid cuts of 1978-79 and 1989-90, as well as the high levels of CMEA aid in the mid-1980s, was mainly determined by internal factors. Given the state of Vietnamese society in the 1950s and the attitudes of the people and their leaders, and given the basic economic realities of the country, external factors certainly seem to have played an important role earlier on. But the interplay between domestic and international conditions has to be analyzed if the period is to be understood.

Furthermore, through the 1980s, the source of inspiration was increasingly not the Soviet Union, but rather the spectacular economic development experienced in the newly industrialized countries in Southeast Asia. Indeed, as the 1991 events in the Soviet Union were to show, the Vietnamese reforms, *when viewed as state policy,* were more economic than political in character--in other words, perestroika rather than glasnost. Despite some political liberalization during the 1980s, Vietnam retained its authoritarian, one-party system. The Vietnamese leaders' lesson from Eastern Europe and the USSR appeared to be straightforward: more perestroika, if the economic collapse of the USSR was to be prevented, and less glasnost, if the collapse of the hegemonic role of the Communist Party was to be avoided. However, once reform is understood as historical process and its origins in the early 1980s appreciated, then the political basis of the Vietnamese transition can be tackled. What were the political forces that pushed the party into changing its position between the Fifth and Sixth Party Congresses, and what was the role in this of the commercial capital built up within the pre-1986 transitional model?[31] Since *after* 1989 it was the state business interest that seemed to dominate state policy, a strong prima facie case can be argued for investigation of the origins of this political power in the pre-1986 period.

The Vietnamese Transition in a Third World Perspective

Development Policies of the 1980s

When discussing the 1980s crisis of transition that faced the Vietnamese economy, it should be borne in mind that a majority of Third World countries, in particular in Africa and Latin America, were also confronting serious economic problems. Inappropriate economic policies and a series of external factors--the decline in export prices and terms of trade for most exporters of primary products in the 1980s and the rise in the international rate of interest--contributed to accentuating economic hardship in the Third World. Many developing countries, with different economic and political systems, suffered (as many still do--unlike Vietnam) from debt crises, accompanied by recurrent balance of payments and fiscal difficulties and the concomitant pressure to adopt austerity measures. Against this perspective, the case of Vietnam was far from unique, although it had its own particular features and--we believe and hope--a more positive outcome in the 1990s and beyond. Although this is not the place to make a comparative study of Third World socialism, many important aspects of the DRV model are strikingly similar to experiences in countries as diverse as Laos, Mozambique, Angola, Guinea-Bissau, Tanzania, Cuba, Ethiopia, China, and even Nicaragua during the Sandinista regime in 1979-89. Vietnam's development policies thus shared, with many other countries, not all of which had socialist governments, certain biases in economic policies. Among these, the following can be mentioned:

- An exaggerated belief in state planning and a pervasive use of administrative allocation of resources.
- An excessive use of price controls and subsidies, with concomitant distortions in relative costs and prices.
- A lack of financial discipline and a neglect of monetary issues.
- A low cost-consciousness within the state sector.
- A high priority given to modern industry at the expense of agriculture and small-scale undertakings.
- A tendency to overoptimistic targets and excessive fixed capital formation (the "hunger for investment"), especially in the early years.
- A neglect of exports.

Most of these countries found themselves experiencing similar problems, partly with similar causes. Widespread recognition of past mistakes created strong pressure to correct them. Self-criticism was common, and liberalizing economic reforms could be found in Tanzania, Guinea-Bissau, Angola, Mozambique, Laos, India, and China. Planning structures, and old ways of thinking, were under heavy attack. Attacks came from below, as the constraints of the old system forced citizens, both individually and in groups, to engage in various forms of fence-breaking, as part of reform programs supported by their respective governments (and, in many cases, by the International Monetary Fund (IMF) and the World Bank). If state planning had once been considered to be the solution to the problems originating from capitalism and market forces, markets were now thought of as the solution to many of the problems besetting the planning system. The wheel thus turned. In only a few of the countries, however, and Vietnam appears to be an example, did the new ways of thinking translate into a real chance of rapid economic growth. We reflect on this in Chapter 9.

Thus, although the transition process started earlier in Vietnam than in most other Third World countries with socialist regimes, it can be seen as part of a general trend--accelerated, but not initiated, by Mikhail Gorbachev's perestroika in the Soviet Union--in which established socialist development thinking was questioned.

Transition or Structural Adjustment?

When comparing the Vietnamese experience with that of other countries, it may be observed that what was occurring in Vietnam was not quite the same as typical structural adjustment programs that attracted support from the IMF and the World Bank. These programs often contained several of the following ingredients:

- A reduction of state expenditures, including real wages in the public sector, and of the fiscal deficit.
- Tax reform.
- Curtailment of state subsidies to public enterprises, and a dismantling of certain state monopolies, such as parastatals responsible for the supply of inputs to agriculture and for the procurement of staples.
- A reduction of consumer subsidies.
- A modification of key prices in the economy, in particular, the rate of exchange (through heavy devaluations), food procurement prices

(which normally were increased), and the real rate of interest (which was raised).

- A liberalization of the foreign trade regime, in particular, a reduction of the role of quantitative restrictions and import licensing arrangements.
- A relaxation of price controls, where these were prevalent, and a revision of the entire price and incentive structure with the aim of "getting the prices right" (or, at least, less wrong), and enhancing incentives for productive activities.

When comparing these familiar reform programs with the transition in Vietnam, it must be stressed that there are many differences as well as similarities.

In Vietnam, the process started from a heavily centralized system in which the private sector played an exceedingly marginal role and where prices mattered little.[32] State monopoly power in the allocation of resources was far more pervasive than in virtually all other Third World countries. "Structural adjustment" in Vietnam thus did not merely signify resource reallocation, but also systemic change. In this regard it is important to recall the economic focus of this book. Thus, our sense of systemic change is based upon our idea of the change in economic system. Clearly, those with other interests, such as the cultural, would define systemic change differently. However, this economic system change certainly implied important social and political shifts, both as prerequisites and outcomes, and amounted to a revolution in the development concept and strategy.

In Vietnam it was not, to use a rhetorical phrase, only a question of "getting the prices right"--it was also, to a large extent, a question of *making prices matter.* Or, to give an example: It was not only a question of providing exporters with proper incentives through a modification of the rate of exchange--it was also a question of first giving potential exporters the right to export at all.[33]

The changes required added up to rather more than at first appeared. One could argue that orthodox structural adjustment has to do with getting a system to work properly, whereas in the case of transition, as in Vietnam, system change was the outcome. Whereas many other Third World countries were modifying--with great difficulties in terms of transition costs, unpopular income distribution effects, pressure from foreign creditors, domestic political opposition, and so forth--certain parameters of the economy in order to achieve the desired combination of growth and adjustment, Vietnam was changing from one development strategy to an entirely new one.[34] This gave an added dimension to the transition, for it required a far more fundamental change in outlook.[35] Any market economy, once established, needs to be made to work effectively, for without active state intervention to overcome monopoly and market distortions, markets cannot function well and rates of growth tend to be slower. Thus the increasing involvement of multilateral donors in around 1989, and the opening up of the economy to foreign direct investment in 1987-88, combined with the experience created by the market economy itself, all helped to create the beginnings of the knowledge base needed to govern a market economy. This happened at a time when CMEA aid was being cut back to a very low level and when the continued U.S. embargo greatly restricted Vietnam's access to Western assistance.

There are, however, aspects of the Vietnamese case that made the process of reform less difficult than in many other countries. Apart from what was said earlier about the vast developmental potential of the country in terms of human and natural resources, the relatively egalitarian character of Vietnamese society made political economy issues less contentious (compared, for example, to market economies in Latin America). To this could be added the "softening" of neo-Stalinism embodied in the political compromises of the DRV model. Also, substantial real income gains occurred at important stages in the transition process--1980-81 and 1989, years that marked seismic systemic shifts.

In fact, many of the most difficult measures to take in the transition from one economic system to another were, in Vietnam, taken piecemeal and over a period of one decade--1979-89. Contrary to the experience in many other countries, it appears that this ex post facto gradualist approach (in contrast to the big-bang approaches seen elsewhere) was one where winners tended to outnumber losers. The package of drastic reforms did not begin with a severe and unpopular austerity program with layoffs and price increases. Rather, the transitional model had created conditions for both extensive structural change and a commercialization of the state and cooperative sectors before the final assault on the remnants of the DRV program in 1989. Note also that effective attacks on macro imbalances were only launched when the process was well advanced and had gained some legitimacy. By 1989, prices mattered and autonomous capital had been accumulated outside as well as within the state and cooperative structures. This permitted the links between macro policies and micro response to work reasonably well. In terms of our focus upon the economic system, the Vietnamese development model "post-1989" was a "new world."

The timing of the policy changes involved in the reform process was thus not only, and perhaps not even mainly, a technical issue but was instead intimately related to political factors such as the credibility of the program in the eyes of the public. During the 1980s, opposition to reform was gradually broken down--or, rather, squeezed both from below and from above. By 1991 popular support for reform was one prop for a regime that had seen the collapse of communism in both Eastern Europe and the Soviet Union.

Given the fact that a large number of countries, in Eastern Europe as well as in the Third World, in the early 1990s were also undergoing a transition to more market-oriented economies, the Vietnamese experience might serve as a useful point of reference for a discussion about problems of transition in general. Reference can be made here to such central issues as

- Price reforms and macro stabilization.
- The role of the state in a transitional economy.
- The likely implications of different sequences of steps in the reform process.
- The nature of the distortions inherited from the old development model and of the new distortions that emerge.

For obvious reasons, given the novelty of the attempts to replace centrally planned economies with market economies, both the theoretical models and the empirical analyses of such processes are weakly developed. The analyses rely upon stereotypical blueprints and standard recipes that fail to take into account the complexities and specific characteristics of each individual case.[36] While trying to avoid making generalizations based on the experience of one particular country, we nevertheless suggest certain interpretations of Vietnam's prolonged process of economic reform (some of which may be rather unorthodox), that may be of wider interest and relevance. Perhaps the most intriguing is the view of transition as historical process rather than top-down reform. There is something appealing, at least in our view, in the idea that transition is a creative and therefore unplannable process.

By 1990, the Vietnamese economy could, in most important respects, be regarded as a market economy--albeit with poorly developed or nonexistent markets for land, labor, and capital (the factors of production). The transition was over. Most transactions were based upon voluntary exchange and mutual interest. This was quite different from the obligatory instructions of the central planning system. Farmers, if they were members of the minority who still belonged to agricultural cooperatives, were no longer subject to their control. As the process continued into the 1990s, Vietnam's development problems would, to an increasing extent, come to resemble those of other low-income developing countries. Problems of transition would lose much of their relevance, as ordinary development issues came to the fore. Without attempting to make forecasts about the future, we also try to indicate some of the key problems related to growth and development that confronted Vietnam in the early 1990s, investiigating how the interaction between the heritage of the past and the economic system toward which Vietnam was moving posed new problems and opened up new opportunities.

Structure of the Book

The book is organized as follows. In Chapter 1 we look at the nature of the transition in greater detail. A simple set of stages is put forward to apply to the period. The chapter contains a short appendix on the economic analysis of transitional economies. In Chapters 2 and 3 we examine the historical context and the human and natural resource constraints that operated during the transition period.

In Chapter 4 we discuss the fluctuating meaning of reform in Vietnam in an attempt to analyze the way in which the debates evolved and how the Communist Party came to support market oriented methods of economic organization.

In Chapter 5 we examine at some length the ways in which the Vietnamese economy changed as the transition took place: the pattern under which markets emerged, the changes in industrial structure, and in agriculture, and so on. We investigate the extent to which what we call "plan distortion," as discussed in Chapter 1, declined.

In Chapter 6 we look at the effect on social life: the changing nature of social relations, authority, and power. We concentrate here on health and education.

In Chapters 7 we reconsider the transition period in terms of processes of accumulation and institutional evolution. We are thus able to place the decade within a longer time frame and assess its impact upon growth prospects. In Chapter 8 we discuss the consequences for the Vietnamese economy of the patterns and habits of rent seeking that were common during the transition. The link is made between such issues and the macroeconomic stability of the country. We explore the likely consequences for the emerging institutions of the 1990s of the combination of the legacy of the transition period and the nature of Vietnam's integration (or reintegration) into the world economy. We conclude the book with Chapter 9. Statistical tables and figures may be found at the ends of chapters.

Notes: Some Definitions Restated

DRV. The Democratic Republic of Vietnam. North Vietnam, 1945-76.

DRV model. The result, in terms of socioeconomic behavior and structures, of the attempt to implement neo-Stalinism in north Vietnam.

DRV program. The program of social and economic change imposed upon the united country after 1976, derived from the North; referred to as the DRV program to bring out distinctly Vietnamese aspects of it and thus differentiate it from the more general elements common to the neo-Stalinist system advocated throughout the communist world in the 1950s.

Hard reform socialism (ca. 1979-1985/86). The ideology dominant in the first half of the 1980s that sought to improve the operation of the neo-Stalinist system without removing its essential characteristics: and therefore hostile to the private sector and "international capitalism." Accompanied by the attempt to rein in and control markets and thus defend the basic institutions of the DRV.

Neo-Stalinism. The traditional socialist development model, derived from Stalin's Soviet Union, but by the 1950s subject to considerable modification in different countries. Essential characteristics: central planning and the use of the basic micro institutions of agricultural cooperatives and SOEs.

Reform. State or party policies designed to change the socioeconomic system, which may or may not have such an effect and which may or may not act progressively.

Soft reform socialism (ca. 1986-1989/91). The ideology dominant in the second half of the 1980s after the party advocated *doi moi.* The Vietnamese attempt (historically doomed) to encompass the contradictions between the desire to maintain traditional neo-Stalinist institutions and the drive to a market economy, with the opening up to FDI and encouragement of the private sector.

SRV. The Socialist Republic of Vietnam. Vietnam, 1976-.

Transition. The process by which socioeconomic systems change from those based upon neo-Stalinism to those dominated by markets.

Transitional model. The hybrid socioeconomic system that emerged in 1980-81, within which unplanned "outside" activities had more opportunity to operate than before; specifically, it included, among other things, passage of legislation that legalized such outside activities. Its extinction in 1989 marked the emergence of a market economy in Vietnam.

Notes

1. See, for example, Barbara Franklin, "AIDS and Vietnam," CARE International in Vietnam, Monograph Series no. 1, Hanoi, 1993.

2. DRV--the Democratic Republic of Vietnam--north Vietnam from 1945 to 1976.

3. Many dazzlingly diverse and esoteric activities can only be understood in terms of "plan"--"market" interactions. See, for example, the article about Nghia Binh Province by Do Quang Thang in *Nhan Dan* (*NhD*) for 2 October 1979 on the development of paper output, when the urban population was supplying shares (1,000 dong each) so that the cooperatives could buy raw materials from the free market to be used by small plants set up within the planned sector--the agricultural cooperatives. A heavy industry model factory-- the No. 1 Machine Tools Factory in Hanoi--was doing well with extraplan activities within the "three-plan" system in the very early 1980s (Guiding 25-CP 1982:25) and was relying upon market-oriented payments in kind to workers *(NhD,* 5 November 1985). It was used as a basis for grassroots reports to the Third CPV Plenum in 1982 (To Huu 1985:83). And the famous French-built textile mill in Nam Dinh had shifted to piecework payments and so-called output contracts in 1979-80. At around the same time, the factory was putting profits from nonplan output into its general bonus fund, while, in some sections 60-70 percent of workers were active in trade. Economic activity had reportedly risen sharply after introduction of the transitional system (*NhD,* 16 January 1979 and 19 November 1980). Note that these occurred both before and during the transition.

4. An additional sense can be had from the saying, "Those who work outside, eat outside" *(lam ngoai an ngoai).*

5. We do not wish to argue that Vietnam was unique in this respect; many, if not most Eastern European economies showed similar deviations from Stalinist textbook norms.

6. We therefore question the value of typical behavioral assumptions in econometric studies that assume that the boundary is set exogenously. For example, it is often assumed that the proportion of state enterprise output in Chinese factories operating according to "two-track pricing" is set by planners (Cao Yong 1992).

7. We do not intend to subsume under the use of these terms the idea that politics were irrelevant and the real polity monolithic; indeed, it may be useful to see these labels as representing the political compromises necessary at the time.

8. The academic analysis of low-income developing socialist countries that have sought to utilize central-planning techniques is underdeveloped, especially in its quantitative aspects. Effective modeling of either macro or micro behavior is poor. In the area of theory, the work of Janos Kornai is valuable for the analysis of those sectors of a developing socialist economy that are centrally planned, with his stress upon shortage indicators, multiple disequilibria, and the institutional origins of such phenomena as "investment hunger" and the soft budget constraint. But since his focus is upon developed socialist economies with strong state structures, his work inevitably tends to ignore the interactions between administrative and voluntary resource allocation methods that lie at the root of the transition process in Vietnam. His work, however, has been of great value to this study (e.g. Kornai 1985).

9. Until the late 1980s the distinction between party and state directives was not fundamental in Vietnam. We therefore include in the term "legislation" the important party decrees that were part of the formal basis of these models (for example, regarding cooperative organization). We do not intend by doing so to argue that these directives were "law" in any of the commonly accepted Western senses, with associated references to notions of "rule of law".

10. By this we mean, at a minimum, a set of prices that was consistent with the generalized use of markets to allocate resources.

11. By rents we mean to indicate here those resources available at low cost to individuals or groups who gain access to positions where they can be enjoyed-- "pork," to use American political terminology. For example, if rice was being taxed or procured from farmers at very low rates of return to farmers, then anybody who gained access to such rice and then sold it at a profit would effectively be accessing the rents created by the combination of cooperativization and state rice procurement.

12. Janos Kornai makes a very similar point in discussing the possibly harmful effects of macrostabilization on CPEs (Kornai 1985).

13. See, to give an outstanding example, Phan van Tiem (1990) for a discussion of the pre-1965 debates and their impact, as well as ed., Chu Van Lam (1992) on rural development policy.

14. The term "hard reform socialism" is a useful shorthand. The term denotes an ideology that seeks to improve the operation of the neo-Stalinist system without removing what we see as its essential characteristics: at root, central planning and the use of the basic micro institutions of agricultural cooperatives and SOEs. We see this as therefore naturally hostile to the private sector and "international capitalism." We contrast this with the ideas that were dominant in the second half of the 1980s after the party advocated "*doi moi.*" The term "soft reform socialism" tries to capture the Vietnamese attempt (historically doomed) to encompass the contradictions between the desire to maintain

traditional neo-Stalinist institutions and the drive to a market economy, with the opening up to FDI and encouragement of the private sector.

15. Tran Phuong's main academic work is his edited study of Vietnamese land reform (Tran Phuong 1968), which shows in passing that most land real-location occurred *before* the formal land reform of the early and mid-1950s; his often-referred-to "initial questioning of the neo-Stalinist system" can be found in a series of articles in *NCKT* (Economic Research) for 1966 and 1967 (Tran Phuong 1966-67). A concealed attack upon Vietnamese agricultural policy can be found in a study of Bulgarian agriculture (Tran Phuong 1979). For an inter-esting analysis of economic structure by his son, Vu Tuan Anh (1985), see the latter's article in Economic Research. Tran Phuong was moved up from a posi-tion as minister of Home Trade to become deputy prime minister in charge of economic affairs in 1982 (SWB--the BBC's Summary of World Broadcasts--27 April 1982) but was demoted in January 1986 in the aftermath of the failed price-wage-money reforms of 1985 (SWB 3 February 1986) to become head of the Long-term Planning Institute at the State Planning Commission. He was basically a patriotic technocrat whose career has, like many others, an almost Shakespearean quality.

16. For a discussion of the class analysis behind the traditional system see Fforde and Paine (1987:43, et seq).

17. Official estimates of the Infant Mortality Rate (IMR) vary between 35 and 64 per thousand (UNICEF 1987:1). To give two examples: According to a 1984 statistical collection, total social output rose by an average of 9.5 percent between 1980 and 1983 (SO 1985a:table 28); but according to a 1987 collec-tion the rate of increase was only 6.5 percent (SO 1987:table 12), a cumulative difference of nearly 10 percent over the three years. Again, according to the 1983 Yearbook, industrial output rose by 5.6 percent in 1983 (SO 1985c:table16), but according to another published in 1985, it rose by over 15.1 percent (SO 1985b:table 27).

18. See, for example, the letter from Hoang Dinh Minh published in *NhD* for 16 December 1983 entitled *Phuong thuc phan phoi tuy tien* (The distribution of goods "at leisure"), which discussed the way in which bicycles intended for incentive sales to farming families in Bac Thai Province had been sold on the free market instead.

19. A secondary difficulty with the analysis at this stage is that the precise relationship between political events on the national stage and their contexts is simply not known. As a result, the state may often appear as a "deus ex machi-na," whose actions are unexplained; this does not mean that we think that this is in fact the case. However, until we know more of its precise origins, policy formation will inevitably appear isolated from the context in which it happens. We hope, though, that the logic of the sequence and nature of events is suffi-cient to show that Vietnamese communist policy was not made in a vacuum,

but rather that policymakers attempted to control events that they frequently not only did not understand well, but that also, even when well understood, were almost impossible to influence.

20. This study draws upon various databases that have covered some of the available secondary sources, especially for state industrial enterprises. It also benefits from extensive collections of papers and legal documents as well as extensive interviews with farmers, workers, and cadres at many levels.

21. Fforde first became properly aware of this in private discussion with Professor Nguyen Tri of the Industry Faculty of the National Economics University, Hanoi, who acted as his supervisor in 1985-86.

22. According to World Bank estimates (WB 1990) GDP per capita was $109, which we believe is an underestimate. It is, however, consistent with estimates made by the Vietnamese authorities in the early 1990s (SO 1992).

23. Indeed, in 1989 the end of the transition period saw rice exports leap to 1.4 million tonnes, placing Vietnam at number three ranking in the league table of world rice exporters.

24. In 1991, monthly wages in labor intensive manufactures were typically US$10-12(i.e., 120,000-150,000 dong); off-season agricultural workers in the northern deltas would work for less than 20 cents a day (Fforde, personal observation).

25. According to Tran Viet Phuong (personal communication to Fforde), it was possible circa 1994 to discern three basic Vietnamese views of just what best categorized Vietnam prior to the 1986 Sixth Party Congress: (1) essentially Stalinist, with elements of Maoism but without significant modifications to Vietnamese conditions, (2) a Vietnamese form of the Soviet model; (3) something essentially Vietnamese, neither a Soviet model nor any other foreign model, although influenced by foreign models. Our notion of the DRV model would seem to fit into the third category.

26. Here, the important differences between Vietnam and Eastern Europe can be seen. The "weak state" associated with the political compromises inherent in the DRV model made fence-breaking less risky for both the participants and those who in authority who did not carry out the textbook Stalinist response-- the use of violence.

27. See Dam Van Nhue and Le Si Hiep (1981) for the first use of the term of which we are aware.

28. In the South, of course, it had had to do so since 1975.

29. A good example of this was the adverse effects upon Haiphong's burgeoning commerce of the departure of liberal Party Secretary Doan Duy Thanh for a ministerial post in 1986 (Joint Publications Research Service (JPRS) 10 July 1986 discusses policy implementation in the city).

30. It had, however, been beaten to this goal by Laos, which had abolished administrative resource allocation in 1985-86 (Funck, in Ljunggren 1993b).

31. This line of thinking is related to the concept of the "state business interest." By this we mean the idea that this diverse and internally divided group made up of SOEs, their superior organs, and other interested parties could nevertheless be seen having systematic impact upon national level political events. One key event that this may be able to explain is the "U-turn" in policy toward the state sector expressed by Decree No. 306 in April 1986 (discussed later on).

32. Here again we stress the importance, in understanding systemic change, of the North as the dominant political center.

33. Theoretically, this means that predictions for transition in Vietnam or any other economy moving from central planning were likely to be false if based upon, for example, Latin American experience, where the starting point is a distorted *market* economy. It is thus interesting to see Eastern European economies that attempted big-bang solutions, based theoretically upon market economies, instead often evolved what were clearly--if sometimes implicitly--transitional models that preserved temporary areas of stability for the old socialist economy. The risks that these would then act as excessive brakes--if not actual reversals-- to the transition process were obvious.

34. Here again it is useful to avoid confusion about the extent to which we argue that fundamental change in economic system and strategy has occurred in Vietnam. To the extent that we define our focus of study as economic system, then fundamental change has happened, since we define centrally planned and market economies as essentially different. This simply stems from the way we define our terms and is tautological.

35. For example, most of the knowledge base of the economic intelligentsia became worthless--cadres trained in central planning techniques, cooperative management, etc. People with training in commercial law, in business administration, etc., were simply lacking (at least in the North).

36. See, for example, Kornai's attempt to classify tens of Third World countries as centrally planned, including Zimbabwe (Kornai 1992, cited in Ljunggren 1993b:44).

1

The Nature of Economic Transition

The Nature of the Transition: Process or Revolution?

From what to what? Process or revolution? In the aftermath of the collapse of communist rule in Eastern Europe in 1989, and in the Soviet Union in 1991, discussion over the meaning and scope of the notion of transition from central planning to a market economy widened considerably. Some very different reform programs aiming to move away from the traditional neo-Stalinist model could be seen; a range clearly existed, from the big-bang approach of Poland to the politically conservative gradualism of China. These differences were both analytically and morally important: analytically, because of the great differences between social systems governed by markets and others, and morally, because of the important links in much human thought between markets, private property and social morality.

Although not widely understood or indeed studied prior to the events at the end of the 1980s, Vietnam, like China and Laos, had already undergone important social and economic change in the direction of a market economy. We argue here that the shift away from central planning to voluntary exchange as the basis for product distribution was the most important part of these transformations. Moreover, we believe that this corresponded to a shift in the characteristic nature of power relations in the society away from compulsion and prescription and toward those more diffuse pressures seen in a market economy. This distinction was largely bound up with the most important mechanisms of change driving the transition, almost as though these polar opposites were locked in a conflict to determine the future of the economy. This process-oriented position is not common in the economics literature.[2]

On a year-by-year basis, the steps in the transition can be viewed in many different ways, each of which stresses important aspects of the change: the emergence of markets; the evolution of pre-requisites for markets such as capital of certain sorts; the political developments that shifted back and forth in their overall direction; and, most important for the welfare of the people concerned, the "winners and losers."

The transition period was one of great confusion. This was perhaps necessary--it was found that a market economy requires both more information, and information of quite different types, than a centrally planned economy.[3] For much of the period, Vietnam's emerging markets were rather isolated from the world economy.[4] Thus there was much learning by doing. It was possible to observe, both directly and through what was being written at the time, that people were struggling to see order and social value in what was new and strange.

But one should not be too abstract. Before reaching general conclusions, it is useful first to look at what and where Vietnam was coming from. The next section therefore presents a summary of the main features of traditional neo-Stalinism and what happened when it was adopted by the Hanoi leadership in the late 1950s. This draws upon other work.[5] The subsequent section outlines the main mechanisms of change, and discussion in the final section concerns the political economy of transition. This sets the stage for the detailed analysis in Chapters 2 to 6. We argue that during the 1980s Vietnam laid the basis for a successful transition to a market-oriented economy. It is important to clarify in a general way what is meant here by transition and its major aspects in order to support the assertion that at least by 1990, and perhaps rather earlier, the Vietnamese economy was best viewed and analyzed as a market economy, albeit with severe distortions largely due to the absence of adequate markets in land, labor, and capital, that is, factor markets.[6]

Traditional Central Planning

The starting point for any analysis of the transition is the traditional central-planning model created in the Soviet Union during the 1920s.[7] Implementing this model involved establishment of a state industrial sector that operated according to a system of administrative allocation of inputs and outputs; quantity plan targets at enterprise level coexisted with a system of "balancing," in which planners allocated to enterprises the inputs required to meet the plan targets, which then became inputs to other enterprises, foreign trade, or the retail network. Agricultural collectivization saw farmers brought compulsorily into collective farms whose output was procured by the state distributive network. A general characteristic of the system was the use of compulsion to extract economic resources and concentrate them in priority areas. The typical transaction between economic agents was not based upon the agents' own calculations of the relative advantages of alternatives between which they would then choose. Instead, transaction meant the delivery and receipt of products in order to implement planners' legally obligatory targets.

This economic system in practice had a number of notable characteristics.

- First, it was capable, at least for some decades, of generating high rates of savings and accumulation. In response to planners' perceptions and desires, supplies of the resources required to generate rapid growth could be obtained, with depressed consumption levels disregarded.
- Second, it lacked technological dynamism since the introduction of new products was not well linked to the incentives structure.
- Third, it had very low static economic efficiency because of the absence both of indicators of relative economic cost and of mechanisms for providing suitable rewards for efficiency and sanctions against inefficiency.

In the wider political arena, the system's reliance upon compulsion corresponded to a general closure of the society, limiting its access to new ideas and the development of social structures that could articulate and resolve competing interests. This is why it is more meaningful to refer to it as neo-Stalinist rather than simply centrally planned.

Perhaps the best-known example of this economic system is that of the Soviet Union itself. During the 1930s the crash industrialization program did succeed in creating a basis for economic development, but with massive costs. Once reserves of so-called extensive growth derived from such measures as shifting the working population out of agriculture had been exhausted, productivity gains slowed. In many countries that tried to implement this model, later attempts to shift toward a market-oriented system showed that much of the hard-won industrial asset stock was grossly uncompetitive in world markets, while as the old system of supply broke down, many workers found themselves with no effective means of acquiring foodstuffs and other consumer goods. This points to the need for major structural change as the transition occurs, and raises in turn the question: How will this come about? What are the mechanisms of change? We argue here that among more general characteristics, certain elements

of the traditional system are of crucial importance in the transition to a
market-oriented economy.[8]

Transaction Types and their Implications

At its simplest, the transition to a market economy requires a qualitat-
ive change in the nature of the *dominant transaction type* within the economy. Transactions have to become essentially voluntary, based upon
considerations by producers and consumers of the relative costs and benefits of alternatives,[9] and we refer to these as "autonomous transactions."
Economic agents therefore have to acquire the freedom and ability both to
make these calculations and to act upon them. This means that they have
to control accumulated masses of something that can act as a store of
value and then as a medium of exchange--in other words, capital. This
need not take the form of money at all times, and in fact is highly unlikely
to do so, especially in the early stages. In their sensitivity to trade-offs and
comparisons of benefits and costs, agents will develop sources of
information and methods of calculation. The shift in transaction type
therefore involves development of price-sensitive supply and demand. It
also requires a radical increase in economic agents' autonomy and independence. This also means that the internal organization of production
units must change to reflect the fundamental shift in the units' goals.

The extent of the internal reorganization required is often underestimated by those without direct experience of the traditional system. For
example, a conventional centrally planned state enterprise possessed a
system of accounting under which could be found entries labeled "profits," "depreciation," "wages," and so forth. It also had bank accounts,
long-term debt, and other attributes reminiscent of a market economy. But
it would be deeply misleading to equate the two sets of categories,
although they have the same names. A traditional enterprise is better seen
by analogy as a totally controlled plant *within* a normal company. Whereas in a market economy the boundary between organizational and autonomous ("market") behavior is the firm, that is not the case in a centrally
planned economy. There, the enterprise neither decides upon its customers
nor its suppliers; it does not control credits and debits to its accounts; it
does not set prices; and it neither decides what it produces nor determines
changes in production technology. The transition therefore requires that
the enterprise establish itself as, among other things, the boundary
between autonomous and organized activities: In other words, it has to
generate independent control over its activities.[10]

Once it is accepted that units within the state sector have to change in
this manner as an essential part of the transition, then it becomes clear
why the property issue is so fundamental and so vexing to thinkers within

the fray. It can easily be said that property rights combine rights to share in generated surplus as well as rights to participate in decisionmaking. In an "ideal" centrally planned system, a state enterprise can be said to be state property since planners decide what is produced, to whom the product is delivered, and what happens to any resulting profits. However, once the unit develops autonomy, as well as the control over capital that enables it to participate in autonomous transactions, then both rights to share in generated surplus and to control decisions are no longer the planners' alone.[11] This is discussed in greater detail in Chapter 5. In Vietnam, these rights were initially shared by a group of interests that included the workers within the unit. As factor markets later developed, these de facto property rights changed and shifted, to become more obviously held either by local politicians and managers as individuals or held by the state in a more normal and familiar form as seen in developed capitalist economies. At the same time, labor participated increasingly as labor, rather than as co-owners of the unit, with wages set mainly by supply and demand for labor. These trends were only strong, however, after 1989. Clearly, this aspect of the transition must have important political economy implications, and these are discussed in Chapter 6.

An illuminating example of the development of state enterprise autonomy from within central planning is the pulp and paper mill built with Swedish assistance at Bai Bang in Vinh Phu Province, in northern Vietnam. It started operations in the mid-1980s.[12]

As a processor, the mill required and depended upon supplies of raw materials from forestry producers in the region. These were of two types: the state forest enterprises, which mainly produced wood; and a bamboo sector that included the state, cooperatives, and individuals. The latter sector also sold to a private market in housing timber. Under the traditional system the mill had no responsibility for these supplies, which were meant to be delivered to it according to the plan's orders. These orders were given both directly to state units and through cooperatives to farmers. Prices were set by central government. Pulp and paper were produced according to a quantity target given to the mill by its ministry (the Ministry of Light Industry), and their prices again set by planners based upon calculations of costs. The accounting system functioned primarily to assist in the control by planners of the overall system. Thus, although costs, prices, and profits all existed, they were not, as in a market system, designed to guide independent decisionmaking by the mill, its customers, or its suppliers. Indeed, under the traditional system the mill was not intended to be an autonomous unit, but rather an element within the overall state economy. It was the development of autonomous transactions during the 1980s that helped shift the mill management toward a greater awareness of markets.[13]

In this study we thus identify the transition from a centrally planned to a market-oriented economy as being the establishment of an economic system in which the typical transaction is based upon voluntary exchange between independent producers and consumers.[14] This will almost always take the form of some sort of market. However, these markets will, depending upon their precise character, be more or less efficient. In this regard, he direct and overly simple link often made between concepts of distortion and their implications for economic efficiency is confusing. It is therefore important to adopt analytical tools that clarify what can be meant by efficiency in the context of different resource allocation mechanisms. This is best done by making a distinction between two different types of distortion.

Distortions

It is widely accepted that the heavy use of compulsion and the creation of the growth pattern typical of a central-planning system leads to considerable economic distortions, of a character particular to that economic system. However, it is asserted here that what results is a pattern of resource misallocation that arguably combines two quite distinct types.

- In the first, the distortions in the underlying factor allocation are relative to all other allocations *consistent with a generalized market-oriented system.* That is to say, factors of production (land, labor, and capital) are situated throughout the economy in a way that is simply inconsistent with any generalized system based upon voluntary exchange. In this sense, a high level of distortion measures the extent to which factors will have to move before the economy can become market-oriented. We call this sort of distortion "plan distortion," since it results from the nature of the central-planning system itself.
- In the second, the distortions in factor allocation are *relative to some economically efficient allocation pattern or patterns.* Economic theory argues strongly that effectively operating markets result, in the absence of externalities and economies of scale, in efficient resource utilization. In this sense, a high level of distortion measures the extent to which resources are used in a way that makes output levels lower than they otherwise could be. We call this sort of distortion "market distortion."

The difference between the two notions, though not immediately apparent, may be clarified by an example. Imagine that planners under the old system had ordered production of a certain type of fixed asset that is used to produce specialized electronic surveillance equipment. Assume that there is no demand for such products under a market-oriented system. In order to reduce plan distortion, the asset must be used in another way. It must move to some part of the economy where it can be used to produce something that can be disposed of to a willing customer. Alternatively, it could simply be scrapped. However, it is possible that it could be modified to produce salable commodities. Assume that this happens--an alternative can be found. Assume, however that the government then decides to create (perhaps through entry barriers imposed through licensing requirements) a substantial monopoly to be enjoyed by the users of these assets in order to protect employment levels, or perhaps to prepare for the sale of state shareholdings, and the assets are not used efficiently. Assume, for example, that they would be better sold off for scrap and the freed capital used to buy more modern equipment. Thus, an eradication of plan distortion will not necessarily eradicate market distortion. What it does do, of course, is reveal it by the very shift to a generalized system of market-based transactions. *The shift to a generalized system of market-based transaction would eliminate plan distortion but not necessarily market distortion.*

The precise nature and extent of plan distortion in any centrally planned economy prior to transition is of great importance, for this arguably forms a basic economic constraint to the transition. In addition, of course, there may be political obstacles. However, the movement of factors of production in ways that reduce plan distortions is a necessary part of the transition. The pattern of labor, capital and land utilization must alter so as to be consistent with the requirement that the transactions that result in them being brought together in production are voluntary.

Mechanisms of Transition

Thus analysis of transition should examine and identify mechanisms that encourage the reduction of plan distortion. It is important here to recall the fact that until market-based transactions have become generalized it is *not* the market alone that determines resource allocation. The very nature of transition dictates that there has to be some hybrid between the old and new, and this hybrid must logically contain mechanisms that reduce plan distortion until a generalized market-oriented resource allocation system pertains. These mechanisms must act so as to shift resources toward areas of the economy where transactions are autonomous.[15] Thus there has to be a mechanism that allows economic agents to compare the relative values of the two alternative transaction types.

The obvious possibility is a coexistence of the two transaction types for the same good. Producers and consumers may thus obtain and dispose of the same goods both autonomously *and* within the plan. If local interests place higher values upon autonomous transactions, then they will be preferred. If this preference influences behavior, the desired mechanism driving the transition and the reduction of plan distortion exists. The origin of this mechanism, however, is the different values[16] of similar goods when thrown into different resource allocation system, that is, planned or autonomous transactions. If these are reduced greatly, or if autonomous transactions are forbidden (which can be viewed as a great increase in their cost), then the operation of the mechanism will become weaker and the process of transition will slow.[17]

To give a concrete example, consider again the Bai Bang Pulp and Paper Mill. The mill was originally required to produce certain sorts of paper for delivery to customers subject to state orders and was dependent upon other organizations for implementation of raw material delivery. During the mid-1980s supplies of raw materials became unreliable, and food supplies (especially rice) were increasingly difficult to obtain through the official state rationing system. At the same time, it had become possible to dispose of paper directly to customers at high prices (or to swap it at high values), thus generating resources that could be used to buy rice and raw materials directly. This the mill did, for example by purchasing rice in the South in 1988 during a period of acute food shortages in the North and also by rapidly expanding its direct purchases of bamboo on the free market during 1987-89.[18]

One consequence of the coexistence of different allocative mechanisms, such as parallel markets, is the existence of highly visible economic rents, for example, through access to scarcity premiums when plan supply is limited. When planners are rigid, fiscal policy lax, markets weakly developed, and economic conditions unstable these rents are likely to be high. During the transition, therefore, capital accumulation based upon access to such rents may be considerable.

Transition Paths

This approach to the transition process embodies a particular view of a market economy. It is an analytical view, within which ideas such as the market are abstractions. This way of thinking also points to the connection between the way in which a market economy is finally arrived at and the particular nature of that market economy. By focusing upon the importance of autonomous current transactions, one can argue that a market economy does not require for its existence extensive and effectively operating capital, labor, and land markets. Even if these prerequisites are lacking, it will almost certainly be a market economy, albeit a highly inefficient one. This will result not only from the likely high levels of market distortion, but also from the implications for competition and dynamic behavior of the absence of capital markets. But we believe that it is still best seen as a market economy. This position undoubtedly allows for an easier analysis of situations where certain elements of the economy are not permitted to operate, but where transactions remain predominantly autonomous. For example, if certain individuals are excluded from modern industrial production (e.g., on racial or other exclusive grounds),[19] then that is an example of market distortion through the prohibition of free entry and exit. Other examples of what appear to be market economies that lack complete and normally operating markets in basic factors might easily be cited.

Sets and Sub-sets

There is a further advantage to be gained from working with the distinction between plan and market distortion. Any given ("distorted") centrally planned economy has, at any point in time, a resource allocation that is the outcome of the various economic processes characteristic of it. This allocation involves an allocation of factors of production. Plan distortion then describes the multidimensional gap between this and the set of possible market-based resource allocations. It might be said that the larger the gap (especially for labor), the greater the social costs involved in the transition.

It is obvious (logically speaking), that there would usually be a number of feasible paths by which plan distortion might be reduced. This suggests that there are subsets of the set of possible final outcomes in terms of market allocations, in other words, one can talk about those outcomes typical of attempts at big-bang policies, those typical of a gradual approach starting with adjustments of state agricultural procurement prices, and so forth. Some might be considered as more accessible than others, implying lower adjustment costs--in other words, easier to get to. Others would be less attainable. For example, one might imagine a subset involving recapitalization of the existing capital-intensive sectors. This would almost certainly lower rates of real income growth in other sectors, thus adding to the costs of labor adjustment.

The sense, therefore, is that the *particular path of adjustment actually followed may itself limit and condition the outcome.* Thus the initial direction taken by the economy, if it is a result of the spontaneous breakdown of the system and pressures for change within the political economy, may shift the possible target subset toward those outcomes with lower social adjustment costs.[20]

In any case, it is worth bearing in mind that the particular process of transition actually adopted, by creating capital and processes of accumulation, will have an important influence on the nature of the resulting market economy. On the day after the abolition of central planning what happens next depends greatly upon how an economy arrived at its current state.[21]

The notion of sets and subsets also helps in discussion of the ways in which the nature of technologies and products conditions the potential for the development of new forms of exchange. Thus, it is typically easier to find a buyer for bicycle spare parts than for heavy girders; and the existence of technologies that permit profitable small-scale production of easily salable consumer goods should also be important.[22]

Transition Indicators

The development of quantifiable indicators of the parameters of the transition is of great importance and not widely researched. This is not least because of the frequent presence of arguments about the desirable speed, timing, sequencing, and political nature of the transition.

Although the distinction between plan and market distortions is easy to make, development of empirical indicators is far from easy. Processes are often easier to identify than levels. This is discussed further in Chapter 7. Here, however, we simply assert the importance of the following:

- The emergence and development of capital, by which we mean resources under the direct control of economic agents and used for financing profit-oriented activities. This includes both liquid capital and human capital, the latter notion expanded to include organizational capacity.
- Autonomous contracting and joint ventures between economic units.
- The evolving consciousness of the people concerned. Language has to develop if it is to be useful under new circumstances. New words, and new meanings, therefore indicate new social forms and mechanisms (Fforde 1990a and 1990b).[23]
- More concrete indicators such as factor mobility, structural change, and so on.

Transition Stages

The above discussion permits a simple periodization of the transition process. We identify four stages.

The Pre-stage. The first stage, the *pre-stage*, is simply the period prior to the emergence of the transitional model and the acceptance of autonomous transactions. During this time there may or may not have been significant expansion of unplanned activities. However, emergence of unplanned activities, if it occurs, creates a platform for their later development.

An important feature of the pre-stage is its effect upon the potential for a rapid and easy transition, that is, the nature and extent of plan distortions. These distortions apply not only to fixed assets (are they relatively concentrated in technologies with limited alternative use?) but also to human capital. Farmers who have spent generations in heavily managed collective farms may have lost the skills needed for independent family farming, whereas those who have enjoyed extensive activity on relatively freely managed private plots will typically have retained and even developed relevant knowledge.[24]

Fence-breaking. The second stage, that of *fence-breaking*, is a period when the process of transition is started through accelerated expansion of autonomous transactions. New and direct relations of a novel type start up between customers and suppliers.[25] This stage may become inseparable from the next stage. However, under some circumstances it is important to differentiate in the analysis between an informal (i.e., illegal) system and a formal (i.e., legal) transitional model. If reform is top-down these two stages are likely to be undifferentiated, whereas if it is bottom-up, and perhaps resisted by the authorities, two separate stages will be identified.[26]

Formal Transition. The third stage, that of the *formal transition*, involves the institutionalized, and, to a certain extent legally sanctioned, development and expansion of market-oriented activities. This typically reduces plan distortions until a generalized system of autonomous transactions becomes feasible.

The Post-stage. The final stage is the *post-stage*, when the main issues are likely to be those of market distortions and the development of nascent factor markets that will typically have emerged in weak and distorted forms. In particular, if the development of capital markets has been delayed, then one characteristic of the fence-breaking and formal transition stages will be that truly autonomous capital accumulation will largely have been confined to individual producers and traders. These will to a great extent be sited within units that were nominally part of the planned economy--SOEs, in particular. There will be no, or very restricted, effective intermediating mechanisms for shifting capital to successful producers. Toward the end of the formal transition, therefore, there will have been substantial accumulation of capital in the hands of certain producers, with a lack of mechanisms for moving it into more economically efficient sites. Combined with the weakness of the state's fiscal base, this will focus attention upon the development of the financial and monetary system (McKinnon 1991). The post-stage may end with the emergence of recognizable factor markets and a reconstructed state whose role has emerged more clearly.

Stages in Vietnam

For Vietnam, an approximate summary of these stages can be dated as follows:

- The pre-stage lasted until around 1979, when the impact of western and Chinese aid cuts, combined with bad weather, led to a spontaneous breakdown of the DRV model. This was to a limited extent sanctioned by the atmosphere change resulting from the Sixth Plenum of the Communist Party, held in summer 1979.
- Fence-breaking lasted until early 1981, with the passage of two decrees that institutionalized the transitional model (25-CP and CT-100, discussed later).
- The formal transition then lasted until the abolition of the two-price system in 1989.
- In the post-stage that followed, factor markets rapidly emerged, helped by the interest rate reforms of 1992 (creating positive margins for banks and positive real interest rates on loans to SOEs), the sharp rise in savings as a percentage of GDP, the Land Law of 1993, and the fast growth of the free market in jobs (see Chapter 9).

Note: The Economic Analysis of Transitional Economies

The Problem

A famous film producer, a Holocaust survivor brought up in communist Poland, was once asked what his most striking initial impressions were of the West. He replied by describing his feelings walking the streets of Zurich, watching what people were doing. He said that the overwhelming impression was one of choice--ordinary people were confronted in their daily lives with a range and variety of choices that for him was dazzling.[27] This observation seems to strike a central truth, for it is the nature of choice that distinguishes economic behavior under central planning, and its residual in transitional models, from that in market economies. Furthermore, the effects of the coexistence of these two types of behavior, and their interactions, distinguish transitional economies from market economies in general.

The problem has three essential aspects.

- First, under central planning, choices are made over a quite different set of variables from those in market economies. Rational behavior--constrained maximization--therefore takes place, in any meaningful sense, using different choice variables, different constraints, and different indicators of trade-offs. This means that the micro foundations upon which any theorizing or modeling is based need to be thought through.
- Second, if central planning coexists with markets, choices are usually contingent: Better implementation of orders received from above leads to better value outcomes in other areas oriented toward the free market. This means that observed prices do not reflect values--the relative costs and benefits that lead economic agents in their constrained maximization decisionmaking are *not* visible as prices. It also means that the balance between plan and market is endogenous and decisionmaking in the two spheres cannot be isolated. Although it may be said that the plan target "has" to be met before free market activities "are allowed," it is extremely unwise to assume that that is actually the case.
- Third, the system of property rights that exists in transitional economies is by nature contradictory and transient. Therefore, the stable and predictable set of property rights needed for traditional equilibrium analysis does not exist. Indeed, the relationship between plan and market is endogenous, not exogenous, so property-rights cannot be assumed a priori to take any particular form. This is a restatement of the endogeneity issue.

Standard Analytical Assumptions and Methods

In standard textbooks on economic decisionmaking in market economies, the analysis views the economy in certain ways. Consumers maximize utility subject to income, prices, and preferences. Producers maximize profit subject to technology, costs, and prices. These decisions result in *ex ante*, or intended, levels of production and inputs (for producers) and consumption and work (for consumers). What happens next can go in a number of different directions, but the core is the simple combination of utility-maximizing consumers and profit-maximizing producers. To quote Edmond Malinvaud: "More generally, 'agents' are the individuals, groups of individuals or organisms which constitute the elementary units of activity. To each agent there corresponds an autonomous center of decision" (Malinvaud 1972:3).

To adequately conceptualize a market economy, different authors stress different areas in addressing the key aspects that allow a market economy to cohere and function in a coordinated manner. These aspects concern the nature of the relationships between different economic agents, which are bound up with discussions about the nature of commodities. To take Malinvaud again as an example, we find that commodities are goods that satisfy human needs, have quantities and a single price, and are subject to the historically very particular requirement that "the social organization of economic activity generally allows individuals to exchange goods amongst themselves . . . [which] conform to prices given to the different goods" (Malinvaud 1972:3). This assumption, it is abundantly clear, does not hold in an economy with central planning, where individuals are not allowed freely to exchange goods among themselves.

The most important point to be made, therefore, about the economic analysis of transitional economies is that what is being studied is *essentially* different from those of the standard textbooks still normally used to teach economics. However, economics has started to move away from these positions, and to look at more basic categories within which transitional economies can more easily be analyzed (e.g., Milgrom and Roberts 1992).

Notes

1. E.g., regarding the importance of private property as a "defense against tyranny."

2. See Fischer (1993). In Chapter 9 other interpretations of the Vietnamese transition are examined.

3. This itself is an interesting finding, since it is often asserted that one of the great advantages of a market economy is the way in which it economizes upon information requirements by focusing on price. Although this reaffirms that many Vietnamese observed that the novel system required them to know many new things, this subject requires additional research and analysis. It may be that, under "real" conditions, a knowledge of markets means an extensive knowledge of suppliers and customers that is in addition to price. To that can be added the observation that when technology no longer comes from above and when the input mix can be altered far more easily, then certainly there is a demand for more information--otherwise how can choices be made?

4. To some extent this was a result of the political economy involved; direct trade with the West did expand in 1979-81 but was subsequently halted as local trading corporations were closed down (see *NhD*, 9 February 1982 for the effect on small-scale industry).

5. See Fforde and Paine (1987); also Spoor (1985); Phan Van Tiem (1990).

6. For this study, the key element is the nature of transactions in current goods and services. Thus, the development of effective factor markets is necessarily a slow and gradual process, occurring later on and therefore taking a secondary position.

7. This has been well studied. See, for example, Wiles (1977), Ellman (1979), and Davies (1980).

8. This draws upon earlier work (Fforde and Paine 1987) that was influenced, like many other works, by Kornai (1980). This work, however, tried to go somewhat beyond Kornai by introducing the concept of "aggravated shortage," whereas Kornai's marketless adjustment coexisted with markets and quasi-markets within the socialist economy. This idea was then used to analyze the North Vietnamese economy prior to 1975.

9. This is an analytical point. Within this view the levying of usurious interest rates upon a willing borrower would be seen as voluntary, yet for many this is morally questionable both in terms of the nature of the society that practices such behavior and of what we as outsiders feel about it.

10. See the literature on the reasons for the existence of firms--e.g., Coase (1988); Williamson and Winter (1991).

11. It can be argued that in practice no CPE could extinguish such peripheral autonomy. Nevertheless, in the pure system this was minimized.

12. The best bibliography on this interesting experiment in confronting Swedish sentiments of solidarity with the realities of aggravated shortage is Skarner (1988); see also Fforde (1989b).

13. Autonomous transactions were to evolve in areas such as inputs (development of a market in wood and bamboo) and outputs (formation of direct relations with customers based upon negotiations over price, quality, etc.)--see Fforde (1989c). The mill in essence acted first to break the state

supply monopoly in bamboo (around 1987-88) and then moved against wood sellers (around 1989-90).

14. A stress on transaction type rather than on the existence of some set of equilibrium prices and quantities evokes memories of Austrian and Institutionalist (e.g., J.C.R. Commons) economics. In fact, it more likely comes from a combination of (now in parts renounced) Marxism among the coauthors and the nature of the subject matter. For, in order to analyze exchange and distribution as "prices start to matter more," *existing* exchange relations cannot be treated in a standard supply-demand Marshallian manner. So, what is the alternative? The note to this chapter examines the theoretical position.

15. In Vietnam, this mechanism relied heavily upon the high differential between planned and unplanned "values" (often prices); inflation, in maintaining and widening this differential, therefore played a positive role. Attempts at stabilization, conversely, could, and in 1985 did, hinder the transition to a market economy. As already mentioned, Kornai (1985) discussed this point in a paper written for the World Bank. He argues, as do we, that *under certain conditions*, macro stabilization may inhibit economic liberalization. The key question is then what those conditions are and the nature of the system to which they apply.

16. By "value" here we simply mean the relative attractiveness to the producer and consumer of the good concerned, which measures the trade-offs involved--i.e., that which would be one of the parameters of a constrained optimization. The problem of how to measure such values presents interesting difficulties for any quantitative analysis of the transition. Interesting applied Ph.D. work by Stephen Seneque in Canberra is pointing to an analysis of allocative efficiency by Red River Delta farmers that reveals clear gaps between implicit value and actual price when farmers are subject to quantity targets (Fforde and Seneque 1993)

17. Since autonomous transactions were not only present in the DRV prior to their legalization through the Three Plan system in January 1981 but also existed in the form of the parallel markets normal in almost all East European economies, it should be stressed here that it is the degree and precise nature and extent of such transactions in Vietnam and under Vietnamese conditions that are important to understanding the transition in Vietnam--in other words, the nature of the DRV model (Fforde and Paine 1987).

18. Personal observations; see also Fforde (1989c).

19. One could recall here treatment of Jews, nonestablishment groups, officers of an army defeated in a civil war, Chinese, Aborigines, Irish, women in Muslim societies, etc.

20. Thus, for example, extensive and spontaneous market development may occur, for reasons based upon the nature of available technology and the existing pattern of demand, in areas of the economy requiring low capital inputs

(perhaps small-scale industry and agriculture). This is likely to generate more rather then less real incomes growth, more rather than less employment, and perhaps most thought-provoking of all, an economic structure more adapted to conditions of comparative advantage.

21. This will help to explain the pattern of events in 1990-92, after the removal of subsidized prices in 1989.

22. Here one is reminded of the ability of primitive artisans profitably to produce and sell crude copies of consumer goods in northern Vietnam in the late 1970s (Fforde, ongoing).

23. Many vivid expressions arose, steeped in the Vietnamese notion of local autonomy and responsibility: "own capital" (*von tu co*); "wages paid by the enterprise rather than according to the state schedule" (*luong do xi nghiep tu lo*); "doing it for yourself" (*to no tu giai quyet*).

24. See Chapter 3; also Fforde and Paine (1987); Fforde (1989a); Wadekin (1973).

25. This will almost certainly draw upon experience gained in the earlier stage. See Fforde and Paine (1987:passim).

26. This issue is bound up with the distinction we make in this book between "models" and "programs"--between reality in combination with policy, and the textbook prescriptions. As mentioned above, one of the many reasons for making this distinction is that we as yet know too little about just how these processes worked themselves out at local and sectoral levels; "the state" is still insufficiently differentiated and the analytical categories somewhat broad. However, we believe that this is, for the time being, the correct approach to take.

27. Fforde--personal recollection from an interview of Roman Polanski by Peter Ustinov, British television, early 1980s. Relating to the discussion of "voluntary" transactions in the preceding chapter, the Pole did not mention that such choice was only available to those lucky enough to be (1) on the streets in Zurich and (2) in possession of enough money to pay Switzerland's notoriously high prices.

2

Historical Context

Unlike many other developing countries, Vietnam is historically a nation.[1] Present-day behavior draws upon national history, and is often explained by Vietnamese through making reference to many centuries of national existence. Since at least the beginning of this millennium, if not for far longer, the Vietnamese have had experience wiht centralized administrative systems. Ideas of the nation-state are not, therefore, the product of Western colonial domination. Furthermore, modern Vietnam is the product of decades of armed struggle both against foreign forces and among the Vietnamese themselves. The outcome of this is, at present, the Socialist Republic of Vietnam, established in 1976 and studied here. Elite and popular conceptions of the meaning of national advance and development are heavily influenced by the particular nature of Vietnamese historical experience. The popular morality and sense of justice draw upon deep historical roots. The Vietnamese facility for avoiding unwanted or inappropriate state policies, or adapting such policies when necesary, would surely be unimaginable without great historical familiarity with such problems. In addition, the apparent inability of central authorities to impose their will inhibits rapid top-down imposition of radical policy reforms. It is therefore hard to understand the pattern of transition in Vietnam, above all the dominant role of spontaneous, or bottom-up, forces, without some appreciation of those elusive phenomena--national character and history.

The only clear development program that the current Vietnamese authorities have adopted so far resulted in the DRV model discussed earlier. This had affinities with traditional thinking, though with obvious differences appropriate to the Marxist-Leninist beliefs of the time. Through the

1970s and 1980s, policy operated through and upon institutions rooted in this model. In this chapter we therefore seek to provide a basis for linking the transition from plan to market to its historical roots.

Traditional Vietnam: The Family and its Environment

The traditional heartland of the Vietnamese is the Red River delta of northern Vietnam. Originally an empty land of swamps and cranes, it was well suited to growing paddy rice, and this became the basis for the Vietnamese culture. As most available land was brought under cultivation, the area filled with people, and so began the long process of territorial expansion known as the March to the South. Blocked by the Chinese from expanding to the north and limited by their reliance upon paddy cultivation to low-lying delta lands, the Vietnamese could only move southward. By around the eleventh century, they had started to move down the coastal strip of central Vietnam. Progress was slow, however, and only by the early eighteenth century did they arrive in the northern part of the Mekong Delta in the far South of present-day Vietnam.

Vietnamese history, as it is usually related, goes back even further, to the period before the centuries of Chinese occupation in the first millennium. The Vietnamese therefore have long experience of a centralized nation-state. Whether they were imperial officials (the mandarins) or peasants in their collective communes, the Vietnamese people were well accustomed to living with ideas of nationhood.

Systems and Subsystems

To simplify to the point of caricature, we believe it useful to maintain that, traditionally, Vietnamese society has revolved around *three basic subsystems*. In premodern times, these were the following:

The Neo-Confucian State. The emperors exercised arbitrary rule through the agents of the centralized bureaucracy--the mandarins. The bureaucracy was a single integrated network capable in principle of a close and detailed implementation of the emperor's commands. This system had been imported from China, and its legitimacy relied heavily upon the bureaucracy's access to allegedly superior foreign knowledge. Its power was ethically justified by the teachings of the neo-Confucian classics that all mandarins had to study--book learning was all-important to the bureaucracy. Rule had to be "virtuous" and disinterested. These maxims, however, could also be judged by results. The idea of the "mandate of heaven" meant that popular uprisings (albeit led by elite families or royal clans) were legitimate if the emperor's rule could no longer be seen as meeting the needs of the nation. The imperial government was held ultimately responsible for basic national tasks, including organization of national defense and territorial expansion. Another important part of its responsibilities was to mobilize the population for military service and work on the massive system of dikes that protected the northern deltas from river flooding.In the ruling neo-Confucian ideology, however, society was perceived as essentially static, and indeed the ideology supported various ways of limiting economic growth. In this respect it differs radically from twentieth-century Marxism-Leninism. Notably, accumulation of capital by merchants was frowned upon and taxed accordingly.[2] Society was formally divided into a hierarchy of classes: literati, peasants, artisans, and traders. Nearly all villages possessed some minor scholar who could teach the neo-Confucian classics to local children. One effect of this was to create the popular respect for formal education that ensured through the 1980s that almost all children went to school. Another was to encourage the sense that intellectuals outside the system could, through their access to knowledge, be just as legitimate as those within it--a concept that built a reliable foundation for some variation or variations of individualistic thinking.

The Local Collectives. The most prominent example of these collectives was the rural commune (*xa*). In a still predominantly rural population, almost all peasants belonged to a commune, which usually contained the center of their emotional and sentimental life--their "home village" (*que huong*). It is almost impossible to overestimate the importance of this institution to Vietnamese society. In a very poor area, where the weather is violently unpredictable, collective organization played a vital role in providing support to peasants, helping to insure against poverty, and protecting them from the demands of the state. In a world made up of such collectives, an individual without one was exposed to enormous risks and dangers. The commune and the home village provided the basic social frame for the rural population (Scott 1976).[3] The commune had important religious functions, for its tutelary spirit was the focus of local religious activity, communal feasts, and so on. The commune's spirit had usually received imperial recognition and approval, and the representative spirit was frequently that of a dead Vietnamese military leader, sometimes one victorious in battles against invading Chinese armies. Local religion therefore linked collective and state. The commune was also responsible for providing the military and labor resources that were the essential prerequisites for the survival of the nation. It is widely reported that in the nineteenth century, however, communes were largely self-governing. The lowest level of the imperial bureaucracy stopped at the district level just above the commune, resulting in the well-known maxim "The writ of the king bows to the customs of the village" (*phep vua thua le lang*); local autonomy was part of the accepted balance of power between the central Imperial Court and the local communes.

Within the commune, a number of institutions contributed to its power. One, of great importance to an agricultural society, was the so-called communal land (*ruong cong,* or *cong dien*; also *cong tho*). The commune allocated this land to its members in order to meet communal needs, and also to help those who lacked land. It averaged over one-fourth of the land area and was often highly valued by the peasantry as a support to the collective and an insurance against risk. In some communes almost all land was communal; in others, there was virtually none--levels as low as 10 percent were common. Collective property, and its use as a basis for the local community, is therefore quite familiar to Vietnamese through their historical experience. Although tax rolls were based upon communal membership recorded by name, communes were collectively taxed, and their members therefore had an incentive to stand together against state officials, traditionally seen as corrupt and grasping, who came to levy taxes.

The commune's important collective functions helped create the sentiments that provided the basis for peasant self-identity. Vietnamese peasants' emotional attachment to their home villages is legendary. In Vietnam today employers must still respect people's feelings for their home villages and the importance attached to returning there for the Tet (Lunar New Year) holiday.

The Family and the Individual. Although the collective sense is strong, Vietnamese society is also traditionally characterized by what could be termed "individualistic" elements. It may be argued that although more traditionally "Vietnamese" ways focused upon the nuclear family, imported neo-Confucian values stressed the importance of larger kin groups. Since the 1945 August Revolution, the underlying stress upon the three-generational nuclear family based upon grandparents-parents-children has continued. But with the effective collapse of neo-Confucian notions, the social role of the extended family (*ho hang*) of people with similar surnames greatly declined. The traditional commune tended to stress the smaller, or nuclear, unit, as does the modern system of cooperatives (largely but not entirely abandoned after 1988).[4]

Individuals and Their Roles

Traditional Vietnamese society, as well as Chinese neo-Confucianism, also asserted the importance of certain stereotypical roles within the family: father-son, husband-wife, elder brother-younger brother, wife--mother-in-law. These were in addition to other relations: ruler-subject, teacher-pupil, and friend-friend. They were said to be the basis both of the natural order and the framework of the state itself. On these grounds, society pushed for the subordination of younger people to their elders and of women to men at the same time that it maintained the individual authority of the Emperor. Hierarchical relations within the family were linked to the hierarchical nature of relations between the subject and ruler.

The dynastic state philosophy therefore stressed the need for individuals to subordinate themselves to the collective and to superiors defined as such by the neo-Confucian system. It should be noted, however, that the popular Buddhist religion exhibited a more contemplative and individualistic view. There was also a strong Taoist influence. The powerful themes created by the tension between fate and talent in an individual's life can be seen clearly in the most important single item in the Vietnamese literary canon, the *Tale of Kieu*. Largely pessimistic about the possibilities for self-determination in traditional Vietnam ("Fate and talent are two words that hate each other"--*chu tai chu menh kheo la ghet nhau*), this story concerns the life of a single person, a woman, whose individuality is profoundly inhibited by her sense of duty and by the powers that surround her.

The sense of personal individuality constrained by duties toward kin and suffocated by the arbitrariness imposed by concentrations of economic and state power strikes many echoes for modern Vietnamese. The Sino-Vietnamese word for revolution, *cach mang*, means, literally, to change fate. It can also be read, in political philosophy, as to "change the mandate of heaven" (*thien menh*), that is, to change the dynasty. For the analysis of reform processes, the point is that it is quite right and proper for the individual to strive against higher powers, especially if by doing so one's immediate family gains; the family is assumed to be right; the higher powers, on the whole, wrong. That it is the nature of the individual to struggle in this way is unquestioned; the heroine of the *Tale of Kieu* is thus a strong character whose destiny is to struggle actively against constraints, not accept them passively.

Some writers point to two other aspects of traditional Vietnamese culture. First, there is the striking strain of romantic individualism that mirrors the Chinese classics and can be seen in bastardized form in modern Kung Fu films (Woodside 1976:5). With sufficient pluck and luck, an individual could transcend the ordinary social boundaries. Second, there is the prevalence of religious and ideological pluralism. Alongside Buddhism there was Taoism, as well as the indigenous religions seen in the communal spirit cults. Chinese neo-Confucianism was, in the last analysis, Chinese and not Vietnamese; its prescriptions regarding female inheritance rights, for instance, were modified to take account of the somewhat less oppressed role of women in Vietnam. The Legal Code of the first Nguyen emperor in the early nineteenth century, for example, said that a widow should keep family property after the death of her husband and until her own death. In the sixteenth century, Western contacts added Catholicism to the brew.

For all the relative pluralism of religion and ideology, however, traditional Vietnam was still highly conservative. Great stress was placed upon the role of collectivities in both realizing and limiting individual self-realization. This was reinforced by the belief in the malleability of personality through correct learning and the importance of knowledge to the legitimacy of the national bureaucracy and imperial rule. However, the 1945 August Revolution and its radical approach to gender and generation greatly weakened the influence of these ideas, quite apart from greatly advancing the processes that removed Vietnam from French colonial domination.

Systemic Reproduction: The Importance of Family

Together, these three subsystems (the neo-Confucian state, local collectives, and the family and the individual) could, under certain conditions, guarantee their common reproduction. In quasi-caricature; the family at the base maintained access to land through the local commune and could unite with others to send young men to fight Chinese invaders, weaker powers to the South, or other ethnic Vietnamese of different allegiances. Reproduction of the whole system containing these subsystems was aided by the role of the state in national expansion and through the easing of social tensions by emigration from the overcrowded northern deltas. The taxes supplied by the largely self-sufficient communes provided the small resource flows needed by the bureaucracy. The lack of development of either markets or cash economy helped to protect the institutions of the commune against land concentration. The system as a whole was only dynamic, however, in its territorial expansion, for economic development and improved technology were minimal. The division of the country during the seventeenth and eighteenth centuries showed the limits of the imperial system in maintaining national unity, and the arrival of the French revealed its inability to undergo rapid reform in the face of this major threat.

Basic to the aggregate system made up of these three subsystems, however, was the focus upon the reproduction requirements of the family at its base. The stress was on family strategy and on the extent to which communes (or their subsequent structural reemergence in the form of cooperatives or state enterprises) could meet the perceived needs of the families whose members worked and lived in them. Familiarity with the nation-state and the right to "restore meaning," that is to rebel against unworthy national leaders, therefore amounted to a political space within which people would operate when and if their economic environment ceased to satisfy and other opportunities opened up. Family psychology and perceptions of opportunities for advancement, especially for children, therefore provided a potent force for major systemic change.

Implications for the Present

To understand modern Vietnam, perhaps the most important legacies of traditional society to observe are as follows:

- First, a belief in the valuable and important role, both managerial and ethical, to be played by a centralized state bureaucracy in national life. The idea that autonomous social "space" should develop spontaneously and free from official guidance based upon ethically sound knowledge was alien. However, the notion that in practice it probably would was as "natural" as the existence of evil to a Christian. Thus the plan-market stand off familiar from Marxism-Leninism could draw upon deep cultural roots.
- Second, a mass historical experience and commitment to collective organization in local villages that covered a wide range of functions--emotional, spiritual, and economic.
- Third, what might be called an "individualism," though different from Western meanings of the term. This individualism was bound up with loyalty to family; it asserted the individual's existence and, under certain circumstances, the right to push against the pressures exerted by collectives and other powers such as the state.

Foreign Models

Vietnam, throughout its history, has been affected by a range of foreign influences. China was dominant for many centuries, but in modern history the West has played the major role in presenting alternative ideas of paths to national advance. In the following section we present a brief examination of the impact of foreign influence and the implications for the process of transition.

The French Impact

The French conquest of the late nineteenth century destroyed many basic assumptions of traditional Vietnamese society (Marr 1971). Above all, the colonial presence had a profound effect upon the status of the ruling elite. Their imported knowledge--neo-Confucianism--was shown to be inadequate as the French proceeded to destroy the Vietnamese armies and put puppet emperors on the throne in Hue. Following tradition, this suggested that a New Knowledge would have to be found to replace the old as the motor of an independent postcolonial Vietnamese state. These ideas would have to be dynamic, concentrating upon the now widely accepted key task of securing the economic development needed both as an essential part of progress and as a foundation for continued national independence. Perhaps more subtly, the French conquest, and the eventual defeat of the French, strengthened the existing tendency toward pluralism: Vietnamese intellectuals, and indeed anybody who could read the spreading number of books in the easily learned Latin script (*quoc ngu*), were exposed to the wide range of Western ideas in addition to those they received from their domestic environment.

The effect of French colonialism upon the impoverished northern and central peasantry was dramatic. The French Union made money, mainly from the underpopulated South, but also from mining in the North, and Saigon became the main source of revenue from exports of such goods as rice and rubber. Internal migration in the 1920s and 1930s was insufficient to reduce the substantial economic differences between the North and Center and the far richer South. Taxes in the North and Center were primarily levied in order to pay for the colonial administration. Thus, a heavy and monetary tax burden coupled with limited opportunities for earning cash forced the poorer peasants to borrow money, and they began increasingly to lose their land. At the same time, population pressures continued to rise in the North. One reason for this was the effects of the *pax francona* (French peace), and the end of the wars of conquest. This led to a reduction in epidemics. Another was the long-term effect of the population boom that had occurred when the long period of civil wars ended in the early nineteenth century. (Fforde and Paine 1987:18).[5]

Popular discontent rose in the 1920s and 1930s. As more and more people started to pawn their land the commune system began to break down. Moneylenders, rice traders and colonial petty officials began to gain control of the communal lands and extended their personal landholdings. As power became increasingly concentrated in the hands of private individuals and elite families, the collective basis of the rural communes was correspondingly eroded. As rural conditions deteriorated, popular unrest increased, culminating in the risings in central and southern

Vietnam of the early 1930s. The 1944/45 famine confirmed to many peasants the dire effects of a breakdown in local collective mechanisms (even though it had little to do with village capacities).

The Search for Alternatives

The Vietnamese, having seen neo-Confucianism undermined, looked for alternatives. It seems that one legacy of colonialism and the question of national self-expression was to pose the problem of modernization in terms of the interrelationship between the nation, the collectivity, and the family and individual (Woodside 1976:passim). As we have argued, state, commune, and family were the basic subsystems of traditional Vietnam. This way of looking at things is still important today and appears clearly in debates about the correct relationship between the family, collectives and the state. But personal subordination as Annamites (the French word for the Vietnamese produced a keen awareness of Western power, which meant that economic growth and development were the unchallengeable goals of any postindependence Vietnamese government.

Traditional thinking encouraged hostile attitudes to private industry and trade, for many reasons. These forms of commerce could be seen as being in opposition to many valued aspects of Vietnamese society: for example, local collectivities (private capital accumulation had attacked the communal system and aggravated processes of land loss); virtue (by encouraging selfishness); and the bureaucracy that was seen as the normal expression of the national endeavor.

This meant that a bureaucratic program that placed constraints on the development of private property and markets was an almost instinctive solution to the burning problem of national development. This was especially true if it gave a major role to rural collectives, which could be used to adapt the communal system so as to create a basis for economic development. Neo-Stalinism seemed to meet these criteria. It would have to cope, however, with the basic poverty of the region, the tradition of ideological pluralism, and the importance Vietnamese attach to the family and the individual. However, it is however clear from Table 2.1 that the level of economic and social development in French Vietnam was primitive.

National Independence, Neo-Stalinism, and the DRV Model

The anti-French struggle was in the first instance patriotic and nationalistic and in the second, social revolutionary and radical, in that it assisted major changes in accepted attitudes to class, gender, and generation. The August Revolution of 1945 and Ho Chi Minh's Declaration of Independence established a break with the past and committed the country to profound social change. Ideals of social equality, democracy, and justice came onto the stage. Many of the anachronistic assumptions of neo-Confucianism were abandoned. These were, however, very much subsumed by the nationalist struggle.

Although the proportion of the Vietminh leaders who came from poor families is not known, the movement had, in the person of Ho Chi Minh himself, a leader with a cosmopolitan and multilingual background. The first generation of communists among them had learned their Marxism during the 1920s and 1930s. They were supported by a wide range of popular forces based in the delta peasantry and some of the upland minorities; in the North, many of the extant local leadership--richer peasants and small landlords--joined the struggle. In the Vietminh army, interpersonal relations were relatively egalitarian.

The position of women was advanced by the new Democratic Republic of Vietnam's adoption of Western precepts of citizenship. For example, women voted in the 1946 elections for the National Assembly. Another aspect of these wide-ranging changes were the literacy campaigns, which rapidly gained success among the previously largely illiterate peasantry.

But this was offset by other, perhaps more backward-looking effects. The advent of the Vietminh in liberated areas reversed the previous processes of land loss and reinforced the collective functions of the communes by using them as a basis for the Resistance Committees that organized the armed struggle as well as logistics services. The unwinding of the processes of commercialization and monetization that had pushed land loss in the 1920s and 1930s was also encouraged by the return to barter economy in many areas. Wartime propaganda started to focus upon the New Knowledge that was, it was expected, to form the basis for the new Vietnamese government. This increasingly came to mean Marxism-Leninism and a development model inspired by Soviet experiences.[6]

Neo-Stalinism Applied, 1957-75[7]

After the defeat of the French colonial forces at the battle of Dien Bien Phu in 1954, the country was divided in two at the 17th parallel. In the North, the DRV, under the leadership of the Vietnamese Communist Party (then called the Vietnamese Workers' Party), commenced the task of economic construction and social development. Until the beginning of heavy U.S. bombing in 1965, there was a period of comparative peace during which the institutional framework of the DRV was used to mobilize resources into the development program.

In hindsight, the DRV development program appears strikingly in keeping with aspects of traditional Vietnamese thinking. This was despite its historical origins in the ideology of the Soviet Union of the late 1920s and 1930s. Granted the radical innovation that the state's main responsibility was seen in dynamic terms--the initiation and management of national socioeconomic development--the program was designed to use a large central bureaucracy to allocate resources directly into what were seen as the priority tasks of national construction. These were understood simply as meaning rapid industrialization, or the creation of large-scale modern industry. At the same time, central planning could apparently ensure the distribution of scarce commodities to those who needed them most.

Central planning and the administrative direction of the economy seemed to promise a pattern of development that would avoid the creation of private--and therefore unethical--economic power. Pressure against markets would ensure that there would be no possibility of land concentration and land loss. The overall picture of development was one in which the New Knowledge behind neo-Stalinist development appeared to offer a moral and ethical basis for integrated national development. The plan, which through administrative orders directly guided the growth of industry and the flows of resources throughout the economy, was to be a visible and concrete manifestation of the New Knowledge. Social order was to derive from the new social classes: a collectivized peasantry, and the growing industrial working class.

The peasantry, securely based in agricultural producer cooperatives, was to supply the food and industrial materials needed by state industry. These cooperatives presented a way of adapting traditional collectives-- the communes and the villages they contained--that offered a solution to the problem of national economic development as it was then understood. Cooperatives could also fulfill the welfare roles that were so important to the relationship between individuals and families, on the one hand, and to the rural collectives, on the other. They could help families in difficulties, for example, if a parent was dead; they could help the families of men in the army; and they could help finance valuable services such as the rapidly expanding medical and school systems.

In this program, the focus of the development effort was the working class--the growing mass of state employees in the factories. Rapid growth in this sector was the explicit goal of neo-Stalinism. At the same time, however, there was a large expansion of state employment in the social infrastructure of bureaucracy as well in such areas as education, health, and culture.

This offered much to families. The state and the collective, in a structural transformation of the old triadic set of subsystems, would supply conditions for advancement. However, much depended upon the conditions and alternatives.

Economic Management

State economic units were set up in accordance with the established Soviet managerial concepts also adopted in such countries as China.

The central planning system, somewhat simplified, was basically intended to operate as follows: Capital resources were supplied by the state to SOEs in order to produce a certain product. These resources were essentially supplied free. Each unit was managed by a level of the state bureaucracy (a ministry, if centrally-managed; a provincial or city department, if locally-managed[8]) that allocated labor to it. The unit was then given a regular production target, in quantity terms, and in order for it to meet this target it was provided with levels of current inputs calculated on the basis of simple arithmetic norms. These inputs were supplied directly to the unit by the state, and its output was also supplied directly to the state. The unit was there essentially to produce for the target, and with almost no freedom to choose either what it produced or who it produced for, the unit had little interest in either the value of what it produced or the real costs involved in doing so. It was also not allowed to seek out better suppliers of its inputs. In this way the planners maintained central control over resources and could hoped to ensure that they went to priority areas.

The system was saturated with the ethos of rapid development, thus plans given to factories were set at high levels. Factories had no difficulty in disposing of their products, which were delivered to the state trading monopolies according to the plan. Managers had strong incentives to hoard inputs so as to maximize output regardless of cost. They were quite free to borrow in order to finance increases in circulating capital, and they were as insensitive to capital costs as they were to the price of output and the costs of inputs. Prices and costs simply did not matter greatly to such resource allocation systems based upon administrative instructions. Shortages were therefore inherent, since sellers' "markets" predominated. This "shortage economy" was accompanied by high levels of short-run inefficiency,[9] whose effects upon popular welfare were partially masked by foreign aid.

The basis of this system was the use of state monopoly power to concentrate resources on the top priority sector--state industry. Forced development meant that free exchange could not be used to secure these resources. The state therefore had to defend its monopoly position by taking administrative measures against those who sought to break it, attacking smuggling, illegal transactions in key goods such as food and fuel, and so on. In principle, this should then have allowed it to supply these resources cheaply to the priority areas of the economy. Distortions (at least relative to market-set levels) in the social valuation of economic resources were therefore an integral part of the development effort and reflected the state's intended use of monopoly power to concentrate resources. It is the spontaneous erosion of this system and its effective collapse in the period 1979-80 that underlies the history of reform and transition in Vietnam. The obvious historical question is therefore: Why did it not collapse earlier? This leads us to a discussion and analysis of the realities of the pre-1979-80 situation and what processes and forces existed to maintain it. Use of the terms "DRV model" and "transitional model" aims to facilitate this. In this case the distinction between the DRV program and the DRV model can best be approached through an examination of what happened when the textbook prescriptions of neo-Stalinism encountered Vietnamese reality.

Implementation Problems

Whereas the New Knowledge stemming from neo-Stalinism arguably fitted well with traditional Vietnamese notions, the attempt actually to implement these ideas in North Vietnam ran into considerable difficulty. The thinking behind it was in fact very limited; it was, in the strict sense of the term, simply "imported." There was little clear conception of how Vietnamese society was developing once the new institutions were put into operation in the late 1950s and early 1960s. The country was also increasingly locked into ideological debate with the Saigon-based Republic of Vietnam. Internal criticism was stifled, especially after the so-called Nhan Van--Giai Pham affair of the late 1950s, when independent analysis and criticism of developments were condemned by the party and driven underground. Both northern and southern governments asserted their own legitimacy, to their own people, if not internationally.

During the First Five-Year Plan (1961 to 1965) the basic framework of the DRV state and its associated neo-Stalinist institutions were used to attempt accelerated industrialization. Large supplies of foreign aid came in to meet this goal. This was essential as there was almost no modern industry in the area. The aid was used to develop modern state industry, which showed impressive rates of growth, as shown in Table 2.2.

But as the First FYP progressed, macroeconomic tensions mounted. One indicator of the pressure of the industrialization drive was the ratio of accumulation to total national income. This reached a peak of 25.1 percent in 1965--a level it was not to reach again until 1995 (see Chapter 9) (Fforde and Paine 1987:table 22).

The tax base failed to grow sufficiently to cope with expenditure needs. The foreign trade position deteriorated. In a poor country, however, the crucial requirement was food supplies for the non agricultural workforce. In this sector conditions were initially deceptive. In the early years, food supplies had been relatively good. State prices were even at times *above* free market prices. But in the early 1960s the lack of attention paid to the overpopulated and impoverished rural areas led to its inevitable consequence and, as the state's rice monopoly failed, food costs rose. *State employees' real wages fell by around 25 percent during the First FYP* (Fforde and Paine 1987:57, citing SO 1978:tables 132 and 136).

There were a number of reasons why food supplies grew too slowly to meet the rising demand from the state sector:

- First, the system of agricultural cooperatives, which almost all northern peasants had joined in 1959-60, was inefficient. Managers had little or no experience. They were meant to work with a detailed system of labor management that was clumsy, allowing little room for rewarding hard work. Rather than farming in the small family units they were used to, cooperators now had to work in large teams, with payment according to a detailed system of work norms and points (see Chapter 5). The numerous supervisory cadres had to be paid and in the end contributed little if anything to output. Their numbers tended to proliferate.
- Second, agriculture, already poor, was starved of resources. Although some efforts were made to improve irrigation, introduce better tools, and so forth, state industry received top priority in the allocation of the foreign assistance that was driving the First FYP.
- Third, as free market prices rose, cooperators increasingly preferred to work on their so-called private plots. These were left to them to farm privately, and they could legally sell surplus output from them on the free market. With insufficient resources coming into the cooperatives from the state, which saw them primarily as tax units, work for the cooperative became increasingly less attractive than work on the private plots. This tended to push resources onto the free market and away from the plan.

Spontaneous Change: Institutional Endogenization

Macroeconomic pressures eroded state monopolies and revealed the underlying distortions in the economy imposed by the DRV development program. This created spontaneous adaptations and, in effect, bottom-up reform processes. Members of agricultural cooperatives and SOEs expanded their own account activities by diverting resources into areas that permitted them to access free markets. These helped to reduce somewhat the short-run inefficiencies of the system but could not cope significantly with structural distortions. As markets and quasi-markets grew in importance within the socialist sectors, the classic "shortage economy," familiar from the Soviet Union and Eastern Europe, evolved into something rather different, which has been termed an "aggravated shortage economy" (Fforde and Paine 1987:chapter 3). Thus an important characteristic of the Vietnamese pre-stage was the coexistence of planned and unplanned activities, quite illegally, but nevertheless to a certain extent accepted.[10] This led to processes whereby the traditional neo-Stalinist institutions adapted, or became "endogenized". Micro level de facto change was therefore on the agenda before reunification in 1975-76. This was a basic element of the DRV model.

A key issue behind the development of spontaneous adaptation processes is the attitude and effectiveness of the authorities in using administrative measures to curb the development of unplanned activities. One clear example is the use of the police to control the free market. This is an area that requires further research, but it is clear that from the very early 1960s onward the DRV authorities showed themselves unwilling or unable to use such measures to the degree necessary, and this permitted the free market to grow and adaptation processes to erode the power of state monopolies. We are not yet certain just why this happened, but it was fundamental to the political compromises that came to define the DRV model. Similar compromises can be seen in other parts of the socialist bloc.[11]

Macroeconomic distortions thus exerted fiscal pressures that were met by inflationary finance rather than by recourse to administrative measures. As free market prices rose, the North Vietnamese economy adapted, and neo-Stalinism was found, in effect, to be unimplementable under North Vietnamese conditions. Just why this was so, will perhaps long remain subject to historical debate, the failure of the authorities to use violence is one key issue to explore. In any case, it had been assumed that the resources needed to operate the newly installed plants in modern state industry could be supplied by the northern economy. But although the abundant labor supply meant that people could easily be found to take the jobs offered, it was far more difficult for the state to find the resources these workers needed-- most important, food, but also other consumer goods as well as raw materials. Aid increasingly filled the gap after 1962-63 and can arguably be seen as another important element of the compromises inherent in the DRV model. Foreign aid thus appears to have reduced the likelihood of social confrontation. However, by doing so it *diminishes* the force behind arguments that maintain that wartime conditions required preservation of elements of the DRV model that were under pressure for spontaneous adaptation, especially the system of centralized labor control in the cooperatives. If aid fed the cities and the army, what did it matter what the villages did?

In the state economy, DRV planners still placed great stress upon the development of production, but without a firm grasp of what this would actually mean for social relations within production units once the system had started to evolve under its own dynamic and outside planners' control.

The forced pace of development meant that output plans issued to factories were set at high levels, perpetuating disequilibria and investment hunger. The plan emphasized strict fulfillment of output targets and the obligation to supply the resources needed to meet those targets. Based upon the direct administrative allocation of resources, planners did not need to compare alternatives by weighing cost against benefit. In such a system there is in any case no clear way of doing so, since the desire to use state monopoly power means that prices (e.g., those paid to farmers) should not reflect the forces of supply and demand. The plan had therefore to ignore the choices people would actually have to make in order to fulfill those directions in a poor area where economic assistance was primarily directed at expanding the fixed capital stock of modern state industry. The breakdown toward the end of the First FYP (1961-65) was not, therefore, either expected or well understood.[12]

The neo-Stalinist model, and its extreme use of state monopoly power, led to considerable waste when the attempt was made to implement it in North Vietnam. Since resource flows had to follow plan directives, only the planners were meant to shift resources from where they were idle to where they were needed. In practice, however, resource supplies became increasingly tight as rising industrial investment and increasing nonproductive state activity pushed up the demand for inputs from the state monopoly trade organs. More and more it was found that the DRV central-planning system could not cope with this task. Some Vietnamese sources use the phrase "simultaneously abundant and short" (*dong thoi thua, thieu*) to describe situations where some input, badly needed in one factory, remained over-stocked in another, since the two factories could not deal directly with each other. This is a classic characteristic of a shortage economy (Kornai 1980:passim).[13]

The macrodistortions revealed themselves in difficulties with the overseas and fiscal balances. Inevitably, therefore, toward the end of the First FYP, aid donors found themselves under pressure to modify the pattern of assistance. This meant supplying the DRV state apparatus and the newly installed state industry with the inputs that should have been supplied from the domestic economy. Consumption goods imports rose in order to meet the needs of the workers; industrial inputs--fibers for textiles, steel for machines, and so forth--had to be brought in to operate the machines.

This trend toward import dependency was increased by the onset of U.S. bombing, after which high levels of foreign aid helped maintain output and consumption. This meant that the underlying value relations of the economy moved away from those typical of a neo-Stalinist system. Levels of surplus extraction through state procurement were never too extreme, and with the cities supported by food aid and state factories and workers supported by commodity aid from the Soviet bloc and China, the weight of the system upon the domestic economy was eased. However, this helped to create a particular type of dependency, in which the "modern" sector could almost detach itself from the rest of the economy and float upon levels of commodity aid that were hidden, in that such commodities became inputs to state production units supplied through the Vietnamese state supply net. This syndrome was reinforced in the late 1980s by the increased Soviet aid program at that time, which is discussed further later on.

Popular Expectations

The priority given by the DRV program to the state and modern state industry created high expectations among the population and a widespread sense that increased economic activity was to take place in the state sector, and in the cities. The pattern of development was expected to lead rapidly to a modern industrialized society that would be essentially urban. The place to be was therefore in the cities, working for the state. This ethos, supported by the ideological apparatus of the DRV state, dominated North Vietnam for the three decades after 1950.

But, before the onset of heavy U.S. bombing and wartime mobilization in 1964-65, state employees were already finding that life was not quite as they had expected. Poor food supplies and high free market prices had eroded real incomes during the First FYP. Despite this, however, access to state employment was highly valued: A state worker was part of the leading sectors of the economy, receiving priority allocations of resources from the state. Housing, medical care, and access to various other facilities were important. State employment therefore came to be increasingly valued for the access it gave to cheap resources, above all to food and social security, as shown in Table 2.3. The weak commitment to labor effort, however, resulted from the existence of free market alternatives or their equivalent.

The Legacy of National Reunification

The DRV model, understood as the socioeconomic system that resulted from the failed attempt to implement neo-Stalinism in the North, was an important legacy of the pre-1975 period for reunited Vietnam. For this reason, much of the policy thrust of the immediate post-1975 period should be seen as having these two aspects:

- First, the imposition upon the South of a system that was suffering severe internal difficulties and was far less powerful than many outside analysts have assumed.
- Second, the need to address the problems in the North imposed by the realities of the DRV model. Here can be found The origins can be found here of much of the early debates about "reform" prior to 1978-79 (e.g., Nguyen Tri 1972).

After 1965, the wartime struggle was closely linked to the issue of "Socialist Construction." This resulted in an assertion by the national leaders of the value of the DRV program and neo-Stalinism. However, as we have argued already, this had been showing strains before the start of U.S. bombing. The political commitment to the model complicated its eventual replacement. From the economic point of view, the main effect of the U.S. bombing was the increased level of imports from the Soviet bloc and China, which, it has been argued, more than compensated for the direct effects of the destruction and actually pushed up gross national income in North Vietnam (Fforde and Paine 1987:70).

Wartime imports aggravated the structural distortions of the northern economy. They permitted a further expansion of the overgrown state sector while hiding the domestic economy's inability to supply needed inputs to it. This meant that the structural origins of basic macroeconomic imbalances were exacerbated. Unless there were major changes in development policy, return to peace would expose the nonpriority sectors (above all agriculture) to even higher pressures from the state to supply cheap resources. The state monopolies would be under greater pressure from competition from other methods of allocating resources, in particular the free market. It would be even more difficult to regain economic balance, and economic issues would be likely to dominate postwar politics.[14]

The trauma of wartime violence created a great desire for peace and prosperity, for demobilized soldiers inevitably sought a stable economic base for their families. Brought up to accept the norms of the DRV model and confronted with poor employment prospects in the stagnant rural areas, they pushed for jobs with the state. Family links were important in gaining access, as were the party's views on what constituted a politically correct class background. Rising popular aspirations were therefore bound to run up against the need to restructure the economy once aid imports were cut back during peacetime.

The Beginnings of Spontaneous Transition

Fundamental to an assessment of the failure of the DRV development program is the fact of North Vietnam's basic poverty. Northern agriculture reflects the region's historical role as the population source for the rest of the country. With rapid population growth and the creation of an overdeveloped state sector, food supplies were bound to be of crucial importance.

The process by which the institutions of a classic shortage economy adapted and evolved toward a coexistence with autonomous transactions was largely spontaneous, for many aspects of aggravated shortage were simply illegal. As the state found it harder and harder to compete with unplanned ways of acquiring and disposing of resources, ways of acquiring additional food supplies became of great importance for units dependent upon supplies from the state. There were basically two ways in which this could be done: The food could be produced by some or all of the workers in the unit, or it could be acquired in some other way, such as by finding things to sell or exchange. This often involved tapping into the frequently rather odd pattern of economic rents created by the DRV model, within which exchange values of the same good could vary enormously as the position of the transactors within the system changed. For example, a state employee buying cloth on ration could then sell it to state workers operating what were essentially free market tailoring services within an SOE, so long as they had the proper "cover."

Both of these options encouraged the units to develop strategies that virtually obliged them to use their resources in ways that the planners did not intend. This required and encouraged utilization of methods of collective action evocative of traditional behavior, since the collective was needed to protect such strategies from superior levels. A state unit was meant to be producing its stipulated output according to the target, not finding ways of generating higher incomes by developing sidelines or growing food. This view, and corresponding hostility to "outside" strategies, was entrenched in the official thinking behind the DRV program. But since supplies through the state distribution system were often inadequate, *fulfillment of the plan often relied upon such activities*. A unit that could increase its workers' welfare by developing activities "outside" the plan could often fulfill its plan more easily than another, more conservative unit, that operated by the book.[15]

This process relied heavily upon conditionality. That is, the management of a unit permitting diversification in this way made such deviance conditional upon fulfillment of the unit's plan targets. A process akin to bargaining therefore took place, as the unit adapted itself to balancing the various costs and benefits that arose from different sorts of outside activity and fulfillment of the state plan. The relative volume and implicit costs of resources supplied by the state--consumer goods rations, industrial inputs and so on--were an important part of this balancing process. Changes in the availability of food, for example, could result in pressure for more freedom to work outside.

Similar developments occurred in agricultural cooperatives, where cooperators sought to extend the family economy, usually by such strategies as working less hard for the collective, extending the private plots beyond the 5 percent norm and concentrating upon them such valuable resources as the manure from livestock (Fforde 1989a). Here again, the unsuitability of neo-Stalinism to North Vietnamese conditions resulted in pressure for its adaptation. Collective support for the agricultural cooperatives was encouraged by their important role in welfare service provision. Furthermore, the North Vietnamese peasantry's ability to force adaptation of this key element of neo-Stalinism in line with local interests (but quite contrary to central state policy) was an example of the continued vitality of traditional collective action.

These processes of spontaneous adaptation to the incentive structures accompanying the DRV model can be interpreted as ways of improving the range of choices available to economic agents. State factories and cooperatives became more aware of the range of economic opportunities available to them. At root, therefore, these processes were linked to the need to improve resource allocation by cutting information and transactions costs through such measures as the opening up of the internal market. The key issue was that of choice. Alliances that cut across official boundaries were formed, laying the foundation for further expansion of commerce when conditions changed, as they would in the late 1970s and early 1980s.

Conclusions

Viewed in terms of its developmental capacity, the DRV at reunification in 1975 was a "weak state." Its functions were in many ways more redistributional than accumulative.[16] Central planning and high levels of aid imports to a significant extent meant the allocation of consumer goods and production inputs to "those who needed them." Despite its proven ability to mobilize the Vietnamese people for the bloody struggle to liberate the South, the DRV was chronically dependent upon imports and faced continual difficulties in finding adequate economic resources from the domestic economy (above all from agriculture) for its needs. The distortions underlying the structural problems of the macro economy were considerable, but the weaknesses of the foreign trade and fiscal positions were masked by high supplies of aid imports that were delivered to state trading monopolies and eventually sold to finance state spending.

The economic management system of the DRV was both ineffective and inefficient; it had created an unwieldy and overcentralized bureaucracy, reliant upon a high degree of state monopoly that was intended to give planners direct control over the allocation of economic resources. As a result, *there were large short-run inefficiencies throughout the economy.*

In practice, however, state trading monopolies were often rather weak, and spontaneous adaptations had taken place that allowed many economic agents to exploit profitable alternatives. This unrehearsed bottom-up adaptation of the neo-Stalinist model often relied upon traditional behavior, linking collective action to family needs in order both to permit an expansion of family-based production and to push for ways of going outside the plan in order to acquire needed resources. Familiarity with such alternatives meant that many economic agents were well placed to exploit the enhanced opportunities that increasingly arose in the late 1970s and 1980s. Prior to 1975, however, these agents had been unable to have more than a marginal impact upon the high level of short-run economic inefficiency and waste that pervaded the economy.

The underlying development ethos was, in doctrinal terms, extreme. As such, it had affinities with traditional thinking, and official commitment to it had risen during the war. It was hostile to voluntary--unplanned--methods of acquiring and disposing of resources and stressed instead the population's obligation to respect direct administrative allocation through the state's system of trading monopolies. This required people to ignore immediate material incentives in order to carry out their duties under the DRV development model. Given actual Vietnamese conditions, the model was almost quixotically oriented toward urban and modern industrial development. This ethos had led to structural tensions that inhibited the efficient long-term development and exploitation of national resources. The DRV model was unable to efficiently exploit the development potential of the area. However, the apparent differences between the DRV model and neo-Stalinist prescriptions show that although the doctrinal position was extreme, in practice official tolerance was granted when the combination of official impotency and local initiatives did not inhibit the attainment of higher goals.

Sectorally, there were two main problems. The primary difficulty was that agriculture had been starved of economic opportunities. Long-term rural economic development policies were weak--credit systems, technical extension schemes, supply of trained personnel, and so forth,--were almost nonexistent, or they operated primarily at the central or provincial level without any real impact at the grassroots level.[17] Rural stagnation had coincided with the creation of an overdeveloped state sector that nevertheless seemed to offer the best employment opportunities. Popular aspirations had also been influenced by the propaganda given by the state to the DRV model. Family investment in human capital and choice of careers had responded to these incentives and created a large number of people well qualified to work in urban state employment. As a result, *both human, fixed, and institutional capital was poorly utilized and misallocated, preventing the country from realizing its growth potential.*

The second main sectoral problem was the lack of attention paid to exports and regional specialization. The ambitious development policies of the early 1960s had stressed autarchic growth and had generally ignored the export sector. Provinces had become to a large extent economically self-sufficient. As a result, *severe barriers to the development of domestic and foreign trade had greatly inhibited the exploitation of possibilities for both internal and international specialization.*

Despite these shortcomings, official commitment to the DRV program remained strong. Having linked it closely to the national liberation struggle, the national leadership was still (at least in public) convinced that neo-Stalinism was appropriate for a reunited Vietnam. They considered anathema any decentralizing and market-oriented reforms that would utilize the considerable potential of the private sector. Proper research into such possibilities was banned, and those involved in economic management were thus ill-prepared for any reform debate. Their experience was in the continual attempt to defend the state's monopoly position from attack rather than in exploration of the best ways of dismantling it: *Market management meant control, not development, of markets.*

The DRV model was therefore ill-suited to a confrontation with the effects of wartime U.S. aid upon the fundamentally far richer South of the country when national reunification followed the collapse of the Republic of Vietnam in spring 1975.

The preceding discussion implies that the emergence of a market-oriented system in Vietnam was likely to lead to considerable ideological tensions. The ethos stating that "rulers ruled on the basis of their understanding and virtue" had reached the extreme doctrinal position of denying to markets and the private sector the possibility of socially productive activity. Markets and the private sector could not be trusted. It would not be easy to abandon such a position, not least because the people thus criticized and reeducated would be there to point to the past.

A striking point about the transition in Vietnam, that has had a major impact upon the final result is the hostility to the private sector and the free market, which continued until late in the process. This meant (see Chapter 3) that markets tended to emerge from *within* the state sector. There was, until quite late in the transition, little growth of the private sector in the strict sense, and therefore the political economy was dominated by relationships within the state apparatus. In the early years, this appears to have created a constituency for further reforms that played an important role in preventing conservatives from reversing the process. After the 1986 Sixth Party Congress, however, the attitude toward the private sector changed significantly.

We return to these issues in Chapters 7 and 8.

Notes

1. See Le Thanh Khoi (1981); Woodside (1976); Marr (1971, 1981). Fforde (1983) contains a lengthy bibliography. We would particularly like to thank David Marr for comments on an early draft of this chapter. We would like what follows to be treated as an attempt to introduce relevant aspects of a complex subject to a nonspecialist audience rather than as a definitive statement on the subject, which is still in many areas underresearched.

2. Recall that private trade only started to become ideologically acceptable toward the end of the 1980s, when the economic transition was already well advanced and hard reform socialism had been replaced by soft reform socialism (see Chapter 3).

3. The distinction should be made between the commune, with its administrative content, and the home village, upon which farming families centered their lives.

4. The standard official household registration unit (the *ho khau*) was based on the married couple, with their children. A three-generation nuclear family could thus contain two households, if the grandparents retained their own separate registration.

5. Such arguments remain somewhat speculative. Longer-term trends should be examined, related to the shift in the demographic structure as population surged with the return of peace.

6. We maintain the position here that it is better to see the attractions of neo-Stalinism in terms of development rather than war. Indeed, Soviet official writers always distinguished what emerged in the late 1920s and 1930s in the Soviet Union from the economic system applied during the Civil War ("War Communism"). In our opinion, as we have already mentioned, it is important to examine the period 1954 to 1964/65 in detail before presenting justifications and interpretations of the situation in the DRV during the following decade in terms of the demands of wartime mobilization. The analysis should probably in fact go back earlier, to the shift in Vietminh economic strategy that occurred when the Chinese communists increased their influence in the late 1940s. It is our impression that there is an implicit revisionist position among Vietnamese historians in which it is argued that cooperatives had not been necessary during the French war, and also that Vietminh strategy, in the early stages, did not employ central-planning techniques (or something that tried to follow them) for industrial management. Wartime mobilization and planning in the United Kingdom, for example, one of the most highly mobilized of all combatants during World War II, did not involve forcing farmers to join collectives that controlled their production; nor did it impose a blanket system of administrative allocation of resources covering produced goods, as Soviet planners did. And the system was rapidly abandoned when peace returned; even the Attlee government's sense of economic planning was quite different from that of Stalin.

7. This section draws substantially upon Fforde and Paine (1987).

8. The Vietnamese state hierarchy had four levels: below the center there were cities and provinces, below them, quarters (*quan*) and districts (*huyen*); and below these, wards (*phuong*) and communes (*xa*). Technically, all of these could act as the superior level to SOEs, but in practice the quarters and districts were the lowest level.

9. It should be pointed out that the main result of an extensive research program into the econometric modeling of macroeconomic disequilibria in industrialized CPEs was that there was in fact very little aggregate shortage (see the work of R. H. Portes, among others).

10. The main focus of Fforde (1989a) is an examination in detail of the effects of this upon rural economic organization.

11. Examples could include: the maintenance of private production rather than cooperativization throughout most of Polish agriculture (apart from the "recovered territories" in the west that had been part of the German Reich), and the liberal treatment by Moscow of Hungarian economic reforms after 1956. For a discussion of Soviet attitudes to the transitional model in the 1980s, see Fforde (1985).

12. Fforde (1986) discusses the effects of systemic unimplementability upon Vietnamese communist thinking. See also Phan Van Tiem (1990). Again,

however, it should be said that the period prior to 1964-65 requires further research.

13. It should be stressed that the term "shortage economy" refers to an economic system that creates situations where in almost all markets the supply side dominates; supply is less than demand. This is different from that in specific historical instances, such as in Germany and Japan in 1944-45, where the shortages were not an intrinsic part of a system but the result of the collapse of supply under wartime conditions. They had not existed earlier to anything like the same extent. "Shortage," in Kornai's analysis, as in ours, is a systemic characteristic.

14. Although there are certainly signs in the published literature that many people were well aware of the existence of fundamental problems (for example some of the pieces in Nguyen Tri 1972, a work that is far from radical in its perspective), the pattern of the debate prior to the "breakout" in 1979 is the subject of other research (Fforde, ongoing, and some of the collaborative work within the Australian Vietnam Research Project). The sacking of Bui Cong Trung (head of the Economics Institute) in the early 1960s and the failure to establish an effective critique of the traditional system increased the personal costs of speaking out, as well as the risks of futile gesture in the face of high-level political conservatism.

15. It is the possibility thus opened up of mechanisms leading to systemic change that make this important. Many organizations--such as armies--face similar problems, but with quite different implications for the analysis of change.

16. Fforde is grateful to Robert Wade for this idea.

17. Mention should be made here of the policy of district building stressed at that time (Le Thanh Nghi 1979; Mai Huu Khue 1981).

Tables

TABLE 2.1 The Legacy of Colonialism: Vietnam in the 1930s

Population	18.8 million
Rice production (per capita)	300 kg
Modern industrial employment (percent of pop).	0.4 - 0.5
No. of hospital beds per 100,000 population	5.3
Doctors per 100,000 population	0.3
Schoolchildren	0.5 million
Schoolteachers	9,300

Sources: SO 1985b:tables 7, 66, 129, 130, 148, 149; Fforde 1983:63.

TABLE 2.2 Economic Growth During the First Five-Year Plan

	Average Annual Percentage Change, 1960-65
Total population	3.0
Total social product	9.1
Total industrial output	13.6
State industry	19.2
Artisanal and light industry	4.0
Total Agricultural Output	4.2
Staples output	3.4

Source: Fforde and Paine 1987:tables 7, 19, 30, 31, 32, 73, 78.

TABLE 2.3 Changes in Output and Employment During the War Years

	Average Annual Percentage Change, 1965-1975
Total population	2.8
State employment	6.1
State industrial employment	4.9
Total social product	4.2
Industrial output	5.9
State industry	6.2
Agricultural output	0.6
Staples output	-0.1

Source: Fforde and Paine 1987: tables 8, 12, 19, 30, 31, 73

3

Basic Constraints: Natural, Human, and Organizational

This chapter provides additional background to the analysis, of Vietnamese social and economic development in the 1980s. It has the following two main goals:

- First, to quantify some of the basic constraints that faced Vietnam in the 1980s. These include both human and institutional aspects. The discussion therefore includes an overview of political and social aspects of the period.
- Second, to examine broadly the evolution of those constraints as the transition to a market economy occurred.

The attempt is made here to assess the structural changes that took place as the Vietnamese economy shifted to a market orientation and also to gauge the extent and trends in plan distortion. Although this sheds much light upon the issues involved, the macro evidence available is in fact rather limited. The trend to the emergence of market-based transactions is clear. However, the data tend to suggest that inter-sectoral structural adjustment did not occur to any great extent: That is, the reallocation of productive resources needed for the emergence of a market economy apparently did not take place between sectors (e.g., from industry to agriculture). This probably reflects the lack of development of national and regional factor markets until the very end of the 1980s, so that factor redistribution largely took place *within*, rather than *between*, economic units. It was these shifts that reduced plan distortion. However, data on the spread of market relationships are far more compelling, showing how the planned part of the economy was squeezed.

The chapter starts with a discussion of three areas: the natural resources of the country; its population, and the basic parameters of the Vietnamese political system. The second section of the chapter then presents the main economic trends of the 1980s.

Natural Resources

Geography and Climate

Vietnam's geography is somewhat unusual. The traditional image of the country is of two rice baskets on the ends of a carrying pole, illustrating the two large deltas of the Red and Mekong Rivers in the North and South, respectively. These two deltas contain around one-half of the population and are situated some 2,000 kilometers apart.[1] The rest of the population occupies the coastal strip running approximately north-south between them, as well as the upland areas. Since the northern deltas were populated first, and therefore have a far greater demographic density, regional specialization was thus a necessary element of any balanced development program. However, since the physical distances are so great, moves to establish national markets suffered from inherent difficulties exacerbated by the poverty of the country and the poor state of the transport system. On the other hand, the high population densities meant that local markets were (and are) correspondingly favored in those areas that possessed them. Regional differences therfore have a tendency to dominate many developmental issues.

The climate is predominantly humid and tropical. Its dominant feature in the North and North-center is its instability, which contributes greatly to the riskiness of agriculture in general, and rice cultivation in particular. Typhoons can easily deposit 500 millimeters of rain in 24 hours, compared with typical average annual precipitation of 1500-2500 millimeters (SO 1987:table 217). In the southern delta areas the temperature varies far less than it does in the North, both throughout the year and from year to year. Average January temperatures in the north are typically 13 to 14 degrees Celsius, compared with 28 to 29 in the summer months of June and July. In the South average winter month temperatures are around 24 to 25 degrees Celsius, compared with 27 to 28 in the summer (SO 1987:table 215). Rainfall in the South is less variable, and the rise and fall in the Mekong River is less than that of the Red River.

In the upland regions the climate is cooler and less humid, although without areas of snow cover or regular frosts. This creates potential for valuable diversification of forestry and agriculture.

Delta and Forests

The effects of Vietnamese geography on the country's history have been profound. The deltas of the Red and Mekong Rivers in the North and South, respectively, provide the majority of the low-lying flat lands required by the wet-rice culture of the *kinh* (ethnic Vietnamese) people. Of the some 5.9 million hectares of rice land in the country in 1989, some 1.1 million were in the Red River Delta proper and 2.4 million in the Mekong delta (SO 1993: table 55).

The Red River Delta itself is surrounded by a frontier region of provinces, such as Vinh Phu and Bac Thai, that have both delta and upland areas. The highland provinces such as Cao Bang are referred to as the Mountains and Hills, and in the late 1990s they had around 0.7 million hectares of rice land. To the south of the Red River Delta there are three traditionally poor provinces with substantial rice areas known collectively as Old Region Four--Thanh Hoa, Nghe Tinh and Binh Tri Thien (around 0.7 million hectares between them).[2] The coastal area south of these provinces (the Central Seacoast) contains around 0.5 million hectares and the Central Highlands, around 0.15 million hectares. Immediately to the north of the Mekong Delta proper is the region containing Ho Chi Minh City and the industrial region of Bien Hoa. This is known as the Southeast and has 0.3 million hectares of land. The basic division of the economically valuable land into delta and upland areas is reflected in the official land classification. The Vietnamese divide the land resources of their country into seven categories (as shown in Tables 3.1 and 3.2). The balance of resources was rather stable in the 1980s, with around 20 percent available for agriculture (of which around 80-85 percent was rice land). *On a per capita basis, the availability of agricultural land is only some 0.1 hectares per head.*

The upland areas are conventionally divided into two regions: the hills, up to around 500 meters in altitude, and the higher mountains. Despite the continuing overexploitation indicated earlier, the country's forestry potential has always remained large.

A major problem was, and still is, the degradation of the country's environment, as population growth and industrialization have put heavy pressure on the resource base. Deforestation has accelerated and was thought to be some 200,000 hectares per year, due to agricultural clearance, forest fires and most important of all, the population's collection of timber and fuelwood. As a result, soil erosion has been rapid, and large areas of land have been converted into barren lands. The lasting effects of U.S. chemical warfare were also serious; in some parts of the South, by the late 1980s forests and wildlife had not yet regenerated, and cropland productivity remained below pre-war levels.

Forestry moved rather earlier than other sectors to accept the importance of the smallholder sector. Under the "land allocation" program (*giao dat giao rung*) substantial areas were moved out of the state sector. By the beginning of 1990 this amounted to 4.4 million hectares, of which 1.5 million were classified as forested (SO 1991:table 93).[3]

Other Natural Resources

As a result of its complicated geological history, the country contains a wide range of mineral resources. These are mainly concentrated in the North and include coal, wolfram, lead, zinc, silver, gold, antimony, asbestos, manganese, bauxite, and apatite. The region remained relatively underexplored in the 1980s but was known to contain silver, copper, lead, iron, antinomy, rare metals, bitumen, bauxite, and chrome. In the South, where deposits are less diverse, the most important mineral resource was the petroleum deposits in the Mekong Delta and the offshore continental shelf. Apart from coal and petroleum, Vietnam's mineral resources remained largely unexploited; gold and silver, though, had been mined for centuries (*BCNCT* 5202 1986:34).

The country possessed raw materials suitable for chemical fertilizer production, but the mines had been badly damaged by the Chinese in the 1979 war. There are substantial limestone deposits that formed the basis for the cement industry as well as for lime used in agriculture.

Energy

Vietnamese energy resources may be divided into a number of groups. Those that are nonreproducible--natural forests, coal, and natural gas-- exist in many regions of the country. Demand for fuelwood was a main reason for the overexploitation of the forests. It was estimated that the hydroelectric potential of the country was around 160 billion kilowatt hours per year, predominantly in the North and Center of the country. Coal production, which remained at around 5-6 million tonnes through the 1980s , made up 91 percent of all energy production, and hydroelectric power contributed another four percent (*BCNCT* 5202 1986:32).

Exploration for petroleum restarted in the late 1970s. Although onshore exploration failed to give any promising results, much hope was placed in offshore areas. Territorial disputes with China and Indonesia hindered progress, but a Soviet-Vietnamese joint venture started production in 1986. Output rose rapidly from the late 1980s on, and started to make an important contribution to exports and central government revenues around 1989/90. Domestic consumption of oil, which until the end of the 1980s was mainly imported from the Soviet Union, remained exceedingly low; per capita consumption was, for instance, only between one-third and one-fourth that of China.

Human Resources

The People

After national reunification in 1975-76, Vietnam's population grew from 49.1 million to around 66 million by the end of the 1980s. Given the weak rise in staples output, population growth was one of the major problems facing Vietnam during the 1980's. However, after the 1988 agricultural reforms, per capita staples output again increased substantially, as shown in Table 5.1.

Demographic densities differed greatly throughout the rice-growing areas in the post-reunification period. In the more densely populated provinces of the Red River Delta, such as Ha Nam Ninh, a rural population of 3.0 million occupied a rice area of some 280,000-290,000 hectares, an area per capita of 950 square meters. This compares with the richest provinces of the Mekong, such as Kien Giang, where a rural population of 1.4 million occupied around 260,000 hectares, an area per capita of 1,900 square meters (SO 1985b:tables 11, 67).

The rate of population increase reportedly declined during the 1980s, although official figures show an average rise of around 2.2 percent during both the Second FYP (1976-80) and the Third FYP (1981-85). From the mid-1970s on, however, the birth rate had fallen from 39.5 per thousand to below 30. There was substantial regional variation in fertility, with the Red River Delta at around 25 per thousand compared with levels still well over 30 in the Mekong Delta and the Central Highlands (SO 1987:table 4).

Life expectation data was unreliable. The reported death rate was around 7 to 7.5 per thousand during the mid-1980s (SO 1987:table 4). It is held that during this period the population suffered from widespread malnutrition and that this was getting worse in the mid-1980s as food supplies deteriorated. Thus: "a shortfall in food production affects the entire [sic] Vietnamese population, who on average manage on a calorific ration of 1,900 Kcal/day" (UNICEF 1987:3). In the opinion of an informed Vietnamese commentator, the average weight of newborn children was falling, and the height and weight of adolescents was also deteriorating.

It appears that attitudes to family planning were changing after reunification. In the overcrowded northern deltas, there is some evidence for rather rapid change in people's attitudes, as falling infant mortality resulted in family sizes well above historical precedence.[4] Parents found that the number of infants surviving was often far larger than expected. Assistance from the local cooperatives was on the whole available to families with many children, with food support and donations of clothing for children common. Furthermore, in many areas children of families in cooperatives were able to attend local schools and, through their membership in the cooperative, could secure access to plots of land at adulthood. This welfare net eroded throughout the 1980s, but it had never been as universal as propaganda maintained (Vogel 1987).

The cooperative system, where it existed, thus helped offset the costs for many peasant families of raising unexpectedly large numbers of children. However, the increasing role of the family economy later in the 1980's raised the demand for family labor, possibly creating resistance to birth control. The reduction in party influence also permitted a return to more traditional and paternalistic attitudes toward women (Allen 1990). Although it is hard to judge, it is likely that such pressures were offset by the adverse effects upon family welfare of family sizes too large for the limited resources. It is reasonably certain that the potentially severe costs of a large family were well known by the end of the decade. This encouraged use of traditional family planning methods as well as more modern techniques. The latter, however, were still not very widely used. According to the United Nations International Children's Emergency fund (UNICEF) the reductions in infant mortality seen over the previous two decades had started to level off by the close of the 1980s (UNICEF 1987:1).

Human Capital

Labor mobilization and utilization changed greatly during the 1980s. In the rural areas, various official surveys reported substantial increases in labor mobilization into production, almost certainly helped by higher real incomes.[5] It also became clear that women, who provided the great mass of the labor force, were working far longer hours (Allen 1990). Participation rates are hard to measure and to a great extent are demographically determined (Table 3.7). However, the table does show that the proportion of the total population recorded as working rose from 36.9 percent in 1979 to 42.8 percent in 1984 and to 44.9 percent in 1989.

The expansion of the state sector and the extensive educational system created a human capital stock that was rather well developed but in many ways inappropriate to a market economy. Two examples of particular note were various metal-working activities, associated with the heavy industrialization program, and construction. As fiscal pressures mounted toward the end of the decade, cuts in state spending, such as in construction, led to severe unemployment among skilled workers in many categories. However, as certain professions became of great importance--for example, accounting and interpreting--their remuneration rates soared (these workers made up only a very small proportion of the population). Demand for English language tuition rose; Russian became of marginal importance.

Education and Health

Education and health services in Vietnam were, considering the low level of economic development, good. But substantial resource misallocation and the lack of support for grassroots activities, above all in rural areas, reduced the impact on the health of the population. Propaganda designed to report a high level of effectiveness revealed the underlying ethos of the state and its concern with establishing the caring role of the state in these areas. Official statistics were unreliable throughout the 1980s and tended to hide the true situation, but they nevertheless reveal the considerable attention paid to these sectors. Although precise figures are unavailable, the population was largely literate; however literacy levels were lower in the Mekong Delta. Even in the poorer rural areas of the North the great majority of people who had grown up since 1960 had had the standard eight years of basic schooling.

Similar problems arose with health issues. These are discussed further in Chapter 6.

Political System[6]

Issues

The political analysis of transitional systems is a relatively new subject. The underlying assumption of much of this book is that the party adapted to the changing political structures beneath it, notably the rising state business interest. It also responded to other social pressures arising from the transition process, of which fear of urban unemployment was probably the most important, leading to delays in reducing subsidies and in support to the state sector (Beresford 1989; Fforde 1993). Attention was paid to the demands of the population, especially to the potential for social disorder at points of great tension, such as the price-wage-money measures of 1985. This notion--of an underlying political reality--confronts the continuation of the old formal structures. However, note that the DRV model itself, as the result of the failed attempt to implement the neo-Stalinist program, also implied systematic gaps between form and reality. What is most lacking from the picture as we understand it in the mid-1990s is the role and importance of individuals: for example, Le Duan, wartime leader and party general secretary until his death in 1986, and Nguyen Van Linh, general secretary from 1986 to 1991.

Basic Structure

Throughout the 1980s Vietnamese formal political institutions remained, in essence, those established during the late 1950s in the DRV. The Vietnamese Communist Party, whose dominant position was laid down by the Constitution, sought to maintain control over political and social power, ideologically based on Marxism-Leninism. This pattern closely followed the Soviet and Chinese models of the time. Control was to be exercised through the party's power to appoint key personnel--the *nomenklatura*--backed up by the system of party cells throughout social (including the army) and economic organizations.

As in many other areas, in practice the Vietnamese political system, and the exercise of power within it, evolved to show significant deviations from the Soviet and Chinese models. The most important factors involved were probably experience of the national liberation struggle; the sense of local autonomy; the tradition of intellectual pluralism; the exposure to the West, especially in the South; and, in the 1980s, the transition process itself. There is a strong argument that the main political effect of the transition was to change the underlying political structure of the country, creating an important business interest initially basing itself upon the increasingly commercialized state sector. In this interpretation, the party, closely linked to such groups, responded in order to maintain itself in power, but at the same time without finding an easy way of adapting to the needs of other parts of Vietnamese society.

Since economic reform involved the development of a commercialized state sector, in many ways this influenced the evolution of the underlying, or "real," as well as the formal, political systems. The society to a degree became less closed, and information became far less subject to ideological control. There was an effective de-Stalinization around 1987-89 after the Sixth Party Congress. As foreign investment and trade mounted as a result of the passage of the Foreign Investment Law in late 1987, contacts with visitors from the West stopped being a threat to individual Vietnamese. However, these important shifts occurred only toward the end of the transition, thus throughout the important and early years the political atmosphere remained controlled and appropriate to hard reform socialism. In addition, starting around 1989 the political atmosphere tightened again, partly in response to the events in Eastern Europe.

The Socialist Republic of Vietnam was a member of the Council for Mutual Economic Assistance (CMEA, also known as COMECON), linked by treaty to the Soviet Union. Almost all military equipment was provided by the Soviet Union, which allowed Vietnam to construct strong defense installations on the Sino-Vietnamese border (Pike 1986; Lockhart 1989). This support enabled Vietnam to maintain--before large-scale withdrawals began in 1988--some 140,000 troops in Cambodia and 50,000 in Laos. Vietnam thus had one of the largest armies in Asia, with an active force strength estimated at 1.26 million. Military conscription of males was compulsory, with a basic three year term of service (SIPRI 1987-88:175-76). Although details are not well known, through the 1980s the army developed substantial production installations of its own, and grew a significant proportion of its own food.[7] Products from the army production became increasingly available on the free market in the late 1980s.

The political institutions of the Socialist Republic thus aimed to ensure the social and political dominance of the Vietnamese Communist Party. The party was hierarchically organized according to Leninist principles of democratic centralism and had adopted Marxism-Leninism as its basic philosophy at its foundation. The party maintained formal control over the state apparatus through a number of mechanisms. This changed somewhat in character as the transition occurred but aimed throughout at securing key appointments.

All candidates for local and national elections in principle had to have the approval of the Vietnam Fatherland Front, an umbrella organization dominated by the party. The front also contained the mass organizations, such as the Trade Union, Peasants' Association, and so on, which were viewed as instruments for the expression of the party's leadership role in society rather than as autonomous associations representing the independent interests of their members. Although there were attempts to increase the number of candidates participating in national elections, these did not go very far. The National Assembly, to which candidates were elected, was not therefore capable of effectively articulating the different interests within Vietnamese society. However, in local elections, especially to communal and cooperative positions, there appears to have been a great range. Within some there was a large number of candidates, whereas in others, elections were quite empty of democratic content, with local party chiefs able to maintain themselves in power with support from superior levels. These issues were debated in the party press.

Since the early 1960's, a major structural issue within the Vietnamese polity had been the high degree of local autonomy (Beresford and McFarlane 1995). The provincial and city administrations, with their People's Committee and party organization, acted as a level within the overall hierarchy approximately equal to a central government ministry. A provincial leader was usually a local man, certainly not a central appointee. The party's apparatus of social control thus usually meant local control, with the center's writ not necessarily running at the periphery. A similar centrifugal tendency could be seen throughout the society, with lower administrative levels tending to become independent of their superiors, competing with them for access to resources, such as aid or procured agricultural products.[8]

Changes Through the Decade

In comparison with the late 1970s, when the DRV program was unchallengeable, from around 1987-89 on the political atmosphere eased.However, although these changes were striking they were largely so in the light of earlier conditions. Differences within the political establishment were very great, and this resulted in access to such outlets as the party press for divergent views within the party.

Around 1987, political reform began to be pushed forward. The National Assembly played a greater role and was given a higher profile, but real power remained with the party. After the events of 1989 in Eastern Europe, however, the party announced its opposition to multiparty pluralism and clamped down on dissent, both within and outside the establishment. A member of the Politburo (Tran Xuan Bach) who had publicly advocated pluralism was summarily dismissed. By the end of the 1980s the Communist Party therefore found itself in the position of being a largely unreformed Leninist party that was responsible for governing a market economy "on the road of socialist construction."

Limits of Political Reform

Despite these advances, however, Vietnam in the 1980s remained far from being a politically open society. In many areas, the constraints placed upon the population were quite unjustifiable. Some crucial indicators confirming this were

1. *The liberty of individuals to express political opinions freely.* The mass media remained under firm political control. Individuals were not allowed to set up newspapers, to have safe access to

telecommunications, or to hold public demonstrations in favor of political policies opposed to those of the party and state. After the closure of the newspaper *Tin Sang* in Ho Chi Minh City in the early 1980s, the relatively open press in the South had to operate through the official media.

2. *The freedom of individuals to travel freely and to have free intercourse with foreign visitors to Vietnam.* In many areas, until around 1988 foreign experts and other visitors found that they were actively discouraged from having contact with Vietnamese, a situation that eased in 1989. However, during most of the 1980s, it remained formally the case that Vietnamese citizens were not permitted to have contact with foreigners without approval from the authorities. From 1986 on, these barriers were increasingly ignored, but they were nevertheless still enforced in some areas. Vietnamese citizens could not travel freely abroad,[9] and it was well known that Vietnamese scholars invited to conferences and other academic pursuits were often denied visas or passports. Again, however, marriages between foreigners and Vietnamese tended to become far easier toward the end of the decade. Illegal departures oof Vieetnamese--often as boat people--rose slightly toward the end of the decade, but not to numbers comparable to the major exoduses of the immediate post-1975 and 1978-80 periods. The number of overseas Vietnamese returning to visit (and occasionally to settle in) Vietnam started to rise in around 1987. Visas were increasingly given without great problems, especially for those wishing to visit in organized groups. This trend also applied to people who had left as boat people.

3. *Other human rights.* According to foreign reports, some 100,000 Vietnamese who had been closely involved with the Republic of Vietnam were put into reeducation camps in the period after the fall of Saigon. They were not subject to any due process of law, but most were released within a few months. By 1986 some 6,000 to 7,000 remained; after the Tet amnesty of 1988, the officially reported number still detained was 159. Amnesty International was critical of the operation of courts in Vietnam; the organization did, however, note that the courts started to function rather better toward the end of the decade.[10] A number of prisoners of conscience existed, often designated as such as a result of religious or journalistic activities.

4. *Access to foreign sources of information.* This improved through the decade, although by 1990 foreign journals were still not freely available. Listening to Western radio broadcasts was, in the 1970s, likely to cause difficulties for the people concerned, but from the

mid-1980s on, the activity was most probably unlikely to do so. Audio- and videocassettes had to be declared at customs on arrival in the country and could be retained for examination if the contents were deemed to be unclear or contentious. Increasing numbers were smuggled in and then copied in quantity.

5. *Freedom to establish or belong to independent social organizations.* Official labor organizations remained entirely dominated by the party-state apparatus. There was no evidence of the creation of independent trade unions. Mass organizations remained strictly controlled. A notable exception was the Vietnamese Red Cross. The Catholic Church at times had a seminary and its bishops were appointed from Rome (with certain review rights held by the Vietnamese government). Catholic priests were sometimes allowed to travel, but the church played almost no independent role in public life.

Conclusions

Through the 1980s the overt political system persisted largely unreformed. The improvement in the social and political climate toward the end of the decade is most striking when compared with the neo-Stalinist and xenophobic conditions of the late 1970s and early 1980s. The most important shift in the political structure was therefore predominantly *within* the establishment. As we argue, the emergence of a commercial interest within the state sector in the first half of the decade played a key role in pushing for market-oriented reform, culminating in the policy changes of the 1986 Sixth Party Congress. This was based upon rather autonomous levels within the state sector--provinces, cities, and ministries, whose relations with state economic units evolved from those of the traditional central-planning model to something closer to capitalist ownership, albeit greatly diffused in the absence of clear property rights. *In particular, the Vietnamese transition was marked by the absence of openly organized extraparty opposition.*

Economic Structure: The Impact of Transition

Despite the shortcomings of available statistics, by ordinary standards it is clear that Vietnam in the 1980s was an extremely poor country. Access to food was a major issue for a large proportion of both the urban and rural populations for most of the decade. Both industrialization levels and the creation of the economic surpluses needed for domestic and international trade were weak. The preceding sections on land and labor have showed that any structural change to remove plan distortion was concentrated mainly on movements of factors within production units. This tends to be supported by other aggregate indicators, the results of which are discussed in the next section and summarized in Box 3.1.

The Food Staples Balance

Figure 3.1 shows the level of per capita staples output through the postunification period. Two elements stand out: the existence of two periods of rapid growth in 1979-82 and 1988-90; and the stagnation and then decline in the mid-1980s.

Changes in Land Availability. Through the 1980s more land was brought under cultivation. Toward the beginning of the decade this was largely carried out by state farms and cooperatives, but later this land was increasingly taken over by family farmers. The property issues underlying this are discussed later. It should be noted that the existence of substantial land-use conflicts, especially outside the delta areas, makes the data unreliable. The problem is further compounded by the widespread existence of "ghost" cooperatives, operated in order to keep higher authority at arm's length (Fforde 1989a).

Measured in terms of land use, in the 1980s there was a rise in the land area put into production of staples, industrial crops, and fruit. Throughout the 1980s, yearly reported increases in the opening up of new land were marginal, at around 30,000-50,000 hectares (SO 1987:table 76).

Land Use. Agricultural land use was dominated by lowland rice cultivation, as shown in Tables 3.1 and 3.2. By the end of the 1980s, both the state farms and cooperatives had lost ground to family-based production. This does not, however, show up clearly in the statistics. The proportion of cooperative families in collectives rose steadily until 1988, when data stopped being published. This was partly because of the effects of Decree No. 10 on the definition of cooperatives and the de facto decollectivization of the Mekong Delta in 1988-89. Table 3.3 gives data on the comparative importance of state farms. Although the cooperative form was maintained in the North and Center, its content altered greatly, so again these figures do not effectively measure the shift from a collective-based to a family-farm-based rural economy.

In the upland areas and food-deficit deltas, nonrice staples crops were grown for food. The predominant crop was manioc, followed closely by various types of potato. The proportion of staples production met from rice tended to fall during the 1980s after a sharp rise in the 1970s. Nonrice crops thus accounted for a national average of around 10-15 percent of total staples production. Rice was, and still is, very much the preferred staple food, thus the substantial regional variation in the proportion of the staples supply coming from rice reflects to a certain extent the population pressure. Nationally, total staples output per capita moved cyclically, related to the ebb and flow of reforms. After a long period of food imports, in 1989 and 1990 there were substantial rice exports. However, these fell off again in 1991. By the end of the decade, gross availability per capita (i.e., net of net imports) remained uncomfortably close to the 300 kilogram per capita level. There was also substantial regional variation in staples production per head and levels of supplies to the state (Table 3.8). This is discussed further in Chapter 5.

Nonstaples Agriculture: Cash-Crop Production. Vietnam possessed considerable potential for development of non-staples crops. Coffee, tea, and rubber could be grown in the so-called *"terres rouges*-(red lands)-." Cash-crop production increased during the 1980s, although there are no data differentiating collective from farmer activities (see Table 3.5).

Aggregate Measures of Economic Growth

Economic growth was rather unstable through the 1980s; patterns of expenditure also showed marked changes. However, during the early part of the decade, aggregate measures of output showed substantial year-on-year gains that then faded away, as shown in Figure 3.2. This suggests that in the middle of the decade something of a turning point occured in the underlying dynamic of the economy. The inflation rate shows a similar pattern (see Figure 3.3), with a period of initial instability in the very early 1980s giving way to more stable prices in 1983-4 but replaced by hyperinflation in 1986-88. Box 3.1 summarizes the overall picture.

GNP per Head. Far-from-reliable estimates of GNP were made that confirm the low level of development. International estimates sometimes give higher figures, but all indicators confirm the picture of Vietnam as one of the poorest nations in the world.

In recognition of this, the World Bank *World Development Reports* placed Vietnam in the group of "low-income" countries but, sensibly in view of the unreliability of the statistics, gave no GNP data. In the early 1980s the General Statistical Office in Hanoi published the estimates of the value of Vietnamese GNP given in Table 3.9. These were updated in the early 1990s and revealed a similar picture.

Other Estimates of Aggregate Economic Activity. Vietnamese estimates, based upon Soviet net material product (NMP) methodology, put total social output[11] per head, which includes some but not all output from the private and individual sectors, at around US$48 in 1985 and US$108 in 1989 if free market exchange rates are used.[12] But there was no adequate measure of the real international value of the Vietnamese dong, and although until 1989 its official value was well above any realistic level, the free market rate was also likely to been have pushed down by extreme shortages of foreign exchange. However, during the decade of transition aggregate estimates of output in Vietnam showed rises of around 50-70 percent in constant prices, while population rose by around 20 percent. Per capita output therefore rose around one-third, or around 2.5-3percent per annum. This is an appreciable level of growth, if low by regional standards.

Savings, Accumulation, and Growth. Low recorded levels of domestic savings were a characteristic of the Vietnamese economy through the 1980s (Dollar 1993). The rather high levels of accumulation were almost entirely financed by overseas assistance. This had a long history in both Northern and Southern Vietnam (Dace 1986; Beresford 1989).

In 1975-76 both the North and South were highly dependent upon overseas support. Through the late 1970s aid was received from the West, the Soviet bloc, and China, but from 1978-79 the Soviet Union became the dominant donor. During the Fourth FYP (1986-90) aid was further increased. This suggests that the increase in aid from the Soviet Union *after* 1985-86 was an important source of support for the subsidized sectors of the economy --the major part of the state sector--that then came under such great pressure after 1989.

The proportion of total national income devoted to accumulation was also unstable. After rising in the mid-1980s it then declined (see Table 3.10 and Figure 3.4; also Drabek 1990), until by the end of the 1980s it was around one-third of the peak levels reached in the DRV in the mid-1960s. Spending cuts in the face of accelerating inflation hit state investment (Table 3.10 and Figure 3.5), and the aid program increasingly played the role of supplying current inputs to subsidized sectors at low prices.[13] Of imports from the non-convertible region, the proportion made up of fuels and materials rose from near 33 percent in 1980 to 57 percent in 1989 (IPM 1990:Appendix).

Investment data was only officially available for the state sector. In the key sector of state industry returns remained low (see Chapter 4). Labor productivity in so-called "heavy" sectors was in aggregate *lower* than in the less capital-intensive "light" sectors.

The absence of any clear relationship between investment and growth suggests the presence of substantial inefficiencies in the Vietnamese economy: Capital investment was *not* the main source of output growth, pointing to an important structural characteristic of the Vietnamese economy. During the Second FYP (1976-80), high rates of investment in industry accompanied a fall in output, and the level of unused capacity rose correspondingly. This suggests that the pattern of growth was not one in which capital accumulation led to increases in productivity and consequent output gains. Rather, it was largely determined by *shifts in the level of utilization of existing assets.* These were not "shocks" to a given economic system, but instead an essential part of the transition process itself. The growth process over the decade was more in the nature of a series of short-run adjustments permitting excess capital stocks in various sectors to be utilized more efficiently. This implies that the analytical focus should be on those inputs constraining output in the short run. In an economy with a very weakly developed and "thin" industrial base that was highly aid dependent, this meant current inputs- labor, agricultural surpluses, and inputs available but scarce within the central-planning system itself. Short-run output changes were therefore closely related to shifts in the plan-market boundary. Also, changes in the level and composition of the capital stock were not very important, since it was variation in the level of other inputs that dominated changes in output from year to year. It could be said that the main engine of growth was the process of system change itself and the associated reduction in plan distortion.

Output and Employment. The output and employment data in Tables 3.7 and 3.11 show that the country remained predominantly rural and agricultural. Price distortions overrecord the output per head in industry, which pushed up the proportion of gross output registered as coming from manufacturing. The share of agriculture in constant-price produced national income (PNI) was around 47 percent in 1979 and around 48 percent in 1989 (SO 1990b:138), as shown in Figure 3.6. This suggests that at the most aggregate level there was no important structural change in the economy, at least so far as the broad intersectoral pattern of production was concerned.

However, if the state, cooperative, and private sector shares of PNI are examined, a pattern of rather sharp change is revealed, but running *against* simplistic notions of commercialization. During the 1980s, the economy was formally dominated by the socialist sectors, whose share of national income continued to *rise* until the end of the decade (see Figures 3.7 to 3.9). Note, however, that there is a trend shift in the middle of the decade, with the recorded state sector *shrinking* as a share of PNI from 1977 to 1983/84, and then *rising* until 1990. *Thus, arguments alleging commercialization must focus upon the changing nature of the so-called planned economy.* The movements in the private sector are particularly interesting, especially the relative declines in the middle of the decade shown in Figures 3.8 and 3.9. This partly resulted from the integration of the South into the unified, socialist economy and the collectivization of the Mekong in the first half the 1980s. However, it again supports views of the process of transition in Vietnam that stress its intraestablishment nature: The name of the game was to be found in the SOEs and cooperatives,--and in their relations with the planning authorities and state trade organizations and not in the private sector, which remained in the shadows. Reviewing the sequence of developments (see Chapter 1), we can see that the systemic changes of the first half of the decade (during which the private sector was by some measures expanding) thus corresponded to the first part of the formal transition. The private sector, in the strict sense, did not play an active role until late in the transition. However, to a great extent this is a statistical nicety, since the definition of private is within the orthodox, neo-Stalinist, class analysis of society (Fforde and Paine 1987). This became increasingly inapplicable as the commercialization of the state sector altered the meaning of state property, and autonomous state commerce became both more important and more like a "private" sector in its economic behavior.

Figure 3.2 and Table 3.12 show the structural instability of the Vietnamese economy. Rates of growth varied greatly from year to year. Table 4.1 in Chapter 4 shows the targets and outcomes of the three FYPs from 1976 to 1990.

It is worth stressing that throughout the 1980s the Vietnamese economy remained predominantly oriented toward subsistence production. There was only a slight trend toward a greater degree of cash-cropping and live-stock production. In agriculture, for instance, although staples cultivation was 58.6 percent of gross output in 1976 (57.0 percent in 1980), by 1985 it was still 54.0 percent and by 1989 unchanged at 54.0 percent (SO 1987:tables 24, 25; SO 1991c:tables 47, 48).

Employment and Population. Since the official price structure under-valued agricultural output and therefore the official output figures under-estimated the sector's contribution to the economy, employment data are perhaps a more reliable indicator.

The data shown in Table 3.7 indicates that only one in ten of the recorded labor force was primarily active in industry, and of these, only around one-third were in the "modern" state sectors. Although low, this is some ten times higher than colonial levels, as shown in Table 2.1. It is interesting to observe, moreover, that the proportion of the labor force employed in agriculture increased during the 1980s.

It is also noteworthy that by the end of the 1980s the 10 percent of the employed labor force in industry was predominantly involved in the small-scale and handicrafts industry, which accounted for around 70 percent of reported industrial employment.[14] Combined with the sectoral employment data, this shows that the Vietnamese labor force was concentrated in areas with low capital intensity, typically producing commodities easily market-able in the face of state monopolies.

Other Development Indicators. Other official indicators of development also confirm Vietnam's poverty and economic stagnation compared with other developing countries in the region. Figure 3.1 indicates that staples availability per head remained around 300 kilograms of paddy equivalent; international agencies estimated that calorie inputs per head were around 1,900 kilocaloroes per day, below widely accepted levels of sufficiency (UNICEF 1987).

Real Incomes and Consumption. Other than anecdotal information, the main source of published data on real income levels was the General Statistical Office's surveys of the expenditure and incomes of the families of workers and farmers.[15] However, the combination of second jobs, nondisclosure of incomes, and the supply of cheap goods and services through the state rationing system create great difficulties in drawing firm conclusions. Certain broad trends can, however, be identified.

Urban Areas and State Employees. Above all, until the very end of the decade, living conditions in the cities were generally felt to be bad: People did not report buoyantly rising real incomes. Life was almost universally said to be difficult. By 1989 certain industrial consumer goods were clearly in better supply than they had been, and markets were visibly operating better. One basis for this popular perception of the 1980s was the high real cost and unreliable supply of foodstuffs, which offset the beneficial effects of better nonfood consumer goods supplies. The combination of rapid inflation and partial rationing created grave difficulties, especially for women responsible for household budgets. The first half of the decade was far worse than its closing years.

A snapshot of 1986 can be seen in Tables 3.13 and 3.14. The data are in current prices. To put this into some sort of perspective, the free market value of the dong against the U.S. dollar started the year at around 150 and ended it at near the 450-500 level. It averaged around 250 to the U.S. dollar, implying monthly per capita spending of around US$2 for urban workers and US$3 for farmers. One indicator of the low level of real income was the large proportion of expenditure on food, for most money had to be spent on essentials.

Food supplies play a major role in determining perceptions of real incomes, and it is notable that the proportion of expenditure on food *rose* sharply in the 1970s, from 71.6 percent in 1976 to 83.0 percent in 1980 (see Figure 3.12). These figures tend to confirm popular perceptions of stagnant, if not falling, real consumption. They also suggest important year-to-year variations in relative food prices.

These figures do not take account of the value to the worker of rationed goods supplied at prices well below open market levels. It has to be stressed, however, that the poor and fluctuating state of food supplies was to some extent offset by better availability of other products.[16]

Note also from Table 3.13 that less than one-half of an urban family's income actually came from official wages. Through the 1980s, workers increasingly relied upon second jobs ("other incomes"). The proportion of total income coming from wages was as high as 73.2 percent in 1976, but had fallen to 66.5 percent by 1980. In reality it was probably far lower. The trends through the decade can be seen in Figures 3.10 to 3.12. We find this evidence rather convincing, not least because we can see no political reason for falsifying the data.

Furthermore, by the late 1980s a large proportion of incomes reported as coming from the state under the heading of "wages" was made up by the bonuses and other supplements paid by factories and other units from their own free market activities. According to usually reliable sources, in the better-off factories during early 1988, something like 50 percent of incomes were pure wages. Although up to 40 percent could come from the outside earnings of the factory, a more common share was 25-30 percent. Rising unplanned activities therefore had a twofold effect upon urban incomes, generating both substantial extra payments at the place of work as well as private earnings on second jobs (this is supported by the data in Table 3.13).

Also, by the middle of the decade it was commonplace for factories and other units of the state economy, especially in the North, to provide income supplements in kind to their workers. These were obtained in a variety of ways, most usually by direct exchange by the factory outside the plan, and provided an important support when the state rationing system broke down, as it did intermittently. Again this points to a reduction in plan distortion and a reallocation of labor effort.

The data from retail sales suggest that real spending rose rather sharply in 1981-84 but then collapsed in 1986, as shown in Figure 3.19.

Rural Areas. Published and reliable information on rural incomes was scarce, reflecting both the great regional variation and the previous relative lack of interest in this area of the economy.[17] Again, however, the Statistical Office's survey data are available for farmers. These show higher average incomes than for urban state workers. These figures are not comparable with earlier data, which dealt only with members of agricultural cooperatives (see Table 3.14).

Distribution, Trade, and Economic Surpluses. Figures 3.13 and 3.14 provide information on the development of the free retail market. Note that the period of hard reform socialism from 1981 to 1985 saw a decline in the free market's share of retail trade and that from around 1987 there was a substantial recovery until by 1990 nearly two-thirds of retail trade was uncontrolled. Note, however, that in practice the private sector was by no means the only operator in the free market, which included a substantial commercialized state and collective sector. Chapter 5 contains further information on the reduction in the disequilibrium in the staples market as state prices moved closer to those on the free market (Figure

4.1), which confirms a similar trajectory (especially the tightening in 1981-85 compared with 1979-80). The trend toward the market is clear.

Both domestic and foreign trade were weakly developed. Total annual officially recorded retail sales in the country, including state, collective, and private trade, were at a level of around 11,000 dong per head of population by 1985, at a time when average state employee incomes were around 12,000 dong (SO 1987:Tables 2,149). The state, which had earlier sought a monopoly in staples trade, usually without success, procured 15.3 percent of staples production in 1976. By 1980 this had fallen to 13.7 percent, but by 1985 it had been pushed back up to 21.5 percent (SO 1987:tables 23, 71, 143). The ratio kept up in 1986, at 21.3 percent, but then slumped to 19.2 percent in 1987 in face of deteriorating agricultural terms of trade and a poor harvest. There was great variation in procurement levels between the Mekong delta and other regions, as shown in Table 5.5. There is no series of official data on levels of staples marketing outside the state sector. However, Figures 3.15 and 3.16 show calculated figures for the levels of staples availability above a notional 250 kilogram per capita subsistence minimum, net of state procurement, for the Mekong Delta and the four provinces of the Red River Delta with a potential for rice surpluses. This shows an easing of procurement pressures in 1981-82 and 1988-89, in the immediate aftermath of the reforms in the agricultural sector.

Foreign Trade. In the mid-1980s total exports were around US$700-800 million a year, of which around US$350 million went to convertible currency areas. These figures almost certainly underestimate the effective openness of the Vietnamese economy. A high proportion of means of exchange and liquid savings was kept in gold and dollars, and economic agents were surprisingly well aware of relative border prices for tradable goods and services.

Despite Vietnam's comparative advantages in foreign trade, as a country wellendowed with cheap and rather high-quality labor, the barriers imposed by the state ensured that the external sector remained weakly developed. A high proportion of imports, albeit hard to quantify, was financed by the economic assistance program. Reported exports per head grew from 4.5 current U.S. dollars-rubles[18] in 1976 to 6.3 in 1980 and to 11.7 in 1985. They stayed approximately unchanged (SO 1987:tables 2, 162) until the rapid increases of 1989-90. It is, however, probable that there were substantial unreported exports and imports toward the end of the decade as smuggling intensified.[19] See Figure 3.17 for the reported trade deficits with the convertible and nonconvertible areas.

The basic structural features of Vietnamese foreign trade in the 1980s thus were as follows:

- First, the chronic deficit.
- Second, the growing role played by regional direct trade,[20] which was in approximate balance (see Figure 3.18). By 1986, direct regional trade had grown from almost nothing (in the late 1970s) to around US$160 million a year, with exports approximately equal to imports. This was despite the pressures upon local authorities to disband their own export-import companies in the early 1980s.
- Third, a rise in the share of imports covered by exports from 1980 until around 1985; there was no further advance until 1989-90. The source of this improvement was exports of light industrial goods, agricultural, forestry, and marine products.

The foreign trade and balance of payments situation is further discussed in Chapter 8.

The State and the State Sector

As we have seen, traditional thinking argued that the state should play a key role in many sectors. However, largely because of the low level of development itself, the relative size of the state sector was not in fact very great. Modern state industrial employment was less than 5percent of total population, as shown in Table 3.7. This created the contradictory picture of an ambitiously expansionary and aid-financed state unable to control an economy still largely based upon subsistence farming and small-scale local trade. Instead, it relied ever more heavily upon external assistance to maintain its levels of activity. As the economy became more market oriented, much of the state sector became less able to compete and more reliant upon subsidies. As market relations became more prominent and control over resource flows within the central-planning system diminished, materials supplied through the centralplanning system became less and less capable of acting as a support to planning in the state sector. After 1989, subsidies more appropriate to a market economy had to be used, taking the form of inflationary credits and tax breaks, combined with entry barriers.

The generally low level of economic development in Vietnam meant that the severe macroeconomic imbalances were in fact being caused by a limited growth of the state sector in production combined with a far greater degree of pressure on distribution and exchange. State employment and productive economic activities were not extensive. Their ability to create economic distortions reflected both the poverty of the economy and the goals set by neo-Stalinist development priorities, above all the use of state monopoly power to directly control resource allocation.

In the 1980s, a fall in the relative power of the central authorities undoubtedly occurred. This could be seen in the rise of regionally organized state foreign trade, the dynamic growth of local state industry, the falling share of retail trade controlled by the authorities, and the slowdown in state employment generation. However, the central authorities remained the main focus and source of the two critical macro imbalances: the budget deficit and the balance of trade.[21] These perpetuated the overvalued exchange rate and rapid price inflation.

Conclusions

The Fundamentals

In the 1980s, the basic resource potential of Vietnam was considerable, especially when compared with many other developing countries at similar income levels.

Vietnam is a large country, and this meant that the scope for import substitution and development of production for the internal market was substantial. With a population of over 65 million, Vietnam was in quite a different position from countries such as Mozambique, with 16 million, or Cuba with 10 million.

The population was welleducated, with literacy near the 90 percent level. It is unusual to find Third World populations that live at annual income levels near US$100 per head but also have eight years of education; this was the norm in the overcrowded delta areas of northern and north-central Vietnam. The number of university graduates was also high, if concentrated largely in urban areas. The population was, in ethnic terms, relatively homogeneous. The Latin-based national script made it easier to learn English, which was already the international lingua franca of the region.

The population had, furthermore, considerable traditional experience with forms of organization at both the collective and national levels. This contributed to such intangibles as the ability to function politically in a sophisticated manner, supporting the development of a national polity that could form the basis for social stability and nonviolent systemic change. It also provided some basis for popular response to incorrect national policies and reduced some of the more adverse consequences of such mistakes. This is clear from the creation of the political compromises inherent in the DRV model, and also from the historical process of transition itself.

The geography and climate of the country also conferred certain advantages. The potential for tropical marine and agricultural production was considerable, especially in such "hard" goods as those salable for convertible currency, such as rubber, coffee, tea, spices, and other such products. The upland areas provided considerable scope for timber production, so long as logging was kept in some balance with replanting. The mineral resource endowment was also good: coal, petroleum, aluminum, tin, phosphates, and iron all existed in exploitable quantities. In the rice lands of the southern delta areas the country possessed a resource that could be exploited to produce staples supplies capable of supporting a far larger population if socioeconomic conditions permitted.

The basic infrastructure of a modern state existed in Vietnam through the 1980s: a transport network, urban centers; post and telecommunications services, and so on. The fact that these were poorly utilized does not deny the point that they existed- in some other developing countries at comparable income levels they did not exist. The massive investments in infrastructure required in the late 1990s as FDI came flooding in were able to build upon this base, which was rapidly shown to be inadequate for a market economy growing at some 8-10 percent annually.

The Fundamentals and the Transition

Viewed in aggregate terms, Vietnam's productive structure did not change that much during the decade from1979-89. What did change was the allocation of resources at the micro level, predominantly within production units. This paralleled the big systemic changes in exchange and distributional relations as market replaced plan. In the first half of the decade, the private retail sector was under severe pressure; in the second half, increasing levels of foreign assistance propped up a state sector that was under great strain from the commercialization process it was undergoing. Although uncontrolled trade reportedly stagnated in the period up to around 1985-86, it subsequently expanded rapidly, both within the private and the nonprivate sectors.

Real incomes probably rose, but not much, again mainly more toward the end of the period than at the beginning. We conjecture that they fell sharply in 1978-79 and 1985, but rose in 1980-81 and 1989.

Throughout the 1980s the produced capital stock- largely aid-financed- was poorly utilized, for reasons analyzed in this book. This was also true of human capital and in combination added up to high levels of plan distortion. This meant that the potential existed to use these forms of capital more efficiently in order to support higher output level, and at the same time make it easier to shift to a generalized commodity economy when and if that point was reached. *During the transition, one of Vietnam's main economic resources was, therefore, the high level of plan distortion itself- the considerable short-run economic slack created by the failure of the economic system to fully utilize the existing factor stock.*

Much of the economic history of the decade therefore has to do with the short-run effects of various discrete changes in resource mobilization. Among these, we argue, were the 1981 and 1988 reforms to agriculture (positive); the introduction (1980-81), tightening up (1982-85), and then easing (1986-88) of the Three Plan system in SOEs (positive, then negative, then positive again); the price-money-wage reforms of 1985 (negative); the collectivization drives of the Mekong in 1978-79 and 1984-85 (negative); the temporary liberalization of foreign trade in 1980-82 (positive and then negative); the opening of the borders, macro stabilization, and generalized commoditization of 1989 (positive); and so on. This is one large part of the macrodynamics of the transition, and it provides yet another explanation of why a transitional economy like that of Vietnam in the 1980s was rather different from the normal market economy.

Notes

1. In 1984, out of a total population of 58.8 million, the Red River Delta (including Hanoi) had 13.1 million, and the Mekong Delta, 13.3 million (45 percent of the total). Note that this definition of the Red River Delta excludes the delta districts of Hill provinces such as Vinh Phu. Indeed, the nondelta rural population of the northern part of the country at that time was around 10 million, reflecting the population movements of the 1960s and 1970s (SO 1985b:table,8).

2. We use the provinces as they were through the 1980s.   Subsequently, many were divided into smaller provinces.

3. The *giao dat giao rung* (giving out land and forests) program had a rather long history in Vietnam. See Ministry of Forestry 1983. Of Vietnam's total area of 33.2 million hectares in 1984, 13.4 million were reported as "in forestry use," with another 6.5 million hectares "with forestry potential" (SO 1985b:table2).

4. E.g., Fforde and Liljestrom (1987) based upon research into the pressures causing migration out of the Red River Delta into the upland forest areas and elsewhere.

5. For example, "immediately after 1981-82, '100 contracts' [discussed later] mobilized 15.6 percent more workers of working age and 10.2 percent outside working age; on average a cooperator's working day rose by 2.1 hours as the quality of work grew, though only in those tasks directly involved with the contract, because the farmers knew how to "balance" their efforts compared with the return" (Nguyen Manh Hung and Cao Ngoc Thang 1990:29).

6. Useful sources are Porter (1993) and Thayer (1993a, 1993b).

7. This had arisen rather early. Dao Van Tap (1980) stresses, uncontentiously, the army's role in the economic sphere and the need for it to act economically. By the mid-1980s 20percent of the national defense budget was reportedly coming from the army's "internal revenue'" (Ministry of National Defense 1985); the military was nevertheless still subject to criticisms for excess subsidies (PV 1986). Like other parts of the state sector, knowledge development had its own solutions; see the handbook "What troopers have to know about economics and economic management" (Pham Huu Huy and Nguyen Anh Hoang n.d.).

8. Mention should also be made of the great efforts made to develop the district as a planning and control level, a policy that gave cadres at that tier great power over the cooperatives. This power was removed by Decree No.10 in 1988. See Le Thanh Nghi (1979); Mai Huu Khue (1981); Appleton (1985).

9. An important marker of de-Stalinization was a Council of Ministers Decree in early 1988 that stipulated that individuals had the right to go abroad for a number of private purposes (see Order of the Council of Ministers No. 48 26 February 1988 in *Cong Bao* 15 April 1988).

10. See Amnesty International (1990).

11. This measure of total output differs from that of the orthodox Western system of national accounts in a number of areas. Two particular differences are that first, it excludes certain nonmaterial services (estimated by the IMF at around 13 percent of National Income; second, it does not include depreciation (again estimated by the IMF, and put at around 5 percent of national income). These figures must be only broad approximations (IMF 1987:6).

12. SO 1991:table 11; population data from SO 1987: table 2 and SO 1991:. Table 1; exchange rate based upon free market rates.

13. This in many cases fueled the process of commercialization by adding to the resources available for "leakage" onto the free market, the profits from which were then added to the expanding capitals of "local interests".

14. See Chapter 5 for a discussion of the changing official definition of this sector.

15. The survey data are extremely valuable since there is almost nothing else available giving such information. However, very little is known about how the results were obtained. The series was published regularly in the annual statistical collections of the SO, for example, SO 1985b:tables 157-160. These give

relative data (i.e., index numbers). The authors obtained absolute figures privately.

16. The traditional problem with "real" incomes figures derived for CPEs from price index data and figures on monetary incomes was that price indices often only took account of rationed goods, which were often not available.

17. From around 1988-89, however, the Vietnamese authorities spent considerable sums of money on surveys of rural living conditions. The earliest (Ministry of Labor 1990) covered 6,905 households in 21 provinces. The later ones (Le Van Toan et al. 1991; Nguyen Sinh Cuc 1991; Nguyen Van Tiem, 1993) took particular interest in the extent and trends in the numbers of households defined as "poor". A good summary of the implications of these can be found in Nguyen Van Tiem (1993: 16-18, on rich families, for poor families pp. 32-44). The basic conclusion reached was that the numbers of poor people had fallen significantly, from around 20 percent in 1990 to 15 percent in 1992 (Nguyen Van Tiem 1992 :43).

18. Vietnamese official statistical surveys measured foreign trade in "dollars-rubles." To quote the official source: "For the socialist countries (area I), calculations are in rubles; for the capitalist and developing countries (area II), calculations are in US dollars. At present we do not yet have the means for converting the data into a single united currency" (SO 1987:357).

19. QDND (1987) gives details of a case that came to light in Hai Phong, involving senior officials.

20. I.e., trade organized by local state authorities, a prime focus of commercial state interests.

21. Local trade was, on the whole, balanced. At root, this was because it was self-financed, unlike centrally organised trade.

22. In terms of the drama of transition, this certainly may be taken to imply that the sheer inefficiency of neo-Stalinism did provide means to assist in its replacement. The key question, however, is how this could in practice be used to secure progress.

Tables

TABLE 3.1 Agricultural Land Use by Area (in million hectares)

Category	1980	1985	1989	1993 (est.)
Total agricultural land	8.25	8.56	8.98	9.98
Annual crops	7.78	7.84	8.05	8.89
Of which: staples[a]	7.05	6.83	7.09	7.80
Of which: sown rice[a]	5.60	5.70	5.90	6.56
Long-term crops	0.48	0.72	0.92	1.08

[a] Note that there is multiple cropping.
Source: SO 1983:table 42; SO 1991c:table 49; SO 1994a:tables 43, 44.

TABLE : 3.2 Land Area (in million hectares)

Category	1980	1985	1992
Land already used for agriculture	6.91	6.95	7.29
Land already used for forestry	11.90	13.40	9.65
Other land	14.40	12.90	16.20
Total	33.20	33.20	33.10

Source: SO 1985a:table 3; SO 1985b:table 2; SO 1994c:table 2.

TABLE 3.3 State Farms

	1979	*1989*
Number of state farms	232	316[a]
Number of tractor teams and stations	209	485[a]
Number of standard tractors	18,667	53,767[a]
Percent of total agricultural gross output	11.6	2.1[a]
Percent of staples production	0.1	0.1
Export crops (thousand tonnes)		
Tea, green leaf	49	63
Coffee, fresh beans	12	51
Rubber, dry	41	50
Animals (thousand head)		
Buffalo	16	10
Cattle	79	68
Pigs (over two months)	2,211	137
Registered workers (million)	0.26	0.37[a]

[a] 1988 data.
Source: SO 1983, 1991c:various tables.

TABLE 3.4 Forest and Forest Land[a]

				Hectares	Percent of total
1979	Land used for forestry			13.40	100.00
	Of which:	Natural forest		12.92	96.40
		Planted forest		0.48	3.60
1985	Total forest land			19.95	100.00
	Land with forest			13.40	67.20
	Of which:	Natural forest		12.92	64.70
		Plantations		0.48	2.40
	Land with forest potential			6.55	32.80
1989	Forested land			9.32	100.00
	Of which:	Production		6.22	66.70
		Protective		2.37	25.40
		Specialized		0.73	7.80
1993	Forest land			20.05	100.00
	Of which:	With forest		9.65	48.00
		Of which:	Natural	8.63	43.00
			Planted	0.76	3.8
	Land without forest			11.42	57.00

[a] Definitions of different types of forest land have varied over time. The table gives close translations of the headings in the original sources.
Sources: SO 1985b:table 3; 1981:table 94; 1991:table 91; 1994c:table 71.

TABLE 3.5   Major Nonstaples Crop Production (in thousand tonnes)

	1979	1987	1989	1993 (est.)
Cotton	2.2	4.3	3.3	16.9
Jute	24.4	55.5	34.3	28.0
Rushes	81.8	98.7	81.2	75.2
Mulberry leaves	75.0	61.1	56.9	160.0
Sugar cane	3,490.0	5,323.0	5,345.0	6,656.0
Peanuts	81.1	237.4	205.8	240.3
Soya beans	20.0	95.7	82.0	81.3
Sesame	4.8	12.0	8.6	n/a
Tobacco	15.3	32.9	23.9	32.0
Tea	20.3	29.7	30.2	39.0
Coffee	5.1	20.1	40.8	73.5
Lacquer	0.2	0.2	n/a	n/a
Rubber	42.5	51.5	50.6	70.0
Pepper	0.3	4.4	7.1	8.5
Coconut	326.5	806.3	922.1	1,207.0

Source: SO 1991d, SO 1994c:various tables.

TABLE 3.6 Basic Population Data

	1979	*1989*	*1993*
Total population (millions)	52.46	64.77	70.98
Men	25.44	31.59	34.54
Women	27.02	33.19	36.44
Urban[a]	10.09	12.91	13.65
Rural[a]	42.37	50.80	56.29
Population growth rate 1979-1989: 2.1%			
Population growth rate 1989-1993: 2.3%			

[a] Note that the urban and rural data refer to registered populations only.
Source: SO 1994a:table 2.

TABLE 3.7 Labor Participation (in millions)

	1979	*1985*	*[a]1989*	*1993*
Total population	52.5	58.6	64.4	--
Urban	10.1	11.1	12.7	--
Recorded employment	19.4	26.0	28.9	32.7
Industry	2.2	2.8	3.2	3.5
Agriculture[b]	13.1	19.0	20.9	23.9
State sector	3.2	3.9	3.8	2.9

[a] Note that data from 1989 are from two separate sources.
[b] Including forestry.

TABLE 3.8 Regional Staples Output Variation

	1979	1984	1989	1993
A. Staples output per capita (kg)				
Vietnam	234	304	333	364
Mekong Delta	411	518	635	720
Red River Delta	209	251	316	456
B. Staple yields per hectare (kg)				*1992*
Vietnam	2.00	2.60	3.00	3.10
Mekong Delta	2.20	3.00	3.60	3.70
Red River Delta	2.30	2.80	3.30	3.70
C. State procurement (million tonnes)				
Vietnam	1.42	3.77	3.00	
Mekong Delta	0.38	1.90	1.25	
Red River Delta	0.43	0.54	0.28	

Note: Data for provincial level output and other data have to be collected from different yearly editions of the *Nien giam thong ke* (Statistical Yearbook). No state procurement reported after 1989.
Source: SO: various years.

TABLE 3.9 Estimates of Vietnamese GNP

	1976	1981	1983	1993[a]
National income (billion dollars)[b]	4.97	5.14	5.78	12.46
Per capita (US$)	$101	$94	$101	$175

[a] 1993 exchange rate put at 10,960 dong to the US$.
[b] By UNO method, as quoted in source, no explanation given.
Source: SO 1983a:table 9; SO 1994a:table 12.

TABLE 3.10 Structure of State Investment

		1976	1980	1985	1989	1992[a]
Total state investment (1982 billion dong)		12.8	16.0	24.8	17.5	
	Percent of total social product	6.2	7.3	8.0	4.6	n/a
Of which (percent):						
A.	Central	62.7	73.6	55.6	70.2	65.5
	Local	37.3	26.4	44.4	29.8	34.5
B.	Industry[b]	31.9	40.7	31.2	49.4	48.1
	Agriculture	20.0	19.0	18.5	12.4	11.1
	Transport	21.1	19.0	17.9	13.1	18.6
	Trade	4.5	1.5	4.2	2.3	0.7
	Construction	5.1	3.4	2.1	0.8	0.7
	Education	3.4	2.6	3.0	2.8	2.7
	Health	1.8	1.9	3.1	1.9	2.4

[a] Rebased 1989 prices.
[b] Presumed to include energy.
Sources: SO 1985a:table 2; SO 1987:tables 105, 106, 107.

TABLE 3.11 Share of Gross Output, by Sector and Component (as percent of Gross Social Product at current prices)

	1979	1985	1989	1992[a]
A. By component				
State	36.1	37.0	34.5	39.9
Collective	25.9	34.9		
Private	38.0	28.1	65.5[b]	60.0[b]
B. By sector				
Agriculture[c]	37.3	37.7	44.8	40.4
Industry	36.0	41.2	33.2	39.7

[a] Constant 1989 prices.
[b] Private and collective data now combined.
[c] Includes forestry.

TABLE 3.12 Growth of Gross Output by Sector (percent per year, constant prices)

	1976-80	1980-85	1985-89	1989-93
Agriculture	2.0	6.2	4.1	4.1
Industry	0.6	9.3	5.4	10.6
Of which: State	-1.5	8.1	6.9	12.8
Central	-3.5	7.8	7.6	16.9
Local	2.9	8.6	5.8	3.9
Non-state	3.9	11.4	6.2	6.2

Source: SO 1988a:tables 13, 25, 86; SO 1991c:tables 13, 24; SO 1994a:table 41.

TABLE 3.13 Worker Household Income and Expenditure Survey, 1986 ("new" dong[a] per month per head of a worker household)

			Dong	*Percent*
A. Incomes				
	Total income per month		506	
		North Vietnam	420	
		South Vietnam	654	
	Of which:	Wages	247	48.8
		Subsidies	52	10.3
		Others' wages	6	1.2
		Pensions, etc.	33	6.6
		Other incomes	167	33.1
B. Expenditure				
	Total expenditure per month		521	
		North Vietnam	431	
		South Vietnam	n/a	
	Of which:	Food	383	73.6
		Clothing	32	6.2
		Other	105	20.2
Net dissaving			15	

[a] The new Vietnamese dong was introduced in late 1985 at a ratio of 10:1 for the old Vietnamese dong.

Source: SO 1988b.

TABLE 3.14 Farmer Household Income and Expenditure Survey, 1986 (in "new" dong[a] per month per head of a farmer household)

			Dong	Percent
A. Incomes				
	Total income per month		744	
		North Vietnam	591	
		South Vietnam	951	
	Of which:	From the collective	215	28.9
		From the family economy	442	59.3
		Other income	88	11.8
B. Expenditure				
	Total expenditure per month		548	
	Of which:	Food	418	76.3
		Clothing	31	5.7
		Culture and Education	5	0.9
		Health	5	1.0
		Other	62	11.3
C. Net Saving			196	

[a] See table 3.13.
Source: SO 1988b.

TABLE 3.15 Domestic Trade: Proportion of the Total Value of Retail Trade Covered by the State-controlled Sector

	1976	*1981*	*1985*	*1989*
Total	55.8	53.5	72.2	--
Staples	n/a	39.9	82.0	--
Nonstaples food	n/a	50.2	62.4	--
Clothes	n/a	51.7	82.3	--
Pharmaceuticals	n/a	81.4	76.5	--
Fuel	n/a	72.1	86.1	--
Construction materials	n/a	69.9	72.2	--

Note: Data in "pure" retail trade (*thuan tuy*).
Source: SO 1987b: tables 151, 152; SO 1988b. Data series discontinued.

Boxes

BOX 3.1 Aggregate Data and the Transition: Summary

Food staples balance: recoveries after the 1981 and 1988 reforms, deteriorations to crisis levels in the late 1970s and mid-1980s; generally low and close to the 300 kg per capita "warning line."

Changes in land availability: minimal.

Changes in physical land use: not great when examined from aggregate cropping point of view.

GNP per capita: low, suggesting generally low capital intensity of production and corresponding ease in changing the output mix.

Savings and accumulation: low domestic savings, high proportion of investment financed from overseas assistance; no clear relation between increases in capital stock and output gains, arguing that output well off production possibility frontier. Household savings collapsed from 1985 with onset of hyperinflation.

Output: unstable growth, averaging around 2.5-3.0 percent through the decade (NMP measures)--rapid growth in first half, slowdown in second; agriculture's share roughly constant; private sector share rose on some measures up to 1985, then fell sharply on all measures.

Employment: mainly agricultural; of the 10 percent of the recorded labor force active in industry, only 30 percent was in so-called modern industry. The great mass of the population was therefore active in sectors with low capital intensity producing easily marketable commodities (mainly food and consumer goods).

Incomes: real incomes stagnant--high proportion of state workers' incomes spent on food--rose in late 1970s and again in mid-1980s but then fell toward the end of the decade; share of state workers' incomes coming from nonwage sources rose steadily but fell back temporarily in 1985-86.

Distribution and trade: show a decline in the free market share of retail trade up until 1985 under hard reform socialism, then a substantial growth from 1987; state share of rice procurement was low--fell from 15 percent to 14 percent 1976-80, then rose to 22 percent in the first one-half of the decade before falling thereafter. Prices accelerated in 1981-82, then slow, but then shifted to hyperinflation (triple digit levels) from 1986 before stabilizing in 1989.

Figures

FIGURE 3.1 Staples Output per Capita
(kg of milled rice equivalent)

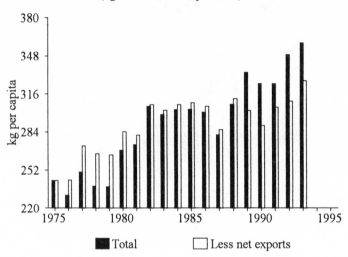

Source: SO various years--mainly 1993 and 1986 for production and trade data. Imports data for 1993 partly estimated.

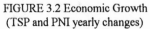

FIGURE 3.2 Economic Growth
(TSP and PNI yearly changes)

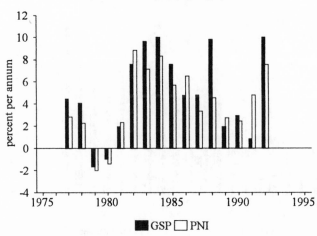

Note: Total economic activity is measured here in terms of the met material product (NMP) system. PNI is produced national income, GSP is gross social product.
Source: SO 1990a, 1991a, 1993.

FIGURE 3.3 Retail Price Inflation
(retail sales deflator)

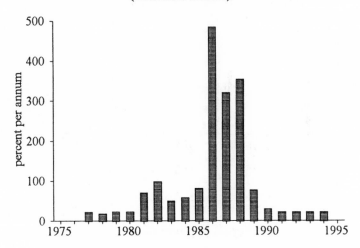

Note: As there was no official data available, for the period 1991 to 1994 the deflator used was the average of the monthly retail price index.
Source: SO 1985, 1990c, 1991b, 1994; SO (HCM) 1994.

FIGURE 3.4 Accumulation
(percent of PNI)

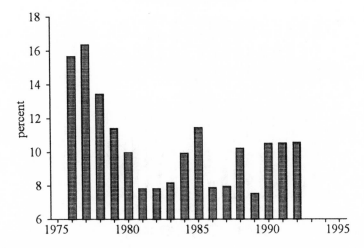

Note: There were large differences in current and constant (not shown here) price estimates, which is not unusual at times of rapid inflation.
Source: SO 1985a, 1990b, 1990c, 1992, 1993.

FIGURE 3.5 Growth in State Investment
(1982 and 1989 prices, yearly growth)

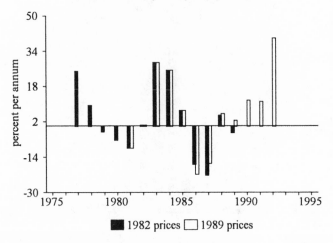

Source: SO 1988a, 1991a, 1994.

FIGURE 3.6 Structural Change
(sectoral shares constant price PNI)

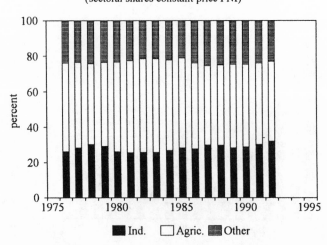

Note: The graph shows the structure of produced national income. Note the appreciable recorded growth in the services--"other"--sector in the late 1980s.
Source: SO 1990a, 1991a, 1993.

FIGURE 3.7 Structural Change
(component shares constant price PNI)

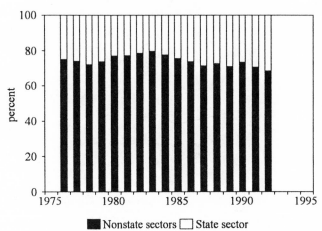

Nonstate sectors ☐ State sector

Note: Graph shows the structure of PNI by "components". Note that the nonstate sectors include cooperatives. The state sector declined during 1978-82 and then grew steadily.
Source: SO 1990a, 1991a, 1993.

FIGURE 3.8 Private Sector
(contribution to constant price PNI)

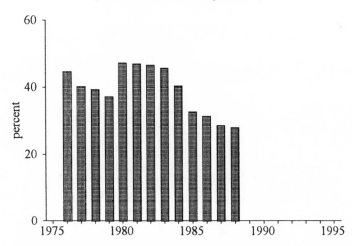

Source: SO 1985a, 1988, 1990c.

FIGURE 3.9 Private Sector Growth Rates
(contribution to constant price PNI)

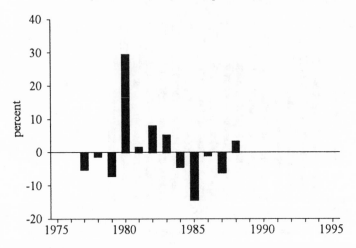

Note: Derived from NMP principles, the data exclude much of the services sector. Note the sharp output increase in 1980 and decline in 1985.
Source: SO 1985a, 1988, 1990c.

FIGURE 3.10 State Worker Other Incomes
(other incomes as percent of total)

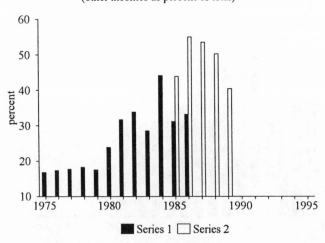

■ Series 1 ☐ Series 2

Source: SO 1984; personal communication. Series 1 is current price data, mainly from SO 1984; Series 2 is at constant 1989 prices and from an informal source.
Note: The graph implies that the main structural shift occurred in the period 1980-85/86.

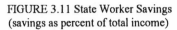

FIGURE 3.11 State Worker Savings
(savings as percent of total income)

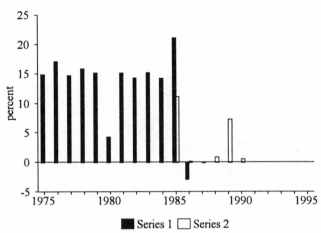

Note: The survey-based series is simply income less consumption as a percent of income; savings do not appear to collapse in the face of hyperinflation until after 1985-86.
Source: As in Figure 3.10.

FIGURE 3.12 Food Spending
(percent of total spending)

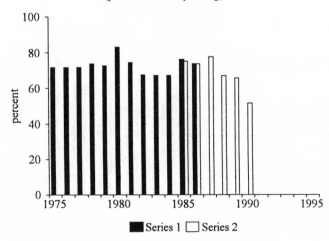

Note: The percent spent on food roughly measures real incomes. Until 1980 this was very high, implying low incomes; it fell after 1980, rose 1984-1987 then fell from 1987.
Source: As in Figure 3.10.

FIGURE 3.13 The Free Retail Market
(structure--private and nonprivate)

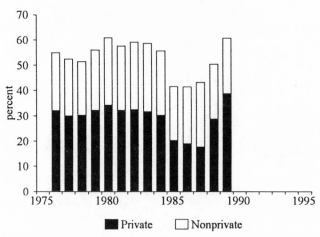

Note: Graph shows the "organized" and "unorganized" (*khong co to chuc*) markets--the latter understood as "free." Data from different series have been averaged for some periods.
Source: SO 1988a, 1991b, 1991c.

FIGURE 3.14 Free Market Retail Sales
(percent of total market)

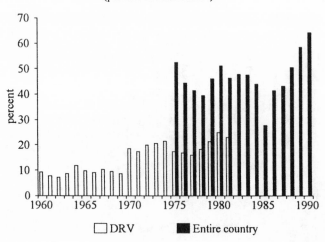

Note: This uses current price data, whereas Figure 3.13 is based upon constant price data.
Source: Personal communication; SO 1981, 1985, 1990b, 1992.

FIGURE 3.15 State Staples Procurement
(percent over 250 kgs per capita)

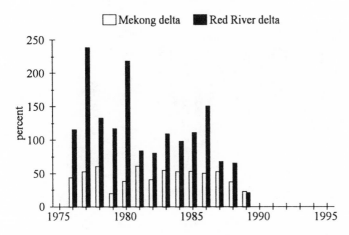

Note: This assumes a 250 kgs subsistence requirement and then expresses procurement
(*thu mua*) as a percent of output above subsistence. No recorded procurement after 1989.
Source: Various issues of SO.

FIGURE 3.16 Net Staples Surplus
(net output)

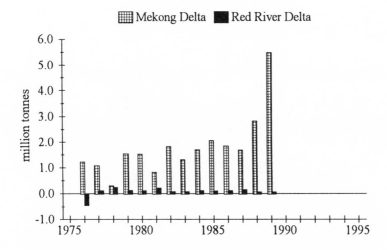

Note: The data show staples left after subsistence and state procurement, approximately
equal to that left for the free market. There was no reported state procurement after 1989.
Source: As in Figure 3.15.

FIGURE 3.17 Trade Deficits
(Ruble and US$)

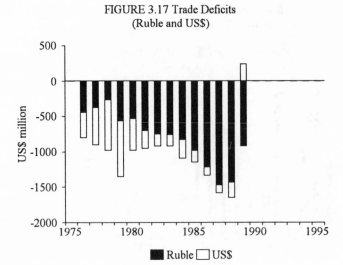

Note: Ruble data is evaluated at the rate of 1 Ruble equals 1 $US.
Source: SO 1985a, 1991c, 1992, 1994a.

FIGURE 3.18 Exports Structure

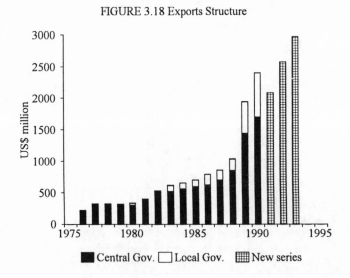

Note: "Local Gov." are so-called direct exports; their growth in 1980, restriction in
1981-82, and then resurgence in 1983 and 1989 mark steps in local capital accumulation.
Sources: As in Figure 3.17.

FIGURE 3.19 Real Retail Sales Growth

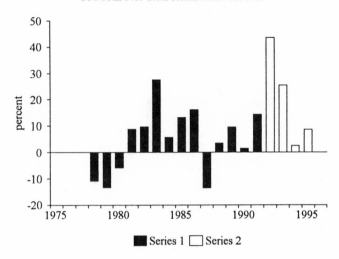

Note: Series 1 is derived from original volume data. Series 2 is reworked from current price retail sales data deflated by yearly averages of the monthly consumer price index.
Source: As in Figure 3.3.

4

Development Strategy

In the previous chapters, we have sought to show how the Vietnamese transition from plan to market can be understood and that it is useful to see it from a historical and process-based perspective. Vietnamese experience can be used to suggest that, in transition of this type, lack of effective central control could have accompanied processes of decentralization and liberalization that possessed a distinctly spontaneous character. We have pointed out in discussing interactions between the macro and micro levels, that grassroots behavior was influenced by the macroeconomic environment, especially by the existence of profitable alternatives to the plan. This was closely linked with the gap that grew up between state and open market prices. However, the macro level also includes state and party policies and their impact, the focus of this chapter.

Reform's Fluctuating Meaning

Spontaneous processes of fence-breaking and the emergence of autonomous sites of accumulation within SOEs may well have been part and parcel of everyday life in Vietnam after least 1979 and the Sixth Plenum. However, such practices were far removed from anything that New Knowledge, advocated by the Vietnamese Communist Party from 1945 to 1986 expressed about Vietnam and Vietnamese socialist development. The world was somehow not as it should have been. Once a return to the logic of hard-line neo-Stalinism was impossible, then the development of autonomous activities, oriented toward markets, posed a series of questions for party thinkers. Yet the textured information available in the press points to the necessity for conservative policymakers to find some way of living with reality. Indeed, one characteristic of Vietnamese communism, it has been argued, was its necessary familiarity with the long distance between textbook theory and the steamy reality of aid-dependent Southeast Asian poverty (Fforde 1986; Woodside 1989). However, government is government, answers are needed, and order depends upon meaning. Thus, the notion of national development had to change.

In this chapter we discuss the ebb and flow of development thinking during the period 1976-93 in the context of economic change. What is the essential problem? To recapitulate: Starting with the pure socialism of the post-reunification period, around 1979-80 there arose a "hard" version of reform socialism that was essentially reactionary, but through tactical concessions to autonomous activities, it acted to legalize the transitional model. This was in its turn abandoned around 1984-85 and was given a final kiss of death by the debacle of the price-wage-money measures of 1985. The Sixth Party Congress of 1986 then introduced a "soft" reform socialism, which heralded de-Stalinization and the opening up of the economy to the private sector and the outside capitalist world. Finally, in 1989 a series of anti-inflationary measures threw the entire reform socialism project into question by introducing a market economy without resolving the issue of state capital. This led to a lack of effective capital markets and weak central government. The resulting system initially revealed itself to be highly inflationary and unstable, as the political economy underlying the transition was greatly dependent upon a combination of subsidy and weak central government. That in turn set the agenda for the 1990s, which was initiated by the 1992 interest rate reforms, the rising inflow of foreign direct investment, the growth of the private sector and strong de facto privatization, and the resumption of multilateral lending in late 1993. How could Vietnamese Marxist-Leninists grapple with, and then explain, such a reality? The simple answer is this: through debate.

This chapter presents the immediate background of the economic crisis of 1979-80, the origins of the transitional model in the economic crisis of 1979-80, and some of the more striking successes and failures of the period up to the Sixth Party Congress in 1986. The policy changes of the period from 1986 until the final abandonment of central planning in 1989 are then examined. Certain key policy documents are summarized in Boxes 4.1, 4.2 and 4.3 at the end of the chapter.

During the economic crisis of 1979-80, increasingly open debate began about the nature of socioeconomic development in Vietnam. The DRV model was criticized, but not without opposition from conservatives, and in the early 1980s new policies still reflected a desire to preserve the basic institutions of the DRV model.[1] Attachment to the New Knowledge that underlay the First FYP (1961-65) was strong. The Fifth Party Congress of 1982 announced a commitment to reorientation of sectoral policy toward agriculture, consumption, and exports that was not, in fact, realized (Vo Nhan Tri 1985:3).

However, after the 1985 debacle, development strategy began to focus on the inadequacies of existing reforms and push for more far-reaching changes--changes that involved a radical reorientation in attitudes toward the private sector, free markets and unplanned economic activities. Through 1987, policy debate increasingly identified the state's central economic management organs as a key factor inhibiting both implementation of the new sectoral priorities and microlevel reforms.

Prior to the 1986 Sixth Party Congress, official critiques were already stressing the issue of bureaucracy (*quan lieu*) and the combination of administrative supply and pervasive subsidization (*bao cap*). Yet this was somewhat misleading and did not necessarily imply a commitment to effective decentralization and liberalization of the economy. It was, instead, often a criticism of the way in which the institutions of the DRV model were operating.[2] Policymakers seem to have believed that stable growth could be attained without further policy reforms--viewed as "concessions" because they would entail quite fundamental changes in the development strategy and an abandonment of central planning and the DRV program.

One logical implication of this was that macrostabilization should have been possible *without* effective micro decentralization. Thus, in the first half of the 1980s, the dominant preception was still of a pattern of change in which the private sector and free markets would play a role *subordinate* to the state plan. Subsidized supply would continue as part of the state's essential central management role,with resources allocated directly into high-priority areas. However, the macro and sectoral distortions proved to be too large, and in combination with other problems, the authorities were unable to restore macro equilibrium. The resulting combination of a high state-free market price differential for domestically traded goods with an overvalued exchange rate was the most important prerequisite for the forces behind the grassroots adaptation mechanisms that were pushing for further de facto decentralization. The partial reforms of 1980-81 had given support to such strategies. The contradiction between the attempt at recentralization combined with macro stabilization and the added pressure for bottom-up commercialization ended with the destruction of the recentralizing strategy in 1985. By the Sixth Party Congress in December 1986, these policies had been rejected and the door had opened to a shift toward far greater formal decentralization.

The Second and Third Five-Year Plans (1976-85)

The Second Five-Year Plan (1976-80)

After national reunification in 1975, the Vietnamese national leadership was composed of individuals whose political education had occurred during the 1930s. People talk about the time just after reunification as being intoxicating, a time when people could seriously imagine that Vietnam could become an industrialized country by the year 2000, "after four to five Five Year Plans."[3] The high targets of the Second FYP reflected this view (see Table 4.1), as stated by Party Secretary Le Duan at the June 1976 meeting of the National Assembly [*NhD* 26 June 1976].

Official commitment to the DRV program in reunited Vietnam is confirmed by a series of early policy measures taken in 1975-76, for example, in the area of agricultural cooperative management reform (Fforde 1989a; Le Thanh Nghi 1977a) and state industrial enterprises (Le Thanh Nghi 1977c; Le Duan 1978; CIEM 1978). It is important to stress the way in which these fitted into the overall development program, based upon neo-Stalinism. Extension of the DRV model to the whole of the country had clear and important implications for the economy of southern Vietnam. Hanoi soon took control of foreign trade, and moved to crack down on the free market in the South. A surprise withdrawal of the southern currency combined with measures against the Chinese merchant community in Cho Lon increased tensions between Vietnam and China in the late 1970s prior to Vietnam's invasion of Cambodia in late 1978 and China's "punitive action" at the Sino-Vietnamese border in early 1979.

Following a similar procedure as that adopted in the North after 1954, the authorities sought to bring about the socialist transformation of the South, which meant imposition of the institutional models of the DRV.[4] In large-scale industry, factories were brought under the direct control of central ministries that sought to manage them according to central-planning methods, allocating quantity targets for output and requiring that production units submit entirely to the administrative allocation of inputs and outputs. Pressure was brought to bear upon the Mekong Delta peasantry to join cooperatives and the production collectives.

In the South-center, for reasons that may have to do with the more traditional rural social pattern, as well as the attitudes of local cadres, these measures were quickly successful. In the South, however, and especially in Saigon, now renamed Ho Chi Minh City, they encountered considerable resistance; by the end of the decade, the Mekong Delta remained largely uncollectivized, and many of the cooperatives and production collectives that did exist had extremely limited functions.

The short-run economic inefficiency implied by these measures is clear, but the macroeconomic effects of the overambitious growth targets were considerable, exacerbating distortions and sectoral imbalances. The data on the subject reveals the effects of the Chinese and Western aid cuts imposed in around 1978. Chinese aid was far more important than Western aid, as China had largely supported the DRV light-industrial sector, as well as directly supplying consumer goods. Thus, whereas total state investment rose sharply in 1977, it peaked in 1978 at a level it was not to exceed again until 1983. However, the sectoral imbalances are quite obvious: During the Second FYP (1976-80) state investment averaged 16.6 billion (1982) dong, of which only some 20 percent (3.36 billion 1982 dong) went into agriculture (SO 1987:tables 105, 107).

The return to capital investment fell during the Second FYP; much newly installed industrial capacity could not be used, and incremental capital output ratios, or ICORs, a measure of the efficiency of the way in which additional capital stock is utilized,) rose. This happened *before* Chinese and Western aid cuts precipitated the major economic crisis.

Prices. Figure 4.1 shows the gap between state and free market staples prices on the eve of the 1979-80 crisis and the increase in "squeeze" between 1975 and 1977. This graph documents, in a striking manner, the degree of distributional tension in relations between state and rural producers. It also shows the extent to which this particular manifestation of plan distortion had already been reduced by 1986-87. Figure 4.2 shows variation in the state's trading margin, showing that the state, not state workers, directly benefited from the output gains of 1980-81.

The 1979-80 Crisis. The economic crisis of 1979-80 had its main impact on the central state- management system.[5] The main problem was the fall in low-price inputs, mainly derived from foreign aid and rice procured with difficulty from both the collectivized and noncollectivized peasantry. Western and Chinese aid cuts directly reduced the volume of resources controlled by the state trading monopolies. At the same time, bad weather and resistance to the collectivization drive in the Mekong Delta made it extremely difficult for the authorities to secure rice supplies.[6] There were falls in domestic supplies of staples to the state in 1978 and 1979 (SO 1987:table 71]. Also at this time, imports fell off as Western countries and China responded to the deterioration in international relations and the Vietnamese invasion of Cambodia in winter 1978-79.

The Chinese army attacked in February 1979. In 1980, total imports fell by 14 percent compared with 1979. By 1982, imports from capitalist countries had fallen to 48 percent of their value in 1979; imports from developing countries were down to 27 percent of their 1979 value, and imports from international organizations,[7] to 18 percent of their 1979 value. The Soviet Union stepped in to replace the shortfall. Whereas in 1979 only 52 percent of imports came from socialist countries, by 1982 this figure had risen to 81 percent (SO 1987:table 166). These supplies, of course, went through the system of state trading monopolies.

The Rise of Autonomous Transactions. As the volume of resources coming through the state administrative supply system shrank, both absolutely and relatively, previously well-established adaptation mechanisms, drawing upon pre-stage experiences, now operated with greater vigor. Suddenly facing cuts in supplies from the state, economic units increasingly started to look for better ways of operating, and this set off a new round of spontaneous bottom-up change, or fence-breaking.

Some examples can be found in the pathbreaking piece by Dam Van Nhue and Le Sy Thiep (1981). To give some more textured information from the DRV heartland, Ha Nam Ninh Province, for example, had started "direct deliveries of materials to producers" by the end of 1979 (*NhD* 21 February 1980). The industrial enterprises in Ha Son Binh Province had established direct relations between units producing artisanal goods in the deltas and agricultural cooperatives in the mountains, "with no intermediaries." By 1979 local SOEs were already setting up small shops to produce "off-list" products and to develop retail outlets of their own (*NhD* 26 July 1979). The Hoang Van Thu paper factory in Bac Thai Province was obtaining inputs "horizontally" as early as 1978 (*NhD* 21 February 1979) but had had to give up by midyear because of material shortages (*NhD* 16 August 1979). The Cau Duong brick factory (centrally managed, just outside Hanoi) was reportedly "stabilizing production" in early 1980 (*NhD* 21 February 1980). The unit had rented transport to fetch coal from Quang Ninh and had bought hundreds of tonnes of firewood from Bac Thai; capacity utilization had reportedly risen.

Although all these examples are from northern Vietnam, similar things were happening in the South. Phu Khanh Province had also permitted "direct deliveries of material to producers" before the 1981 legislation (*NhD* 21 February 1980). Many other examples can be found from the press and academic journals of the time: fence-breaking, under protection from local authorities and line ministries, was rampant.[8]

Coming on top of the military crises of 1978-79, it proved impossible for the government to resist these pressures and it therefore gave limited political support to such practices. In August 1979, five months after the Chinese invasion of Vietnam's northern provinces and the subsequent Chinese withdrawal, the Sixth Plenum of the Party Central Committee suggested that it was acceptable for units to experiment in order to find ways of making output increase sharply (*bung ra*). At the same time, the drive to collectivize the Mekong was temporarily abandoned. However, formal policy changes did not arrive until 1981, after the start of the Third FYP.

The policy debates are reflected in the open literature (CPV 1979a, 1979b and 1979c). For example, Nguyen Duy Trinh (1980:2) took a conservative position, arguing against "the tendency that said that all sectors, especially the individual and capitalist, should be allowed to expand"; furthermore, "the scope for relying on markets should be limited by the need to subordinate them to the plan--the basic reason for failure is the slow pace of change in methods of planning and management structure." This can be compared with the radically promarket (at this stage) Nguyen Lam (1980a and 1980b) who argued against "planning everything," favoring the use of markets and multiple planning levels. Nguyen Lam's work defended the individual and stressed the need to pay attention to the material interests of peasants, regions, and so on, and he pointed to and attacked a key indicator of the existence of planning-induced shortage--excess stockholdings in state industry. He also argued that production should be near to the market and based upon direct contracting, as was later advocated by Dao Xuan Sam (1986).[9] The economic data describing this period is particularly weak; many of the experimental methods tried in the year and one-half between the Sixth Plenum and the promulgation of new policies in early 1981 were illegal. However, it is notable that agricultural output started to grow again in 1979 after falling in the previous two years (SO 1987:table 24). Certain sectors of industry grew rapidly, although reported total output was falling, as shown in Table 4.2 and Figure 3.2.

The Third Five-Year Plan (1981-85)

From Fence-breaking to Transition. The economic history of Vietnam during this period has been studied far less than that of around 1986 onward. This is mainly because the country was still largely closed and also because the purely private sector was still anathema.[10] It is also because of the orthodox analytical focus upon reform per se, and its identification with the slogan *doi moi*, as introduced at the 1986 Sixth Party Congress.

The period of twelve to eighteen months from the Sixth Plenum of September 1979 and January 1981, when the decisions that led to 25-CP and CT-100 were made (the defining documents of the transitional model), is of great interest. During the months immediately after the Sixth Plenum, there seemed to be some hope of a rapid acceptance of markets at high levels--as eventually decided by the Sixth Part Congress. A crucial area was domestic trade, where initial liberalizations were soon reined in (see Box 4.2). However, sometime in 1980 there seems to have been a U-turn in policy, and a Politburo decision (No. 26, 23 June 1980) pointed to the eventual policy stance, calling for stricter controls on private staples trade.[11] To some extent this is dealt with elsewhere (Fforde 1989a), but the period remains under-researched. In any case, hard reform socialism seems to have emerged sometime in 1980.

Macro-Micro Interactions. During the early 1980s the Vietnamese economy started to evolve rather rapidly. Short-run output gains were quite large (Figure 3.2). Grassroots changes interacted with policy concessions and periodic drives to clamp down on outside activities and the free market. These processes generated certain rules of the game that, although close to those that had operated in the DRV during the pre-stage, differed in the important respect that unplanned activities were now not always illegal. A de facto as well as now legally reformed--through the content of 25-CP and CT-100--system became well established and much experience was gained. The overall effect was to show the scope for sharply improved short-term resource utilization in some areas, where output increased *without* significant additional inputs. An important factor here was the effect of higher incomes upon labor inputs, especially in agriculture. Plan distortions were reduced. However, the effects of such liberalizations soon started to wear off, and distributional conflicts mounted.

The 1982 Fifth Congress: Attempted Recentralization. The hard reform policy of attempted recentralization and the accompanying program of concessional reforms was approved at the 1982 Fifth Party Congress (CPV 1982). The leadership made a severe self-criticism, accepting that peacetime construction was a task for which it had too little experience, and leaders introduced certain key theoretical innovations (Dao Duy Tung et al. 1982; Le Xuan Tung 1985). In hindsight, the two most important of these were the following:

1. The idea that the period of transition to socialism had to have two stages. During the first, Vietnam would, it was said, lay the basis for industrialization in a prosperous agriculture and a balanced foreign trade position. The economic surplus would be created without which industrialization and urbanization would be impossible. This meant that the DRV model's priority of state industry and urban development would have to be abandoned and investment resources transferred to agriculture, consumer goods, and foreign trade. It also meant that macroeconomic balances should be restored.
2. The notion that there were "three interests" (*ba loi ich*) in Vietnamese society--the state, the collective, and the

family/individual--*and that each was legitimate.* In any economic venture, they would have to be brought into harmony.

This position allowed a bridge to be made between the transitional model and traditional thinking about the three subsystems of Vietnamese society (see Chapter 2). *The position was deeply ambiguous, and in this ambiguity in part lay its progressive nature.* It meant that the absolute priority that neo-Stalinism had given to state factories over agricultural cooperatives and the family economy had been abandoned. Such priority was now conditional, dependent upon such ideas as balance and harmony. The position therefore supported and encouraged those with less conservative attitudes and thus permitted support for the private and family economies in many areas. But it also allowed conservatives the justification for continuing preferential treatment of the old priority sectors and for attacking the free market and a return to collectivization of the Mekong Delta.

Indicators of Policy Stance. The main consequences of the DRV model were listed at the end of Chapter 2, and it is in regard to these that the hard reform policies of the Vietnamese authorities in the early 1980s have to be assessed. These hard reform policies introduced decentralizing reforms aimed at improving static economic efficiency and should have granted producers freer access to suppliers and customers, both in the domestic and overseas sectors. Sensitivity to costs and prices would have to have increased at the same time that macroeconomic stabilization and sectoral adjustment shifted prevalent costs and prices closer to values that reflected social costs and benefits while being consistent with generalized commodity production. Crucial among such indicators were the exchange rate and the terms of trade facing farmers. A prerequisite of such price-wage reforms, however, would have been an effective abandonment of administrative resource allocation methods in order to make economic units sensitive to price and costs--to "make prices and costs matter." This would have entailed abandonment of central planning, and that was not acceptable.

Attainment of better long-term efficiency would also have required a reallocation of resources toward those sectors that had suffered from the distortions induced by the DRV model. This meant, first, agriculture, but also exports. A positive attitude to small-scale industry was also required and therefore far more liberal policies toward the private sector. Furthermore, such a sectoral re-orientation of the development effort would have needed a profound shift away from the human capital and institutions of the DRV model, with attention paid to development of the financial system, rural development in the wider sense, such as extension schemes, and other elements of the less tangible aspects of efficient and sustainable growth. "Outsiders," both from the old regime in the South and in the North, would have had to be permitted to involve themselves more fully in the economy if human capital were to be effectively mobilized. None of this would have been easy.

Agriculture and Agricultural Collectivization. The overall policy stance taken toward agriculture prior to the 1986 Sixth Party Congress was one in which the "output contracts" system (see discussion later on was viewed as a way, not of shifting to family economy but of improving the internal efficiency of *cooperatives.*[12] Although farmers were in principle free to market a higher share of output than before, the state did *not* try to move out of staples trade and, indeed, sought with some success (as shown in Figures 3.15 and 3.16) to increase its share of output.

The terms of trade facing agriculture did not improve greatly (see Table 5.6). The share of state investment going to agriculture did not rise, and there was no fundamental institutional shift toward creating the dense network--of rural credit and so forth--needed to accelerate technical progress in agriculture.

The Fifth Party Congress' commitment to defending the institutions of the DRV model meant that there still had to be a socialist transformation of the entire country. The drive to collectivize the Mekong Delta was therefore restarted, and by 1985 official data reported that this had been successful: In the delta, some 77.2 percent of peasant families were in production collectives and a further 3.7 percent were in cooperatives; these two collective forms therefore covered over 80 percent of the population (SO 1987:tables 79, 81).[13] Collectivization of the main grain surplus area, no matter what lessons had been learned from the Red River Delta, was still part of Vietnamese development strategy.[14]

In the crucial sector of agriculture, the reforms of the early 1980s did little more than create a temporary improvement in the static efficiency of the collective sector.

Greater autonomy for family producers undoubtedly improved prospects but was not enough.[15] The effects upon output per capita have already been noted in Figure 3.1. By 1985 output growth had slowed, and per capita staple production had started to dip alarmingly again.

Attitude to the Free Market and Nonsocialist Sectors. The hostility of the DRV program to the free market and nonsocialist components continued. Although small-scale industry was to a certain extent liberalized, this usually meant locally managed state industry. More serious, periodic drives against the free market occurred. In the South, especially in 1984-85, these were bound up with the collectivization drive and the attempt to control rice.[16] Not until after the Sixth Party Congress of late 1986 is it possible to see a radical change in the attitude to the free market and the private sector.

Despite this, the growth of autonomous market-oriented transactions within the state sector (see discussion later on--the Three Plan system) meant that the relative importance of the central-planning system declined. Also, it appears that the systemic unimplementability of policies aimed at complete eradication of the free market increasingly created confusion and space for private producers, cooperators, and others to go about their business, albeit quasi-illegally.

Foreign Trade. One spontaneous development in the aftermath of the Sixth Plenum was the creation of local export-import companies, the most important of them in Ho Chi Minh City. Hard currency earnings grew rapidly outside the direct control of the central authorities. In 1982 a task-force was sent from Hanoi to Ho Chi Minh City that, according to foreign press reports, had these companies shut down and brought criminal charges against those responsible. Export earnings from the city temporarily ceased to grow (*NhD* 9 February 1982).

The evolution of policy toward foreign trade decentralization remains complex and difficult to summarize (see Box 4.3). This must to some extent have reflected Ho Chi Minh City's growing political power.[17] State enterprises' rights to retain part of foreign exchange earnings in principle probably date from the 1970s, but this was almost always made conditional upon the approval of their superiors, an outome that was dependent upon bureaucratic tussles and was frequently denied.[18] There was not, at this time, a firm commitment to the development of a decentralized foreign trade network, and the administrative procurement structure aimed at obtaining resources for exports according to the plan remained intact. However, both local and central authorities could use their power to command supply of exportable goods to expand exports.

It is not surprising, therefore, that one of the more positive points of the period is the development of exports, which showed an average growth of 15.6 percent over the period 1980-81 compared with 1.6 percent between 1977 and 1980 (SO 1987:table 164). After 1981, growth slowed.

Erosion of the central state monopoly of foreign trade had similar effects as the grassroots changes affecting state industry and agricultural cooperatives. The combined result was a reduction in the strength of state trading monopolies and a corresponding increase in the levels of administrative pressure needed to defend them. That pressure was not to be forthcoming.

Macroeconomic Imbalances: Inattention to Structural Causes?
Despite the micro reforms of state industry and agricultural cooperatives, the sectoral misallocations discussed in Chapter 2 on the whole did not show great improvement during the Third FYP (1981-85). Furthermore, toward the middle years of the plan there are strong signs of a resurgence of the macro-structural tensions characteristic of the DRV model.

The share of "accumulation" (i.e. gross investment) in total national income fell in 1981 to 7.2 percent but by 1985 was back up to 12.3 percent. State investment, having fallen some 18 percent between 1978 and 1981, then rose by some 70 percent over the next four years, compared with a 22 percent gain in produced national income. Although rising accumulation was insufficient to choke off increasing aggregate consumption, there was no strong reorientation of production toward consumption and away from investment (SO 1987:tables 15, 16).[19]

State sectoral priorities were also unfavorable. The share of state investment going into agriculture fell further, to around 16.5 percent in 1982 and 1983, before recovering slightly. After a pause in the early 1980s, state employment started to rise again, and in 1985 was 27 percent above the 1981 level (a year-on-year rise of 6 percent, far higher than the rate of population growth) (SO 1987:tables 7, 105, 107).

The Fiscal Crisis of Transition: The Road to 1985. In Vietnam during the early 1980s, the increased de facto commercialization of the economy certainly reduced the monopoly power of the state. In the absence of severe and effective budgetary cuts, this meant that the authorities had to pay higher prices for supplies of goods and labor, widening the fiscal deficit and increasing monetary inflation. There was pressure to increase both state employees' wages and the prices paid by the state to obtain commodities. Failure to resist this pressure, which would have required institutional and structural changes that were neither politically acceptable at the time nor likely to be implementable fast enough, led to a series of wage and price hikes (Phan Van Tiem 1990). These pushed the budget into increasing deficit. A cycle developed where such concessions to the subsidized sectors of the economy were followed, after a lag, by further open market price rises that eventually precipitated another series of price reforms.[20]

These processes, when combined with the increased role of unplanned activities both within and outside the socialist sectors, themselves driven by high state--open market price differentials, squeezed those sectors that had previously relied upon the state for access to cheap resources. Almost the entire state system was subject to this process, for state employees had long been dependent upon food either taxed out of the impoverished northern agriculture or supplied free by aid donors. In a similar position to factory management, state employees found themselves encouraged--if not forced--to find ways of generating additional funds so as to acquire resources on the free market. Workers who managed todo this were able to buy food on the free market. They developed their family economies, working in their spare time or taking time off from their paid work. This increased the demand for employment in those sectors that required low capital inputs such as petty industry and trade. This pushed further against the state's prohibitions on the free market and exacerbated the tensions within the remnants of the DRV planning model.

The Third FYP: Conclusions. During the Third FYP, the authorities failed to address the fundamental problems of the Vietnamese economy. Attempts at macroeconomic stabilization relied upon an ability to enforce state monopolies and direct resources into exports and agriculture by administrative command that lacked the requisite power and authority. The breakdown of that system, and thus of the DRV model, ensured that stabilization could not be attained. The authorities, as the indicators show, were not committed to effective decentralization and structural adjustment and retained a basic commitment to the urban and state industry orientation of the DRV development program.[21]

The deterioration in the fiscal position accentuated spontaneous processes within the economy, leading to decentralization and commercialization, and therefore tended to increase the difficulties facing policymakers. On the whole, events during this period resulted primarily from the spontaneous development of the economy rather than fron state policy. The continuation of the weak state phenomenon inherited from pre-1975 laid the foundation for the pattern of economic development in the late 1980s.

Institutional Foundations of the Transitional Model

Micro Reforms of the Early 1980s

It is best to look at these developments in two areas: the operation of state factories and the management of agricultural cooperatives. Changes in these areas were of great importance and contributed much valuable experience. Theoretically, it is important to look at the interaction between production and distribution by examining first the changing behavior of economic agents.

State Industry. The Chinese and Western aid cuts of 1978-79 had sharply reduced the volume of supplies coming through the state trading monopolies. However, there was substantial slack in the system, which came from three main sources: the static inefficiencies created by the central-planning system, for instance, many provinces had substantial stocks of materials; underutilized resources outside industry in agriculture and forestry; and the potential for deals with foreign companies keen to maintain economic links with Vietnam.

State factory administrations therefore knew that there were underutilized resources elsewhere in the economy that they could use to increase output if they could find some way of getting at them. They also knew that they could make profitable deals with foreign suppliers to obtain materials and inputs but that this had often been stopped by central ministries. And they knew that diversification of output into lines that could generate high incomes could give them a way of increasing worker incentives and so increase the output of goods that they were obliged to supply to the state. Encouraged by the 1979 Sixth Plenum resolution and pushed by the cuts in aid-financed supplies through the state system, many factories set about breaking through the constraints of the DRV planning system and rapidly found profitable ways of doing so, in other words, they engaged in fence-breaking (*pha rao*). Goods could be swapped or sold on the free market in order to raise cash to buy materials or pay bonuses to workers. Deals were made with other factories, or with agricultural cooperatives, to supply materials.

On the whole, these processes had two main effects. First, they took up the considerable slack that existed in the economy as a result of the waste created by the DRV planning system, and output recovered surprisingly rapidly in some areas. Second, they placed the factories' old customers under pressure to pay higher prices in order to compete with the free market. For instance, a thermos factory could find that its old suppliers were short of rice or other resources because of the aid cuts and thus could not meet their plan targets. It could then start to pay high cash prices for supplies from other units and finance these purchases by sales on the free market. But this would mean that it would have to pass some of the higher costs on to its old customers, who would object. Thus the mechanisms reducing plan distortion could be seen operating, not least in their political economy aspect. *As the economy became freer, the subsidized sectors of the economy therefore came under pressure for further changes.*

The Three Plan System. The key decree governing state industry under the transitional model was 25-CP of January 1981 (see Box 4.1). According to this decree, state factories were required to register their "unplanned" activities and were forced to give priority to meeting their obligations to the plan (CM 1981).[22]

The decree formalized this in the so-called Three Plan system, under which a state factory had to have a single plan, with three elements. Most important was the First Plan (or Plan A), under which the factory was to produce using inputs supplied by the state and supply the resulting output at low prices to the state. This aspect of production had to have absolute priority over any other activities, and permission to carry out any other activities was conditional on fulfillment of Plan A.

However, the decree also legalized other productive activities. If a factory was freely disposing of products that it had been established to produce ("list" goods subject to the state monopoly), these activities were now called the Second Plan (Plan B). In htis case the factory was now legally permitted to acquire resources by itself, more or less free from planners' instructions, and could then dispose of them as it wished, *but only in order to acquire additional inputs.* It was not allowed to set about freely expanding its activities, buying and selling as it wished.

Under the Third Plan (Plan C), the output in question was the "minor" products that resulted from the unit's own attempts at diversification. This production was free from outside control, largely because such products were not meant to be supplied to established customers, so there was less demand within the planning system for their continued subsidized supply. However, priority was to be given to state trading organs when the unit disposed of these products.

The Three Plan system contributed to the recovery in state industrial output of the early 1980s. However, industrial recovery was initially most clearly marked in areas sensitive to market demand and where there were domestic sources of input supplies (see Table 4.2).

Collective Agriculture. In collective agriculture, local adaptation of the old method of cooperative management had been to extend the area of the family economy by increasing the private plots beyond the statutory 5 percent limit (Fforde 1989a). This occurred in responde to such pressures as the inefficiency of the old centralized cooperative management system and the attraction of high free market prices. As grassroots change progressed in late 1979 and 1980, this process was simply extended.

In order to prevent the cooperative system from breaking down altogether, CT-100 took two main directions.[23] First, by partially decentralizing management of production within cooperatives, it sharply increased both the static and (to a lesser extent) the dynamic efficiency of agricultural organization. Second, by granting cooperators greater freedom to sell on the free market, it improved the terms of trade facing agriculture, thereby improving producer incentives. However, by leaving the management superstructure of the cooperatives intact and by not providing an effective market for local collective inputs, the inherent problem of controlling rural cadres was not addressed. Furthermore, by failing to address the key issue of macro intersectoral relations, momentum in agricultural growth could not be maintained once the initial effects of the improvement in static efficiency had passed.[24]

Output Contracts. In collective agriculture, a new model was found that managed to preserve the basic structure of the cooperatives, creating a basis for their collective functions, such as welfare services. This model was the "output contract" *(khoan san pham)* system. It also, unfortunately, preserved many of the old inadequacies of the cooperatives.[25]

The output contract system was a modification of the earlier management system, which had used the brigade within the cooperative as the basis for organizing collective production, with the brigade responsible for directing labor to work in th ecooperative's fields. The brigade was given plan targets by the cooperative and was meant to give up all its output to the cooperative. The system relied upon a detailed framework of labor categorization and norms in order to decide upon the required labor inputs and other inputs that would be needed to meet the output targets, as well as to calculate labor remuneration. It was a clumsy and inefficient system, which generated widespread opposition (Fforde 1989a; The Dat 1981). Brigade cadres were supposed to directly control a labor force of over one hundred farmers, but this was very difficult. Cooperators preferred to work on their private plots, which were frequently extended to more than the prescribed 5 percent of the cooperative's land. The system as a whole was designed to give considerable economic power to the Management Committees of the cooperatives; such power was usually resented and resisted. However, the system had received strong political support at the highest level.

The output contract system decentralized control of much of the labor process, benefiting the cooperators, usually the family. Each family was given land by the cooperative, and the average output over the previous three years formed the basis for the contracted amount of output to be produced (CPV 1981a, 1981b; Le Thanh Nghi 1981). This was divided into two on the basis of the old system of work norms and labor categories, so that the cooperative was paid for performing certain tasks-- usually caring for the water supply, seeds, and land preparation. This practice ensured that women with absent husbands could get their land plowed and harrowed, since by custom the men usually did such work. The cooperator family was paid, on the same basis, for the remaining jobs--caring for the growing plants, weeding, applying fertilizer and harvesting. Taxes and deductions for the local schools as well as other less popular fees imposed by the local authorities also had to come out of the contracted amount. The cooperative in principle therefore retained the ability to increase or reduce the cooperators' share of the contracted amount by altering the system of payment for the inputs assigned to both itself and the cooperators.

Because the years immediately prior to the introduction of the output contract system had been poor harvest years, the initial output contracts were rather easy to fulfill. Since all output in excess of the target was treated in the same way as output from the private plots and was therefore freely disposable and could be sold on the free market, there was a strong marginal incentive to increase production. This resulted in large short-run output gains. In the local economy, labor and other resources were reallocated more evenly (and somewhat away from the private plots) and they also both increased in supply as higher incomes and rewards led to increased inputs. Typical increases in output reported at the micro level were of 25-30 percent, which shows clearly in the aggregate data in Table 5.1.

Introduction of output contracts throughout the North and Center from 1981 on led to a sharp jump of around 20-25 percent in staples output, revealing the inefficiencies of the old system. Output contracts gave considerably greater freedom to cooperators' family economies and therefore represented a certain acceptance by the government of the value of this sector to the economy as a whole. Output growth slowed around 1983-84, however, and thereafter stagnated. This showed the importance of two basic issues:

1. Economic slack existed, the exploitation of which could produce short-term output gains.
2. Without additional support, further growth was limited.

The fact that output contracts acted *within* the collective economy meant that they did not have to be seen as private. They could therefore be viewed, if necessary, as a modification rather than an abandonment of the DRV program.

Foreign and Domestic Trade. These two areas are dealt with together because they both relate to the issue of state control over distribution. As has been shown, foreign trade policy in 1980 permitted SOEs, especially local units, considerable freedom to bypass the central foreign trade monopoly. In 1980, there was also a temporary easing of restrictions on the domestic retail market (see Boxes 4.2 and 4.3; policy in this area is not as clearly documented as in the cases of SOEs and agricultural cooperatives).

Both of these policy positions were subsequently reversed. The key resolution accomplishing this was Decree No. 312 (CM 1980b), which was clearly opposed to fence-breaking and all that it implied. High incentives had to be paid to enforcement agents with 5-10 percent of the value of hoards, fines, or taxes given for disclosure, and 10-15 percent for direct arrest. Details of experiences in Hoan Kiem, in the center of Hanoi, can be found in Hoang Lien (1980).[26]

Hard reform socialism can therefore be seen as hostile to markets, as unwillingly supportive of participation in autonomous transactions by agricultural cooperatives and SOEs, as lacking the power to enforce its desires, and therefore, as fundamentally unstable.

The Death of Hard Reform Socialism

The Price-Wage-Money, Currency Reform, and Inside-Outside Interactions of 1985. Until 1985 the recentralising pressures from central ministries were hard to resist. Ho Chi Minh City's export-import corporations had mainly been closed down, and as pressure was brought to bear on the free market and outside activities, output growth had slowed from 1983. The government responded to pressure from state employees--one of the most important subsidized sectors--and granted excessive wage increases, which helped push up prices on the free market still further. The situation became increasingly unstable, and opposition mounted as the central ministries continued in many cases to act as ineffective fetters on local initiatives.

By 1985, spiraling inflation forced an attempt to solve the problem of high free market prices "at a stroke" (To Huu 1985). A combination of currency reform, increased state prices, and higher wages was introduced. This served only to stoke the flames of inflation still further, partly because the revenues were not forthcoming to offset the increased outlays and partly because state enterprises were free to borrow almost without limit in order to continue their purchases on the free market.[27]

However, these measures did cause the number of rationed goods to be cut back. The shifting of price subsidy payments from the state retail trading network to the wage funds of state employers (*bu gia vao luong*) meant that there was an opportunity to take goods off ration. As free market prices rose sharply through the 1985/86 winter, the five key commodities--rice, sugar, kerosene, fish sauce and meat--all came back on the ration list in the North. Other goods, however, perhaps the most important of them being clothing, remained off ration, and this allowed the retail market to continue to develop and widen.

The events of 1985 suggest strongly that there were important interactions in the transitional economy between planned and autonomous activities. See, for example, Figures 3.13 and 3.14 on the retail trade shares.[28]

An Assessment. The 1980s began with the economic crisis of 1979-80 and the conservative concessions made to spontaneous bottom-up changes--the Three Plan and output contract systems. These showed that better resource utilization could lead to substantial short-run output gains, that is, that there was significant economic slack in the system. Producers, especially in the state system, became more price and cost sensitive. Important areas of retail trade, for example, clothing and bicycle spare parts, became effectively transformed, with markets dominated by buyers' needs rather than those of sellers. Aggravated shortage, however, remained the basic characteristic of the Vietnamese economy.

However, the attempt to defend the central-planning system and the DRV program became involved with the effects of the transitional model upon the subsidized sectors of the economy. The state's inability to enforce state trading monopolies eventually forced it to concede large price and wage hikes that pushed the budget further into deficit and perpetuated an accelerating inflation. The state was unable to address the price and wage distortions accompanying widespread market disequilibria, and the increased price and cost sensitivity resulted in large windfall gains to those well placed to exploit scarcity premiums.

At the same time, the failure to move decisively to restore macro and intersectoral balances meant that long-run efficiency remained low. The overvalued exchange rate perpetuated the bias against exports, and investment priorities hardly changed. State industry was able to preserve high rates of investment despite declining returns, and agricultural stagnation returned once the short-run impact of reforms had worn off. Export growth was too slow.

The Sixth Party Congress: Toward a Market Economy

After the 1985 measures failed to restore fiscal balance, it was clear that political support for hard reform socialism, as embodied in the recentralizing package introduced in 1980-81, had all but vanished. By 1985-86 disenchantment had reached critical levels. After his death in July 1986, Party General Secretary Le Duan was temporarily replaced by Truong Chinh until Nguyen Van Linh, a somewhat younger man with a liberal reputation, was elected at the Sixth Party Congress in December.[29]

The precise political events leading up to the Sixth Party Congress of December 1986 are still unclear. Three currents appear to have come together to produce the promarket outcome that was reflected in the majority decisions of the congress including,

- Strong pressure from technocrats and promarket reformists for a "final solution" to the DRV model, based upon the political collapse of hard reform socialism after the 1985 debacle.
- Support from rising commercial interests within the state sector, to which reform meant even better access to economic benefits.[30]
- Support from southern liberals who wished to see a return to the pre-1975 system.

Without these three currents it is unlikely that the opposition and strength of those opposed to a full-blooded market-oriented economy would have been strong enough for the congress to have gone even as far as it did in its support for the free market and the private sector.[31] The growth of the free market, especially in grain, had important implications for the overall balance between North and South. With a shift away from the distorted value relations implied by reliance upon state staples procurement, the North and other deficit areas would have to find ways of paying for their rice.

International events were also important, in that Gorbachev had come to power in 1985. Certainly, the attitude of the Soviet Union as the major aid donor appears to have been one of deep discontent with the confusion, lack of clarity, and allegedly downright mendicant attitude to foreign support (see further on in this chapter).

The congress thus introduced soft reform socialism, within which the free market and private sector producers were now acceptable. A series of decrees through 1987-88 pushed for this. One of the first measures taken after the congress met in 1986 was the abolition of interprovincial trade barriers, after which rice prices declined.

The Sixth Party Congress

The 1986 Sixth Party Congress thus heralded a more forward-looking approach to economic reform. It was increasingly accepted that the basic institutions of the DRV model and the macro imbalance of the economy had to be tackled and dealt with effectively. Criticism of the period since the Fifth Party Congress of 1982 attacked the following three key questions (CPV 1987a; Tran Duc Nguyen 1988):

- The attitude to the nonsocialist components and the way in which excessive priority was still being given to the state sector. This was interpreted in some quarters as a shift toward the freedoms granted by Lenin's New Economic Policy (NEP) to the private sector.
- The role and position of central economic management organs. In his speech to the congress, Nguyen Van Linh had even argued that the centralized system of resource allocation contradicted the principles of Marxism-Leninism.
- The failure to implement agreed-upon decisions to reduce sectoral imbalances by reorienting resources toward agriculture, consumption, and exports. In other words, it was necessary to do something about the effects of the DRV model upon the sectoral misallocation of resources.

After the congress the authorities moved to address these issues. In early 1987, important areas such as Hanoi, Ho Chi Minh City, and others made substantial concessions to the free market and private business. These had quick and visible effects upon their local economies. Around the same time, a major step was taken to improve the internal market by instructing provinces and cities to close the internal customs posts that were preventing the flow of goods.

The congress was followed by a number of plenums of the Central Committee during 1987 that developed various key concepts and laid the ground for a series of policy decrees that began to be issued at the end of the year. These covered such important areas as foreign investment; land; foreign trade; state industrial management; the private, family and individual sectors; and agriculture. The movement away from the deterministic central-planning ethos of the DRV program was expressed in the metaphor of the state as conductor of the national orchestra, rather than as controller of the economic machine.

However, by the end of 1987, as economic conditions deteriorated in the wake of the sharp fall in staples output in that year, the Fourth Plenum of the Central Committee of the Communist Party met to discuss the economic situation and the program for the coming three years. It was deeply critical of the pace of reform.[32] Although,

During 1987 we had all started to shift our activities in line with the reforms decided upon at the Sixth Congress . . . and experience had been gained . . . the program was still uncoordinated and without a firm basis. The economic situation had deteriorated and incomes per head had fallen . . .. [The reasons for this were complicated, but] in the implementation of policies in 1987 the main shortcoming was the slow pace with which policies had been established in order to change the structural balance of the economy toward fulfillment of the three targets [of staples and food; consumer goods and exports], above all staples and food. Concrete policies aimed at stimulating all economic components were promulgated slowly. The policies agreed upon in early 1987 concerning a number of areas--such as those toward farmers, toward the changing of economic activity toward socialist accounting . . . have not yet been carried out well. (Nguyen Van Linh 1987).

The six main targets laid down by this plenum are outlined later in this chapter. In early 1988, however, it is clear that as the economic crisis was worsening the authorities were responding by pushing for a faster pace of reform. In this regard they seem to have had the support of the dominant source of foreign assistance, the Soviet Union.

The Soviet Union: Major Aid Donor Through the 1980s

The Soviet Union was from 1978-79 not only the dominant source of foreign assistance. It had also been the ideological source of the neo-Stalinist inspiration of the DRV program and, through party-party links, had provided an important input to the evolution of Vietnamese Marxism-Leninism. Gorbachev had come to power in 1985.[33]

In the context of the contemporary policies of glasnost and perestroika, and the collapse of the USSR in August 1991, this adds in hindsight a certain piquancy to the assessment of the role the Soviet Union played in the Vietnamese transition. Like many others, the Soviet Union seems to have pushed Vietnam in the direction of a market-oriented system. However, the Soviet Union and Vietnam were deeply enmeshed in the basic and largely insoluble contradictions of the basis for bilateral links in state-to-state relations, which guaranteed that Soviet resources could easily be used simply and primarily to support the Vietnamese state sector. This was, in fact, what was happening.

The process of transition in Vietnam, with its largely bottom-up and autonomous character, combined with a formal political conservatism, made the Vietnamese situation very different from that of any other member of CMEA. But the wide range of changes throughout the communist world after the accession of General Secretary Gorbachev, combined with the firm alliance relations with the Soviet Union and its role as the dominant source of foreign assistance, meant that considerations of Soviet thinking have to play a major part in any analysis of developments in Vietnam. Vietnam, moreover, remained almost totally dependent militarily upon the Soviet Union, both for the continued military presence in Cambodia (up until 1988) and for the defense of the border with China. In Chapter 2, we argued that the ideological role played by the DRV program in providing a New Knowledge was in keeping with some traditional Vietnamese notions of national life.

Soviet thinking indeed changed radically (if insufficiently) toward the end of the 1980s. However, before then, although conditions in the Soviet Union were still somewhat conservative, informed Soviet observers were noting similarities between conditions in the Soviet Union around 1920 and contemporary Vietnam: the strong role played by premodern "traditional" behavior, the extensive war damage, and the dominant position of the peasantry (Bogatova and Trigubenko 1987). This was then combined with Lenin's theses on the national and colonial question, which asserted that backward colonial countries could successfully construct socialism because, inter alia, they had the support of developed socialist countries. From this, it was then argued, came the applicability of Lenin's New Economic Policy (the so-called NEP) to Vietnam under contemporary conditions. The key to this policy was identified as the abolition of the rigid administrative resource allocation of War Communism. In its place, the market was given free rein, ushering in a period of rapid economic recovery that ended with the violent collectivization of agriculture and other consequences of Stalin's rise to power.

In the early and mid-1980s, Soviet thinking had thus advocated--at least in public--a development strategy for Vietnam quite different from that which led to the neo-Stalinist DRV model, above all in that it encouraged free domestic trade and the private sector. The key relationship, it was argued, should have been the development of free exchange between the peasantry and urban industry, organized in whatever way was economically advantageous.

Indeed, the case can be made that Soviet economic assistance had been geared in the early 1980s toward encouraging greater economic efficiency and had provided some support for the first steps of the transition (Fforde 1985). The sea change at the Sixth Plenum of 1979 is seen as having started a process whereby the Vietnamese could learn through experience, as in fact happened. Rapid shifts in well-established ways of thinking were probably not expected. A large increase in aid was forthcoming for the 1986-90 FYP, but with substantial changes in the structure of assistance.

1. In the area of policy advice, pressure seems to have been applied to move away from the DRV program; strong approval was expressed for the ideological shift toward the idea that the primary task was to create domestic sources of accumulation and the premises for future industrialization--the "two-stage" theory of the transition process. Yet the Soviet Union, at this time still operating an essentially unreformed central-planning system of its own, was ill placed to provide detailed advice on the management details required. Project personnel had reportedly been unclear as to whether to support or criticize the Three Plan system as it arose in the early 1980s.[34] It was, however, generally supported within CMEA. There is no evidence whatsoever that the important changes heralded by the Sixth Party Congress, above all the liberalization of internal trade and the stimulation of the private sector, were opposed by the Soviet Union; indeed, the contrary seems to be the case.

2. Project assistance was changed so as to limit further expansion of the fixed industrial stock, stressing infrastructural investment in sectors such as energy where rapid increases in output would not put

strain on domestic input suppliers. Improved energy supplies also promised better utilization of existing installed capacity. Support for coal production, for example, was justified because of the resulting ability to increase supplies for direct sale to the peasantry.

3. Import support was shifted away from such areas as food and toward fertilizer and pesticides that were positive contributors to domestic output. Prices seem to have been raised selectively, heightening Vietnamese perceptions of the costs and benefits involved.

4. Economic cooperation in other areas was moved increasingly onto a basis of "mutual advantage," allowing the Soviet Union to reduce the net cost of its aid commitment as well as improving the efficiency of aid utilization by the Vietnamese side. Thus the exploitation of Vietnamese offshore petroleum reserves used a joint venture model, the Vung Tau project, rather than solely Soviet enterprises. The basis for this shift was argued to be an increased utilization of joint ventures Vietnamese processing of raw materials sent from the Soviet Union into products for export to the Soviet Union, and other forms of cooperation aimed at exploiting Vietnamese labor resources and agriculture.

This overall stance both supported and inhibited the commercialization process. It was inhibitive in that it continued to provide cheap inputs to the central-planning structures as well as state industry and trade. It was supportive in that it gave a further twist to the dynamic of commercialization by putting rents into the hands of those who had shown that they would use them to create capital within the state sector. Its ideological stance was soft and certainly not supportive of hard-line conservatives.

Conclusions

The soft reform socialism of the Sixth Party Congress appears to be have been underpinned by both the attitude and the activities of the major aid donor. This was probably true in both economic and political fields. However, the slower pace of economic reform in the Soviet Union meant that institutional assistance was limited.

By 1989, with the imminent breakdown of the Soviet economy, a steep reduction in the aid program was occurring. Between 1989 and 1990, the recorded trade deficit had been cut back substantially (see Figure 3.17). The effects of this upon the macro economy are discussed in Chapter 8, but the expectation of this shift almost certainly had a major effect upon the 1989 Vietnamese decision to abolish central planning entirely.

On the Brink: Development Strategy on the Eve of the Market Economy

By far the simplest way of understanding the reformists' strategy during the second half of the 1980s is through the slogan of the "commercialization" *(thuong mai hoa)* of the state economy, and internal and foreign trade, in other words, the intention that resources should be acquired and disposed of through markets rather than through administrative means. Since the basis of the DRV model had been its dependence upon state trading organs to ensure the direct allocation of resources through administrative order, this amounted--if implemented--to a profound change. Such a radical shift away from long-accepted orthodoxy created opposition from many quarters, and this slowed the pace of transition. This opposition was both ideological and, as we have seen, was tied up with political economy issues. At that time, in the opinion of an informed Vietnamese commentator, there were three areas where reform had advanced reasonably well, and one where there had been little progress. This throws interesting light on the thinking behind the soft reform socialism of the period.

In the area of micro advances and the change in the economic mechanism, legislation was reportedly now available. This was also true for the liberalization of the private sector and the beginnings of structural readjustment. However, effective macrostabilisation measures were still lacking. This position therefore ignored the important implications for any market economy of factor markets--especially capital. In some ways, therefore, soft reform socialism was overoptimistic and ignored the interactions between institutional reforms and structural readjustment on the one hand, and micro reforms, on the other: Capital had a voice, but without a solution to the SOE question, this voice had to be heard from within the state apparatus.

An authoritative statement concerning the reform process can be found in the Vietnamese *communist party* journal, *Communist Studies,* for February 1988. This stressed that the essence of the program initiated by the Sixth Party Congress was "to stabilize the economy; to continue to construct the prerequisites needed for socialist industrialization in the next stage" (CS 1988b:1).

To this end there were six interlinked target areas, which the Fourth Plenum of December 1987 had reaffirmed.[35]

1. *The three key programs*: development of staples and nonstaples food production, consumer goods production, and exports.
2. *Shifting economic activities over to the utilization of "socialist accounting and business."* The basis of this was "voluntary exchange based upon calculation by both parties of the economic costs and benefits involved." This formulation underlines the wide differences between the soft reform socialism package and the DRV program. The aim was "gradually to stabilize socioeconomic relations, within which the most important is to establish stable exchange relations between the state and farmers, so that farmers receive means of production and consumption at stable prices and without difficulty, while the state secures reliable supplies of grain and other agricultural commodities."
3. *Strengthening of the state and collective economies* while exploiting the potential of other economic components. It is clear that there was intended to be a commercialization of the activities of state economic units: "Those state production and business units that incur long-term losses that cannot be strengthened so they can make profits . . . must either be wound up or moved out of the state sector." With regard to the nonsocialist sectors, "the state encourages and accepts the long-term existence and positive effects of the family, individual, and private economies active in production and services; it guarantees the rights to property, to inherit, and to legal incomes for people active in these sectors; it accepts their legal incorporation/identity and equality before the law in their production and business activities."
4. *Attention to social problems.* The main object here was "to create work for the millions of workers who do not have stable employment by utilizing widely the potential of all economic components so as to absorb labor into small-scale industry in both the towns and the cities, as well as to break new land in the regions and the new economic zones, to expand service activities, work on infrastructural projects, and work abroad."
5. *Meeting the requirements of the armed forces.*
6. *Preparation for the 1991-95 five year socioeconomic development plan.*

The plan for 1988 gave some idea of the pace intended, as well as the limits to the notion of commercialization. Planned staples output was set at 19 million tonnes, with increases in industrial consumer goods output of 12.5 percent and in the value of exports of 17.6 percent, compared with 1987.

However, although it was proposed to "develop the positive potential of all components of the economy in production and services" it was also intended to "continue the socialist transformation and strengthen the management of the market." There was, therefore, still a strong desire in some quarters to retain a controlling position in certain markets, above all rice. This is discussed further later on. The two key issues presented by the logic of the growth of "autonomous activities"--private trade and capital markets--were therefore not only still unresolved, but subject to strong conservative pressure.

The Role of the State: Economic Management Organs

Such statements appear to express a shift to a normally developmentalist state. However, it is worth recalling that by this stage rather sophisticated methods had evolved to permit state employees working in line ministries and provincial departments to gain access to economic resources created by the partially commercialized state economy. Apart from the simple creation of various "funds," into which payments from SOEs could be made, there were also a number of actual transfers of administrative workers into commercial activities under the protection of their state organs. These were typically referred to as "living standard units" (*xi nghiep doi song*) and were legally permitted. In the early 1990s, the need for considerable efforts to separate them from their sources of support in the state apparatus was perceived.

The reform of state economic management is an area where the interaction between macro and micro intentions was very clear. In the opinion of an informed Vietnamese commentator, the level of surplus employment circa 1988 was around 30-50 percent of the staff of economic ministries, provincial economic offices, and many factories. The program of ministerial amalgamations and staff cuts therefore went hand in hand. By early 1988, the following had already taken place:

- Establishment of the Ministry of Agriculture and Foodstuffs from two separate ministries.
- Absorption of the State Basic Construction Commission by the Ministry of Construction.
- Amalgamation of the Ministries of Labor, War Invalids and Society, into a single ministry.
- Establishment of the Ministry of Energy from the two Ministries of Coal and Electricity.
- Absorption of the Electronics and Information Department by the Ministry of Engineering and Metallurgy.

- Establishment of the Ministry for "External Economics" (*kinh te doi ngoai*) from the Ministry of Foreign Trade and three committees (Committee of External Economics, Committee of Cooperation with Laos and Cambodia, and Committee for Cooperation with Foreign Specialists).

Similar but more limited changes were taking place at provincial and city levels, where the avowed intention of central government reformers was to abolish many of the provincial and city offices, such as the Staples, Industry, Forestry, and Financial Offices, and therefore to abolish the units responsible for issuing plan targets to locally managed production units. This paralleled the attempt to radically alter the relationship between centrally managed production units and central ministries by shifting the source of plan targets.

Unfortunately, the tendency had been for people to be shifted from the central ministries and provincial offices to lower levels in the factories and unions; furthermore, there was considerable resistance to laying off officials. Central authority was not strong enough to overcome this resistance. This tends to confirm the overall balance of power underpinning the trajectory of socioeconomic change. Events in 1990 were to show the potency of the forces created by the commercialization of the state sector in the period since 1979.

This overall strategy--of simply abolishing certain state management levels--was also intended to apply to other important areas such as foreign and domestic trade. The number of material supply companies was to be cut back so as to reduce costs; this should have been of great importance to agriculture but was resisted by local state interests. Similarly the number of import-export units was also to be reduced. This effort was directly aimed at many regional companies and therefore was an early sign of the recentralization that came to the fore as an issue after 1989.

Cuts in state employment in production units were aimed primarily at nonmanual employees, who, in the opinion of informed Vietnamese commentators, typically made up 20-25 percent of total staff numbers but could reach 30 percent. The target was for a reduction to 8-12 percent. These numbers were based upon estimates that the number of surplus employees in Hanoi alone had reached some hundreds of thousands. However, around 1988 on the eve of the abandonment of central planning, there had in reality only been early retirements. In one ministry, 12 percent of the workforce had been thus pushed out, while some 50 percent were thought to be surplus.

There was, therefore, a strong link between the cuts in state employment and reforms elsewhere, especially in the relationship between units of the state economy and the organization of domestic and foreign trade.

Development of the Legal System

Associated with reform of the role of the state was the attempt to bring socioeconomic activity under legal control. This need not have meant a rigid subordination of economic life to the economic interests of the state. It was clear that one consequence of the failure both of the DRV model and the hard reform socialist attempt to defend it had been great confusion as to what was legal and what was not, as well as confusion over the procedures for settling legal issues. The rules of the game were not quite the way they were set down in the government's Statute Book. Indeed, one consequence of the combination of a formally unreformed central-planning model with extensive bottom-up decentralization was a state of near anarchy in many areas of economic life.[36]

The changes in policy stance during the 1980s greatly contributed to this instability. The shift to a commercial basis for economic relations required a legal infrastructure that was lacking. However, such a shift would have entailed attacking areas of economic life that were too strong: Local control[37] over the state economic sector would have been greatly threatened by the development not only of a capital market, but of a rule of law in economic matters.

Minister of Justice Phan Hien had presented himself as a reformer in this area, advocating wide-ranging legal measures. He emphasized the point that most contemporary legislation dated from the 1960s--and therefore the DRV--and was based upon social norms that were no longer operating (Phan Hien 1987). The Land Law, promulgated in 1987, had the main intention of simply ensuring that there was a national system of land law rather than the substantial local variation that had grown up over the years. However, pointing out the need for change is one thing; obtaining the requisite political power to pass and implement it is quite another.

An area where problems came to the fore was that of economic contract law. Such influential authors as Dao Xuan Sam (1986) stressed the importance of contracts as a basis for development of socialist business methods and raising the independence of economic units. By 1987, the State Arbitration System had indeed begun to be able to reject illegal contracts on the basis of practical results, but there were few signs that this area had been able to advance with any great speed.[38] The shift to labor contracting in the state sector was creating great difficulties for employers who, although eager to move away from a treatment of labor seen as overgenerous, often had little experience to draw upon in the technicalities of labor contracting (see Chapter 5).

However, the reform documents from the 1987-88 period reveal a far better understanding than before of the limits of administrative decree as a basis for legal control of a decentralized economy. This was, of course, one way of attacking the hard reform position.

Nonsocialist Components[39]

A big difference between the hard and soft reform socialists was in their attitudes to the private sector and the role it could play in production and trade. As we have seen, the traditional enmity of neo-Confucianism toward "unproductive" groups had supported the more extreme position taken up by neo-Stalinists toward "anti-socialist" elements. A move back from this to a more accommodating attitude was necessary if the way to a market economy was to be opened. The overall commitment of the authorities to support for the nonsocialist components is clear from the statements cited above. Two decrees promulgated in early 1988 covered the private and individual, and the family, economies (CM 1988a, 1988b).

The Family Economy. Policy toward the family economy--understood to be that of state or collective workers carried on in addition to their main work--was strongly supportive. The decree on the family economy, published in the official party daily *Nhan Dan*, stipulated that the organ responsible for seeing that families register and act in compliance with law--the local People's Committee--was not allowed to interfere directly in their production or business activities (CM 1988a). No taxes were to be paid on these activities (Clause 9), and people had the right to

- Freely sell any products that they had, once they had fulfilled their contracts with state or collective economic units.
- Freely sign contracts with any export or import organization, in order to sell or purchase products.
- Select the bank at which they opened their bank account; withdraw their cash from that account; borrow capital; and receive foreign exchange sent by family members abroad for them to invest in production.

According to Clause 10, the decree was to apply to the entire country.

The policy of encouraging the family economies of state employees was also intended to ease the difficulties involved in cutting staff.

The Private and Individual Sectors. The policy toward the individual and private sectors was far more significant, and the positive attitude now taken was quite different from the hostile assumptions of the DRV model.

The decree on the subject (CM 1988b) asserted that "the state accepts the positive role and long-term existence of the private and individual sectors" (Clause 1). And that "the state accepts and guarantees the rights to property, inheritance, and income of units and individuals in these sectors."

These units were understood to be self-managing, deciding for themselves upon production and business activities, which were not to be planned by the state. Any citizen with capital or means of production who was not a state employee or cooperative member had the right to carry on economic activities in this sector. Private enterprises were understood to include companies, private groups, and other forms that had grown up over the years. The means of production were seen as belonging to the owner(s) of the enterprise, which did not need to be a single individual. The basic distinction between private enterprises and small family businesses, on the one hand, and the individual sector, on the other, was that the former could hire labor--this was explicitly permitted (Clause 3). The income from the enterprise, after paying taxes, belonged to its owners.

Private enterprises were quite free to have joint ventures or almost any other kind of economic relationship with state units or cooperatives. They had to follow state regulations on keeping accounts and pay their legal taxes. They had to have a registration paper, and it was the responsibility of the People's Committee of the province or city to issue this. These levels of government had the right to supervise the enterprises to see that they were acting legally but explicitly neither had the right to get involved directly in production nor to levy special taxes.

There was a list of products and services that were to remain a state monopoly. This included such items as publishing, printing, gold and precious stones, alcohol, cigarettes, port transport and long-distance road transport. Apart from these, certain areas where the private sector could operate would be more closely regulated: pharmaceuticals, food, drinks, exploitation of wood, forests, marine products, minerals, large-scale construction, interprovincial transport, shipbuilding, large-scale electricity consumption, jewelry and electronics repairs, production of car and bicycle tires, production of electrical cooking stoves and similar equipment, production of electric fans, electric motors, bicycles and bicycle spare parts (Clause 9).[40]

Private enterprises and individual producers had the right to use any materials they could find within the country, subject to their being registered to do so--they had to be producers rather than traders. They were expressly forbidden from dealing in materials subject to state monopoly.

They were free to borrow funds, including foreign currency, from any source within or outside the country (Clause 17). They were allowed to sell their output freely once they fulfilled any contracts they may have had with state or collective units (Clause 13).

They were free to choose the state trading organization they would deal with if they wanted to export or import (direct relations with overseas markets were still not allowed). They could receive foreign investment in accordance with the Foreign Investment Law. They could select the bank within the province or city in which they wished to keep their funds but could have only one bank account at a time.

The hiring of labor was, in large cities, to be in accordance with the policy of priority recruitment from the locality and the population registration system (the family registration document, or the *ho khau*). However, the maximum number of employees permitted in each branch would be established by the People's Committee of the province or city in accordance with conditions in the area.

Internal Trade. Although there was no direct guidance on the reform of internal trade, it is clear from other decrees that "the list of major products produced under legally binding plans or orders for goods from the state would be decided upon annually by the state *with the aim of gradually reducing to a necessary minimum the number of products listed in that list*" (CM 1987:clause 2, emphasis added). This pointed to the abolition of central planning.

However, in contrast with this clearly stated intention, the policy with regard to staples distribution still aimed to retain as far as possible the state monopoly over rice trade. In many areas, as has been already emphasized, this monopoly was already very weak.

Foreign Trade. The freedom of a state enterprise to trade directly with foreign customers was also still rather loosely defined. The two main conditions seemed to be that the endeavor be export oriented and have rather a large volume of exports and sufficient well-qualified personnel. The situation was rather unclear. Furthermore, although exporters were clearly allowed to retain part of their foreign exchange earnings, the proportions involved also appeared to be "subject to negotiation." In the opinion of one commentator, central government was typically paid around 10 percent, with the remainder shared between the enterprise and its superior level.

Agriculture

In April 1988, the party published an important decree on agriculture (Decree No. 10) which, inter alia, announced certain intentions that, if implemented, would have amounted to a radical shift in the actual treatment of the rural areas--a "New Deal." These measures were designed to increase output and the mobilized agricultural surplus; improve material incentives, above all in rice cultivation; reduce the coercive impact of local collectives by improving their democratic content; and clean up the same organizations by sacking or moving incompetent or corrupt cadres. This decree was one of the most important policy innovations of soft reform socialism, and it largely solved the agrarian problem that had been plaguing the party. It did this by sacrificing around 50 percent of the rural cadres who had depended upon the cooperatives for their jobs and positions. It is of more than passing interest that the decree originated in the agriculture department of the party. By prohibiting the cooperatives' superior levels (the districts) from issuing orders to the cooperatives, it finally destroyed the rural basis of the command economy.[41]

In collective agriculture generally, the decree stated that there was to be an end to the pressure for cooperativizing of the Mekong, where the simpler production collectives were to remain the accepted form of collective organization. A model cooperative statute was planned for 1988, but it never appeared.

There was, however, at this time no open intention to formally abandon the collectivized system. Instead, cooperatives were to be given far greater economic independence. They were to be equal before the law with all other economic units, free to buy and sell all economic assets apart from land. Cooperatives were allowed to raise capital, including foreign currency, from their members and to pay a return for it. Cooperatives and production collectives were free to buy and sell in any place they chose, after paying taxes and meeting economic contracts with the state.

Cooperative-cooperator relations, expressed in a new "output contract" system ("No. 10 Contracts"), changed greatly. The proportion of the contracted amount to be left to the cooperators should "not be less than 40 percent." The land allocated was to be left for fifteen years at least, and the norms and unit prices in the contract, as well as the contract itself, had to be fixed for five years. Cooperatives and cooperators were in principle free to decide which work would be done by the collective and the cooperator, respectively. Good farmers were to be encouraged by giving them more land, with those who had lost land to find work outside rice cultivation. The cooperative was to retain duties to support the families of wardead and others. Cooperative management expenses were to be kept as low as possible. It appears from other sources that the contracts were to be signed directly between the family and the cooperative, whereas previously the local production brigades had been involved.

The Role of the State in Agriculture

The redefinition of the functions of the state envisaged by Decree No. 10 and other policy documents of the time was an issue of great importance. As the decade came to an end, soft reform socialists in Vietnam were arguing that the role of the state in rural development, as in other areas, was to change in two main areas:

1. State activities should shift from direct management of production and economic activity to "state management of the economy." As a concrete example, districts were no longer allowed to give direct orders to cooperatives or production collectives. Their official role, as we have seen, was instead to provide guidance through indicative plans. The People's Committees of the communes were also to keep out of cooperative affairs. That this did not happen everywhere and at once is not to deny the intention.

2. There were to be major institution-building initiatives. There was to be increased state investment in agriculture and the "immediate" establishment of an Agricultural Development Bank. The state was to carry out a major pruning of the system of trading companies involved in supplying agriculture and purchasing from it. This was designed to increase the power of central monopolies by reducing competition and the perceived excessive number of intermediaries between the state and the producer. The basis for economic relations between the state and farmers would, however, remain two-way barter contracts until conditions allowed the use of money.

Tax concessions would be made: There would be no tax liability on long-term crops or trees before they were harvested. Other measures to boost material incentives included the reduction of labor duties, especially for women. Measures would be taken to develop rural markets; regions would no longer be allowed to levy local customs duties or taxes on goods circulation. Finally, in order to develop scientific and technical support services, research units would shift their activities over to an economic basis. Schools and universities would be reorganized so as to increase educational facilities for rural cadres.

Industry

In state industry, the final reformist decrees prior to 1989 were Decree No. 217 (CM 1987) on state enterprise management and a new but generally meaningless statute on state enterprises (CM 1988c). The former was clearly part of plans for dismantling the central-planning apparatus.

The basic thrust was, as had been the case since 1986, to *reduce* the rights of state economic management organs. Apart from around thirty-five key enterprise unions, the traditional apparatus of control would be dismantled and SOEs would only be liable for taxes. The residual group, however, was large, covering around 50 percent of total output. It included a wide range of areas, from coal, electricity, steel, chemicals, and fertilizer, as well as transport and communications, to textiles, paper, household goods, and electronic products. For these units, the state, it was argued, had to be in a position to guarantee material supplies. The others were primarily involved in consumer goods production and the tax target in this area was seen as being almost the same as a profit target.

It was unclear whether the thirty-five units might receive their plan targets directly from the State Planning Commission (SPC), thus further reducing the importance of their "owning" ministries. According to the new statute (CM 1988c), the planning level of an enterprise was now its union, if it belonged to one (Clause 19). In a similar way, the People's Committees of provinces and cities could take over the planning function from the old industry offices. In the hiatus of 1989 and the abandonment of physical planning, this issue remained, as far as can be told, unresolved.

The basis for calculating an enterprise's profits was changed completely. Previously, and except for unmonitored activities, profits were meant to be a percentage markup on approved input costs. Higher costs therefore resulted in higher profits. Now, profits were simply to be the difference between allowable costs and the value of sales (Clause 46).

The value of wages paid by the enterprise was previously laid down in and limited by the plan given to the enterprise by its superior. Now there was no limit. Thus enterprises were in principle free to recruit workers as they wished--there was no plan given.

With regard to the acquisition and disposal of resources, enterprises were in a still freer position. For example, they could sell their assets. However, the basic distinction between Plan A and Plan B (see previous discussion) appeared set to continue, in that enterprises belonging to the central thirty-five unions were required to comply with the system of Three Plan Targets for high priority goods "under conditions where the supply of essential materials is guaranteed by the state" (Clause 3.1). Otherwise, the intention was to have only one legally binding target--the value of budgetary contributions to the state. This was similar to a profits tax. An additional defense against pressure from higher levels to secure additional low price supplies was the stipulation that "the superior level can only approve and issue legally binding targets or state goods orders if it can guarantee the requisite material supplies, and [the SOE] only has the duty to implement those targets if those supplies are forthcoming" (Clause 25).

The relation between the banking system and the enterprise was improved to the advantage of the enterprise. It could now choose where it kept its bank account. It could also keep all its money in a single account in order to avoid regulation of part of its activities through the earlier practice of forcing it to keep separate accounts for different areas of activity (Clause 48). The enterprise now had the right to choose the way in which it settled accounts with its customers, although it had to use checks if the customer also had a bank account (Clause 50).

The enterprise was now increasingly responsible for obtaining its own capital and was no longer simply supplied with resources on a grant basis by the state. Apart from recently established large units, it kept all its depreciation costs (this position was reversed in the years of fiscal reconstruction after 1991-92).

Conclusions

The soft reformist position of the late 1980s was ambitious by Vietnamese standards, and in many ways it marked both a substantial break with the past and a high degree of continuity.

In industry, the maintenance of some quantity planning targets and, therefore, the retention of cheap deliveries to the state in some ways perpetuated the Three Plan system. Static inefficiencies would therefore remain. But the greater freedom of enterprises in general, and of those outside the thirty-five key unions in particular, was marked. The simple definition of profits as revenue less real costs was particularly significant. In agriculture, although the cooperative system remained intact, the cooperatives had been given greater freedom both in terms of their relations with higher levels as well as in their dealings with their members.

There was a clear intention to push through structural readjustments and improve the position of agriculture, consumer goods producers, and exports in line with the Sixth Party Congress' decisions.

The main weaknesses of this position were

- The lack of stress on capital markets and the necessity for them in a world of independent capitals.
- The survival of the agricultural producer cooperatives as an integral part of rural development policy.
- The unresolved issues surrounding the role of the state and its political base.

- The contrast between the gradualist approach taken since 1979 and the gathering inevitability of fundamental systemic change when and if the two-price system was abolished.
- The lack of understanding of the extent to which active government intervention and regulation (or the lack of it) influences the efficiency of markets, highlighting questions about the role of the state in a market economy governed by the Vietnamese Commuist Party.

However, as should now be clear, Vietnamese policymakers and the Vietnamese economy had already come a long way from 1979 (or, indeed, 1957). In Chapter 9, this position is compared with what was to follow in the post-stage after 1989.

Notes

1. See Ministry of Labor (1981) for an early exposition of hard reform policies for the period up to June 1981; see also Hong Ha et al. (1980) for the public positions of most social scientists; and, for a classic "leather-jacket" managerial position from the old school, Hoang Cam (1984). Dao Xuan Sam (1982) takes the opposite, proincentivist position--the "administrative and supply based way of operation is closely allied with an ignorance of the role of economic interests. Such people ignore reality and were opposed to the *'khoan'* system in agriculture." Alhtough *khoan* here may be understood to mean the "100" contracts introduced by Order No.100 in January 1981, it may also refer to the premature efforts to introduce the system in Vinh Phu in the late 1960s, or in other places even earlier.

2. The intellectual foundations of this position are of great interest in that the hard reform position was, from a neo-Stalinist perspective, viable in a united Vietnam in a way that it was not for the DRV. Access to the South's large potential economic surplus had created favorable conditions for neo-Stalinist forced industrialization. See To Huu (1985) and Le Thang Nghi (1977a, 1977b).

3. For a more detailed examination of the shifts in policy immediately after reunification and a somewhat less critical view, see Tan Teng Lang (1985:14, et seq.). See also Ljunggren (1993a) for an insider's account of the attitudes of Vietnamese planners when dealing with a sympathetic Western aid donor.

4. See Beresford (1989) for an appraisal. The relative absence of critical analysis of this period from many Vietnam scholars is striking. Vietnamese government legislation bears detailed study and is very revealing, showing as it

does the desire both to impose the DRV model on the South and to strengthen implementation of its values in the north.

5. Fforde would like to thank the late Professor Nguyen Tri for pointing this out to him in 1985/86, when he was at the Industry Department of the National Economics University, Hanoi.

6. Beresford (1989). In the North, staples procurement fell off in 1979 but recovered in 1980 (Figures 3.15 and 3.16).

7. This is the table heading in the source--presumably it means non-CMEA aid bodies.

8. We have no information regarding the existence or otherwise of higher-level "umbrellas."

9. Nguyen Lam was at the time head of the important Industry Department of the Central Committee, a position from which he moved in 1982 to be Chairman of the State Planning Commission for a very short period. He was replaced there by Vo Van Kiet (Prime Minister temporarily in 1988 and then from 1991 on until the time of this writing). He was head of the Economics Department of the Central Committee in the mid-1980s. His 1980 article is outstanding for its liberalism at the time. Nguyen Duy Trinh, by contrast, played a major role in criticizing the so-called explosion (*bung ra*) of economic activity that followed the Sixth Plenum. He had been Chairman of the State Planning Commission in the early days and foreign minister in the late 1970s.

10. One of the most striking lacuna is an institutional study of the effects of the 1991 Order No. 100 on agricultural producer cooperatives. Too many studies simply assume that the 1988 reforms acted to increase short-run economic efficiency, attributing subsequent success to the institutional reforms without a solid understanding of what they were starting from. Fforde (1989a) deals mainly with the North and does not really have much to say about the period after 1981.

11. A hard reform interpretation can be found in *NhD* (1982a): "The determining factor is strengthening the direction by all levels of agricultural production, especially of staples, in a centralized, etc., manner."

12. Le Thanh Nghi (1981); there is a substantial literature on the topic in Vietnamese, including the "debate" in *Economic Research* during 1980 (Fforde 1989a). Order No. 100 was summarized in *NhD* for 20 January 1981 as well as appearing in pamphlet form (CPV 1981a). Implementation was guided by such documents as those issued by the Central Agricultural Cooperative Management Department (CACMD) (1982) and the Ministry of Agriculture (1981).

13. There is considerable anecdotal and other evidence to suggest that a very high proportion of these organizations existed on paper only. However, as an indicator of policy stance and the conservative foundation of hard reform

socialism, the continued desire to collectivize the Mekong is rather conclusive evidence.

14. Similar mistakes were made in upland development. Also, the focus upon the district as a planning level and source of obligatory targets for cooperatives was maintained throughout the rural areas, weakening incentives for cash-crop and upland intensive development and storing up problems for post-decollectivization policy makers.

15. A poor farmer from Vinh Lac district in southern Vinh Phu reported to Fforde in 1988 that his family had produced some tonnes of refined white sugar in the early 1980s for sale privately but had been unable to sell them at any price. This suggests that to the important systemic effects should also be added the simple need for higher real urban incomes to support effective demand for products, although the Soviet and Cuban sugar supplies available on low ration prices to urban consumers at the time would certainly have weakened the domestic producers' position.

16. The early attempts to reform the state price structure were admittedly of some importance. Decree No. 26 of the Politburo had, as reported in *NhD*, raised agricultural purchase prices, stimulated use of two-way contracts in procurement, pushed for reform of distribution in cooperatives and raised the bonus share of state wages (NSKDGN 1982). Furthermore, as Phan Van Tiem points out (1990), these brought distributional questions into the debate when they had not previously been addresses). The clampdowns and collectivization drive of 1985 were closely bound up with the price-wage-money reforms, about which discussion follows.

17. Note that Vo Van Kiet, prime minister from 1991 on, and longtime party leader in Ho Chi Minh City (although by origin from the Mekong Delta), was a full Politburo member and chairman of the State Planning Commission from 1982 on.

18. See Hoang Luu (1980a, 1980b); details were also publicized in CM (1980a). According to Hoang Luu, policy at that time had been clearly stated: Exporters were to receive materials necessary for fulfillment of their export and production plans, while agricultural cooperatives were to get staples allocations to enable them to develop exports. There would also be foreign currency loans. There were three sorts of commodities: "special exports," requiring government permission for each trade; "norm exports," for which the government would issue yearly plan targets; and "regional exports," using local resources that were subject to a "special system" if output was above the plan issued by the state. For the last, the local authority (the city or the province) was to get 70 percent of the foreign exchange earned from exports, "so that they can import goods to serve the local economy". Apart from the specialized trading companies of the Ministry of Foreign Trade, all units were allowed to contact foreign markets either directly or through participation in the Association of

Exporters and Importers of the Ministry of Foreign Trade. This is a similar two-track system to that of the Three Plan mechanism applied to SOEs.

19. The data almost certainly does not capture investment outside the scope of the statisticians' model of what constituted measurable economic activity, for example, accumulation based upon extraplan activities by SOEs. However, the data does show the direction of state policy, which continued with developmental priorities consistent with the DRV program and hard reform socialism.

20. Note that these price reforms maintained administrative controls over key products but did, in fact, narrow the list of goods whose distribution was rationed.

21. This begs the question to whether macroeconomic instability was a *necessary* consequence of the DRV and transitional models.

22. 25-CP 1981 was followed by 146-HDBT (1982) and 156-HDBT (1984). The two latter decrees attempted to reinforce the planners' rights to have obligations to them met before the unit worked on its own account. The most straightforward description of 25-CP can be found in a book coauthored by one of its drafters (Le Trang and Duong Bach Lien 1983). Other sources are Van Dac (1983) and a conference reported in *NCKT* (1981) that discussed the effects of this opening up of market relations upon the centrally-planned distribution system.

23. In its implementation, this party decree was accompanied by a number of guiding documents, which could vary from province to province. The pace of implementation was far from uniform and was openly reported as such. A justification of output contracts as a means of retaining control over rural production can be found in a study by the Ministry of Agriculture (1981).

24. This was reflected in the lack of any penetrating analysis from conservatives on these aspects of the Vietnamese economy in the 1980s.

25. CPV 1981a and 1981b are the basic sources. See also Le Thanh Nghi (1981) and other citations in footnote 12 of this chapter. As hard reform socialism extended its reach in the early 1980s, early successes in arguing for the ·household as the "base unit," or for some synonym, were rolled back. This led to difficulties with the state's rural development service net that were to last into the early 1990s, since the object of activities, if it could not be the household, had to be the cooperative.

·26. Rather full details of the results of Resolution No. 312 (1 October 1980) were given, only some five weeks after it had been passed. Incidents such as these were etched deeply into the minds of the urban population, contributing to the slow pace with which capital was brought back into the open toward the end of the 1980s and indeed even into the early 1990s. After the 1979 Sixth Plenum, as part of the "production explosion" (*bung ra*), there had been a sharp jump in restaurant numbers. Ten thousand small traders had started up in early 1980, with many people coming from other regions to trade. In this way Hanoi showed its natural position as entrepot and commercial center for the Red River Delta. During the crackdown, the Economic Registration Committee of the City re-approved around 7,000 applications, an effort that caught many people operating illegally and dodging taxes, which rose from 0.6 million to over 1.7 million dong.

27. This historical episode, like the period between the 1979 Sixth Plenum and the emergence of 25-CP and CT-100 in late 1980, deserves deeper study. The debate in the editorial column (*Xa Luan*) of *NhD* in the second half of 1985 makes fascinating reading, revealing the depth of understanding, and misunderstanding, of the economic logic of the extant transitional model. It is reported that "the army said that either Tran Phuong should be fired or they would shoot him," so great were the tensions created by the price-wage-money measures. Fforde was a visiting scholar at the Industry Department of the National Economics University Hanoi from September 1985 to April 1986.

28. The typical Vietnamese urban household was deeply involved in both plan and market, usually with a strong gender dimension. Evidence for free market activities on the part of SOEs is fascinating, for example, the discovery was made in 1985 that 50 percent of the large cash stocks built up by economic agents were in fact held by SOEs (Le Khac Thanh 1985). This meant that reductions in real incomes from unplanned activities had an immediate effect upon real labor supply through income effects, therefore cutting the labor effort available for official plan fulfillment. In addition, higher demand for free market supplies increased pressures to appropriate low price materials intended for the plan.

29. Truong Chinh, previously identified with a pro-Chinese hard-line approach typified by his opposition to output contracts in Vinh Phu in the late 1970s, moved at this time to support reforms. An early speech of his in office (Truong Chinh 1986) discussed Draft Resolution No. 306 on SOE autonomy, which ended the recentralizing efforts of earlier measures such as 25-CP, 146-HDBT, and 156-HDBT.

30. Note here Party Secretariat Decree No. 306 ("Draft") of 8 April 1986 which predated the Sixth Party Congress and reversed the earlier pattern of reform-favored planners as opposed to SOEs (CPV 1986). This is discussed further on in this chapter. Equivalent measures for farmers had to wait until 1988.

31. A crucial element of this was the alliance between northern technocrats and state business interests, which was somewhat vulnerable to the subsidy issue. This came home to roost after 1989.

32. Details of the plenum can be found in *NhD* for 20 December 1987 (CPV 1987b).

33. The main sources for this section are Fforde (1985) and interviews with Soviet experts in Vietnam during 1988.

34. Personal interview, 1988. Note that Soviet experience of the Vietnamese personalities and practices dated back to the 1950s and earlier.

35. The following is largely drawn from the *Communist Studies* article just mentioned.

36. There were a number of perceptive articles in the otherwise rather dull *Legal Studies* journal (*Luat Hoc*) during the 1980s that greatly illuminated the issues, notably the issue of nonimplementability. Nguyen Nien (1974a, 1974b) reveals early understanding of "aggravated shortage" and the contradictions implied by it for reform socialist undertakings; Nguyen Nien's 1985 work is a concise and hard-hitting critique of the existing economic system and of the reasons for the slowdown in output during the mid-1980s.

37. Here, "local" should be taken to include ministerial; by the end of the 1980s ministries had accumulated major capital holdings, and were responsible, for example, for the building of the Thang Long Hotel in Hanoi. They held most of the share capital of the Export-Import Bank set up in 1989 (*Cong Bao* 31 May 1989).

38. This organization was to play an increasingly visible role in attempts in the early 1990s to establish a system of business courts that could be more independent of local political interests.

39. The Vietnamese term *thanh phan,* here rendered as "component," is extremely hard to translate. It refers to the neo-Stalinist class system, therefore the word "sector" (e.g., "private"), if chosen, has to in corporate the personal aspects, i.e., the "component" into which one's family was classified at the Land Reform (for example, "poor peasant" or "landlord").

40. A list of the so-called list goods subject to central planning in the early 1960s can be found for comparison in Fforde and Paine (1987).

41. But contracts signed with state bodies still had to receive "priority." This was mainly relevant in areas where there were international agreements, above all with CMEA countries (CPV 1988).

Tables

TABLE 4.1 Five-Year Plans: Targets and Outcomes

	Percentage Rates of Growth		
	National Income	Agricultural Production	Industrial Production
Second FYP, 1976-80:			
Plan	13-14	8-10	16-18
Actual	0.5	1.9	0.6
Third FYP, 1981-85:			
Plan	4.5-5	6-7	4-5
Actual	6.4	4.9	9.5
Second FYP, 1986-90[a]:			
Plan	4.3	1.4	5.6
Actual	4.4	3.5	4.3

[a] Data for 1990 from SO 1992:tables 12,15.
Source: Tetsusaburo Kimura 1987 quoted in ISEAS 1987.

TABLE 4.2 Fencebreaking: Areas of Rapid Industrial Recovery, 1979-82

Sector	Percent Annual Growth
MSG	8.2
Alcohol	9.2
Cigarettes	26.0
Sugar	29.9

Source: SO1983:tables 110, 111.

Boxes

BOX 4.1 Key Documents of the Transition (1)

A. State-owned Enterprises (SOEs)

CM, 21 January 1981, 25-CP: Introduces "Three Plan System," thus legalizing SOE market activities.

CM, 25 August 1982, 146-HDBT: "Supplementing and correcting" 25-**CP**, tightened up in interests of plan implementation. Stipulated superior level as responsible for approving nonlist output plans of enterprises.

CM, 30 November 1984, 156-HDBT: On "Problems of management reform in State industry," again tighter, like 146-**HDBT,** reducing profit retention on market-oriented output. But SOEs allowed to have foreign currency accounts and loans, and still permitted to keep back some output based upon own-source materials and minor output; however, price-fixing almost entirely taken out of hands of SOEs. Unimplementable but revealed policy intent.

CPV, 8 April 1986, 306-BBT: U-turn--encourages SOE autonomy but fails to attack interference from higher levels.

CM, 14/11/87, 217-HDBT: Further encourages SOE autonomy and outlines plans to reduce target indicators, etc.

B. Agricultural cooperatives

CPV, 13 January 1981, CT-100: Introduces output contract system; maintains cooperatives intact, along with workpoint system.

CPV, April 1988, NQ-10: Decollectivizes the Mekong; remaining cooperatives should now be service organizations, paid for work done-- abolition of workpoints system. Land allocated on long leases.

BOX 4.2 Key Documents of the Transition (2): Internal Trade

CM, 2 August 1979, 279-CP: *"Ve chinh sach khuyen khich san suat va luu thong nhung mat hang khong do Nha nuoc quan ly va cung cap vat tu, nhung mat hang san xuat bang nguyen lieu dia phuong va phe lieu, phe pham"* (Policies to encourage production and circulation of goods not managed by the State, and the supply of raw materials or the use of raw materials from the regions and waste and by-products) (*NhD* 7 August 1979). Initial liberalization.

CPV Politburo, 23 June 1980, NQ 26-NQ/TW: *"Cai tien cong tac phan phoi luu thong"* (The reform of distribution and circulation). Stressed the need to expand socialist trade in staples, encourage private trade to move "in the right direction" etc. (see *NhD* 26 November 1981 and 24 March 1982). Party directive marking reversal in attitude to free market after the lull in policy from the 1979 Sixth Plenum.

CM, 1 October 1980, Quyet dinh 312: *"Ve tang cuong quan ly thi truong"* (Decision on the reinforcement of market management). See *NhD* 27 October 1980. Stress on: expansion of state and cooperative trade to control almost all of wholesale and most of retail trade, pressure to register and pay taxes, enforcement of the Trade tax, price control, further reform of capitalist trade, prevention of spontaneous rural markets, reorganization of urban markets; Control of speculation and hoarding--no private trade in "List" products, all carriers to have papers; price increases to compete with the state were forbidden, as were sales at prices above the state. Expression in state policy of the June Politburo Decree No. 26.

CM, 21 November 1982, 188-HDBT: *"Ve Tang cuong thuong nghiep XHCN va quan ly thi truong"* (On the need to step up socialist trade and market management). See *Cong Bao (CB)* 15 December 1982. Further tightening up during the high tide of hard reform socialism.

CM, n/a, 1987 (?): Directive ordering abolition of control posts inhibiting internal trade (*Thi Truong* 50, 10 January 1990). The shift to a national free market.

CM, 14 or 2 December 1989: *"QD 195 HDBT ban hanh nhung quyet dinh bo sung 217 HDBT"* (Resolution 195 promulgating various decisions supplementing CM 217), not in *CB*, Hanoi. Abolishes two-price system.

BOX 4.3 Key Documents of the Transition (3): Foreign Trade

CM, 7 February 1980, 40: "*CP ve Viec ban hanh Quy dinh ve chinh sach ve bien phap nham phat trien san xuat hang xuat khau*" (On the promulgation of regulations on policies and measures to stimulate exports goods production). See *NhD* 26, 28 February 1980. Crisis measures during the post-Sixth Plenum (1979) lull, designed to stimulate exports through liberalization.

CM, 26 May 1981, 200: "*CP Quy dinh mot so diem cu the ve chinh sach va bien phap nham phat trien san xuat hang xuat khau*" (Fixing a number of concrete points and measures to stimulate production of export goods)-- tightened up on exporters' autonomy. See *Summary of World Broadcasts* 1 July 1981. Reversal of liberalization.

CM, 15 June 1985, 177: "*HDBT Ve chinh sach, bien phap day manh xuat khau va tang cuong quan ly xuat nhap khau*" (On policies and measures to strengthen exports and reinforce management of foreign trade), *CB* 15 July 1985. Assigned quotas to localities, backed up by investment by the central government; above-quota output of export goods could be exported, and the SOE owned the resulting foreign exchange; all localities active in foreign trade were strictly subject to the Ministry of Foreign Trade "in accordance with" the state's much-desired monopoly. See also JPRS 26 June 1985 and 25 June 1985. Attempting to hold the tide.

CM, 10 June 1989, 64: "*HDBT Ban hanh ban Quy dinh ve che do va to chuc quan ly hoat dong kinh doanh xuat nhap khau*" (Resolution of the Council of Ministers No. 64 promulgating regulations on the management of export-import business), see *Cong Bao* 30 June 1989. Liberalized the system. Shift to freer trade, but incomplete--further measures in early 1990s.

BOX 4.4 Illustrative example

Problems with the Tri An Hydro-electric Scheme

The Tri An installation, aimed at improving power supplies to Ho Chi Minh City, exemplified the Soviet attitude. This large scheme saw the first (105 M Watt) turbine commissioned in February 1988. Two days later the turbine had to be stopped because of leaks in a ferro-concrete water conduit close to the junction with the power unit. A *TASS* report blamed this on noncompliance with the procedure for pouring concrete. It also cited interbureaucratic tussles between the three Vietnamese Ministries involved--those of Power, Construction, and Irrigation. Furthermore, "the bureaucratic mechanism of management, which is not surrendering its positions despite all the efforts which are being made in the country to overcome it, could not fail to affect the course of construction" (Blagov et al. 1988). This was blamed for the problems caused for Vietnamese workers by the instability of prices and nonpayment of wages. However, a Soviet engineer, M. Neminskiy, also pointed to the lack of design attention to such factors as the peculiarities of the Vietnamese climate, the experience of the Vietnamese workforce, and the lack of control and inspection of work quality.

This example confirms both the general attitude of the official Soviet press and the difficulties that such large-scale projects still face.

Figures

FIGURE 4.1 State Staples Buying Prices
(percent of free market prices)

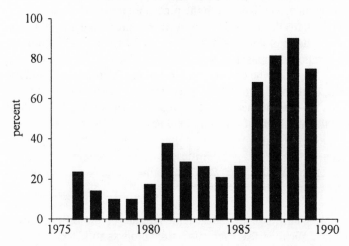

Note: Official data are index number form; a 1:10 ratio was imposed for 1978, corresponding to personal observation. The trends are clear. Free market prices are retail prices.
Source: SO 1983a, 1985a, 1987, 1990c, 1991c, personal communication.

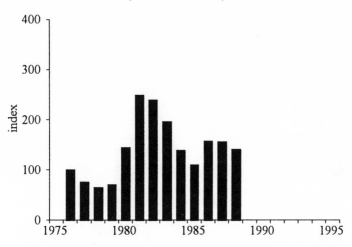

FIGURE 4.2 State Staples Trade
(controlled markets)

Note: The data show the ratio of state staples procurement prices to retail staples prices on
the controlled state market. The ratio is arbitrarily set at 100 in 1976.

Source: SO 1983a, 1987, 1988a, 1990c.

5

Markets and Sectors

In this chapter, we first examine the emergence and development of trade and markets in Vietnam during the transition, so far as the data permit, and then discuss in more detail the two key sectors of agriculture and industry. The effects of the 1980s transition path upon growth prospects in the 1990s, are stressed, preparing the ground for the discussion in Chapters 7 and 8.

Trade and Transactions: The Emergence of Markets

The transition to a market economy in Vietnam was, as discussed earlier, based upon a process whereby autonomous transactions grew up within the central-planning system. These transactions originated within the pre-1975 embryonic transitional model that had existed in the DRV, with its problems of aggravated shortage. During the period of fence-breaking (ca. 1979-80) in response to external shocks, which shifted incentives against planned transactions, autonomous transactions grew rapidly. Then, after 1981 and the legalization of the institutions of the transitional model, they coexisted openly with the system of administrative resource allocation. After the 1985 debacle, the political dominance of hard reform socialism was replaced by the soft reformism expressed by the 1986 Sixth Party Congress, and the subsequent introduction of policies favorable to the private sector and free markets. Finally, in 1989, as Soviet aid started to collapse, anti-inflationary measures coincided with the abolition of the two-price system, which had been the essential characteristic of the transitional model.

This process was accompanied by rather high rates of inflation, which, we have argued, had a positive effect. Inflation perpetuated a high differential between free market and state prices in the face of price reforms that were--at this time--opposed to 100 percent commercialization. However, the reported collapse of urban household savings in 1986 as inflation accelerated to triple digit levels in the aftermath of 1985 has also been noted, as shown in Figures 3.3 and 3.11.

A number of graphs and tables have already been presented that point to some of the visible aspects of these trends. For example, Figure 3.14 shows the proportion of retail sales controlled by the free market. This demonstrates rather clearly the decline of the free market's position in the late 1970s as the traditional model was imposed, followed by a recovery in 1979-80 during the period of fence-breaking. In the early 1980s, under hard reform socialism, there was again a decline, which was then reversed from 1986 onward.

A similar pattern can be seen in the evolution of the disequilibrium in the staples market. Figure 3.15 shows the variation over time of the volume of staples production that remained after state procurement and a notional 250 kilogram per capita subsistence requirement was fulfilledin the Red River and Mekong Deltas. Again, there are indications early in the decade of rather large surpluses on the free market (e.g., nearly 3 million tonnes in 1983), which then fall away and do not return again until 1989-90 after the introduction of Decree No. 10. Figure 4.1 is particularly revealing. It combines the two available indices for free market and state procurement staples prices. Usng a ratio of 10:1 in 1978,[1] the figure then shows how an approximate balance (i.e., 1:1 or 100 percent) had been attained by 1989. This suggests what tends to be confirmed by other sources--which is that state and free market prices had moved far closer together by the end of the 1980s--indeed, by 1986-87. However, what is also suggested by the figure is that the disequilibrium worsened in the period 1981-84, after the introduction of Order No. 100. Thus, the basic logic of the DRV model, perpetuated by the hard reform socialist line, is confirmed. Following the same line of argument, Figure 4.2 is derived from indices for state staples procurement prices and state retail prices. Using a base of 100 in 1976, this figure shows changes in the retail margin charged by the state. It therefore suggests that the state greatly increased its margin in 1981, presumably in order to capture the gains from increased rice surpluses achieved through its forced procurement mechanism.

The evolution of the free market is also shown by the increased role of "other" incomes in state employee families' incomes (Figure 3.10). Note that this started to rise in 1980. It is also shown by the sharp increase in the early 1980s (followed by declines through the end of the decade), in the volumes of state procurement of some products--beef, pork, and fish--whereas the fresh vegetables sector stagnates before rising in 1985-86. (Figures 5.1 through 5.6). Note also the marked declines in the state's ability to obtain supplies of key goods such as pork, beef, and fish in the crisis years of 1980-81.

The development of commercialized methods of input supply in place of administrative allocation is confirmed through two sources. Table 5.10 gives some information on levels of self-balancing for a number of products in the late 1980s. There is also information on the levels of "own capital" in state enterprises around 1988-89, which are rather high in quantity. This was the outcome of relatively autonomous capital accumulation within SOEs through the 1980s (IPM 1990).

These quantitative statistics are supported by a large volume of evidence from individual enterprises and cooperatives. Taken as a whole, they tend to support, strongly but far from conclusively, the interpretation of the overall pattern of events discussed in this study. They show that the focus of the analysis upon market emergence and development is fruitful but that much more research is needed, both on the detailed evolution of the institutions involved and the parameters of the economy.

1989 and Markets

The events of 1989 were of historical importance. Prior to 1989, as part of the process of reducing plan distortions, a number of major price imbalances had been cut back: Lowering the level of subsidy inherent in rice rationing was an important example.

Inflation, which had been one of the main causes of the downfall of the hard reform strategy in 1985, started to accelerate again early in 1989 (see Figure 5.7). In response to this and in order to confront a steep reduction in Soviet assistance, the authorities sharply increased nominal interest rates, which then went well above monthly rates of inflation. At the same time, the borders were opened and high-quality imported consumer goods came onto domestic markets in large volumes. The result was a major shift in inflationary expectations, large movements out of stores of value such as gold and dollars and into dong, much of which were deposited in the state banking system, and a steep fall in the rate of inflation.

At this time, the authorities increased a number of important state prices--dollars, fertilizer, and coal were notable examples--and markets generally shifted into supply-demand balance.[2] The previous excess supply in the centrally planned areas ebbed away as prices were increased. By the end of the year, a decree from the Council of Ministers formally abolished the two-price system, but in practice it had ended prior to that date.[3] Thus, by the end of 1989 consumer rationing was not really important in urban workers' lives. A review of the events of 1989 that came out in 1990 suggested that a museum be set up to preserve ration books and other such artifacts of the time "so that the young should not forget." [4]

Many aspects of the events of 1989 are very interesting, especially compared with 1985. Of particular interest are the different supply responses. In 1985 the combined effects of the clampdown on the free market with the reduction in cash liquidity reduced economic activity in both planned and autonomous areas. The deflation in the latter had important effects on the former. The planned economy was shown to be relying heavily on the unplanned sectors, mainly through the effects upon workers' real incomes.[5] A general deflation followed, until inflation, by recreating the price differential between the two sectors, permitted the basic dynamics of the transitional model to start up again. In 1989, however, market supply increased, helped by imports and consumers' portfolio shifts, leading to an overall output gain and more buoyant economic activity generally. Winners outnumbered losers, which had not been the case in 1985. Plan distortion had arguably been reduced to a level at which the social adjustment costs of shifting to a generalized market system were lower than the immediate benefits.

In any case, whatever further study reveals, it is certainly the case that after 1989 the central-planning element of the transitional model no longer existed. We argue, therefore, that from then on the Vietnamese economy is most usefully considered as a market economy.

Savings

Whereas during the 1980s the development of factor markets was inhibited by the particular transition path followed, there were important moves to encourage financial intermediation in 1988-89. The state banks were allowed to offer positive real interest rates, and a number of private credit cooperatives were permitted to operate. As a result, rather large volumes of funds were attracted. In the short term, the absence of normal investment opportunities and strategies (both in the state and private sectors) meant that there were considerable losses. The state used much of the funds to prop up the state sector and create new economic rents; the cooperatives were typically operated fraudulently. Whilst this pushed home some important lessons, and revealed the existence of rather large stocks of mobilisable capital. The state banks succeeded in borrowing some thousands of billion dong in 1989, worth hundreds of millions in U.S. dollars. However, it is important to have some idea of the underlying savings flows of the population at this time. These were rather small, perhaps equal to around 1 percent of GDP but were to grow rapidly in the next few years. Portfolio effects seem to have dominated financial behavior in 1989.

The available government data on household savings rates are revealing but almost certainly rather unreliable. The findings from the survey of farmers' incomes and spending suggests that in 1989-90 aggregate savings from the entire family farm sector were unlikely to be more than US$40-50 million a year (see Figure 5.9). The state employee survey implies that per capita monthly savings (measured as income less spending) were 2,695 dong in 1989, a year in which the dong averaged a value of 4,600 to the U.S. dollar on the free market (see Table 5.11).[6] Assuming a dependency rate of 2:1 and noting that state employment was around US$4 million in that year, this suggests an aggregate savings flow of around $80 million. Even allowing for a likely downward bias in reporting, this gives a total of annual household savings flow for the entire country in 1989 of the order of only US$150-200 million (equivalent to around 1-2 percent of GDP). At root this was due to the problems facing the rural areas.

Agriculture

Earlier chapters have described how the institutions and development priorities of the DRV model had devastated the already poor areas of North Vietnam. At the same time, the model had stultified growth in the regions of high potential surplus--especially the Mekong Delta and the Central Highlands.

The Parameters of the Transition

Transition parameters have been reviewed in Chapter 3. Apart from one-shot increases in staples output in 1981-2 and 1989, there were no really important aggregate structural changes in agricultural production during the 1980s. Input availability did not alter very much, and the overall picture is of two shifts to higher levels of static and dynamic efficiency as the collective system was progressively unwound. However, in the economic history of the transition, the failure of the first reform package to cope with the basic constraint of slow per capita staples output growth was of importance in explaining the shift from hard refrom to soft reform socialism.

The Failure of the 1981 Reforms: Origins of the Mid-1980s Food Crisis

The package of policies introduced after 1981 combined the output contract system and the temporary abandonment of the collectivization drive in the Mekong with measures designed to have a longer-term impact, such as increased supplies of fertilizer and other inputs, stabilization of procurement targets, price changes, and policies designed to stimulate livestock and poultry production. Performance through the 1980s showed that these were poorly implemented and had little impact. Micro changes, such as sacrificing rural cadres' jobs, were far easier to implement than macro shifts that attacked the rents and subsidies enjoyed by the urban and state sectors.

Between 1980 and 1985, the gross value of agricultural output rose by an average of 4.9 percent annually: 4.1 percent for cultivation and 7.8 percent for livestock. From 1985 until 1988, however, cultivation stagnated, showing no growth at all between 1985 and 1987, whereas livestock output continued to grow at the same rate (SO 1987, 1988a). Livestock output, however, was almost entirely controlled by the family and private sectors; the growth between 1980 and 1985 was predominantly in meat cattle--an average growth of over 11 percent a year compared with 2.3 percent for buffalo and 3.4 percent for pigs (SO 1987:table 67).

Staples Output

As has been seen above, regional differences remained of great importance to Vietnamese agricultural performance. This difference had an organizational dimension, for during the 1980s the North and Center still had operational collectivized agricultures, whereas the Mekong Delta remained far less affected by such transformations.[7]

Until 1988 the trend of aggregate staples output per head was as follows: after a precipitate decline between 1976 and 1978, there was then a sharp rise that halted around 1982, after which there was a period of stagnation around the 295-300 kilogram per head level until 1987, when output slumped to near 280 kilograms(Table 5.1). The 300 kilogram level is a simple indicator of the level of staples output required for approximate balance, with 250 as the minimum subsistence amount (see also Figure 3.1).

The division of the origins of output gains between yield and area increases is shown in Table 5.2. There is a rather substantial decline in the reported staples area after 1982, which was offset until 1985-86 by improvements in land yields. This was mainly the result of changes in rice cultivation rather than other staples crops. In 1982, 82.0 percent of the staples area was taken by rice, and by 1986-87 this indicator had risen to around 83.5 percent; for the same years, rice's share of total staples output rose from 85.5 percent to around 87 percent (SO 1987:table 27; SO 1988). These rather small changes suggest that the deterioration in national per capita staples output after 1982 resulted from the combination of a declining cultivated area with poor yields growth. The fall in area suggests major incentive problems, especially when the regional data are examined, for the relative stability of the national indicator hid growing regional disparities. Table 5.4 shows that the gap between output per head in the two deltas rose from around 60 percent in the late 1970s to around 100 percent in the early 1980s, then started to widen further as the situation in the North deteriorated in the middle of the decade.

Examination of the regional data thus provokes depressing conclusions. For the Red River Delta, the 1986 performance showed that both the cultivated area and the land yield were indeed little better than in 1976. Furthermore, 1986 yields and area were well below the peak years of the early 1980s, such as 1981, the year when the cultivated area reached its maximum, and 1984, the best yield year.

The picture was, therefore, of deteriorating performance prior to the bad weather of 1987 and 1988, which served substantially to depress staples production per head. When these figures are combined with the continuing population growth, the result was an almost uninterrupted fall in production per head over the six years from 1982. This was the background to the 1988 crisis (see Figure 3.1).

For the Mekong Delta, the only major region of the country where staples output per head was well above 300 kilograms a year, the picture was also far from good. By 1988 there had been no significant rise in the cultivated area since the beginning of the decade, and indeed the average in the mid-1980s was below the 1980 level. Output gains resulted from increased yields, and by 1987 these were well above both those of the late 1970s and those experienced in the Red River Delta. The growth was sufficient to keep pace with the rising population until around 1984, after which staples output per head stagnated.

Since the major basis for regional disparities in Vietnam remained the differences between the two large deltas, it is of interest to compare the ratio of staples output per head. Table 5.4 shows that in the very early 1980s there was a substantial narrowing of the gap, which then tended to widen steadily from around 1982 on. The underlying basis for the regional problem was therefore deteriorating.[8]

The decline in the staples area below the 1981 peak in the Red River Delta--a food deficit region--also implied major disincentives to staples production. The failure to expand the staples area in the Mekong Delta until the end of the decade is also striking.

The Incentives Problem

The discussion has emphasized the point that the incentives question has two distinct aspects: first, the role of prices and costs (how much do they matter?); second, whether pertinent prices and costs are distorted. The arguments given at the beginning of this chapter suggested that after a temporary recovery at the turn of the decade, the free market only became important again toward the end of the decade and that the pressure from the state procurement system and the corresponding price disequilibrium *widened* in the first half of the decade after easing around 1979-80 (see Figure 4.1). The opening up of the national market for rice in 1988 preceded by one year the large expansion of exports in 1989. The dollar equivalent of the domestic retail rice price moved substantially upward in the second half of the 1980s (see Figure 5.13) and, indeed, by 1991 was actually well *above* world market prices at over US$ 250 per tonne.[9]

However, here again there are substantial regional differences. In the high surplus areas of the Mekong the influence of collectivization upon the rural population was, on the whole, far less than in the North and Center. It was widely accepted that farmers were well accustomed to economic decisionmaking based upon the reality of a large potential and actual marketed surplus.[10] Prices and costs on the whole therefore did tend to matter, and the incentive problem primarily had to do with the adverse effects of state policy upon the value and volumes of goods and services moving into and out of agriculture. The dominant collective form, the "production collective," was one (where it existed and had any relevance) that permitted distribution of output according to the value of assets supplied by its members, thus providing a return to nonlabor inputs and scope for a more effective incentive structure. Furthermore, there is considerable evidence that these collectives were often weak, acting more or less as simple interfaces between the farmers and the state. In practice, production remained largely in private hands.

State Procurement and Pricing Policy: The Rice Market

The inefficiencies of the state distribution system were great.[11] Accurate data are not available, but according to broad estimates, only some 50 percent of the staples supplied to the state actually reached ration recipients. Similar observations existed for supplies of materials to farmers. Table 5.5 shows the margin between the volume of staples secured by the state and that delivered by the state retail system, but this includes stock changes and other legitimate elements. Figure 4.2, however, shows that the state greatly increased its margin in 1981, effectively taxing output gains resulting from implementation of Order No. 100.

The combination of the cooperative system and the inefficiencies of the state distributional network adversely affected the terms of trade facing farmers. Although data on the terms of trade actually facing farmers are unclear, the aggregate picture confirms the lack of progress in improving incentives when agricultural product prices are compared with consumer goods prices as measured by retail prices. The more favorable picture given vis-a-vis the index of prices for state sales of agricultural means of production showed no improvement between 1985 and 1988/89 (see Table 5.6).

The Legacy of No. 100 Contracts

No. 100 Contracts were originally designed in 1980 to prevent the spontaneous breakdown of the unpopular agricultural producer cooperatives by making tactical concessions to farmer families. The cooperatives, however, remained the ideologically "correct" unit in the rural areas. Also, reflecting the ethos of the DRV program, the allocation of state investment did not alter in agriculture's favor, and prices and margins were moved in favor of the state. After an initial sharp increase in the rice harvest (of the order of 25 percent),[12] staples output stagnated, eventually precipitating, when bad weather came, the food crisis of 1987-88. This element of the hard reform strategy therefore foundered upon the twin rocks of micro level economic inefficiency and a refusal or inability to unwind the macro distortions of the traditional model. However, the concessions made, added to the effective "endogenization" that had occurred during the pre-stage, permitted family farmers to gain more experience and build up capital. In the poorer areas, however, continued population growth further eroded the underlying subsistence margin, with implications for the future.

On the eve of decollectivization in 1988-89, Mekong Delta agriculture was what should be expected from its history: After the abandonment of the collectivization drive in the late 1970s, followed by the return to such policies in the early 1980s and announcement of their formal completion in late 1985, the collectives were usually weak and informal. The official figures, showing that 69.7 percent of the entire rural population of Vietnam were members of cooperatives, and a further 23.6 percent in the production collectives, a total of 93.3 percent (SO 1988), should be treated with considerable caution.

In the North and Center, however, the rural population, with its collective tradition (see Chapter 2), largely belonged to producer cooperatives where the cooperative management's control over production was potentially and often actually far higher. The combination of high climatic risks with poorly developed markets resulted in unreliable supplies and outlets for goods, creating strong disincentives for diversification away from staples production. The high value placed upon local collective welfare consumption, in areas such as health and education, also had the effect of reducing the resources available for economic development in the local economy in the short term. This was, however, offset by the positive effects of such services upon labor productivity. However, apart from the underlying issues of poverty and risk avoidance, the lack of sensitivity of the producer cooperatives to prices and costs had been exacerbated by other factors as follows:

- First, rural producers' long experience of being viewed as a low-cost source of extracted resources for the urban and industrial areas. This drained available surpluses and actively discouraged investment and diversification in favor of subsistence-oriented production.
- Second, the effects of the cooperative system itself. Here the work-point-based method of distributing resources operating prior to 1988 allowed each cooperative to insulate itself from the outside world; the work-point system created an internal pricing structure, based upon staples production, which made it difficult for even the better managers to make rational economic calculations. In cooperatives where management was less committed, the effect was to permit the development of severe disincentives as the value of work associated with rice cultivation was systematically undervalued, allowing resources--rice--to be moved into other areas. This led to a situation where the value of a day's labor in rice cultivation was usually well below that in other areas of cooperative work. Since the cooperative remained the tax unit in collectivized areas, its position vis-a-vis its members continued to be highly ambiguous. Increases in output, it was widely feared, could lead to higher taxes or procurement, or both. However, it was reported in 1988 that the accumulated level of unpaid taxes in Vietnam was nearly 250,000 tonnes, of which over 200,000 tonnes were owed by southern provinces.
- Third, the lack of development of local rural credit and other institutions designed to make it easier for local producers to take risks, to develop market strategies, and generally to move away from subsistence-oriented production.

Conclusions

Prior to Decree No. 10 of 1988, the organization of staples production in Vietnam acted, largely unconsciously, to accentuate, if not accelerate, regional differences. The richer Mekong Delta was more price-cost sensitive and had a far less extensive system of collectives; this tended to raise its ability to utilize resources effectively. Furthermore, state procurement policy almost certainly concentrated available inputs on the Mekong as a high surplus area where the effective cost of rice to the state was lower. In the North, the cooperative system weakened the sensitivity of producers to prices, costs, and economic opportunities, while creating a local tax base used both for legitimate local welfare services as well as for "extractions" by local cadres and superior levels. Staples output stagnated, leading to the food crisis of 1987-88.

The effectiveness of the entire collective system therefore fell into question. Although popular support for local collective services was probably both present and strong, the economic role of collectives was gravely inhibited by the lack of effective democratic institutions that could prevent their exploitation by both local cadres and state procurement agencies.

The 1988 Crisis and Party Decree No. 10

In April 1988 the Communist Party published Decree No. 10 on agricultural reform, which introduced what was probably the final set of rural organizational reforms. These have already been discussed in Chapter 4. The decree presented an analysis of the situation and the reasons for it that was devastating, and it presented a soft reform position highly critical of the institutions of the traditional system and their operation. In particular, the lack of effective attention to rural conditions was brought to the fore and trenchant criticism was made of "new rural despots," who had based themselves upon the cooperative structures to exploit the peasantry.

Agrarian conditions were reportedly--and largely accurately--characterized by

- Stagnation in agricultural development.
- Slow growth of agricultural surpluses.
- Persistence of a situation where large parts of Vietnamese agriculture were still essentially subsistence based.
- Falls in agricultural output since 1985.
- Forest destruction and poor environmental protection.
- Increased social problems such as superstition, gambling, and drunkenness.

In the decree, the causes for this situation were atributed as follows:

- There had been no proper socioeconomic development policy aimed at creating a rational industrial-agricultural structure; agriculture had received too little attention in the past, leading to lack of domestic suppliers of agricultural means of production and of agricultural processing; research and dissemination of new techniques were inadequate; there was great waste in the utilization of investment and inputs in agriculture, and both irrigation and materials supply were poor.
- Collectivization had been carried too far and too fast; people had been forced into collectives, which had been too large and too hostile to the family economy.
- Failure to abolish the system of administrative supply and problems with local cadres had had a severe effect upon producer incentives; cooperatives neither functioned efficiently nor could they be relied upon not to tax rice production excessively.
- Mistakes in macro policy had biased incentives against staples production and had been exacerbated by the failure to implement policies designed to improve the situation.
- State materials supplies to agriculture went through too many intermediaries and therefore increased the price to the producer.
- The organization of agricultural support from the center to the base was ineffective and clumsy; technical cadres were concentrated too far from the producer, and local cadres received inadequate training and encouragement.
- Rural educational programs were ineffective.
- Local party organizations were often based upon family connections or particular areas within the communes, and they contained bad elements that exploited the local population (*NhD* 12 April 1988).

This indigenous critique should be assessed keeping in mind the very high margin that had opened up in early 1988 between the Hanoi and Ho Chi Minh City rice prices (see Figure 5.14).

The main policy changes have already been described in Chapter 4. These changes were designed to reorient state policy in order to assist structural readjustment, and they gave substantial increased freedoms to farmers. However, as before, the micro sacrifices were easier to attain than the structural adjustment.[13]

Freed from the state--the district was no longer allowed to issue instructions to cooperatives--and free to reallocate land to better farmers, cooperative management was in some ways put into a stronger position. In the opinion of an informed Vietnamese commentator, the intention was to cut the cooperative's right to make farmers pay for inputs that the cooperative had to supply but usually supplied poorly or not at all. Thus, other elements of the policy were as follows:

- Disputes over contract violations would be resolved in favor of the cooperator or producer.
- Cooperators would keep all contract overfulfillment. In the past there had been a tendency for cadres to eat into this margin by various means, including pressure from the district for higher staples deliveries from the cooperative.
- The work-point system used to calculate the various inputs laid down in the contract would be abolished and contract costs fixed in terms of money or rice. Cooperatives would be allowed to sell any of their assets to their members.
- Fertilizer and insecticides supplied by the state would still go through the cooperative, but there would be a move away from obligatory sales to the state, to be replaced by taxes and voluntary sales.

It was hoped that introducing these policies would encourage better agricultural performance while also allowing rapid employment growth in small-scale rural industry. The early impact of these policies is discussed further later on.

The North and Product Diversification

It was in the area of product diversification that the weaknesses of Decree No. 10--as implemented--were quickly to become apparent. Although output gains and better markets (especially the far more reliable and stable rice market) helped push up real incomes, future improvements for northern rice farmers, now effectively competing with the lower cost Mekong Delta farmers had to depend upon expansion of other crops and activities. In this respect, the presence of commercialized state trading companies and processing factories, owned by and subject to state influence, often in the form of local authorities, tended to act against farmers' interests.

In the fully collectivized areas, nonrice production often remained a mixture of collective and family-based organization. The local cadres' positions enabled them in many cases to attempt to play entrepreneurial roles for which they were not well qualified. Family-based diversification was inhibited by the diversion of resources into the collective sectors but showed some positive signs, especially in such branches as pork and vegetable production. These trends were clearly visible around the major cities, where the liberalization of the private sector and the development of a national market in rice supported growth processes and diversification.

On the whole, state investment resources still tended to go to the state sector and the state farms. Despite rhetoric to the contrary, there was little hard evidence of much state support to agriculture, and as we discuss in Chapter 8, state policy ensured that the emerging capital market of 1989-90 was strongly biased against the rural and nonstate sectors.

The State Sector: State Farms and Forestry Enterprises

Like other units of the state economy, the state farms tended to be basically inefficient and often highly adapted to take account of resource shortages within the state supply system as well as opportunities outside it. The situation of the forestry enterprises was rather different from other sectors, as state policy had moved rather early to grant concessions to the nonstate forestry sectors (Ministry of Forestry 1983).

One consequence of the primitive and unreliable development of domestic markets was the tendency toward a diversification by specialized state units into subsistence production. This was, for example, an important part of the way in which forestry enterprises operated in northern Vietnam. For example, the large state-enterprise union set up in the Central Highlands to grow coffee as part of the Vietnamese-Soviet cooperation efforts, actually farmed, in addition to its coffee, some 30,000 hectares of rice, 18,000 hectares of maize, and 3,000 hectares of sugarcane; each year it cut down and processed 7,000 cubic meters of wood, and produced some 31 million bricks and tiles and 2,500 tonnes of lime. That union possessed nearly 8,000 head of cattle and 2,000 beehives (Mai Huong 1987).

Rural Differentiation as the Transition Came to an End: The Gathering "Rural Question" of the 1990s?

No. 10 Contracts and the rapid development of markets had important implications for the pattern of rural differentiation. Although the powerful criticism of the "red rural bourgeoisie" in Decree No. 10 should be treated as propaganda to a certain extent, there is no denying the fact that compulsory cooperativization had put rural cadres in a very ambiguous position. As the interface between the rural population and state structures seeking to "mobilize surplus," they were forced to face in two directions.[14] The commercialization of the 1980s meant that, on the one hand, they were under pressure from state trading companies to ensure that supplies from farmers were provided at the most favorable price, while, on the other, there were increasing opportunities for accumulating and investing their own capital. This could (and did) translate into pressure for policy changes to permit private landownership, opening the way for land concentration.

In 1989 the party commissioned a major survey of socioeconomic conditions in the rural areas (Nguyen Ngoc Truu 1991). This produced some extremely interesting results. The conclusions of the report were:

The factors restricting the development of artisanal lines and services in the rural areas, at root, are: raw material prices (jute, rushes, sugarcane, mulberry, peanuts, beans, tea, coffee, rubber, pineapple, fruits, wood, marine products, . . .) are in general kept below their real value,[15] especially those that can be processed and thereby create employment. Taxes upon rural sideline activities, in some places and for some lines are too high, leading to their extinction. The trading network is "tangled," leading to many corrupt activities such as purchases on credit, forced credit, forced supply, price gouging . . . (Nguyen Ngoc Truu 1991:19)

It is worth noting that this refers to the situation prior to 1989, when the market economy was given full rein. However by 1989-90 rural incomes on average had definitely improved (see Figure 5.12). The other side of the coin of this pattern of development was, however, the emergence (perhaps to view, rather than to existence) of a group of richer farmers with substantial savings and a smaller group of poorer farmers who were net dissavers. Figures 5.8 through 5.12 show this rather clearly. The poorest groups (groups IV and V) making up 65 percent of the population, were net dissavers. The richest group, with 15-20 percent of the population, were net savers. *This suggests that over one-half of the rural population was likely to be losing control over assets.*

Under such conditions, the role of the collective in preventing rapid land loss and likely social disorder in the rural areas was crucial. However, the levels of savings of the richer families were still rather small, amounting to little more than US$30-40 per household per annum. Thus, because of the underlying poverty of the region, rather extreme social differentiation was not creating very large levels of increased savings.

The situation was therefore not likely to be stable in the longer term. This is discussed further in Chapter 9.

Long-Term Development Issues

Behind the new policies and the market economy was a slow acceptance of the need for social competition, but by the beginning of the 1990s official reexamination of the arguments for a system in which the state would play a strong role were underway.

One intention of the 1988 reforms had been to pressure rural cadres to manage their cooperatives effectively. To accomplish this, it was proposed that structural readjustment and institutional support would operate through cooperatives that acted as light-handed coordinators and investors in the local economy, which would be greatly decentralized and rely upon the family economy, supported in turn by inputs from or through the cooperative. If implemented, this would have required substantial changes in local personnel, who would largely be replaced from above. This contradicted the calls for local democracy and would have interfered with long-established links between local cadres and superior levels. Its implementation would therefore have been extremely difficult.

Furthermore, the reemergence of a group of richer peasants, whose prosperity was in part based upon moneylending, and the appearance of the corollary, an increasingly indebted group, suggested that powerful socioeconomic processes familiar from the 1920s and 1930s were surfacing. However, the traditional solution--use of collectives to ensure residual land access rights--was still valid. Its efficacy, however, would depend upon the pattern of economic development that is, on the ability of urban and rural industry to soak up landless groups and the relative power of central government. Decree No. 10 therefore provided only a temporary solution to the social problems posed by the overcrowded deltas of northern and central Vietnam. The future would depend greatly upon those elements of the decree that were *not* implemented. The radical reorientation of priorities--the "New Deal" for the rural areas--implied a reorientation of the development effort toward agriculture. This was strongly supported by Western international agencies (which as yet had no money to back up what they advocated).[16] However, it is worth noting those elements of a traditional rural development package that were, in the aftermath of Decree No. 10 and the abolition of the two-price system in 1989, strikingly absent.

Extension and Information Services

The long-term effects of the low priority attached to agriculture under both the DRV and transitional models had extremely serious consequences for the development of agricultural technology. The central organs of the state, on the whole, showed themselves to be inadequate agents for the key task of disseminating technical information through viable and sustainable models suitable for local utilization.[17] It is striking that the Institute for Science and Technology Management did not have any special department responsible for agriculture and the special needs of rural areas.

There had been some success in the area of seeds, where high yielding varieties supplied illegally from abroad had been widely adopted, leading to and facilitating the development of the harvesting pattern.[18] Apart from this, however, the official systems for supplying information to the rural areas were extremely poor. To quote informed but anonymous Vietnamese commentators from 1988: "Information [for rural producers] is very bad; most cooperatives have an information center but the peasants don't use it. . . . One might judge that 70 percent of peasants neither read newspapers [of any form] nor listen to the radio." Farmers felt the value of official sources of information on new techniques was very low.

Major Conclusions

A combination of cooperative and family-based production need not, under favorable circumstances, be excessively inefficient. However, this will be the case if cooperative management does not become technically and economically efficient enough to provide valuable economic services to its members. In Vietnam this was an extremely difficult task. Profound alterations in the rural economy were an enormous shift away from the assumptions and rules of the game of both the DRV and the transitional models. Such changes would require honest and effective administration combined with a willingness to move away from the general ethos of control. This would be extremely difficult to implement. It would be even more difficult to implement in the overcrowded northern deltas once the efficiency gains from the introduction of No. 10 Contracts wore off, unless--which was unlikely--there was extremely rapid employment creation outside agriculture to absorb the growing numbers of effectively "landless," cut off from traditional land access rights in their home communes.

Industry

Through the 1980s, recorded industrial performance in Vietnam was far better than in agriculture. Rather rapid growth was experienced, and this rate was maintained in the mid-1980s when agricultural output was falling. The shift to a generalized market economy in 1989, however, revealed that perhaps 50 percent of northern state enterprises were nonviable.

Industrial gross output data confirms these high rates of growth. The acceleration that began in the early 1980s continued through the mid-1980s. There was a substantial reorientation of the pattern of growth toward consumer goods production, so that the share of consumer goods in total industrial output rose from a trough of less than 55 percent in 1981 to nearly 70 percent in 1987 (SO 1985a:table 27; SO 1988b). Local state industry grew faster than centrally managed industry, and it recorded exceptionally rapid growth in 1987 (see Table 5.7). Note that these data are gross output, rather than value added, and were therefore supported by the increasing levels of Soviet aid during the period.

As state industry became more sensitive to market demand, and therefore to the high prices for consumer goods that reflected the structural distortions of the economy, local industry tended to benefit, as it was often better placed to satisfy such demand. However, the lack of effective demand for agricultural inputs, as opposed to consumer goods and exportables, meant that these limited responses could not meet the restructuring needs of the economy. After 1989 local industry faced far greater pressures than central industry.

There were also important regional differences in the structure of industrial output. Total industrial output in the Ho Chi Minh City subregion (the southeast section, containing the industrial city of Bien Hoa) was approaching twice that in the Red River Delta (which included Haiphong as well Hanoi) in 1985. By the end of the 1980s, industrial output in the southern half of the country was probably double that of the North.

In the South generally, and in the main urban areas especially, the proportion of industrial output coming from nonstate industry was higher than in the North. During the 1990 adjustment, there was a strong correlation between the relative size of the nonstate sector and its rate of growth (see Figure 5.15).[19]

Performance

Indicators of comparative performance are limited. Table 5.9 shows the abysmal record of large-scale industry in utilizing the increased fixed capital stock. Further investigation may have to wait for econometric modeling. However, it is clear that SOEs were operating at efficiency levels that were well below what was attainable under alternative economic systems.

Reforms Through 1989

The overall tenor of reforms as the economy went into 1989 has already been discussed in Chapter 3. Reforms were said to have four major aims:

1. To allow the enterprise itself to formulate its own plan, based upon its appreciation of market demand, which the enterprise alone was in a position to gauge properly.
2. The need to expand horizontal relations between enterprises, thus widening and deepening product markets.
3. Democratization, so that enterprises' collective interests would be respected. One element of this was the plan for workers to elect their managers, subject to approval of the relevant authorities.
4. A clear definition and limitation of the functions of the state, so that there would be no direct state involvement in the activities of the enterprise.

The weaknesses of this policy set are revealed by the radical changes implied by the strongly pro-SOE Decree No. 217 (14 November 1987). For the thrity-five central unions that whould still receive quantity output targets from the state, the intention appears to have been that the over-sight bodies should be the State Planning Commission (for central enter-prises) and the Provincial or City People's Committee (for local enter-prises). This measure was aimed at drastically reducing the authority of the economic ministries and was viewed as a way of pushing through decentralizing reforms. The effort was effectively a dead letter, as line ministries retained their position into the mid-1990s.

The Legacy of the 1980s

On the eve of the abolition of central planning, the effects upon SOE behavior of the experiences of the 1980s were reasonably clear.

The Vietnamese SOE was by now market sensitive and profit oriented. Most product markets were demand constrained but subsidies of various forms were still widespread. The lack of a firm financial basis for the reforms--above all the weak basis for extending credit to enterprises--eroded their effectiveness, perpetuating the "soft-budget constraint."

Here, however, it is worth adding to the implications of the data cited above. We can see the extent to which Vietnamese industry had already (and, to a large extent, spontaneously) been restructured so as to become far more sensitive to open market demand. This trend showed in various ways:[20]

- First, in the proportion of inputs supplied by unplanned, or commercial, transactions in various important branches (see Table 5.10).
- Second, in evidence of the spontaneous development of financial intermediation. By 1989, many state enterprises were accustomed

to utilizing their foreign exchange holding rights to acquire scarce resources on a swap or barter basis. The poor development of goods and financial markets meant that there was much scope for profitable arbitrage and other operations. Effective bankers could expect to make large profits: According to reports, one local "experimental" bank in southern Vietnam found it profitable to lend depositors' funds to market traders on a daily basis. In the mid-1980s there were reports of a developing market in liquid funds between state enterprises at high and positive rates of interest.

- Third, in "own capital," which was a substantial proportion of SOE resources.
- Fourth, in side payments for workers.
- Fifth, in the shift away from heavy and toward light industry.

Opposition to Reform and the Pattern of Interests in the Transitional Model

Under the typical 1980s conditions of market disequilibria, the right to impose a quantity plan target upon a factory or cooperative, corresponding to an obligation to deliver goods at a low price, was an obvious potential source of material gain. There was, therefore, great opposition to the abolition of this right, which effectively ended the particular state monopoly position of the source of the factory's plan--its "owning" ministry in the case of the central enterprise, or the province or city in the case of a local unit (or a district, in the case of an agricultural cooperative).

The examples given in Boxes 5.1 and 5.2 concerning the problems of industrial refrom reflect widely publicized sentiments that were far from unusual. They show up clearly the tensions involved. The tone, which is common in such sources, reveals the general familiarity to both readers and participants of the problem, which dated back at least to the introduction of the Three Plan system in 1981.[21] Through the decade, the direction taken by the economy on the whole favored those units that were more efficient and better placed to capture higher prices and so maintain adequate supplies of labor and nonlabor.

The Dilemmas of Foreign Aid

A prerequisite of the DRV model was the willingness of foreign aid donors to supply the needed resources. Until national reunification, this meant the Soviet bloc and China, but in the late 1970s substantial Western aid was supplied before the cuts that followed the Vietnamese invasion of Cambodia. As we have argued, at that time the Vietnamese authorities were attempting to implement the DRV program in the reunited country, and by accepting the priorities of the Vietnamese government, Western aid donors contributed to sectoral and institutional distortions (Ljunggren 1993a). The evolving attitude of the Soviet Union has already been discussed.

The almost complete monopoly of central government over access to foreign economic relations was drastically reduced over the years as direct local[22] foreign trade developed. However, among the less commercially oriented provinces of central Vietnam, the lack of attention to costs and benefits characteristic of the DRV development model continued. This was particularly true of welfare-oriented departments. Box 5.1 illustrates behavior that was typical during the DRV model on the part of the Ministry of Health. The mere fact that the ministry was involved in economic management at all, as an "owning Ministry," is noteworthy.[23]

In sum, throughout the 1980s the pattern of reform in Vietnamese state industry was deeply permeated by its historical origins and, above all, by the interactions between the ebb and flow of policy and spontaneous bottom-up changes. The boxes show the way in which the rules of the game of the transitional model balanced the attractions of commercial unplanned activities with the requirements of superior levels. These varied enormously. The contrast with the norms of the DRV program could not be more striking.

One outcome was certainly the growing sensitivity to market demand and market opportunities. By 1988-89, the successful Vietnamese SOE was capable of exploiting both. Just as experience with such strategies gained prior to 1979 had helped accelerate fence-breaking in 1979-80, so the Three Plan system had since 1981 encouraged rather optimistic expectations of the ability of Vietnamese industry to adapt. The effects of the macroeconomic and institutional environment in the post-1989 period are discussed in Chapters 7 and 8.

Small-Scale Industry

The official attitude toward small-scale industry (strictly, "small and handicraft industry," or *tieu, thu cong nghiep* changed radically during the 1980s. This was bound up with the U-turn in attitudes to the private sector marked by the Sixth Party Congress in 1986.

Originally, the phrase was understood purely in terms of property relations: Small-scale industry was identified as nonstate industry, a label that was both incorrect and deeply confusing. By 1988 a cooperative in Bien Hoa reportedly had over 1,500 members operating with simple artisanal technology. However, according to orthodox DRV thinking, the high priority given to state industry meant that the phrase "industry" (*cong nghiep*) often meant "state industry."[24]

The policy changes introduced in the late 1980s increasingly stressed the social value of the nonsocialist sectors. Small-scale industry thus came to include cooperatives, private business, individual business, the family economies of cooperative members and state employees, and the joint state-private companies.

Despite this, however, through the 1980s the small-scale industry sector played a major and increasing role in the Vietnamese economy. The data given in Table 5.7, however, still reflect the old distinction based upon property relations rather than technology. The sector showed rapid growth over the period 1982-85, when annual real output growth rates of 12-15 percent were seen in Ho Chi Minh City, compared with 8-12 percent in Hanoi and some northern provinces.

The relative sensitivity of small producers to local demand-supply conditions meant that they were well placed to take account of increased economic opportunities as unplanned activities developed from 1979-80 on. Furthermore, despite the sea change of the Sixth Party Congress, policy had been rather supportive from an early date. Since at least 1979, official policy toward small-scale industry had included the following measures:[25]

1. Freedom to buy and sell inputs both within the sector and with state industrial enterprises (recall that this freedom was only granted to the latter in 1981 with decree 25-CP). A proportion of the supplies of "list" goods and imports available to the state was allocated to them. Previously, 100 percent of products and inputs was meant to be controlled by the state.
2. Freedom to borrow foreign exchange. In practice, however, banks continued to give priority to the state sector.
3. Freedom to contact and do business with economic units outside the province or city where they were registered.
4. Freedom to negotiate better prices for products and inputs.

However, these policies were inadequate and often unimplemented, therefore during the first half of the 1980s the sector remained heavily constrained. Thus tax policy oscillated between confiscatory levels and ineffective rates set rather low. In many cases producers in the sector were brought under close bureaucratic supervision under the name of "socialist transformation" (*cai tao xa hoi chu nghia*), cutting incentives and efficiency. The attempt to limit this from 1979 on was ignored in many areas. In practice, many state factories were not allowed to sell to the sector. The inhibitions upon domestic trade and the "internal customs" barriers also had a strongly negative effect.

Thus, although in many ways so-called small-scale industry was much freer than the state sector, the state's continued strong monopoly position in materials supplies had adverse effects. One clear example, still apparent at the end of the decade, remained the supply of cloth to small-scale producers, in which "a multitude of intermediaries between state and producer," pushed up costs. However, in Ho Chi Minh City this had not prevented a substantial reequipping of the small-scale clothing industry, begun in the early 1980s, using non-CMEA equipment.

In practice, some local branches of state banks began lending to the sector in response to profit opportunities. In the opinion of an informed Vietnamese commentator, by 1988 this could be seen, for example, in the case of the local quarter banks in Hanoi. Charging a monthly rate of 9 percent "which neither state enterprises nor cooperatives would pay," most of their funds went to the nonstate sector.

Against this background, by 1988 official policy stressed the following:

1. The basic equality of nonstate components with the state sector. The sector should be allowed to develop freely.
2. As a support for this, the "family" economies of agricultural cooperators and state employees were allowed to use the assets of their units to develop production *without paying tax.*[26]
3. Cooperatives were allowed to pay rewards to members in accordance with the capital contributed by them. Previously, returns to any input other than labor had been frowned upon.
4. All units operating in the sector were meant to be free from direct managerial interference from local authorities, who were only allowed to enforce registration and levy taxes. They were free to have direct relations with suppliers and customers; this included foreign economic organizations.

A major element of the problem of small-scale industry was the development of rural industry. Perhaps 80 percent of workers employed in small-scale industry lived in rural areas and were often part-time agriculturalists. Policies introduced in the late 1980s were geared to eliminate the previous inhibitions imposed on development of rural industry outside the control of the cooperatives.

A major institutional constraint remained the lack of an effective rural credit system. Although the proposals for establishment of an Agricultural Development Bank pointed in the right direction, as did the experiments with independent district-level banks, time would tell whether these would be able to reduce the "softness" of the state banking system and redirect lending away from the areas of traditional property.

The Nonagricultural Economy and Wider Development Issues

The evidence appears to suggest that by 1989 the basic issue of price-cost sensitivity was, through a number of mechanisms, largely solved. It follows logically that SOEs--or rather, their de facto owners--had control over significant volumes of sufficiently autonomous capital. The issue was not whether enterprises could operate in a market environment, but whether the authorities could, or would, implement tax and credit policies that would reduce economic rents, heighten economic efficiency, and accept the consequences in terms of enterprise closures. Market rather than plan distortion was now the key issue.

Thus, as has been emphasized already, balanced and sustainable growth would require a removal of the structural and macro origins of price-cost distortions. In addition, related to the issue of bankruptcy, the problem of the insufficient rewards and mechanisms driving innovation had not really been tackled. This question was bound up with the problem posed by the nature of the Vietnamese fixed industrial capital stock, which was on the whole both too large and of poor quality.

Installed Capital Stock

By the end of the 1980s, the Vietnamese economy suffered from the structural problem of a supply of fixed industrial capital that was, in many areas, simply too large. The overinvestment of the past had caused factories to be constructed that could not operate at their installed capacity because of the limited supplies of inputs (in particular, raw materials, power, spare parts, and skilled labor) available from the rest of the domestic economy. As long as aid donors were willing to foot the bill, some could be met from imports, but with the collapse of Soviet assistance in 1989-90, that option was no longer available. Subsidies, therefore, would have to come from within the Vietnamese economy (at least until other aid sources filled the gap). After 1989 their form was to change, from cheap low-price inputs to subsidized credit and tax breaks.

The capital stock in state industry was not only too large but also qualitatively poor. Research at the Institute of Science and Technology Management (Hanoi) revealed that this problem had a number of different aspects.

- First, the capital stock was old. Apart from assets left over from the French period, which by 1989 were almost museum pieces, investment in the North had come in two main stages. During the

First FYP (1961-65), installed technology essentially dated from the levels attained in the Soviet bloc during the 1950s; this was particularly true in the Viet Tri and Thai Nguyen industrial complexes. Most remaining large-scale industrial technology in the North dated from the 1970s, and with the exception of such installations as the Bai Bang Paper and Pulp Mill, financed by Sweden and equipped with Swedish technology, the Hoang Thach Cement works and the Hanoi Fiber Factory (discussed later), was derived from China or CMEA countries, or both. In the South, the extensive industrial investment in Bien Hoa dated from the 1960s but was, of course, Western technology, primarily Japanese (Brundenius et al. 1987:27-30; see also Beresford 1990). Two major consequences of this were that material input utilization rates were high, as were energy costs.

- Second, the capital stock was extremely heterogeneous. Almost entirely supplied by bilateral aid, each donor country had tended to deliver its own national products, so that there were a large number of different marques, and spare parts supply was thus particularly difficult. The termination of aid from China and the West in the late 1970s had greatly exacerbated the consequences of such aid-financed investment and illustrated its vulnerability.
- Third, imported capital goods were geared toward autarchic development. Most aid was therefore oriented to satisfying domestic demand rather than exports. Development of exports in the 1980s had therefore been inhibited by the lack of such important inputs as, for example, facilities for drying artisanal products such as furniture.

These problems had to some extent been eased by selective reinvestment toward the end of the 1980s but nonetheless remained a major issue.

Patterns and Mechanisms of Innovation

The rise of relatively autonomous profit-seeking capital naturally implied a shift in the locus of technical choice. When competition increased, this would result in normal problems of innovation. However, by 1988 state policy toward technology and innovation remained essentially dualistic as well as activist. This reflected the general pattern of the reform process and the continued desire for a close central control of "priority" sectors. So long as Vietnam remained largely isolated from Western markets, the main source of new industrial technology would remain cooperation with CMEA countries. That option was largely removed after 1989-91. The underlying hope of many reformers was that as the autonomy of economic units grew, so the demand for technical information would increasingly reflect market requirements mediated through potential satisfiers of those demands. However, by 1989 no explicit policy could be seen that encouraged development of consultancies and other organizations to help supply such information. Inthis area, institutional weaknesses limiting the emerging new role of the state were all too clearly visible.

In the DRV and transitional models, a combination of policy biases toward high-tech and large-scale projects with a high degree of aid financing (implying a very low perception of the cost of capital) inevitably resulted in the choice of inappropriate technologies. The shift to a market economy in 1989, and the effective dependency upon private direct investment that resulted from the combination of a collapse of Soviet aid with the lack of a Bretton Woods assistance program, brought these issues into sharp relief. However, the institutional shortcomings remained very great. In the opinion of an informed Vietnamese commentator, "Research on the nature of different foreign technologies, and on project assessment through the use of cost-benefit analysis techniques, has been very weak."

This judgment was confirmed by numerous examples of project proposals, such as that for the expansion of the No. 1 Pharmaceutical Factory in Hanoi (see Box 5.1) as well as others.

At the local level, however, provinces and cities as well as SOEs and other businesses were increasingly involved in utilizing their retained hard currency earnings to expand exports and stimulate the local economy. In these rural locales, where perceptions of the opportunity as well as the immediate cost of capital were often higher than at the center, where aid was more important, the choice of technology was more effective. In some areas there was a trend toward purchase of small modern machines designed to attack identified bottlenecks in the utilization of the existing capital stock in order to stimulate exports. This was also visible in the development of the private sector, above all in Ho Chi Minh City, but also elsewhere.

Prior to 1989, the 1980s had undoubtedly shown an increase in the efficiency of investment by existing production units and by conglomerates within the state economy. However, the delayed development of the private sector and capital markets meant that by 1989 the authorities had not built up significant experience with the key issue of innovation based upon private-sector initiatives. The experience of two Vietnamese entrepreneurs is revealing. One, inventor of a hand-driven batteryless torch, was allowed to expand activities until he employed several hundred workers. The Binh Minh factory, was, however, situated in Ho Chi Minh City, where the attitude toward the private sector was more liberal. The director of the factory had received support from the highest level

(Nguyen Van Linh 1985). Noteworthy by comparison, however, are the experiences of an inventor of an improved tractor in northern Vietnam, Mr. Le Duc Loi, whose product was reportedly far better than that of existing state units. As late as 1988, however, he remained under pressure to submit to state management since the limit set to private employment remained, allegedly, five workers. His access to inputs such as power and materials continued to be problematic. Obtaining bank capital was even more of a problem as state bank lending policy continued to be biased firmly away from the private sector.

Conclusions

By 1988-89 the basic issues of poor static and dynamic economic efficiency were well on the way to being improved through a number of mechanisms. Relatively autonomous capital, including that in the SOE sector, was the basic cause of this. However, the underdeveloped role of the state and embryonic factor markets (especially for capital) ensured that crucial problems arose after 1989. These included the following:

1. Acceptance of bankruptcies caused by a hard budget constraint and an effective system for supplying credit.
2. Widespread adoption, except in a minority of units, of single plan target relations betwen units and their superiors.
3. A move toward a hands-off indicative planning approach to large state enterprises (the residual thirty-five key units).
4. An equal treatment of the private and cooperative sectors.

These issues are discussed further in Chapters 7 and 8.

Notes

1. Based upon personal observation at the time (Fforde 1989a).
2. However, these figures are not very convincing.
3. Although what were called "fevers" (*con sot*) were to occur intermittently for various goods (such as cement and fertilizer) during the early 1990s, these had to do with the normal problems associated with state intervention into a basically market economy, rather than with the residual elements of central

planning: Such goods were not allocated by planners seeking to "balance" the inputs and outputs of the endusers.

4. See Decree No. 195 (14 or 2 December 1989). Two others of relevance abolished the internal rate of exchange for rubles and also ended the system of bartering rice for fertilizer (CM Decrees No. 43, 3 March 1989 and No. 150, 31 May 1989).

5. See Nguyen Manh Hung and Cao Ngoc Thang (1990), which also contains an interesting survey of the institutions of late soft reform socialism generally.

6. Personal observation by Fforde of Hanoi in autumn 1985, after the currency reform, which contrasted sharply with 1989. People were depressed and cast down, whereas in 1989 real incomes and life generally were improving rapidly.

7. Survey data are taken from informal notes on official sources supplied to the authors in 1988.

8. This returns to one of the eternal problems facing historians of the period, which is the precise impact, in reality, of collectivization upon the Mekong. There are rather well-documented arguments about the high proportion of "ghost" collectives to put beside party statements regarding the "complete" collectivization of the Mekong Delta announced in 1985. See also Chu Van Lam (1992). According to a foreign report, a Hanoi Radio broadcast of July 1987 asserted that "only around 30 percent of reported collectives in the South worked according to set procedures." In the remainder there was very little stress on "socialist collectivized work." One major reason for this was that the organizations set up at district level to push for conformity with management norms had by this time been disbanded, so the local level had reverted to behavior more in accordance with local interests. However, it was also reported that there were many instances of corruption and misuse of resources.

9. The data are consistent with suggestions that state fertilizer distribution policy favored the Mekong Delta, although the authors were unable to obtain reliable data on this issue.

10. Note that Figure 5.14 also reveals the great tensions within the divided national rice market during the food crisis of early 1988, with Hanoi prices reaching far higher levels than those in Saigon. From then on the differential rarely went above 20-30 percent.

11. For example, when compared with farmers in the North, Mekong Delta farmers were seen as far more willing to sell to middlemen and less unwilling to become staple deficient in order to devote resources to cash crops. Northerners were notorious for their apparent willingness to bear high transaction costs in order to avoid middlemen--probably because of their experience of high levels of "gouge."

12. Total paddy rice production rose from an average of 11.5 million tonnes in 1979-80 to 12.4 million tonnes in 1981 and 14.4 million tonnes in 1982, the first complete year of operation under the No. 100 Contracts system (SO various years).

13. Interestingly, this decree (No. 10) has not been much discussed in the secondary literature, contributing to the misleading picture. Some party reports on its implementation blamed poor execution on the fact that it had originated in the party agriculture and propaganda committees but had had to be carried out by state structures. A "New Deal" for agriculture had therefore turned into another series of micro reforms. By 1993, many farmers were still subject to pressures and directions from producer cooperatives, although the regional picture varied enormously.

14. This is discussed further and in greater detail in Fforde (1989a)

15. I.e., there was significant monopsony or other asymmetry in the market.

16. See the reports of the World Bank (1990) and FAO (1990).

17. An exception might be made for the so-called "V-A-C" program, which encouraged peasants to integrate gardening with livestock and pond-based fish-rearing in their own family economies.

18. See Brundenius et al. 1987:22. This source ignores--revealingly--any other aspects of agricultural technology.

19. The line in the graph is a simple ordinary least squares regression line.

20. The measurement, in a systematic manner, of commercialization processes in Vietnamese state industry is discussed in other work (Fforde, ongoing).

21. If not before--see criticisms of profitseeking by SOEs in the DRV during the early 1960s (Fforde and Paine 1987).

22. That is, state trade organized by local authorities.

23. The devaluations of the official dong in 1989-90 drastically reduced the level of effective subsidy to the state pharmaceutical sector.

24. Thus, various editions of the textbook *Industrial Economics* issued by the Economics and Planning University, Hanoi, ignored small-scale industry.

25. It is highly possible that many of the measures applied to state industry in 1981 had been tried out earlier in the industrial cooperatives. See CPV (1979a) and Decree No. 134 (1976) in CM (1976). Fforde (ongoing) looks at these issues in greater depth.

26. This passed into law with promulgation of a decree in March 1988, Clause 9 of which stipulated that these activities should not be taxed (CM 1988b).

Tables

TABLE 5.1 Staples Production in Vietnam

Year	Staples Output (million tonnes paddy equivalent)	Population (million)	Output Per Capita (kgs)
1976	13.49	49.16	274
1977	12.62	50.41	250
1978	12.26	51.42	238
1979	13.98	52.46	266
1980	14.41	53.72	268
1981	15.00	54.93	273
1982	16.83	56.17	300
1983	16.99	57.37	296
1984	17.80	58.65	303
1985	18.20	59.87	304
1986	18.38	61.11	301
1987	17.56	62.47	281
1988	19.58	63.73	307
1989	21.51	64.77	332
1990	21.49	66.23	324
1991	21.99	67.77	324
1992	24.21	69.40	349
1993 (est)	25.50	70.98	359

Source: SO 1983:tables 2, 41; SO 1994a:tables 2, 44.

TABLE 5.2 Aggregate Staples Production: Areas and Yields

Year	Sown area (million hectare)	Yield (tonnes per hectare)
1976	6.2	2.2
1977	6.6	1.9
1978	6.8	1.8
1979	6.9	2.0
1980	7.0	2.1
1981	7.0	2.2
1982	7.0	2.4
1983	6.8	2.5
1984	6.8	2.6
1985	6.8	2.7
1986	6.8	2.7
1987	6.7	2.6
1988	7.0	2.8
1989	7.1	3.0
1990	7.1	3.0
1991	7.5	2.9
1992	7.7	3.1
1993 (est)	7.8	3.3

Source: SO 1983a:tables 41,42; SO 1994a:table 44.

TABLE 5.3 Regional Staples Production Performance

A. Red River
Delta

Year	Average Land Yield (tonnes)	Average Land Area (million hectares)	Staples Output Per Head (kgs)
1976	267	0.9	2.7
1977	290	1.0	2.2
1978	289	1.0	2.3
1979	268	1.0	2.3
1980	268	0.9	2.4
1981	318	1.0	2.6
1982	334	1.0	2.9
1983	318	1.0	2.9
1984	300	0.9	2.8
1985	296	0.9	2.8
1986	283	0.9	2.7
1987	309	1.0	2.9
1988	342	1.0	3.1
1989	379	1.0	3.4
1990	321	1.0	3.3
1991	292	1.1	2.8
1992	403	1.1	3.7
1993	456	n/a	n/a

Source: SO:various years.

TABLE 5.3 Regional Staples Production

B. Mekong Delta

Year	Average Land Yield (tonnes)	Average Land Area (million hectares)	Staples Output Per Head (kgs)
1976	454	2.1	2.3
1977	369	1.7	2.0
1978	317	2.1	1.7
1979	411	2.2	2.2
1980	453	2.4	2.3
1981	419	2.4	2.2
1982	499	2.3	2.6
1983	474	2.3	2.6
1984	518	2.3	3.0
1985	512	2.3	3.0
1986	516	2.3	3.1
1987	462	2.2	3.0
1988	535	2.4	3.3
1989	635	2.5	3.6
1990	658	2.7	3.6
1991	700	2.8	3.7
1992	727	3.0	3.7
1993	720	n/a	n/a

Source: SO:various years.

TABLE 5.4 Staples Output Per Head: Ratio of
Mekong Delta over Red River Delta

Year	Ratio (in percent)
1976	51
1977	38
1978	9
1979	42
1980	69
1981	32
1982	49
1983	49
1984	73
1985	73
1986	83
1987	49
1988	56
1989	68
1990	105
1991	140
1992	80
1993	58

Source: SO:various years.

TABLE 5.5 Food Staples Imports: State Procurement and Distribution (million tonnes of paddy equivalent)

Year	Domestic Staples Production	Staples Exports	Staples Imports	State Procurement	State Distribution	Net Current Losses[a]
1976	13.5	0.0	1.0	2.0	2.1	0.9
1980	14.4	0.0	1.4	2.0	2.1	1.3
1985	18.2	0.1	0.6	3.9	3.8	0.6
1988	19.6	0.1	0.7	3.4	3.4	0.6
1989	21.5	2.2	0.3	3.0	2.0	1.8
1990	21.5	2.5	0.3	n/a	1.4	n/a
1991	22.0	1.6	0.4	n/a	1.0	n/a
1992	24.2	3.0	0.4	n/a	0.8	n/a
1993 (est)	25.5	2.6	n/a	n/a	n/a	n/a

[a] Distribution plus exports less imports less procurement.
Source: SO:various years.

TABLE 5.6 Agriculture: Terms of Trade

	1980	1985	1988	1989[a]
Agricultural terms of trade, state procurement				
A. Against agricultural input prices	1	0.9	1.1	
B. Against all retail prices	1	0.9	1.0	0.8
Price index of state procurement	1	13.2	1605	2353
Price index of state staples procurement	1	12.7	1918	2148
Price index of agricultural means of production	1	10.9	1471	
Price index of all retail sales	1	14.2	1580	2782

[a] Note that after 1989 no state procurement was reported.
Source: SO:various years.

TABLE 5.7 Industrial Output Growth: Annual Rates of Growth

		1976-80	*1980-85*	*1985-89*	*1989-93*
Total		0.6	10.0	6.6	10.6
State		-1.5	6.8	6.9	12.8
Of which:	Central	-3.5	4.7	7.6	16.9
	Local	2.9	11.1	5.8	3.9
Small scale industry		3.9	14.9	6.2[a]	6.2
Of which:	Collective	11.0	20.5	-5.9	-25.1
	Individual	-6.8	6.1	18.7	15.8
Means of production	(Group A)	1.1	6.4	5.8[b]	n/a
Consumer goods	(Group B)	-0.6	11.2	7.0[b]	n/a

[a] Called "nonstate" from 1986 onward.
[b] Different source used from rest of column.
Source: SO 1985a:tables 84, 85; SO 1987:tables 82, 83; SO 1992:table 256; SO 1994a:table 17.

TABLE 5.8 Regional Structure of Industrial Output in 1985 (billion 1982 dong)

	Total	*Central*	*Local*	*Nonstate*
All Vietnam	105.3	35.6	23.9	45.8
North and North-center	38.9	18.0	8.7	12.2
Northern mountains and midlands	11.2	7.4	1.8	2.0
Red River Delta	21.7	9.5	5.3	6.9
Old Region 4	5.9	1.1	1.6	3.2
South and South-center	66.5	17.6	15.3	33.6
Central Coastlands	10.1	1.9	1.8	6.4
Central Highlands	2.1	0.4	1.0	0.7
Southeast	38.2	14.1	8.8	15.3
Mekong Delta	16.0	1.2	3.6	11.2

Source: SO 1987:table 88.

TABLE 5.9 Capacity Utilization in Industry: Output Gains and Increases in Installed Capacity in Some Branches of Industry

	1976-80	*1981-85*	*1985-89*
Electricity			
1. Capacity gain (million kWh)	0.116	0.456	1.291
2. Output gain (million kWh)	563.1	1389.9	2718.2
1. / 2.ª x 10,000	2.1	3.3	4.75
Fertiliser			
1. Capacity gain (1,000 tonnes/year)	69.2	275.7	4.7
2. Output gain (1,000 tonnes)	-74.5	171.2	-163.2
1. / 2.	--	1.6	-0.03
Cement			
1. Capacity gain (1,000 tonnes/year)	573.0	2410.4	18.7
2. Output gain (1,000 tonnes)	-110.7	948.9	584.5
1. / 2.	--	2.5	0.03
Fibers			
1. Capacity gain (1,000 tonnes/year)	16.3	33.1	4.7
2. Output gain (1000 tonnes)	-6.2	20.3	5.1
1. / 2.	--	1.6	0.92

ª 1. divided by 2.

Source: SO 1987:tables 89, 117; SO 1989:table 139; SO 1991c:tables 31,

TABLE 5.10 Proportion of Total Inputs Obtained Commercially, 1988

Branch	Percent of Inputs Obtained Commercially
Cigarettes	ca. 60, 100 in some factories
Vegetable oil extraction	ca. 80, 100 in some factories
Soap	ca. 100 (although such inputs as power still come from the state)
Pesticides	ca. 100 (mostly in the form of foreign exchange)
Textiles	ca. 30 to 40
Bicycles	ca. 80 in the South; around 20 in the North
Food processing	ca. 50 (can tend to come from socialist countries so they are supplied to factories by the state)
Beer	ca. 80 in the South

Source: An informed Vietnamese commentator.

TABLE 5.11 Dong to Dollar Exchange Rates 1985 to 1994

Year	Free Market Rate	Official State Rate
1985	70	1.2
1986	261	14
1987	883	107
1988	n/a	135
1989	4,618	3,971
1990	5,595	5,045
1991	9,705	
1992	11,233	
1993	10,659	
1994	10,962	

Source: Personal observation, 1985-88; Institute of Prices and Markets, Hanoi: 1989-94.

Boxes

BOX 5.1 A Conservative Position: The No. 1 Pharmaceutical
Factory, Hanoi.

The No. 1 Pharmaceutical Factory in Hanoi provides an example of
some of the difficulties confronting the issue of industrial reform in
northern Vietnam. Here, as a result of foreign consultancy reports,
information was relatively abundant.

In essence, the problem confronting the sector was one of an apparent
excess of installed capacity compared with the available resources.
Because the factors leading to "investment hunger" had continued, the
authorities submitted requests for foreign assistance in order to further
expand capacity. The rejection of such requests (in this case stemming
from the Ministry of Health, which had long received Swedish assistance) by a foreign consultant (Persson 1987) was the natural response
to the situation:

" . . . the conditions for pharmaceutical production at Factory No. 1
are not satisfactory . . . the premises are so bad that a rehabilitation is
neither technically nor economically justifiable. It cannot be economically and technically justifiable to build a new production unit at
Factory No. 1 when the existing factories are utilized only to 20% of
their capacity. A rationalization of the pharmaceutical industry ... will
in the current situation have to result in a winding up of some of the
existing factories for pharmaceutical production. The factories to be
selected for winding up are of course the factories with the worst standard. Factory No. 1 belongs to these.

In spite of [the Government's policy of self-sufficiency in pharmaceuticals in the north of the country] the construction of a new production
unit for tablets is not recommended as two new pharmaceutical
factories are under construction in Hanoi together contributing about
8,000 sq. m. of production area (Factory No. 2, 5,000 sq. m. and
Union of Pharmaceutical Enterprises, Hanoi, 3000 sq. m.) . . .

During the briefing it was told by the representatives of the Ministry of
Health that the new Factory No. 2 is intended for production of traditional medicine for export and that *the other factory is not under the
control of the Ministry of Health.*" (Persson 1987:16-17, emphasis
added.)

The argument that the other factory was "not under their control" is
revealing, suggesting the persistence of "investment hunger."

BOX 5.2 The Thang Long Paper Enterprise, Ha Son Binh

The Thang Long Paper Enterprise was a locally managed factory belonging to the Red River Delta province of Ha Son Binh, immediately south and west of Hanoi. The proportion of unplanned materials used by the enterprise was expected to rise in the short-term after being stable for the past three years. These "Plan B" and "Plan C" activities reportedly accounted for some 30 percent of output. The enterprise was expecting to start receiving its plan targets from the State Planning Commission either in 1987 or 1988, since it was a key unit. The enterprise had moved over to the new definition of profits as total sales less actual costs. It had no limit on what were described as "supra-norm" loans from the bank but paid 8 percent a month for these compared with 4 percent for "norm" credit. This was felt to be costlier than other sources of funds, so that the enterprise tried not to borrow and instead to use its own capital. Its manager, Dao Cong Hieu, published a strongly critical article during early 1987 in the journal of the Ministry of Light Industry (Dao Cong Hieu 1987). He cited the industrial management decrees of 1986 that had sought to increase the autonomy of enterprises by cutting the number of plan indicators.

The Desire for Production Autonomy: "(These decrees) have been promulgated but in their implementation many enterprises still meet great confusions (*lung tung*) . . . in our own enterprise we put forward proposals to all relevant levels (in line with these decrees) from as early as April 1986, but they have not yet been approved. . . . In the plan, since we were not being supplied with materials needed to produce goods such as cartons, printing paper, writing paper--indeed we had to 'run' for these for ourselves--we proposed that we should only be given a single plan target--"budgetary contributions." But when we received the plan, the superior level not only did not reduce the number of plan targets . . . but actually raised them. Apart from the usual three--the realized value of merchandised output, principle products and budgetary contributions, we also received a target for "the value of total output." As a result, we could not declare that we had met our plan until the 26th December although we had fulfilled the three usual indicators by the 15th . . .

(continued)

BOX 5.2 (cont.)

The Need for Cash: "With regard to raw materials to produce paper--although we were not supplied with any we still have a plan target of 150 tonnes (of paper) that we had to supply to "trade" [i.e., the provincial trading company] . . . this is simply the same as "cooking rice without any rice" (*nau com nhung khong cap gao*) . . . the main raw materials used by the enterprise, such as straw and waste paper, are almost all bought from individuals so that we need around 1 to 1.5 million dong every month; however, the bank does not supply us with all the requisite cash. We have to beg at the bank every day . . . this is being the 'servant of the bank account' rather than the 'master . . . '"

"The products of the enterprise, such as cartons etc. are delivered to central enterprises such as the Rang Dong light-bulb and thermos factory, and the Thang Long and Bac Son cigarette factories. To do so, the enterprise is paid by cheque (literally "through the account") whilst it has to meet very high cash outlays in order to obtain inputs. We propose that . . . part of the output of these customers should be sold to the provincial trading company so that it can sell them for cash and supply that cash through the provincial bank for distribution to the enterprise so that it can buy materials . . . "

The Desire to Market Output at Free Prices: "[The enterprise is capable of producing a great variety of paper products of different sizes, qualities and costs.] We therefore think: in place of the present system of price control the enterprise should be allowed the right to negotiate prices actively with customers."

The Desire to Control Labor Inputs: "With regard to labor there are also many complications. The factory produces many new and complicated commodities that demand high skills and so it cannot simply recruit "children and nephews." But in order to hire labor it has to go through complicated and lengthy procedures with many different levels. We think it should be allowed freedom to recruit and pay workers . . . and not be limited to the value of the wage fund given to it."

Figures

FIGURE 5.1 Pork Procurement
(thousand tonnes live weight)

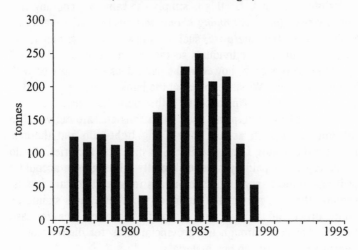

Source: SO 1981, 1983a, 1987, 1988a, 1990c, 1991c.

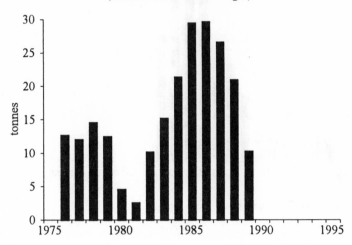

FIGURE 5.2 Beef Procurement
(thousand tonnes live weight)

Source: SO 1981, 1983a, 1987, 1988a, 1990c, 1991c.

FIGURE 5.3 Fish Procurement
(thousand tonnes live weight)

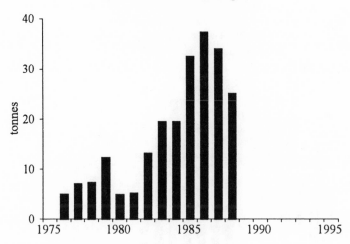

Source: SO 1981, 1983a, 1987, 1988a, 1990c, 1991c.

FIGURE 5.4 Fresh Vegetable Procurement
(thousand tonnes)

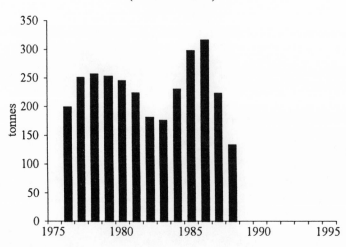

Source: SO 1981, 1983a, 1987, 1988a, 1990c, 1991c.

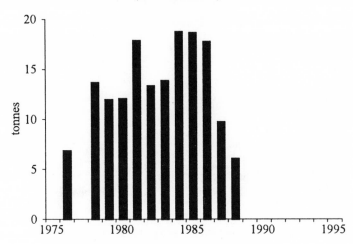

FIGURE 5.5 Tea Procurement
(thousand tonnes)

Source: SO 1981, 1983a, 1987, 1988a, 1990c, 1991c.

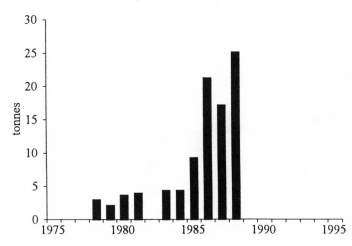

FIGURE 5.6 Coffee Procurement
(thousand tonnes)

Source: SO 1981, 1983a, 1987, 1988a, 1990c, 1991c.

FIGURE 5.7 Monthly Rate of Inflation
and Monthly Interest on Sight Deposits

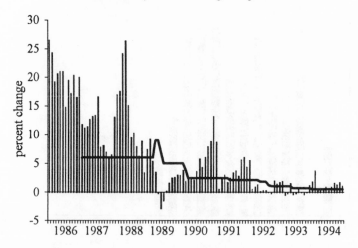

Note: Interest rate is monthly interest paid on private savings deposits.
Source: Institute of Prices and Markets, various years and publications, Hanoi.

FIGURE 5.8 Rural Family Groups
(saving as percentage of income)

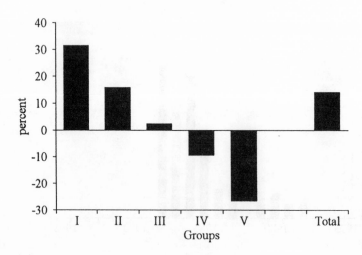

Source: Le Van Toan et al. 1991.

FIGURE 5.9 Rural Family Groups
(savings in US$ per annum)

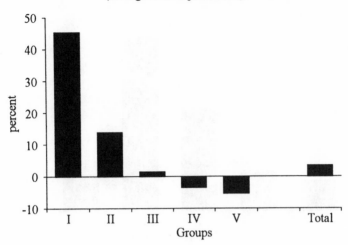

Note: Exchange rate calculated as yearly average of weekly data on free market rates from Institute of Prices and Markets, Hanoi.
Source: Le Van Toan et al. 1991.

FIGURE 5.10 Rural Family Groups
(savings in US$ per annum)

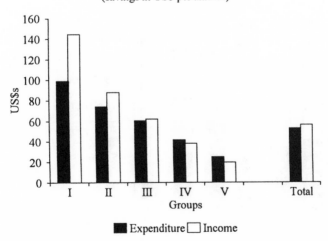

Note: Exchange rate calculated as yearly average of weekly data on free market rates from Institute of Prices and Markets, Hanoi.
Source: Le Van Toan et al. 1991.

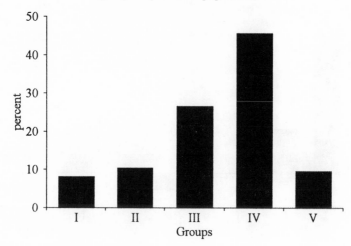

FIGURE 5.11 Rural Family Groups
(groups as percent of population)

Source: Le Van Toan et al. 1991.

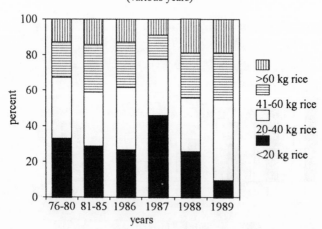

FIGURE 5.12 Rural Incomes Distribution
(various years)

Source: Le Van Toan et al. 1991.

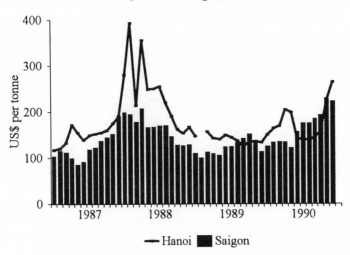

FIGURE 5.13 Retail Rice Price in US$
(Hanoi and Saigon)

— Hanoi ▮ Saigon

Source: Institute of Prices and Markets, various publications and years, Hanoi.

FIGURE 5.14 Hanoi:Saigon Rice Prices
(percent gap)

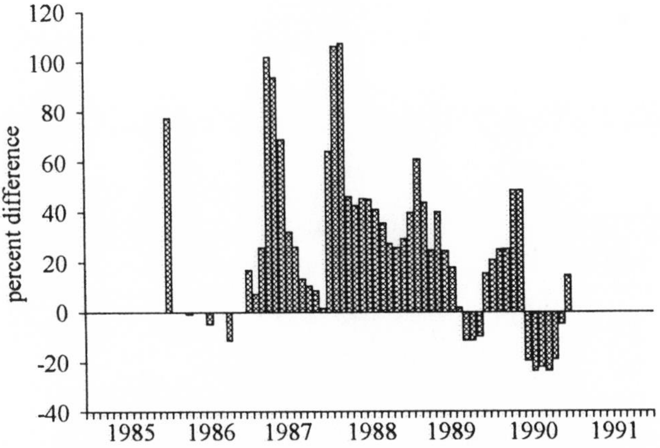

Note: The graph shows the percent premium of Hanoi prices on those in Saigon.
Source: Institute of Prices and Markets, various publications and years, Hanoi.

FIGURE 5.15 The "Break-out" of 1989-90
(growth and the nonstate sector)

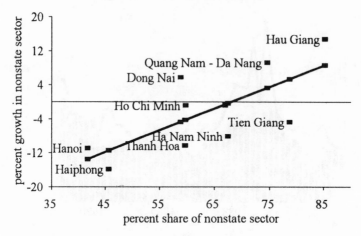

Note: The graph shows, for some provinces, a simple OLS relationship for the nonstate sector between its share in locally managed industry and its real growth in 1989-90.
Source: Personal communication.

6

Social Aspects, Equity, and the New Development Model

Equity issues are of considerable importance, not only for moral reasons but also to maintain some sort of social stability under the great pressures created by rapid economic development. However, although certain ethical values are probably sufficiently universal for two non-Vietnamese to comment on them legitimately, others clearly are not. In the text that follows, we try to balance such considerations.

Equity and Differentiation: The Vietnamese Population Under and After Transition

Markets inevitably imply capital, so for the mass of the Vietnamese population the shift to a market economy meant a shift in the nature of the class relations within which they worked and lived. Initially, state workers appear to have been in a position to share in the rents acquired by their units and used as a basis for the creation of autonomous capital. The position of cooperators in many instances appears to have had a similarly dual nature.

In many ways the DRV state, although certainly weak, had been successfully redistributional in its functions. The resources that were channeled through its institutions (cheap rice and Socialist bloc aid were the most important) were distributed to those to whom it gave priority--state employees, in the main. However, the state also ensured that education and health were rather well supplied to the general population. If it is a mistake to underestimate the commercial acumen of the North, as well as the sheer economic power of the South, it is also wrong to undervalue the developmental impact of the DRV model in social areas. The results, in terms of social welfare, life expectancy, the position of women, and mass education, had pervasive effects long after the model had gone. Similarly, the large investments in human and physical capital that went into building up the rural districts as instruments for socialist construction again had powerful effects, both positive and negative. Non governmental organizations (NGOs) and bilateral rural agencies offering support activities in the late 1980s and early 1990s sought to build upon this potential, and organizations that were strongly opposed to the political assumptions of the Socialist Republic of Vietnam found themselves working closely with the party-state apparatus. This was partly because there was little alternative but also because these organizations seemed to be aiming to meet goals that donors could accept and support.

The varying popular attitudes toward the socialist goals of the DRV state and what happened to these attitudes after 1976 are well beyond the scope of this study. They are also politically highly sensitive issues and not addressed lightly by foreigners. Our subjective assessment is that elements of the DRV program were of considerable attractiveness to large parts of the population, but that bitter experience of the reality of life under that system rapidly led people to change their minds. Support for armed struggle was not simply separated from such considerations; but people could and did change their minds. In some ways, the decade and one-half after 1975 can be seen as one of a series of "rapprochements" (*thich nghi hoa*, in a loose translation) not only between North and South, but also among generations, values and ideas. Perhaps the greatest success of the Vietnamese during this time was to change the dominant social system without spilling blood, despite the violence that preceded reunification and the strong elements of compulsion within the neo-Stalinist program that had been experienced by the population as a whole.

In this chapter we look at two limited areas of great importance to any poor population close to subsistence: the mobilization of resources into education and health, areas that are also important elements of development policy and state activity. The two-sided nature of rural collectives can be seen if it is realized that the collectives were simultaneously channels for surplus mobilization for heavy industrialization and mechanisms for financing education for village children.

The Wider Social Meaning of Collectives in Poor Rural Areas

The economic rationale for supporting strong collective economic organizations is often associated with the problems created by high risk, coupled with the social value attached to welfare services such as education and health. A basic problem facing cooperatives was that they were also part of neo-Stalinism and its Vietnamese expression, the DRV model, and therefore were mechanisms for extracting surplus and enforcing socialist norms. It thus proved hard to prevent their manipulation by unscrupulous local leaders. Such activity came increasingly into the open as the ground was laid in 1988 for Decree No. 10, the herald of decollectivization.

However, the importance of welfare services was, and still is, also closely bound up with the important role played by women in the agricultural labor force. The pattern of migration out of rural areas resulted in family strategies where women remained in the villages while their husbands moved away in search of work. Thus, during the 1980s in many areas in the North, the proportion of women in the rural labor force averaged around 70 percent. These split families, which usually seemed to result from rational economic choices, revealed in part the social costs of the urban and industrial orientation of development policy. Men left to find work; women stayed behind to rear children and farm.

Rural women often depended greatly upon the local collective in order to meet certain of their needs. Educational facilities were a key issue, since without them, it was thought, their children would never be able to "escape" (*thoat ly*). Since they were often living at or near subsistence and at the same time were carrying out heavy farming work, good health services were also important. Furthermore, less tangible inputs to the family economy, such as cultural activities and measures to promote equality between the sexes, or at least reduce inequality, relied upon local administrative-collective structures, of which the cooperatives were an important part. For this reason, it was often argued that it was almost impossible to have adequate farm labor productivity *without* such collective services. Such important issues as the slow reduction in pressure for early marriage, the extension of family planning, and the development of better informal or postformal education all depended upon the local community and local resources, which were dominated by the economic activities of the local cooperatives.

From this perspective, which is not intended to be a defense of the economic inefficiency created by the cooperative system, one consequence of a return to more family-based production might be the following: Weakening the collective would require greater work effort on the part of the female labor force without producing corresponding improvements in their welfare. A small number of families would be able to increase their incomes at the expense of supplies of collective goods, which would then result in a deterioration in the position of women generally.

The solution to this apparent dilemma lay--and lies--in the tolerance of social differentiation within a rural socioeconomic structure that provides welfare services and insurance against risk. This is almost impossible without some sort of local democracy acting as a check on the powers of local cadres, and this in turn depends upon state policies that are supportive of agricultural development. A combination of collective action with encouragement of family-based economic activities appears to be the most likely way of generating sustainable and equitable rural development.

Education: The Overall Picture

The basic successes of the Vietnamese educational system, prior to, during, and immediately after the transition, have already been indicated in Chapter 3. There existed, in a very poor country, the structures of a universal educational framework resulting in rather good indicators, for example, in the number of students and literacy levels. In the North and Center, illiteracy had been almost eradicated, and in the South, much progress had been made, although literacy rates lagged behind the other parts of the country. The most backward areas were the isolated upland regions containing minority groups.

The educational system in Vietnam was divided as follows: primary school (grades 1-9 in the South; in the North, grades 1-8), secondary school (grades 10-12), and vocational and university education. The number of pupils and students in the different educational levels in 1986 is given in Table 6.1.

The dropout rate was appreciably higher in the South and Center than in the North. Altogether, some 70 percent of all children finished eight years of primary school, and 20 percent finished secondary school. Of those who finished secondary school, between 15 and 20 percent went on to either vocational schools or universities. By the end of the 1980s, there were around 300 vocational schools and 100 universities or colleges in the country. In contrast with the situation in many other developing countries, school enrollment rates in primary and secondary levels were almost the same for boys and girls.

Acceptance at higher education institutions was based upon competitive examination. Priority was given to certain applicants, for example, to children from upland areas whose secondary education was assumed to have been lower standard. Compared with the high rate of participation in primary and secondary school, a rather low proportion of schoolchildren continued on to the tertiary level--some 21 per 10,000, compared with 130 per 10,000 in Mongolia and 232 per 10,000 in Cuba, the two other less-developed members of CMEA (Crosnier and Lhomel 1987:27).

Some 3 million children between six months and five years in age attended a kindergarten or preschool, which corresponded to 35 percent of all children of this age. In primary school, the average number of children per teacher was around 50. For the entire primary and secondary school system, there were around 0.5 million teachers.

Around 4 percent of the state budget went to education. Teachers' salaries and textbooks were partly financed through the budget, whereas the construction of the schools was normally the responsibility of the respective communes, or districts. However, local resource mobilization was significant and was a necessary element of the story.

Fiscal Considerations

There were six major sources of revenue for the educational system:

1. State and local government budget,
2. Voluntary contributions from the population, that is, parents,
3. Voluntary contributions from other ministries, state enterprises, and so forth,
4. Proceeds from the sales of production taking place at the school (furniture, textile products, vegetable products, etc.),
5. Donations from international organizations, and
6. Fees.

Prior to the introduction of an official fee system in 1989,[1] the first two of the sources in this list were the most important, whereas the other four played a rather marginal role in most areas.

Adaptations

It was at the local level that the deep-rooted problems surrounding the overall Vietnamese educational system were to be found. The country still essentially modeled its educational system upon the systems of developed countries, with their strong drive for central control of curricula and a reliance on local initiatives only in order to respond to shortcomings in state financing. As central authority weakened and the lack of opportunities within the state became clearer, the question of the direction and value of education at all levels was exposed.

The ethos of the DRV program in education had been appropriate for priorities that aimed to produce citizens ethically and technically qualified to participate in rapid urban-based industrialization. This provided the theoretical underpinning for the Vietnamese educational system. Once this model had been abandoned, a fundamental reexamination of the rationale of the educational system was needed.

As a result, as local initiatives had to factor positively role in providing financing for schools and support for students, there was enormous variation in the quality and nature of educational services. Since teachers--like others on salaries fixed by the state--badly needed additional income, there was considerable scope for obtaining unofficial access to their services at open market prices. This became more important through the 1980s as the fiscal crisis deepened. Two clear examples from the capital, Hanoi, were the ready market in language tuition and the open advertising for revision classes aimed at university students. Other instances of the expansion of the market for educational services were the short-term contracting by enterprises and others (at high fees) of university lecturers in such subjects as industrial management and accounting, and the use of special tutors by parents eager to get their children into a good position for the competitive examinations for entrance at institutions of higher education.

Many teachers had also begun to leave their profession in order to engage in other activities, such as petty business, on a part-time or full-time basis. Or, as formulated by a high official at the Ministry of Education, "Teaching is often the second profession of the teachers." In poorer communes, where rice supplements were inadequate, in closing years of the decade there was a large exodus from schoolteaching.[2]

As a result of these trends, by 1991 it was no longer true that education in Vietnam was free. In the state system, schools had to be supported financially by the pupils' families. This support was organized on an ad hoc basis, supplemented from 1989 by officially sanctioned fees (CM 1989d). Without such extra subsidies, teachers would not be expected to turn up for work. In the rural communes, the cooperatives and the local authorities had to find ways of feeding and housing the teachers, whose positions therefore depended greatly upon the local resources available, the value attached to education by the local community, and the local capacity for organizing ways of supplementing teachers' official incomes.

It appears almost certain that the rural population placed an extremely high value upon education. A commune without schools was almost unheard of. Migration from the poorest delta areas to the Central Highlands and other regions was normally very difficult to organize unless there was a school in the new village. As rural people were confronted rural stagnation and traditionally had great respect for formal learning, their strong desire to enable their children to escape from the countryside was quite understandable.[3] However, these perceptions had tended to introduce bias within the education system against teaching subjects suitable for rural development and toward teaching of things believed suitable for urban state employment. Thus, as the balance of the development effort shifted, a reorientation of local demand for educational services toward a different and more suitable pattern of knowledge might have made it relatively easy to generate the local resources needed to pay for the teachers.

It is striking to consider the real costs involved for a food-deficit commune to provide universal primary education. As has been shown, prior to Decree No. 10, in a typical delta commune of perhaps 5,000 people, unproductive administrative and economic management cadres numbered perhaps over 50 and were seen as unnecessarily burdensome. Yet with over 1,500 schoolchildren, the commune might have been feeding 30 teachers.

Thus, if economic trends of the very late 1980s were to continue, it appeared as though the admirable progress made in basic education in Vietnam would be endangered. Budgetary austerity at both central and local levels was likely to affect education, making it increasingly difficult for the communes and parents to provide their teachers with food. Regional differences in access to, and quality of, education were set to continue to widen in Vietnam's traditionally highly egalitarian basic educational system.

Health

By the end of the 1980s, the most serious health problem in Vietnam was almost certainly lack of adequate food. According to data provided by the Ministry of Health, malnutrition affected, in varying degrees, over 50 percent of children. The estimated daily calorie intake, as found in different surveys of the Nutrition Institute, was around 1,900 kilocalories, which signifies a 20 percent shortage of the recommended level of some 2,300 per head. Furthermore, some 85-90 percent of energy was derived solely from consumption of cereals, mainly rice, while the per capita intake of fat, proteins, and other vital components was far below the minimum standard (Vogel 1987).

Accompanying this were nutritional deficiencies of all kinds, which particularly affected the most vulnerable groups, that is, children, and the poorest people. The data are scarce, and often contradictory, but common symptoms were these: a large percentage of newborn children with a birth weight below the norm of 2,500 grams, a very low average weight gain during pregnancy (8-9 kilos, on average), many mothers with lactating problems and insufficient breast milk, children and adults weighing appreciably less than in countries where nutritional standards were adequate, and so on. A significant proportion of the population had low physical resistance, and childhood malnutrition was responsible for a large number of deaths from diseases like diarrhea, measles, and respiratory infections. These problems were regionally concentrated.

As shown by the data presented earlier, the nutritional situation had not significantly improved since 1975. During the mid-1980s, there were clear indications of a serious food crisis. In the very difficult years in the late 1970s and in early 1988, the Vietnamese government had had to introduce emergency measures in order to prevent starvation and informed the international community that the country was facing a large deficit in the amount of grain required to meet the basic needs of the population.

However, despite the chronic food shortage, indicators show that the health situation in the country improved during the decades after independence. Life expectancy at birth reportedly rose from 42 years in 1960 to 59 years in 1983, and the infant mortality rate declined from 165 per 1,000 live births in 1960 to somewhere between 35 and 64 per thousand in the mid-1980s (infant mortality rate (IMR) data are particularly unreliable, and various official sources give quite different figures).

The Formal Health System

In theory, the Vietnamese health system of the 1980s was impressive. From the central level--the Ministry of Health and affiliated medical institutes--through the provinces, districts, and communes, there was a network of institutions that catered for the population's needs in both preventive and curative health services (Vogel 1987).

The primary health care network was based on communal health care centers. Ideally, there should have existed, in each commune (with approximately 3,000 to 7,000 people) one health Center, with the following staff: one medical doctor, one assistant doctor, one nurse, one midwife, one pharmaceutical worker, and one assistant. This whole staff complement was very rarely available, however, and staff usually only worked part-time.

Although the primary health centers formed the backbone of Vietnam's health system, in actual practice, a strong urban bias existed in the delivery of health services (although probably less pronounced than in most other Third World countries). Thus, although virtually the entire urban population had access to health services, only some 90 percent of the population of rural provinces in the Red River Delta, and 40 percent in the Mekong Delta, were covered by functioning health centers.

Altogether, there were around 10,000 primary health centers in the country. Local authorities were responsible for the supply of medicines and for investments in buildings and equipment, with the communes responsible for--but often unable to manage--financing all salaries of personnel. The national and provincial hospitals (approximately 700) were financed by the central and provincial governments.

Superficially, the Vietnamese health service system had several interesting features that received international recognition. It was, by Third World standards, egalitarian in nature and oriented toward primary health care. Much emphasis was put on preventive measures; the late Ho Chi Minh himself directed large campaigns like the Three Hygienic Measures. The formal structure was, however, highly centralized and far less oriented toward primary health care, in the true sense of the term, than has often been asserted (Vogel 1987). This makes it easier to understand why such a socially valuable sector should have found itself in such difficulties when state finances deteriorated, as they did in the 1980s. As in many other developing countries, it proved to be easier to mobilize local resources for education than for health. As in other areas, the investment bias of the DRV model led to an overexpansion of capacity.

The Vietnamese hospital system often lacked such basic commodities as syringes, serum, blood, and drugs. More strikingly, it lacked the human resources needed to effectively utilize what it did possess--and this despite a major overhang of underpaid and underemployed professional medical staff. Major sacrifices were imposed upon those members of the caring professions who wished to continue to work full-time in the medical services, as their real salaries were steadily reduced to levels inadequate for survival. More often than not, they were forced to take up additional jobs in order to make a living.

The system's problems in generating additional resources from the community also inhibited the development of efficient local medical materials production. The Ministry of Health retained central control over drug factories that were relatively unreformed, and the lack of attention paid to developing the domestic market for equipment also reduced supplies. An additional factor, depressingly familiar from other developing countries, was the effect of exposure to modern technology, often provided by aid donors, upon central authorities' demands for medical equipment. As elsewhere, compounded by the underlying "modernizing" ethos of the DRV program, this also inhibited development of domestic suppliers of effective, low-technology resources that the country could afford.

As a result, it appears that top policymakers often felt that increased expenditure on health services was simply too expensive; material production had the first priority. One off-the-cuff example provided by a Vietnamese commentator, was that of the choice between investing in a hectare of coffee or in a hospital bed. The lack of basic development in the rural areas meant that this was both the inevitable and the incorrect comparison to make. We agree fully with the opinion of Vietnamese researchers who studied the conditions of women, concuding that women made up the majority of the agricultural labor force and would make or break the policy of priority being given to food production. Attention to mass health services, viewed in terms of prevention and community-based care, would thus have a high impact on labor productivity in the long term. Health serviceswould have to operate through the local community in order to be cost effective and implementable. Reliance on the overcentralized structures of the DRV model, to a large extent fueled by foreign aid, meant that when resource constraints were met there was no formal system for mobilizing resources at the grassroots level.

Adaptations

Strategies designed to secure local resources for health service provision contrasted strongly with education. Whereas it was almost unknown for a commune not to have schools, empty and inactive health stations were depressingly familiar. This reflected the lack of a clear means of expressing and articulating the value of health services to the local community, which had, as in the case of education, to find the resources-- above all food--to pay the personnel involved. To view the question as simply one of getting more resources out of central government was naive and ignored the major lesson of the failure of the DRV model; local resources were typically the major constraint upon implementation of any given project, whether industrial investment or anything else. This was especially true in the area of local health.

Experience from many other countries suggested that there were many relatively cheap ways of improving community health. What was striking, therefore, was the lack of success of the Vietnamese national health system in coping with the gathering problems of the 1980s. This failure is only understandable in terms of a reevaluation of the real nature of the primary health care content of the DRV system (Vogel 1987), and its lack of attention to creating local finance through generating local demand for such services.

Towards the end of the 1980s, the spontaneous adaptation of the system was therefore taking the following directions:

1. Defensive bureaucratic response by the Center of the state system, often based upon access to foreign resources, aimed at defending such institutions as its own production centers, high-technology installations such as hospitals and research centers. User charges at hospitals were introduced in 1989 (CM 1989e).
2. Simple abandonment by the local population in many areas of the peripheral structures of the centralized health system. Local dispensaries were ignored, and health services became a combination of privatized access for cash on the part of the better off, with acute problems attended to at the remaining regional clinics and hospitals. Since medicines were often unavailable through the official network, many people turned to the parallel market for drugs, without bothering to try to get a physician's prescription.
3. Local defense and support of services viewed as having high social value (child delivery was one possible example) heavily constrained by lack of knowledge of the potential for high cost-benefit spending in certain areas, such as simple mother and child care.
4. Decentralized, discriminating support for selective health services for particular groups, such as support by profitable economic units for hospitals in their area that could supply acute services to their workers. Certain provinces were starting to initiate their own reforms, often in sharp conflict with central government.
5. Extremely patchy and limited development of Vietnamese pharmaceuticals and medical equipment production, inhibited by the defensive strategies of the central medical authorities. This meant that medical authorities were not well placed to meet local demand coming from the more advanced local communities and better-off local hospitals.

Policy Measures of the Late 1980s

By 1988-89 this evolving picture was reasonably clear. It was then influenced, in 1989-90, by a number of important policy decisions. Both Vietnamese policymakers and foreign aid donors needed to take great care in assessing any plan for restructuring the health service system in order to meet new circumstances. The Vietnamese primary health care network had certain deep-rooted shortcomings that prevented the country from developing and changing it rapidly in response to changed conditions. The strength of local financing abilities, revealed clearly in the educational sectors, was not exploited in the case of health. Despite this, the fact that there was a well-educated population and the need for better labor productivity in agriculture suggests that the opportunity was there for creation of a more effective and socially profitable health system.

Continued support for the unreformed DRV model of centralized control and high-tech medical facilities would only inhibit this process.

Implications for the 1990s

The Role of the State and Notions of Social Justice

Three main elements stand out from the experiences of the 1980s:

- First, the strong popular and governmental commitment to mass health and education.
- Second, the complicated and proactive way in which resources were mobilized to meet the demand for such services.
- Third, the frequently bottom-up nature of initiatives in this area, as in others. In many instances a process could be observed within which local state apparatuses responded to opportunities and ideas rising from below, sometimes in contradiction with central government prescription.

A general observation that follows from this is that under favorable conditions production of "public goods" in Vietnam is remarkably easy. The role of the state is sufficiently malleable and porous for the strong underlying popular notions of social justice and personal advantage to find expression. The key issue--as yet far from well understood--is what characterizes favorable conditions.

This suggests that through the 1990s similar patterns will pertain. In areas where there are strong popular sentiments and it is (for whatever reason) possible to organize effectively, public goods and other services will become available. It is unlikely that these will be the result of top-down initiatives, but sympathetic responses at the local or even central level will be necessary.

Socialism Viewed as Redistribution

Robert Wade has suggested (as a passing remark) that in the 1990s, whereas most of the East Asian NICs found themselves confronting the need to change their state structures from essentially accumulatory to redistributional in function, for Vietnam the process was the other way around. This is an idea worth pursuing.

It is certainly true that strong elements of neo-Stalinism were, from the point of view of state workers, cadres, and others, highly redistributional in nature. The presence of the socialist bloc aid programs, combined with the administrative distributional functions of the central-planning system, gave the state extensive resources for allocation to priority areas. The softening (*mem hoa*) of the rigors of the pure model when applied in Vietnam, resulting in the DRV and transitional models, gave this another twist, for low price resources provided an important source of economic rents to finance the development of autonomous capitals.

It is also true that, in comparison, for example, with North Korea, Vietnamese central planning was, in some senses of the word, hardly serious. At crucial points (the early 1960s, the late 1970s) the Vietnamese leaders turned away from the violent logic inherent in the neo-Stalinist program, refusing (or unable) to shed the blood needed to curb the development of the free market. This tolerance of autonomous activity led directly to the DRV model and the 1980s hybrid system, which were both, according to ideologues, doctrinally unacceptable. Hanoi, in this sense, never pushed to the extreme required for the state it governed to be accumulatory in the centrally planned sense. That this was understood by the population perhaps helps to explain the tolerance of the slow pace of transition to a market economy. Still, the strength of the security apparatus, especially in the South, is not to be denied.

In the 1990s, with a far different economic system, what would it mean for the Vietnamese state to become accumulatory? Such a reorientation would presumably require relative support for capital in its relations with labor and stress upon other measures designed to harness national resources to the task of rapid growth and development. However, time will tell whether this is a fair reflection of the dominant political choices facing the Vietnamese leadership in the early 1990s. Certainly, as discussed later on, fear of suffering the same fate as the Soviet bloc encouraged caution and economic success as a means of cementing support. Regime survival was perhaps only to be ensured by having as much redistribution as possible within the overall accumulatory strategy.

Notes

1. Fees were first legally permitted by Decision No. 45 of the Council of Ministers, "on recovery of a part of medical hospital fees," 24 April 1989.

2. Although the district was in principle responsible for paying teachers' salaries, in practice the local commune usually had to make up the frequent shortfalls.

3. Regional differences were marked in this area and levels of nonmatriculation and nonattendance were differing markedly among different parts of the country by the end of the decade. See Table 6.1.

Tables

TABLE 6.1 School Attendance in Vietnam 1986: Number of Children in
Each Grade

Grade	North Vietnam	Rest of the Country	Total
Primary school			
1	1,036,000	1,294,000	2,330,000
2	852,000	931,000	1,783,000
3	771,000	760,000	1,532,000
4	692,000	652,000	1,344,000
5	593,000	540,000	1,134,000
6	635,000	524,000	1,160,000
7	527,000	414,000	942,000
8	448,000	343,000	792,000
Secondary school			
10	200,000	137,000	338,000
11	177,000	103,000	280,000
12	152,000	80,000	233,000

Source: Ministry of Education, 1987:direct communication.

7

Accumulation, Savings, and Market Development: Processes of Change Reconsidered

As argued earlier in this study, after 1989 the Vietnamese economy is best analyzed as a market economy, that is, after the abolition of the "two price system" and the dismantling of the system of central planning based on state allocations of inputs and obligatory production targets for the individual enterprises. The year 1989 signified the entrance into the post-stage in the process of transition (see Chapter 1). The vast majority of transactions were now voluntary in character, and except for a very limited number of products--electricity, petroleum, housing, and a few others--prices were established in accordance with supply and demand. Farmers were, on the whole, largely free to decide what to produce and how to dispose of it. Still, there were many salient features that clearly distinguished Vietnam in the early 1990s from an ordinary market economy--and even more so from an *efficient* market economy. The main purpose of this chapter is to discuss some of these differences, with a view to examining prerequisites for the emergence and development of efficient markets.

Events and Issues in 1989-94

Although the post-1989 Vietnamese economy, we argue, was a market economy, its most important characteristic was the nature of the economic processes that determined the allocation of factors of production--land, labor, and capital. These processes were not recognizably similar to those in most other market economies. Through the early and mid-1990s the rapid emergence of institutionalized and "normal" factor markets occurred, paralleling a steep rise in domestic savings levels. A second major issue of transition was the nature and role played by the state. This was related to the emergence of factor markets and the nature of accumulation processes: What institutional forms would emerge? What would happen to the relationship between SOEs and the state? And what role would the state play in supporting accumulation processes as it moved away from its distributional functions; in this respect East Asia offered fertile ground for comparison, helped by the large levels of FDI that started to come in during the early 1990s.[1]

Figure 3.2 shows the outstanding growth performance, 1989-93. GDP increased in 1994 by around 8 percent or more. This shows very little of the recessionary "J-curve-effect" experienced in many other transitional economies, with absolute falls in output. This was mainly because--as we argue--Vietnam post-1989 was not a transitional economy. It should also be recalled that Vietnam lost around US$1 billion in Soviet bloc aid in the period 1988-90. The micro response to the macro changes of 1989 was predictably that of a market economy, with rapid increases in output as market access improved radically with the opening of the borders and shifts in inflationary expectations and general confidence. The detailed year-by-year history of the period is complicated, not least because of the political conflicts associated with the attempt to recentralize authority and focus upon state rather than party power as part of the Rule by Law (*nha nuoc phap quyen*) project. This will not be dealt with here, as justice cannot be done to it in the space available. Also, the situation in the mid-1990s was still far from clear.[2]

After 1989, there followed a period of rather rapid growth of around 7-8 percent annually. This was accompanied by an increase and then a decline in the rate of inflation; fiscal payments and the balance of payments followed a contrary path, improving until 1991 and then deteriorating. Figure 5.7 shows the rate of inflation and the rate of interest paid on sight savings deposits. Until the interest rate reforms of 1992, real interest rates in the state banking system were not only negative, but lending rates were lower than borrowing rates. As Vietnam prepared for the resumption of IMF, World Bank, and Asian Development Bank lending in 1994 (and digested the impact of the end of the U.S. embargo in early 1994), prices were stable, as was the exchange rate, but the fiscal and current account positions were deteriorating fast, as shown in Table 7.1. After the interest rate reforms of 1992, the macro economy was, in terms of its main macro prices, rather undistorted: there were single prices for

U.S. dollars, and labor was generally paid its market price (but see the further discussion later on). A major source of economic rents was land, which, especially in urban areas, rose rapidly in value, until by the mid-1990s prices were comparable to or higher than those in other regional centers. Large areas of urban land were under state control and so conferred substantial returns upon those who could gain access to them. FDI joint ventures were mainly with SOEs, whose main capital input was land. By 1994, FDI was coming in at rates reported at over US$1 billion annually. At the same time, as Figure 3.18 shows, exports rocketed.

However, the detailed pattern of growth through and immediately after 1989 was, on the surface, rather strange: The state sector grew relative to other sectors, as did heavy industry relative to light industry (see Table 7.2). State industry increased its share of reported industrial output. We believe that these figures masked a pattern in which mobile commercial capital (of various types) was simply moving into areas where rents were highest and transactions costs associated with corrupt state regulation lowest--around 1989-92, this was the state sector. However, from 1993 on, the private sector as measured started to grow far faster. This was almost certainly helped by other factors, such as the earnings made by private individuals in trade and then property and also the growing trust in the policy statements made by the Communist Party.

The tendency toward urban and industrial focus in the growth pattern, supported by state activities, was clear. The November 1993 Donor's Conference project priorities showed this, as they demanded very little stress upon rural development.[3] The Inter-Congress Party Conference of January 1994 called for industrialization and modernization of the economy, as well as for the continued implementation of the program of Rule by Law and state administrative reform.

Agriculture, however, despite this relative neglect, showed rather rapid growth of between 2 and 4 percent per capita. This growth was concentrated in areas closest to markets, and in central coastal Vietnam and the northern mountainous areas output stagnated (see Table 7.2).[4] However, the various studies made of income distribution and poverty showed that the market economy and the various consequences of Decree No. 10 were helping large numbers of farming families to move out of poverty.[5]

As a working hypothesis, given the events in Eastern Europe and the Soviet Union, it is useful to note that maintenance of macro stability was probably associated with regime survival: Bank failures and inflation could perhaps have initiated uncontrollable popular unrest and demonstrations. However, within the regime political economy, considerations argued for the maintenance of economic rents, within limits set by goals of economic growth and economic efficiency. From this perspective, the gathering issues of corruption in the early 1990s have to be examined in the context of the fine balance sought and attained in 1990-92, when interest rate distortions and tax breaks were sufficient to enable the state sector to emerge as a powerful economic force in the new Vietnamese market economy, though not at such high levels that overall macro economic stability was threatened. This development should also be viewed in the context of technical issues, such as the creation of the treasury and a more effective tax system.[6]

Foreign Comments on the Vietnamese Transition to a Market Economy: An Overview

This section presents a rapid overview of what is a quickly growing literature. In performing such an exercise the authors can only try to extract what we see as the key elements of the studies reviewed, applying the same ideas used in this book to examine the Vietnamese transition. We can thus see how some recent foreign work on Vietnam, especially by economists, may be criticized for ignoring the study of the Vietnamese economy itself in favor of focusing on government and party policy, in other words, focusing on reform. Most studies take a top-down approach, using the assumption that state activities are key and central to change in Vietnam.

In particular, the meaning of the events of 1989 is of importance in the different interpretations. These interpretaitons are typified in statements made by people who have been highly active in the delivery of policy advice to the governments of countries moving away from central planning. Brian Van Arkadie, for example, sees Vietnam in 1989 as possessing an economy that had already been undergoing important change: "By 1989 the situation was such that . . . the economy was already capable of a much more flexible response to market opportunities than the highly bureaucratized and centralized Soviet system" (Van Arkadie 1993:437).

This view is of particular interest in that the author was an important source of advice on the management of the transition to a market economy in Vietnam. His opinion, however, is diametrically opposed to that of Jeffrey Sachs and Wing Thye Woo: "Vietnam, which is an overwhelmingly peasant economy like China, raised its growth rate by 4 percentage points in 1989 when it instituted big-bang-style microeconomic liberalization and macroeconomic stabilization" (Sachs and Woo 1994:274).

This juxtaposition highlights the importance of the question whether reform should be viewed as process or as government program. Had the economy had time to adapt prior to 1989, thus explaining the success of that year, or was it all to do with "big-bang style" measures taken then? Although Sachs and Woo present little evidence to support their assertion and the accompanying article by David Dollar (1994) also does not do so either, such judgments complement a policy focus.[7]

Most economists, although with some important exceptions,[8] take this position, and they are supported by influential political scientists who also put the state and party in a central explanatory role. There may be philosophical underpinnings to this. Gareth Porter (1993), for example, utilizes the notion of "authoritarianism" as a key explanatory tool. This is counterpoised with "liberalism" as a primary theme of the book (p. xiv); and the notion of an antidemocratic authoritarian political structure is "linked inextricably" to the Socialist Republic's "economic and social crisis" (p. xiv). Porter makes an association between "political structure" and the world of Vietnamese farmers and urban dwellers through the idea that Vietnam since 1986 has been undergoing an "unprecedented process of economic and political change," but he argues that it is the top party leaders' lack of accountability that has slowed and blunted the regime's policy response to socioeconomic crises (p. xv).

Yet if Vietnamese society is viewed as passive *prior* to the changes of 1989-90, subsequently Porter easily admits to the existence of "powerful domestic and international forces beyond the power of the SRV regime to control or direct" (p. xv). And this is related to the opening up of the economy and society to the outside world. Within a view that sees Marxism-Leninism as powerful and "strong," when working through the traditional economic system, it is thus natural to conclude that the regime in the 1990s is now "notably weaker . . . than it was earlier in its history" (p. xvi).[9] Again, this focus upon formal structures and the idea that the regime has been weakened by the shift to a market economy lead to a view that it is the official sanctioning (or not) of extraparty political participation that is central to an examination of political participation (Porter 1993:chapter 6). However, although informal activities are brought into the analysis, they come in as a resistance to policy implementation and through "creat[ion of] socioeconomic realities to which the state must adjust" (p. 152). Again there is the polarization between an active and repressive "state"--authoritarianism--and a reactive "society," to which implicitly only a democratic liberalism can grant an active role. This approach thus reinforces the top-down view of the majority of economists writing on Vietnam, for in the continued absence of such a liberalism it is implicit in the argument that "policy is king." The contrast with the intentions (if not the reality) of the present study should be clear. The task of "bringing society back in" has naturally been attempted on the Left. By the mid-1990s the two main contributions from the Left were

Gabriel Kolko (1995) and Gerard Greenfield (1993). Both of these analysts focus squarely on the internal politics of the party and state and their relationships with other elements of Vietnamese society. Neither has much time for treatments that ignore the material interests of those in power; neither has much good to say about what happened in Vietnam during the first half of the 1990s. Kolko takes this to the point of putting into play the idea that in some sense the Vietnamese political leadership has betrayed not only those Westerners who supported the anti-U.S. struggle but also large parts of the Vietnamese population--"The war was won, but the peace is quickly being lost" (Kolko 1995:3). Interestingly, Kolko argues that "few if any of Communist Vietnam's economic policies from 1955 to 1975 differed in principle from what nations normally do when locked in mortal conflicts" (p. 9). The reader could consider whether the various institutions of neo-Stalinism--agricultural producer cooperatives, nationalization of modern large-scale industry, and the particular distributional and exchange implications of central planning--really do not differ in essence from what happened elsewhere, for example in the United States and Britain during World War II. In our opinion, Vietnamese history since 1975 and the way in which the transition to the market (as we term it) took place cannot be divorced from the realities of neo-Stalinism and the DRV model (in our terminology). Kolko's position is not uncommon; it has to be considered in view of Vietnamese arguments about the absence of cooperatives and other elements of the DRV model during the successful anti-French struggle, and also, in our opinion, it needs to address the political and economic events of the early 1960s, when the political compromises of the DRV model were worked out. Phan Van Tiem (1990) perhaps presents one of the clearest views that in the closing years of the First FYP (1961-65) the basic elements of the post-1976 battleground were laid out in the open. These are, however, historical questions.[10] Kolko and Greenfield present a refreshing alternative to the reform-oriented approach of the majority of foreign writers on the topic. When these writings of the majority are critical, criticism is posed in terms largely of the failures of government and politicians. The approach is deeply top-down in its philosophy of the nature of change and its causes, as will be seen.

Top-down assumptions about the nature of change seem to go well with interpretations of events in terms of rapid and rather discontinuous change: big-bang reforms are seen to have taken place in Vietnam. Dwight Perkins, at the influential Harvard Institute of International Development, has this view: "[B]oth Vietnam and Laos have chosen what amounts to an across-the-board, big bang approach" (1993:9). This is colored, however, by an admission that the reasons for the policy changes are "not obvious" (p. 2). In the same volume, Adam Fforde (1993) advances the concept of the "state business interest" as a way of explaining the effects upon the Vietnamese political economy of the processes of change in 1979-80 and the introduction of the Three Plan System in early 1981.

In the same volume, Dollar (1993) points to some fundamental questions. In examining the 1989 stabilization program, he points out that there were two good reasons to be skeptical about the efficacy of the 1989 measures: first, that "these tools do not necessarily have the same effect in a socialist economy as in a market economy" and, second, that the measures lacked external support (p. 211). Yet Dollar's main explanation for the resurgence of inflation in 1990-91 is the market economy, the lack of fiscal control. It can be noted that this begs the question why such control was lacking, but it is still pertinent to ask whether the "unusual" success of the 1989 measures would not lead to the conclusion that by 1989 Vietnam *was not a normal socialist economy*. We argue in this study that this was in fact the case: Micro level adaptation and the reduction of plan distortion had by 1989 prepared the Vietnamese economy for a shift to generalized market-based exchange without too much upheaval. Indeed, much of Dollar's informative analysis of the monetary processes that occurred in 1989 (pp. 212-216) is a story of events in a market economy, *not a socialist one*. Dollar further developed his ideas in his 1994 work. Again, in our view, he successfully straddled the fence, arguing (p. 374) that because of the favorable basic endowments in Vietnam, "the good policy introduced in 1989 engendered an immediate supply response."[11] If Dollar, with an implicitly historical sensitivity, thus sidesteps the big-bang version of events, David Dapice (1993) has little to say about the nature of Vietnamese commerce "at the starting point." There is little in Dapice about the micro level histories of emergent capital and capitalists and their associated macro institutions that would be the point of departure for the increasing involvement of Vietnamese business in the international economy during the early 1990s.[12] Adrian Wood (1989), the author of a very early paper, agrees with Dollar in painting a picture of a "nearly post-transitional economy" circa 1988, especially regarding the state of the banking sector and the implications for the existence of informal capital markets (pp. 568-570, on the political economy of 1989).

The work of the great majority of economists writing on Vietnam, however, maintains the basic duality inherent in "policy analysis," where the focus is on state and party actions, or both, as the central origin of change. This is consistent with both the political science view exemplified by Porter[13] and the leftist position of Kolko.

Nick Freeman (1994) sees reform as the motor of change, dating from the Sixth Party Congress (p. 76). His comments on the differences between Chinese and Vietnamese experience of FDI (pp. 76-89) are perceptive. They arguably show a *less* policy-driven approach in Vietnam, where the stress on exports rather than the domestic market joined in a more natural sequence of events to permit a far more rapid growth of FDI if measured as a share of GDP.

A view that attempts to bring policy and the role of the state back into the analysis, to "endogenize" it, can be seen in Grzegorz Kolodko (1990). He conceptualizes "post-socialist economies" and thus places stabilization programs in a "broader context of systemic conditions and transformations" (p.10). He sees the situation in Vietnam at the end of the 1980s as one where the basic goal of the regime was to maintain itself in power through a market-oriented reform (pp. 11-12). Again, like Dollar, he believes that the stabilization measures of 1989 were close to IMF orthodoxy--with a strong reliance upon monetary measures. Writing with colleagues several years later, he observes elsewhere that there was little or no fiscal tightening in 1989 (Kolodko, Gotz-Kozierkiewicz, Skrzeszewska-Paczek 1992:129).

However, many writers place an orthodox stress upon "reform." Among them are James Riedel (1993), Ian Jeffries (1993), Markus Diehl (1993), Marie-Agnes Crosnier and Edith Lhomel (1990), Per Ronnas and Orjan Sjoberg (1990a and 1990b), Vo Nhan Tri and Ann Booth (1992). These writers, however, choose this focus consistently, taking the reality of policy measures as given and then examining their impact and associated problems. A good example is Jozef Van Brabant (1990), who talks about "Vietnam . . . reforming itself ever since political reunification in mid-1976" (p. 210). However, in section 2 (pp. 212-216), he describes the "protracted reform experience since 1979" (p. 212) almost entirely in terms of policy, viewing Vietnam as being reformed by changes in policy. Thus, he argues that "the core dilemma of the reform movement in Vietnam . . . revolves around central control and macro-economic coordination." (p. 223). Granted that the planning mechanism was removed without being replaced by an equivalent, it follows that "marked change . . . can emerge only through gradual changes in economic structures with the purpose of cushioning palpable socio-economic costs. . . . (T)he speed of this adjustment is a policy variable" (p. 224). It is hard to see how Vietnamese reality reveals that those who formulated policy in any sense controlled the pace of adjustment so that its pace could be described (for example, like tax rates) as a "policy variable." This is not to argue that important factions of the "elite" were ignorant of the processes going on around them and thus affected the pace of change. The actions of the state, we argue, influenced and were influenced by the pace of change, but they did not control it. In any case, Van Brabant remains consistent in his analysis, within which society and the economy are at root *reactive* to policy change, which therefore, as in many other studies, is the main source of change.

Apart from David Dollar's work already mentioned, a number of papers came from the professional staff of the Bretton Woods institutions. Two such are authored by Zdenek Drabek (1990) and Gabrielle Lipworth and Erich Spitaller (1993). Lipworth and Spitaller assert that the policy measures of 1989 are "a bold and comprehensive program of structural reform" (p. iii). They therefore logically seek an explanation of the quick supply response in 1989-90 in the macro structure of production (p. iii). This can be compared with the analysis here which looks instead at the processes of micro adaptation under the transitional model and the reduction of plan distortion. Interestingly, this leads Lipworth and Spitaller to ignore the growth of informal capital markets during the early 1990s out of the commercialization processes of the 1980s, focusing their discussion of finance solely upon formal structures, that is, banks, and so on. Yet the rapid growth of domestic savings rates in the early 1990s appears to have bypassed formal financial systems, fueled instead by other intermediations. Drabek (1990) attempts to examine the pre-1989 period in terms of the failed reform during 1986-89, which is largely attributed to macroeconomic management shortcomings. This has an interesting historical echo, for it could also be argued that the period prior to 1986 had already gone through adequate microlevel adaptation and macro reduction in plan distortion for an easy shift to generalized market-based exchange in 1985-86. In other words, from an economic point of view "1989 was possible in 1985." This view is not uncommon in Vietnam, and if pressed, we would probably agree with it.

Danny Leipziger (1992) takes the position that Vietnam "embarked on an ambitious program of economic transformation, beginning in 1989 with widespread price, exchange rate, and interest rate reform coupled with a cutting loose of state enterprises from fiscal subsidy" (p. iii). The argument is put strongly *against* possible suggestions that earlier changes had been positive: "[T]he Vietnamese reforms of 1989-91 followed an earlier half-hearted attempt at reform, which was largely unsuccessful, except perhaps for the fact that it may have whetted the appetite of the reform-minded" (p. iii). The paper reveals clearly the policy focus and the confidence of that time and place.[14] The subsequent evolution of the bank's public thinking can easily be seen from its published reports (see reference list).

Among political scientists, William Turley (1993) takes a more intermediate position on the top-down issue. He argues that "[w]hile economic renovation had certain spontaneous features, on the political side it was initiated entirely within the party, on approval from the top" (p. 333). A similar but more nuanced position was taken by Borje Ljunggren in various writings (e.g., Ljunggren 1993a). Carlyle Thayer, one of the best-informed Western political scientists working on Vietnam, takes a thoroughgoing empiricist standpoint. Lacking access to information on the precise pressures upon politicians and political decisionmaking, he has shifted from a collegial characterization of Politburo activities to viewing them increasingly as a "regularization" of politics, with social constituencies playing important roles and politicians' strategies designed to create and strengthen support (see various works cited by Thayer in the reference list). Porter also addresses some of these issues.

As analysts grew closer to what they were writing about, in terms of contacts and time, so the top-down perspective eased. Ronnas' (1992), excellent and early empirical study of emerging commerce is a good example. Another is by Raymond Mallon (1993 and 1992 (?). N.d.), refers to "grassroots moves (in the early 1980s) toward the use of market mechanisms interact[ing] with policy concessions and periodic clamp-downs" (1992 (?). N.d.:2).[15] Mallon concludes that "Vietnam has shown that a gradual shift from a centrally planned economy to a more market oriented economy can work" (p. 17). In his conclusions (pp. 17-19), he is well aware of process and uncertainty: "With the advantage of hindsight, it would have been preferable to have had a clear idea as to what sort of economic system would evolve at the end of the reform process . . . However, even if decisionmakers had a clear vision . . . the very enunciation of that vision could have reduced the likelihood of the reform process succeeding" (p. 19).[16] This is a conclusion, although certainly vague, with which the present authors have great sympathy.

Thus, if a trend can be seen away from the overly hasty conclusions and policy recommendations that follow from a natural but excessive reliance upon prior assumptions, there is still considerable scope for debate about specificities. One here is the timing of sequencing of change. For example, Arkadie (1993:440-441) views SOE reform as having been *less* successful than agricultural reform, as does Ljunggren (1991:394). A comparison with Prabhu Pingali and Vo Tong Xuan (1992) shows that it is very important to distinguish between the changes of the early and mid-1980s, when SOE "reform" was arguably more effective than Order No. 100 and events post-1988. Arkadie (like Mallon) was also personally very close to the difficulties posed by SOEs during the early 1990s.

Conclusions

This rapid review of the emerging literature on the transition to a market economy in Vietnam reveals an expected structure. In our opinion, the weaknesses of the literature reflect wider issues: the focus upon policy rather than economy, the willingness to make assertions based on strong prior assumptions and theories rather than on a reasonable analysis of Vietnamese reality, and the lack of basic theoretical rethinking in order to confront the novel nature of what was happening in Vietnam. After all, it is not common that countries undergo such changes.

To be even more critical, we believe that big-bang metaphors are meaningless when applied to Vietnam: For example, the supply and other economic responses to the policy changes of 1989 make no sense without some understanding of the history of the 1980s and the nature of the DRV model in the way we discuss it. We also believe that the normal policy focus of much modern economics falls into a trap when it is applied to Vietnam, for it appears that the pattern of events was so heavily influenced by the evolving interest group patterns and the power of the state so limited and circumscribed that the question of policy implementability has always to be borne in mind. And if policy was not necessarily implementable and *"politics (as ever) was the art of the possible,"* then pragmatic rather than dogmatic policy advice is likely to be recorded by history as having been the most valuable.[17] Finally, for economists, we suggest that the single greatest risk involved in confronting transitional economies is the possible failure to reexamine and reformulate notions of microeconomic behavior--the micro foundations upon which any macroeconomic judgments have to rest.

The Meaning of "Commercialization": The Role of the State

In the literature dealing with the transition from central planning to other economic systems in Eastern Europe, the term "marketization" is usually preferred to "commercialization." The two concepts are sometimes used synonymously; in our opinion, however, the latter is more relevant to analyzing the transition process in Vietnam (or at least, the stage that ended in 1989). By commercialization, we mean the following: the replacement of the direct and compulsory methods of input and output allocation through a central plan by the voluntary and decentralized interactions of individual agents (households, enterprises, etc.). A development of factor markets--markets for land, labor, and capital--is not a necessary condition for an economy to be commercialized in this sense, although nonexistent or poorly functioning capital markets and an absence of private property over the major means of production would prevent the economy both from becoming marketized in the full sense of the word and, thus, of course, from becoming a *capitalist* economy.

It is striking that the most powerful and significant reforms in the transition period--25-CP (1981), on the Three Plan System, and CT-100 (1981) and NQ-10 (1988) on internal cooperative management and farmer family economic rights--were essentially "micro" in their focus. Indeed, at least in the case of agriculture, these reforms were associated with statements of intent to reprioritize state activities to support the sector, which in practice was not implemented. This suggests a pattern of change within which micro initiatives, combining autonomous forces with policy shifts, subsequently impacted at the macro and national policy levels in various ways.

One of the key questions confronting the Vietnamese after 1989, therefore, was what would happen to state property. As we have seen, on the eve of full-scale commercialization, policy toward SOEs had still not addressed this issue, preferring instead to enhance the independence of SOEs,, reduce the number of plan targets, and so on. However, as we have argued, relatively autonomous capital had to have arisen to act as the prerequisite for stable commercialized (e.g., market) transactions in goods and services. The question, therefore, was how this capital would evolve and whether and in what manner the issue of a transition to a capitalist system, in the analytical sense, would be solved.

Similar issues arose in the context of rural development. The persistence of high distributional margins pointed to the continued existence of entry barriers. In some areas, these could be attributed to the interaction between local *nomenklatura* and commercialized SOEs. In others, local monopoly reflected the absence of strong state intervention to ensure markets that operated well.

Limits Imposed by the Nature of the Post-1989 Vietnamese Market Economy

Unclear Status of SOEs: Problems of Ownership, Accountability, and Conflicting Goals

In 1990-91, the state was still the dominant owner of the means of production within industry. The nonstate share of industrial production was estimated at 23 percent, while that of retail trade had increased from 30 to approximately 70 percent during the last years of the 1980s.[18] In banking, mining, and communications, and many other sectors state ownership dominated completely. Furthermore, the state sector was reportedly increasing its share both of GDP and industrial output (Table 7.2).

Thus, the economic transition had entailed a process of commercialization of the state sector, with state units acting with greater and greater autonomy according to increasingly commercial criteria. Outright privatization was playing a marginal role (if the far-reaching process of decollectivization of agriculture is disregarded in this context).[19] The question should then be asked: What forces existed to push for the emergence and development of factor markets?

The nature of state property was, to the insider, clear. In any particular unit, it had little to do with the formal system. Capital inside SOEs could, in some analyses, be divided into a number of types: state budgetary contributions, the unit's "own capital," bank loans of various types and conditionality, private capital "in the shade" (*nup bong*) of the SOE, informal joint ventures with Vietnamese commercial capital (either state, private, or some combination thereof), under-the-table investments by foreigners (usually regional, if small-scale and informal), capital contributed by individuals within the unit, and capital from the unit's workers. This was the reality; legal classification into "state" and "private" did not help to reduce the transactions costs involved in assisting those who controlled the unit and the allocation of profits to reconcile their competing interests. The natural solution was for a period of de facto privatization and confusion. This was helped by the Company Law promulgated in January 1991, which laid down how private companies of various sorts could be established. The middle period of the mid-1990s was therefore set to be one in which much mobile capital would leave the state sector for other forms. Although this situation was the underlying reality, its surface appearance was rather different. Here, however, the basic mechanism can be seen that was pushing for the emergence of capital markets-- earnings looking for profitable outlets.

The question of privatization was thus not only, or even primarily, an ideological issue in Vietnam. Budgetary considerations appeared to be more important; the state wanted to get rid of loss-generating companies, while keeping those that were able to contribute to state revenues. The former constituted the majority, but there were few buyers. With the natural development of increasingly powerful and mobile capital and the emergence of formal capital markets (see furhter on), privatization, both informal and formal, was likely to accelerate. The issue of who would become the future owners of privatized companies could not easily be resolved. Members of the Vietnamese *nomenklatura* were, like their East European counterparts, strong candidates for becoming Vietnam's future businessmen if and when privatization took place.[20]

Policy Toward the State Sector

In order to facilitate future reforms of the ownership of state enterprises, a law on share companies was promulgated, and the value of all assets of state enterprises was reassessed. New legislation attempted to clarify the ownership status of state enterprises and to define the legal procedures for the transformation of state property into private or mixed forms of ownership. Although this process is far from easy to interpret, it appears as though various decrees[21] basically set forth four different options:

1. Establishment of a management board (accountable to the state);
2. Establishment of the unit as a share company, or "equitatization" (*co phan hoa*);
3. Leasing or contracting out the unit; and
4. "Allocating the capital of the unit to the unit." See Decree No. 22, January 1991 (*CB* 15 March 1991). The exact meaning of this was unclear, but the procedure, aimed at increasing the management's accountability vis-a-vis the state, required the management to preserve the value of the unit's assets.

These attempts to define property rights within the state sector most certainly did not clarify the many issues involved. Laws regarding creditors' rights and bankruptcy proceedings were in the process of being enacted, but to judge from other areas, the fact that a new law was promulgated did not necessarily mean that it would be implemented.

A crucial issue was the problem of accountability. The function of the state had changed, and the authority and power of central government had been eroded. Sometimes a multiplicity of agencies represented the owner of a state enterprise, i.e., "the state", and conflicts between the owning ministry, State Planning Commission (SPC), local government, and local People's Committees were common. Trade unions often formed alliances with local government to protect employment, at the expense of the profitability of the enterprise. Also, workers often accounted for 50 percent of the members of the Enterprise Councils, or Management Boards; clearly, there was often a conflict--well-known from the old debate about "self-management'" and "market socialism" and from practical experience in, for example, former Yugoslavia and Poland--between the desire of workers to raise their wages and the right of the formal owner ("the state") to receive an adequate return or at least reduce state subsidies to the enterprise.

It should also be stressed that the Vietnamese state at this time (1990-93), although weak in many respects, was still far more interventionist than was the case in many modern market economies. Many ministries were still attempting to give detailed directives to their (or "their") enterprises. The role of state contracts, which often had the character of compulsory deliveries, also reduced the voluntary nature of a large number of transactions with the state sector. Other examples could be given; as recognized by the Vietnamese leaders, a heavy bureaucracy was a characteristic legacy of the past. The "dirigiste" attitude of cadres from the Communist Party, the responsible ministries, and local authorities was deeply entrenched and could not be expected to change overnight. State enterprises were essentially run by the same people who had been managers during the transition period, and they maintained close links with the higher echelons of the state and party apparatus; indeed, good personal connections in the state system remained an important ingredient of profitable behavior.

A clear line of demarcation--with important political implications-- between the party and the state and between the state and the enterprises (whether private or state-owned) needed to be drawn. Reforms limiting the scope for direct, vertical control from above were likely to be insufficient as long as managers were appointed by the center, supported by the center, and faced no threat of corporate takeover.[22]

Within the SOEs, certain factors--unclear property rights; weak and confused accountability; conflicts of interest between different parts of the state and between the state, management, and workers; selective interventions from cadres and bureaucrats; and the lack of authority of central government--led to state enterprise objective functions that were quite different from those of private enterprises in a market economy, where "the firm" is a well-defined legal and economic unit and the firm's profit is the overriding, transparent criterion. In the immediate post-1989 period, therefore, enterprise behavior in Vietnam differed, in important respects, from textbook maximization rules. Simple transactions could, of course, still be handled with the help of ordinary economic theory--by and large, Vietnamese state enterprises wanted to buy cheap and sell dear--but in matters related to employment, new investment, accountability, and so forth, conflicts of interest not only arose but were also difficult to solve. Bargaining, in which the profit motive was only one component, was still the rule, to a much larger extent than in Western market economies.

A comparison with the defunct neo-Stalinist system may be appropriate. The planned economy is often described as a "command economy," with a general at the helm and tiers of underlings who blindly follow the orders issued. In practice, however, the rules of the game in centrally planned economies tended to be rather fluid. In the DRV model, the profit motive had largely been replaced by directives formulated in terms of physical production targets, but--and this is important--with significant and major restrictions, secondary objectives and room to maneuver. Especially in an aggravated shortage economy like Vietnam's before 1989, it was comparatively easy for the director of a state enterprise or an agricultural cooperative to produce excuses: the raw materials or spare parts had not arrived in time, the power supply was irregular, and so on.

The DRV model was emphatically such an "excuse economy." It was, as we have stressed earlier, the outcome of the unimplementability of neo-Stalinism in North Vietnam, and central control was much less strict than it looked on paper. Generally, there were uncountable legitimate problems that hindered the fulfillment of plan targets. Even as these targets were established, the affected units at lower levels were pointing out how unrealistically high the goals were and were negotiating, as they always had, for lower targets and larger allocations of subsidized inputs and capital.

There are many arguments that support a view of the DRV model as a bargaining economy (rather than as a command economy), in which the position of the state manager was often more comfortable than it would have been if that manager, like his capitalist colleagues in market economies, had been confronted with a single goal (profit) and with a binding budget constraint to force inefficient (or unfortunate) companies to go bust.

The point to be stressed is that, after 1989, Vietnamese state enterprises not only discovered they were in a legal no-man's-land but that traditions inherited from the DRV model also weighed heavily on them. The budget constraint had certainly been hardened and the authorities repeatedly declared their intention to phase out remaining subsidies. Yet with over 50 percent of central state enterprises and an even higher share of province and district enterprises, taking a loss, these enterprises were still, as a rule, being bailed out (by the state banking system rather than, as before, directly through the state budget). State enterprises were asked to be profitable and to deliver part of their profits to the state. However, not only did they generally fail to make profits, for which they were not sanctioned, but they actually managed to evade most taxes and import duties.

Interest rate distortions, tax breaks, economic rents, rent-creation, and so on were thus all key elements of the Vietnamese market economy in the very early 1990s. In summary, the post-1989 syndrome, in which weak legislation led to confused rules of the game and weak enforcement of existing legislation, meant that state enterprises in Vietnam continued to bargain with their owners (and even about who their owners actually were) and with workers, creditors, and customers--even about things that should not have been negotiable. Actual enterprise behavior had changed, of course--to make money was now far more important than in the past--

but the legacy of the DRV model, in addition to uncertainty about property rights and lack of experience of a market economy, meant that simplistic notions about free competition based on the profit motive would have been inappropriate.

It is difficult to find quantitative indicators to substantiate the above assertions about the confused objective functions of state enterprises. Aggregate data on hard indicators and proxies, such as the percentage of firms making losses year after year, the extent of excess employment, tax evasion, nonpayment of loans, and so on, were difficult to get, and in-depth micro studies would have had to be carried out in order to assess the importance of various conflicting goals in actual enterprise behavior. Still, it should be stressed that market behavior by a state enterprise in Vietnam post-1989 was certainly not as transparent as that of "typical" Western capitalist enterprises for example, the American firm Johnson and Johnson Inc.

Weak Institutional Infrastructure

In discussing the likely Vietnamese responses to the above situation, it is useful to reflect on the role institutions can play in reducing transactions costs. In the very open Vietnamese economy of the 1990s, any significant difference between Vietnam's key prices for tradable goods or mobile factors and those in international markets led to rapid cross-border shifts. Competition to attract capital and support Vietnamese business therefore had to focus on institutional aspects: better markets, better infrastructure, better human capital, more reliable contract enforcement, and so on.

The bias in favor of hardware in the traditional model also acted as an obstacle to the further development of markets. There was a serious shortage of market-supporting institutions in areas such as information, marketing, commercial banking, foreign trade, insurance, consultancy, and the like. The intellectual infrastructure had been built up to serve the ideals of neo-Stalinism; as a result, people with skills suited to a commercialized economy (accountants, managers, lawyers, economists, commercial bankers, interpreters, marketing professionals, and so forth) were sorely lacking.

Economic information was weak, and markets lacked transparency. As has been stressed earlier in this study, knowledge about prices, alternative suppliers, distribution channels, and so on was insufficient, in particular in rural areas, which facilitated exploitation of producers--not least by state trading companies. In the DRV model, economic agents were supposed to obey orders and were not meant to know what was happening in the economy in order to do their job. As commercialized behavior spread, demand for economic information increased and soon outstripped its supply; as a result, people with access to information could reap substantial rents. It is striking that capital investment strategies after 1989 still favored trade and services as opposed to manufacturing.

The tradition of secrecy in economic matters, sometimes justified with reference to "national security" was still clearly present within the Communist Party, although there was a clear recognition from the government of the importance of disseminating more economic data as markets developed.[23] The entire "information industry"--of paramount importance for a modern market economy--found itself in its infancy, and the public sector's statistical services (i.e., the information published by the General Statistical Office) was likewise poorly equipped with resources and suffered from the biases inherited from central planning.

An issue related to the weakness of market-supporting institutions was the high degree of market fragmentation.[24] Different enterprises and households faced different effective prices for similar goods and services; the embryonic and segmented credit market (discussed later) was an obvious example, access to hard currency was another. Transaction costs were high, not only because of the deficient physical infrastructure and lack of information but also because of unclear property rights, the prevalence of restrictions, red tape, and outright corruption.

It must, in this context, be stressed that the prevalence of local, regional, and even national monopolies was far higher in Vietnam than in most other low-income countries, as a result of the particular import-substitution policies pursued during the DRV model. The DRV model was characterized by a strong belief in economies of scale, and typically, the pattern was to create one major supplier of many commodities in each district or province. When such units became "commercialized," they naturally enjoyed a virtual monopoly; in the absence of competition, the relevant regulatory functions of the state--to control abuses and to encourage competition--assumed a greater importance.[25] This was especially true when local authorities supported "their" SOEs' local monopolies.[26]

The development of *good* markets is, in short, cumbersome, expensive and, from the government's point of view, a rather different proposition from the unguided emergence of unregulated markets. It takes time and requires huge outlays, including investment in human capital and market-oriented institutions with long gestation periods.[27] The South of Vietnam had an obvious advantage over the North in this respect, which was one reason why income differences were likely to increase further in the future; not only was the resource endowment of the South superior, but the skills and institutions necessary for a process of "marketization" were also much better developed than in the North.

We will return later to the issue of the role of the state. Suffice it here to conclude that the post-1989 weaknesses of market-oriented institutions in Vietnam and of the state as supporter of such institutions gave rise to imperfections that slowed down the further marketization of the economy. They also, as has been shown in earlier chapters, led to high transaction costs and inefficiency and to the preservation of economic rents due to local monopolies and monopsonies and information asymmetries. Or, to use the distinction introduced in Chapter 1: Although plan distortion had largely been eliminated prior to 1989, market distortions remained significant and strongly influenced by the events of the 1980s.

Factor Markets

Land. Private ownership of land was still ruled out in· the post-1989 period. According to the Constitution, all land belonged to the state, which, however, could allocate use rights to economic units, that is, to households, cooperatives, state farms, foreign investors, or other agents. Since the right to *use* land privately had been acknowledged, there existed, however, a "gray"--tolerated, but not legally recognized--market for use rights, enabling farmers to lease land from other farmers who for some reason were willing to lease it out.

In order to provide some long-term security for farming families and give incentives for maintenance and new investment, lease contracts could be extended to fifteen years for rice land, longer in the case of cash crops.[28] The right to inherit use rights was also acknowledged. The virtual dismantling of the traditional cooperatives after Decree No. 10 was announced in 1988 created a confused situation as to landholding and property rights, and land use conflicts became increasingly common. Regional differences were still large; in the North and Center of Vietnam, land-use rights had traditionally been subject to more collective restraint, aimed at reducing risk and excessive social differentiation, than in the comparatively land-rich South.

One important corollary of the absence of a normal market for land was that the development of a formal rural credit market was hampered by the lack of collateral for agricultural credits. This may not necessarily be bad--a Bangladeshization of the impoverished Red River Delta, with an increase in the numbers of indebted smallholders forced to sell their land in case of a bad harvest, would be a disastrous scenario that the emergence of a land market might lead to in a rather short period of time. But developing such a market in rural areas requires special efforts to facilitate a process of capital accumulation and diversification of production. With the old access mechanism of the state--the producer cooperatives--gradually withering away, the state largely withdrew from rural areas, leaving behind a vacuum in terms of extension services, access to improved technology, access to rural credit, and so on.[29]

Labor. There was a pronounced tendency toward a "commercialization" of labor relations after 1989. Compulsory allocation of labor to state enterprises belonged to the past. The private sector's vital role in absorbing the high and rising unemployment was acknowledged by the authorities, and there was no upper limit to the number of workers that a private enterprise could hire. There were minimum wages, but for any wages above this level, enterprises were free to negotiate with their workers.

Although there were many legal restrictions reducing the mobility of labor, it was already possible to talk about a labor market.[30] One such restriction was the law against spontaneous migration; in order to restrict migration to urban areas, a special permit issued by the local authorities was needed for permanent settlement. For those with employment, registration in the early 1990s appeared relatively easy. As was common in many areas, enforcement of legislation was lax, and the authorities readily acknowledged the existence of large numbers of job seekers who had come to the major cities without registering with city administrative officers.

The evolution of the labor market in the first half of the 1990s appears to have been rather healthy. The widespread land access guaranteed by the land allocation practices supported by the party was important in helping to provide income entitlements to poor farmers, whose bargaining position as migrant workers was thereby enhanced. Employment creation was substantial, with services and small-scale producers creating job numbers well above the rate of job loss in the state sector. However, although the macroeconomic underpinnings of the labor market were thus sound, the costs involved for workers in obtaining information meant that there was a rapid growth of "people markets" (*cho nguoi*) in the main cities.

Within the SOEs, in 1989 many workers were in a position to share in the economic rents enjoyed by the state sector, in terms of access to the benefits derived from access to Soviet aid, cheap credit, and so forth. As de facto co-owners of the SOEs, they also often shared in the commercial profits derived from outside plan activities in the form of additional wage supplements. Through the first half of the 1990s, there is some evidence that these earnings levels above what was obtainable in the general labor market were eroded. The lack of worker opposition to this may be explained by the tendency for real wages to rise and also by the very high levels of competition experienced as budget constraints were hardened and imports flooded in.

The labor legislation of the immediate post-1989 Vietnamese economy put a heavy premium on job security, and a strong case had to be made by any employer wanting to shed workers. It was, however, generally recognized that the number of workers employed by SOEs was excessive, despite large staff reductions in the late 1980s and around the turn of the decade. In late 1989, the government issued regulations providing incentives for early retirement with one-time, lump-sum payments to redundant workers, and a large percentage of state employees were dismissed during 1989-92.

Capital. In the early 1990s, the lack of development of a normal capital market was probably the most serious obstacle to a continued marketization of the Vietnamese economy. The situation also conserved inefficiency. Given the distorted capital structure inherited from the 1980s transition and the DRV model, there was an urgent need to carry out a drastic restructuring of the economy, which would require huge financial resources. The historically low level of domestic savings (see Chapter 8) had to be raised and the efficiency of investment increased.

Vietnam's financial system was poorly equipped to meet these challenges. It was almost entirely credit-based, with the state banks playing the major role. It was extremely inefficient; for example, a simple clearance between Hanoi and Ho Chi Minh City could take twenty days or more.[31]

Despite several reforms of the banking system and the creation in 1989 of various specialized banks with multipurpose banking functions,[32] the state banks still functioned largely as money distributors for the government. Although banks had been given more autonomy and were "in principle" requested to assess the financial viability of their debtors, they were still told to provide subsidized credit to loss-generating state companies. Lack of clear rules about creditors' rights greatly increased the risk to banks lending to state units. The State Bank of Vietnam, also called the Central Bank, was forced to finance a large part of the fiscal deficit.

After a brief period in 1989 when positive real rates of interest were established, the interest rate structure in Vietnam remained seriously distorted. In real terms, the rate of interest tended to be negative through 1990-91, as it had been in the past (see Figure 5.7), which resulted in an inability to attract deposits and a continuation of subsidies to recipients of credits, in other words, the state sector. Also, official deposit interest rates were higher than lending rates, leading to a need for direct subsidies and state support to the banks. The negative spread between deposit and lending rates made banking a very bad business, since losses necessarily increased with the scale of operations. Banks were thus forced to take heavy losses on their loans to state enterprises (even when the loans were being serviced, which was not always the case).

Actual interest rates sometimes differed from the official ones, however. The usual lending pattern appeared to be that state units were allowed a certain quota at a low level of interest, after which they paid a rate closer to that on the free market. This dual structure thus resembled the old two price system and was likely to be abolished as pressures for further reforms of the banking system mounted. The fact that banks were allowed to make profits "at the margin," by charging higher interest rates than the official ones, was likely to encourage more commercial attitudes in the banking system and improve risk assessment.

One can, in this context, draw a parallel with the 1980s Three Plan system in industry, which had greatly enhanced market-oriented behavior within SOEs and thereby helped to erode the DRV model from within.

As outsiders, the newly emerging private sector faced a harder budget constraint than state enterprises. Foreclosure on nonperforming loans to the nonstate sector, leading to asset seizure, was widely reported in 1990-91, but the rights of the banks vis-a-vis the state sector appeared to be weak, as they were not equipped with the normal powers of creditors in countries with more developed capital markets.[33]

The hardening of the soft budget constraint, which was an important part of the 1989 package of stabilization measures, was reversed somewhat in 1990-91. Cases of district and provincial state enterprises forced into bankruptcy were not uncommon, but to our knowledge, no major central state enterprise went bankrupt. The fear of unemployment was the most important reason given by the government for its reluctance to force unviable enterprises to close down, but behind the continued bailing out of companies operating at a loss was the strong political influence of state enterprise managers.[34]

In view of the fact that approximately 95 percent of all bank credit went to state enterprises, of which over one-half were failing to make profits, it is tempting to conclude that there was an inverse relationship between financial viability and access to credit: The larger the losses, the more assistance was provided. Finance was, in short, extended to cover past losses rather than future investments.

This inverse relationship was accentuated by the fact that the treasury remained heavily dependent on enterprise profit transfers for the state budget (or local government budget, for locally owned enterprises). As will be further discussed in Chapter 8, this source of state revenue had diminished drastically during previous years. The few economically successful companies thus saw their profits being siphoned off, which was likely to act as a powerful disincentive against making profits that were "too high." The exact mechanisms for profit transfers were not quite clear; the system lacked transparency, and there was much room for bargaining. The fact that state companies were notoriously poor taxpayers indicated that there were many different ways in which the soft budget constraint still operated.

Since state enterprises and the central government absorbed the lion's share of available bank credit, access to loanable funds during 1990-91 by individual entrepreneurs and small-scale private companies was largely limited to village credit cooperatives and the informal credit sector. The role of the banks for financial intermediation--channeling savings into productive investment--therefore remained very limited.

For the future, it was expected that private enterprises would be allowed to raise their own capital.[35] The law on share companies had been tested in selected areas following the Vietnamese practice of experimenting before letting new legislation come into force on a national scale. A functioning stock market could not be expected to be established before the mid-1990s.[36] Other financial instruments--such as treasury bonds--played a subordinate ongoing role.

One major conclusion that emerges from the above brief overview is that the financial system inherited from the DRV model had not yet been transformed into a capital market. Incentives to save in financial assets were weak; interest rates were often negative in real terms, confidence was lacking, and poor services and bureaucratic procedures in state banks made most people prefer gold and dollars. There was a poor (indeed, an almost nonexistent) diversification of financial instruments in terms of risk, choice between long-term and short-term instruments, and so on. As for lending criteria, it should be observed that credit practices strongly discriminated against the nonstate sector and played an essentially conservative role by protecting an obsolete capital structure and reducing competition by preventing both free entry and free exit in the productive sectors. Rents and distortions were thereby conserved, and the Schumpeterian process of "creative destruction," badly needed in Vietnam as the country embarked upon an entirely new development strategy, was hindered.

The Financial Crashes of 1990: Premature Marketization

During the latter half of the 1980s, the government allowed hundreds of private credit funds, or credit cooperatives, to start doing business, as an alternative to the formal banking system. The cooperatives provided funding for private enterprises unable to get credits from the state banks, but some state enterprises also became involved both as borrowers and as depositors. In 1990, before the crash, there were approximately 300 credit cooperatives in operation, controlling deposits of around 400 billion dong, or almost US$100 million.[37]

Many of the credit cooperatives operated like pyramid schemes, attracting deposits by offering interest rates of up to 15 percent per month. Beginning in Ho Chi Minh City in March 1990, a number of credit cooperatives--largely unregulated and poorly supervised, with no system of reserve assets or deposit insurance--started to go bankrupt. Some of the worst cases of pyramid schemes--involving grossly fraudulent behavior on the part of the owners--were closed down by the authorities, and several well-known cooperative managers were arrested.[38] The scandals panicked depositors, who rushed to withdraw their money, forcing many cooperatives out of business. The bankruptcies also caused the collapse of more than 2,000 small private enterprises.[39] Angry depositors staged street demonstrations, demanding that the government cover their losses. In August 1990, the financial crash reached Hanoi.

Only a few of the urban credit cooperatives survived the crisis. Even fewer could be regarded as solvent, as even the well-managed ones suffered from lack of confidence and deposit withdrawals. In the aftermath of the crisis, a number of high-ranking government banking officials accused of slack supervision or outright fraud were arrested. The government also recognized the need for regulation of the secondary credit market, for measures that included minimum reserve requirements and closer supervision. New legislation came into force, and from 1990 on, the State Bank of Vietnam engaged in the slow and difficult process of examining and certifying the cooperatives one by one.

The financial events of 1989-90 illustrate that the development of a capital market takes time and, more important, that it *should take time*. The premature financial liberalization, taking place before the legal and institutional setup had developed sufficiently and before monetary credibility had become consolidated, easily led to speculative "bubbles" and pyramid schemes of the kind briefly discussed here.[40]

The major effect of the crash of the secondary credit market in 1990 was probably psychological. The public's faith in the financial system was seriously damaged, and the issue of corruption and economic crime in general came to the surface. The confidence crisis--and, of course, the negative real rate of interest all through 1990 and 1991--also affected the formal banking system; many people withdrew their deposits to buy gold and dollars, as illustrated by the sharp increase in the price of these assets during the latter half of 1990 and 1991.

The contrast with events in 1989 was remarkable. Whereas the policy measures introduced in 1989 resulted in a drastic increase in bank deposits, as people switched from gold and dollars to savings accounts in the state banks and the value of the *dong* actually appreciated against gold and dollars on the free market, the tendency was reversed in 1990-91.

The changing expectations had serious macroeconomic implications and threatened the achievements of the stabilization policies of 1989 (see Chapter 8).

The Role of the State in Support of Market Development

Processes of Change and the Meaning of Policy

Much of the emerging literature on the Vietnamese transition focuses on the post-1986 and post-1989 periods and thus attributes the primary role in explaining the changes that have occurred in Vietnam to policy. This is not the approach that we have taken. We acknowledge, however, that in the 1990s the role of the state--and debates as to what this should be--took on a new dimension: if in the 1980s positive responses could be had from liberalization, in the 1990s a more active position was needed if the state was to create a more stable political base for the ruling Communist Party. An example that we were given anonymously by one Vietnamese colleague was that of the difference between the emergence of a stock market and the emergence of clothing markets. The latter, if unregulated, would not have the likely major effects of an unregulated stock market. Experience of the consequences of the 1989-90 secondary financial markets crash was vividly in people's minds. Thus, as factor markets emerged, based on the underlying growth patterns normal to a market economy, the state was under pressure to become more effective and more active in playing its role as a participant in Vietnam's socioeconomic development. What role was this to be? By the mid-1990s, there was no clear answer to this. If there was a choice between the more interventionist philosophies of the region and those of the "Anglo-Saxon" persuasions espoused by the Bretton Woods institutions, then it was not as yet clear where Vietnam stood.[41]

In a mixed economy of the Western kind, the balance between the private and public sectors can indeed vary. But everywhere, the state is strong. It is not necessarily large in terms of ownership, share of employment, or other conventional measures, but it is strong in the sense that central government controls the key levers of state power--the army, the currency, the bureaucracy, the state budget, and the rest. By and large, the state supports an enabling environment by providing public goods such as stable rules of the game, an appropriate legal framework, and defense of property rights. Also in successful Asian market economies, the actual role of the state has little in common with laissez-faire-- indeed, the NICs can in many ways be seen as examples of state-directed development strategy.[42]

The potential role of the state as defender and even creator of markets should be stressed in this context. For post-1989 Vietnam, this was a new role. Historically, the DRV state had mainly disrupted or destroyed markets and the issue then was how the public sector could be transformed into a supporter of markets and competition. Adam Smith commented upon the tendency of private capitalists to conspire against the free market whenever they got an opportunity, and he stressed the importance of creating a proper legal framework and public regulation in defense of competition. Or, as Karl Polanyi commented about the emergence and development of markets in the modern industrialized countries, "The road to the free market was opened up and kept open by an enormous increase in continuous, centrally organized and controlled intervention."[43]

In post-1989 Vietnam the inheritance of an economy with numerous local monopolies, information asymmetries, and barriers to entry meant that the reduction of monopoly power and various "rents" required a massive regulatory effort, albeit of a completely different kind than attempted in the past. A large number of market distortions could only have been eliminated by public action. Effective political support for this was lacking. However, macro stabilization, with its implications for regime survival and foreign capital mobilization, was a different matter.

In rural areas, this new role for the state would have entailed concerted efforts to improve the operation of marketing bodies, to reduce excessive price differentials, to protect rural households from exploitation by local monopolists and monopsonists, and to facilitate and assist the creation of rural credit, information, and extension services.

For the development of a capital market, the need for public supervision--and, perhaps, for the provision of public deposit insurance, lender of last resort facilities, and so forth--was obvious. Indeed, the importance of prudential supervision by central banks and other state regulatory bodies had been clearly demonstrated by recent experiences with financial liberalization in both developed and developing countries, including Vietnam.

In the export sector, to use another example, the potential role of public agencies--support to marketing, transmission of information, quality control, and the like--was great, as illustrated by the heavy involvement of state institutions in export-promoting activities in successful export countries.

In view of the important tasks confronting Vietnam, it is thus important to stress that after 1989, the Vietnamese state remained weak. In this regard, it is necessary to understand the importance of the slogan Rule by

Law, with its implication that the state bureaucracy should "get off the back of business" by making decisions based upon procedures and general directives, rather than performing ad hoc interventions that opened the way to corruption and favoritism. This required a recentralization of state power, so that economic decisions could be taken by businesses within the market economy. Such government policies therefore ran quite against the trends toward the commercialization of the state sector and the decentralization of state power that had occurred prior to 1989. This is somewhat paradoxical for those who assume that in centrally planned systems political power is highly centralized.

A brief historical digression may be useful in understanding the inherent weakness of the state even during the height of the DRV model.

Communist Vietnam: A Weak State?

As shown in preceding chapters, the development strategy outlined after national reunification and reflected in the Second FYP of 1976-80 was a failure. Central government derived its apparent strength from suppressing certain behavior that did not correspond to the New Knowledge and modernizing ethos underlying the DRV model, but it was unable to achieve its development objectives. The economic base of central government was foreign aid. As this assistance was drastically curtailed in the late 1970s, the unimplementability of the DRV model forced the leadership to make concessions.

During the early stages of the transition process (hard reform socialism), central government tried to reimpose its will in order to preserve the DRV model. The outcome was, however, rather the opposite: lower-level units of the economy became increasingly successful in utilizing state resources for their own purposes. Generous assistance from the Soviet bloc was channeled into state enterprises--many of which were leaky buckets--to be distributed among various local groups: managers, workers, local government, and so forth. As discussed earlier, Soviet aid, somewhat paradoxically, thus facilitated the spread of commercial behavior.

There were important regional differences. With an outdated capital stock derived from the socialist world, the northern state sector relied more heavily than the South on input supplies from the Soviet aid program. This was also true of the northern agricultural cooperatives, which received virtually all their inputs from the Soviet Union, with the Vietnamese state as intermediary.

In the South, the asset base was more competitive. In a common pattern, units within the state economy sought out extra inputs through deals with hard currency earners that enabled them to import of needed goods, which fetched a high price on the Vietnamese free market. This pattern, less common in the North, led to the growth of highly profitable state trading companies, often provincially or city-based. But there also remained large areas of the southern economy integrated into the system of state subsidization through the allocation of cheap goods and cheap credit.

In this process of erosion of the DRV model, central government tended to be the loser, and lower administrative levels the winners. High profits accrued to any unit that could meet two conditions: first, acquire cheap resources supplied through the state system and, second, divert those resources onto the free market.

Thus, the transitional model created a powerful constituency within the state apparatus for further commercialization and reform, at the same time weakening an already ineffective central government. The state became increasingly confused in its objectives as line ministries and local authorities became more and more involved, through the state sector, in business activities. Economic discipline in lower-level units was deteriorating, as shown in the central authorities' mounting difficulties in enforcing existing economic legislation such as tax laws, recovery of debt, collection of import duties, and so forth. It is noteworthy, for example, that the main agents smuggling industrial goods into the South--thus creating severe competition for Saigon manufacturers--were the Mekong Delta provincial authorities.

The weakness of central authority even in the face of de facto theft[44] was thus part of the traditional model. At its roots were profit-seeking individuals in the state and collective sectors aiming to squeeze more subsidized resources out of central government (and, in the final analysis, foreign donors). A possibly large but unknown share of the subsidies channeled through the system "trickled up" to individuals at high levels of authority in the form of side payments, that is, gifts and bribes of various kinds.

As part of the eroding discipline, shirking, corruption, and secondary occupations spread throughout the public sector. The appallingly low real wages for public employees encouraged outside activities; few public servants were able to make a living during the transition without resorting to all kinds of outside activities, which often absorbed the lion's share of state employees' working time.

This process, briefly indicated above, greatly undermined the effectiveness and efficiency of central government. In financial terms, it also undermined its solvency. Instead of being able to accumulate capital by absorbing an investable surplus from the rest of the economy--a characteristic of several centrally planned economies in the past--the state became a large dissaver. Transfers from state enterprise to central government, traditionally the dominant source of state revenue, declined--gradually, to begin with, and rapidly, from 1989 onward. As a share of total state revenue, state enterprises' profit transfers declined from 80 percent in 1980 to merely 30 percent in 1989, whereas subsidies from the state to the enterprises showed a rising tendency (see Chapter 8).

The virtual elimination of Soviet assistance in 1988-90 can be seen as the final blow to central government *in its old role*. The state, by 1989, was no longer able to distribute subsidized resources to the rest of the economy.[45] Perhaps paradoxically, this gave the state an opportunity to strengthen itself. The state was forced to withdraw from a wide range of loss-generating activities, and in order to become stronger, the state needed to reduce its role. Or, rather, it had to do fewer things, but do them better. In many ways this project was successful, spurred by the need to secure macroeconomic stability and mobilize resources for national development.

It was, however, difficult to envisage an overall reduction in public expenditures in the 1990s, only-- it was hoped--a drastic reorientation. The role of public support in the emergence of markets was important, but the state also needed to clean house in order to assume its responsibility for the maintenance and improvement of the country's weak physical infrastructure. The deficiencies were to be found everywhere, but bottlenecks were likely to become particularly pronounced in areas crucial to the success of a more outward-oriented development, in telecommunications, port capacity, civil aviation facilities, hotels, and other services capable of accommodating foreign trading partners and investors.

Developments within the social sectors, in education and health (see Chapter 6), also gave rise to government concern, and showed the need for a stronger public sector. The backlog of investment in social infrastructure--including water and sanitation--would require massive public funds. Targeted support to the poorest--the urban unemployed, the impoverished peasants in the Red River Delta, and others--would be needed to alleviate poverty and ease the social cost of structural adjustment. In their enthusiasm for market solutions, in a time of budget austerity, there was an obvious danger that the Vietnamese leaders would "throw the baby out with the bathwater" and forget, in spite of everything, the strongest elements of the traditional model: equality and a minimum of social security for (almost) everyone. However, the dismantling of the collective social security system was going ahead at full speed. The rural cooperatives had lost a great deal of their social insurance functions, and public financing for health and education had been reduced. User charges were being introduced, or raised, in health clinics and primary schools. Illiteracy returned to areas where it had been eradicated before.

The margins were small in Vietnam; one year of poor harvests could have disastrous consequences. Concerted public action to assist the most vulnerable groups was thus probably a necessary condition for a successful transition.

The Issue of Political Credibility

Whether the state would actually succeed in the profound transformation required was to a large extent a political question. The weakness of the Vietnamese state in the early 1990s was the result of a prolonged economic process, some aspects of which have been analyzed in this book, but it was also a reflection of the erosion of ideological coherence within the Vietnamese Communist Party (Ronnas and Sjoberg 1990a, 1990b). Although the long-term irreversibility of the process of economic reform appeared certain--as confirmed, for example, by the Seventh Party Congress in June 1991--the break-down of the traditional development model and the global crisis of Marxism-Leninism had left the ruling party in a confused and uncomfortable position.

The constituency behind a continuation of the reform process was large but heterogeneous. As discussed elsewhere in this book, the winners easily outnumbered the losers and a return to neo-Stalinism had little or no political support within or outside the country. Still, many people questioned the authorities' intentions, and the government's credibility was weak. Clear-cut and unambiguous statements--and actions--that showed that *doi moi* was leading to a market economy were necessary in order to dissipate insecurity about the objectives of the ruling Communist Party. The traditional model was dead and buried, but the political leadership's continued rhetoric about the "construction of socialism" and their defense of the one-party system was riddled with double messages likely to hamper the process of economic reform and discourage both domestic and foreign investors.

Political insecurity and an incapacity to correct macroeconomic imbalances (see Chapter 8) could, in a pessimistic scenario, lead to a Latin Americanization of economic policies in Vietnam through the 1990s. This would signify, inter alia, large fiscal deficits, galloping inflation, a generalized lack of stability in the macroeconomic environment and stop-go stabilization attempts, a further erosion of the capacity and coherence of central government, widespread corruption, capital flight, a lack of productive investment, and other phenomena characteristic of a vicious circle of Latin American dimensions. In order to avoid this, the Vietnamese government needed both political definitions and credibility--and more financial resources.

Conclusions

We do not address the post-1989 post-stage in the same detail as the transition that preceded it. It has as yet no definable end point. Key issues during this period were the emergence of factor markets and the role of the state; we argue that factor markets could and did come into the open, and they supported rather rapid and stable growth. They emerged from within the commercialized state sector, and this influenced the processes of capital accumulation within what had become a highly open economy. What is particularly interesting is the way in which the pattern of economic rents, in what was a highly rent-sensitive economy, shifted: The interest rate reforms of 1992 meant that there was no longer such an attraction for mobile capital to seek a state "shell"; and the rapid increase in land prices meant that SOEs and those with good connections were well placed to acquire very large assets rather cheaply. Whilst most FDI joint ventures were with SOEs, from around 1993 on,the nominal private sector emerged strongly. The tricky issue of the relationship between the state and SOEs was further eased by the way in which the labor market, helped by better-than-expected rural incomes growth and rather good land access, shifted in a healthy direction: Real wages grew, and job creation was rather fast and was good enough to soak up those losing their jobs in the state sector. Thus it was easier than it otherwise might have been to meet the need for a recentralization of political power, permitting the state to carry on meeting its responsibilities for securing basic functions, even the most minimal ones such as law and order. Macroeconomic stability helped, which was in turn supported by the fears for regime survival, should inflation return. This may have been one of the key arguments behind the 1992 interest rate reforms, which effectively removed SOEs from a major source of sectoral support. Indeed, in the world of hindsight, one of the most interesting aspects of the period is the way in which the state sector managed to attain a competitive capacity.

There is a final remark to be made about processes of change and the role of the state: If we examine the sequence of change in Vietnam, we see that rural areas did not start to show really significant income growth until very late, from around 1989-90. Although the earlier changes did produce output increase (in 1980-83), there was no sustained improvement in rural incomes. For SOEs, however, the process was quite different, and big changes in attitudes and behavior came far earlier. *This meant that once Soviet aid was lost, there was very little domestic economic surplus that the state could use to support SOEs.* After 1989, the inflationary cost of fairly small levels of interest and fiscal subsidy to SOEs was rather high. If Vietnam had "started with agriculture," then it is possible that by 1989-90 rural mobilizable savings would have been enough for the state, which was then still highly sensitive to the needs of SOEs, to have found ways of channeling those funds into the state sector. This could have been done through price intervention (slowing the shift to a free market in staples), through credit (through a network of state-controlled rural savings banks) or some other mechanism. That this did not happen, offering therefore the prospect for the emergence of a true private business sector and a relatively level playing field, can surely only be attributed to good fortune. At least, it suggests giving further thought to the optimal reform sequencing arguments that advocate starting with agriculture. On a more realistic plane, it also suggests that the most important thing to appreciate about what happened in Vietnam between 1979 and 1994 is that it was a "process", which is perhaps clear in hindsight, but like all human creative processes, it was confused and confusing at the time.

Notes

1. These three topics--the emergence of factor markets, the role of the state, and the process of internationalization of the Vietnamese economy--were all subprojects of the Australian-Vietnam Research Project involving Fforde, with David Marr and Melanie Beresford, which started fieldwork in late 1994.

2. For two commentaries see de Vylder (1990, 1993); see also the commercial six-monthly report "Vietnam: Economic Commentary Analysis" started by Fforde in 1992.

3. David Mellor pointed to this, in a "dissenting" report for the FAO prepared for the 1993 Donor's Conference (FAO 1993).

4. See Fforde and Seneque (1995).

5. The surveys of the very late 1980s and early 1990s were essentially Vietnamese initiatives. The earliest (Ministry of Labour 1990) covered 6,905 households in 21 provinces. The later ones (Le Van Toan et al. 1991; Nguyen Sinh Cuc 1991; Nguyen Van Tiem, 1993) took particular interest in the extent and trends in the numbers of households defined as "poor." The Le Van Toan survey was carried out in December 1989, the Nguyen Van Tiem exercise in 1992, and the Ministry of Agriculture's (Nguyen Sinh Cuc) in 1991. A good summary of the implications of these can be found in Nguyen Van Tiem (1993:16-18, on rich families; for poor families, pp. 32-44). The basic conclusion reached was that the numbers of poor people had fallen

significantly, from around 20 percent in 1990 to 15 percent in 1992 (Nguyen Van Tiem 1992:43, using specified definitions). These surveys contain extremely interesting analyses of rural conditions. For example, Nguyen Sinh Cuc (1991:78, et seq.) discusses the spiritual life *(doi song tinh than)*--under headings of education, health and democracy.

6. The Department of Treasury and the Tax Office were founded in 1990 and are key early examples of the institutional development of the Vietnamese state "post-1989."

7. The debate between the big-bang and the gradualist approaches is far too large to be covered here. It should be clear from the present study, however, that our own assessment of both the reality and the potential of events makes it hard for us to take seriously a hard-line big-bang position. In reality, time to adjust meant that social costs--for example, in terms of unemployment--could more easily be borne, thus that period could more easily lead to positive changes permitting further progress: "winners" would outnumber "losers."

8. See Turley and Seldon (1993); this contains a piece by Le Duc Thuy, ex-Harvard scholar and onetime personal assistant to Do Muoi, which commences with the following sentence: "[t]he exact starting point of economic reform is open to question, but it is generally agreed that it was under way by 1979" (1993:97).

9. It should be clear to the reader that we feel that there is much about the post-1989 situation in Vietnam that argues for viewing the regime as in fact *stronger* than before; this, however, as yet lacks strong justification.

10. This section deals solely with work with an overt and direct bearing upon the transition to a market economy. Utting (1992) provides another analysis from the Left. See also Wiergesma (1991) for analysis of the failure of rural collectivization in terms of relations of reproduction, presented as essentially those of patriarchy. Spoor (1988), White 1985) and Beresford (1988, 1989) do not address the issue of transition to a market economy directly.

11. It may be useful for the reader here to be aware that David Dollar was a key World Bank staff member working on Vietnam in the early 1990s.

12. We do not discuss here the Harvard Institute of International Development's work, aimed solely at a Vietnamese audience and unavailable in English (see Perkins et al. 1994).

13. Porter (1990) provides a less "theorized" and more open analysis of the "politics of 'renovation.'" However, although he points to certain formalized constituency pressures upon politicians (for example, the "long-standing contacts between Chinese merchants and the party" mentioned in fn. 36, p. 76), the dualistic confrontation between authoritarianism and liberalism as analytical categories remains. Pressures "on the regime" are seen as coming from "demands for greater freedom and political participation" and from the "antagonism . . . toward pervasive party control over every aspect of intellectual and

political life . . ." (p. 88). It is hard to see such control in the mid-1990s: With economic power increasingly decentralized, in our opinion there was a new ball game. But this has not been analyzed in great detail here.

14. Much of the somewhat overdone position taking by Leipziger and others, done in hindsight, appears to be related to a natural and fair disenchantment at the time with what in Vietnam we have termed "hard reform socialism," that is, policy stances common in the socialist bloc that purported to be "reform" but in reality contained no intention of abandoning the essential elements of neo-Stalinism.

15. Brummitt and Winton (1993) provide a somewhat inaccessible but clear analysis of Vietnam's situation and prospects and the implications for Australian interests.

16. Mallon was resident economist at the Hanoi United Nations Development Program Office in the early 1990s and then worked as a World Bank adviser to the Vietnamese government on SOE reform.

17. For some informal reflections by Sachs--perhaps the most famous Western advocate of big-bang solutions--on such matters, see Sachs (1992).

18. Figures given by SPC to de Vylder, 1990. The discussion below refers to the period up until 1993.

19. In fact, large-scale privatization of already existing enterprises was not yet high on the agenda; according to the SPC formal privatization would largely be confined to the taking over by the private sector of certain loss-incurring state companies.

20. For a discussion about privatization policies in postcommunist countries in Europe, see, for example, Hare (1989), Kaser (1990), and Aslund (1991a).

21. The most important of these decrees was Resolution No. 143 of May 1990 (*CB* 31 May 1990).

22. For a useful discussion about the limits to "managerial reform" in transitional economies, see Grosfeld (1990).

23. See the March 1992 CM resolution on secrecy (CM 1992).

24. For a discussion of market fragmentation in the context of rural China, see Edlund (1991).

25. Soviet bloc aid was also responsible to some degree for the scale problem, since aid was typically part of the Soviet Union's own investment production schedule, aimed at Soviet technical conditions. Fortunately, in the case of Vietnam, the decontrol of prices in 1989 had coincided with import liberalization and increased smuggling, which in some sectors compensated for the lack of domestic competition. Not surprisingly, complaints from commercialized state enterprises against cheap Thai and Chinese goods flooding the Vietnamese market were common.

26. It is striking that not only was the state share of industrial production rising through 1989-93 but that this was happening in food product processing.

27. A concrete example illustrating the costs of market creation is provided by Carlton (1990:6). Observing the high costs of running the futures markets in Chicago in terms of large office buildings, expensive real estate, and the many people involved, Dennis Carlton makes the following observation: "A significant fraction of the economy of the city of Chicago is devoted to the making of markets. If a magic spell could be cast to make transactions cost-less, the Chicago economy would be devastated, at least in the short run. This emphasizes how far from costless the making of markets really is" (quoted by Gordon 1990:1128).

28. The 1993 Land Law pushed this process along powerfully, although party prescriptions regarding land allocation had already had a strong impact.

29. Small village-level credit cooperatives, dating back to the 1950s, were estimated to number about 7,500 in rural Vietnam. They were typically formed by individuals or cooperatives and provided a link between the state bank system and village-level clients. A large part of the credit went to cooperatives and was regarded in 1990/91 as uncollectible, as most producer cooperatives had been dissolved. The new banking law (May 1990--see *CB* 30 June 1990) envisaged future rural credit cooperatives to be independent from the state bank system and to be run as credit unions managed by the members themselves. It remained to be seen whether these new credit cooperatives could become more important than their predecessors, which had only played a marginal role.

30. Naturally, the labor market in almost every country is surrounded by institutional constraints such as minimum wage and job security legislation. The difference between the labor "market" of Vietnam and those of developed mixed economies is a difference of degree rather than kind.

31. According to well-informed Vietnamese observers, the long delays normally characterizing bank payments in Vietnam were more the result of corruption than of inefficiency, however; vast sums of money blocked in the banking system were said to be lent on a short-term basis by dishonest banking officials.

32. For a discussion of the 1988 banking reform, see, for example, Asian Development Bank (1989:23 et seq.). See also World Bank (1991).

33. This problem was eased as foreign banks started to come in from around 1991-92.

34. Fforde (1990b), provides a list of examples showing that the state sector was still given privileged treatment through, inter alia, access to cheap loans, tax exemption when an enterprise was in difficulties, and debt relief when a state unit faced bankruptcy.

35. In 1990-91, with Soviet aid gone and little yet to replace it, the invest-ment fund available to the SPC for productive investment had shrunk to little more than $200-300 million.

36. According to statements by the SPC to de Vylder, October 1990.

37. SPC to de Vylder, October 1990. The cooperatives developed fastest in the South, but they also spread to Hanoi and other major cities. Small-scale private credit funds had also been established in some rural areas.

38. Murray Hiebert (1990a, 1990b) gives a vivid account of the scandals and of the corrective measures the government had to take in order to restore the badly eroded confidence in the financial system.

39. Hiebert (1990b). In order to safeguard the interests of the depositors, the authorities in Ho Chi Minh City demanded enterprises repay their loans immediately, thereby forcing many of them to turn over production equipment purchased with the loans.

40. For a discussion of similar phenomena in a Latin American context, see, for example, the classic article "Good-bye Financial Repression, Hello Financial Crash" (Diaz-Alejandro 1986).

41. See, for example, World Bank (1993a); Wade (1990).

42. For a useful and well-researched--if slightly polemical--study on the role of the state in the development strategies of Asian NICs, and in particular Taiwan, see Wade (1991).

43. *The Great Transformation*, 1945, quoted by Wade (1991:378).

44. Theft is the correct term; time after time, government decrees criticized and forbade state units from diverting plan resources to commercial use.

45. However, from around 1992 on,increased bilateral aid was received, followed in 1993-94 by a resumption of lending from the IMF, World Bank, and Asian Development Bank.

Tables

TABLE 7.1 Fiscal and Balance of Payments Positions, Early 1990s

	1989	1990	1991	1992	1993
Current account					
US$ million	-584	-259	-133	-8	-869
percent GDP	-8.0	-3.6	-1.8	-0.1	-7.4
Fiscal position					
Revenue and grants					
percent GDP	16.0	16.1	14.8	20.6	24.4
Current spending					
percent GDP	21.2	19.4	15.8	18.3	23.5
Capital spending					
percent GDP	6.7	5.6	3.1	6.3	7.7
Fiscal balance					
percent GDP	-11.9	-8.8	-4.4	-4.9	-7.6

Note: 1993 data are preliminary.
Source: IMF 1994 "Vietnam: Recent Economic Developments," table 3.

TABLE 7.2 Industrial and Agricultural Output Growth, Early 1990s

	1989	*1990*	*1991*	*1992*	*1993*
Total industrial output	-3.3	3.1	10.4	17.1	12.1
State industry	-2.5	6.1	11.8	20.6	13.3
Central state	5.9	15.3	15.5	23.1	14.1
Cooperative	-36.1	-20.0	-41.6	-31.1	-2.3
Private	34.5	10.4	26.7	16.9	10.2
Total agricul-tural output	7.5	1.7	2.9	8.1	3.9[a]
Cultivation	7.7	1.5	3.7	7.1	3.8[a]
Livestock	6.8	2.3	0.7	11.2	4.3[a]
Industry: share of GDP		19.0	19.8	21.7	21.5

[a] Estimates.

Source: SO 1993:table 18; SO 1994a:tables 13, 17, 40.

8

Macroeconomic Stability: The Role of the State

In preceding chapters, we have attempted to analyze the political economy aspects of the erosion of central government authority during the 1980s transition. We have stressed the limits surrounding the marketization of the Vietnamese economy, as well as the need that emerged in the early 1990s to strengthen and transform the state in order to support, rather than disrupt, emerging markets, both for factors of production and products. In this chapter, attention is focused on macroeconomic developments and resource gaps in more traditional terms. The emphasis is not on macroeconomic theory; rather, the main issue is *macroeconomic stability as a prerequisite for national development and for the consolidation of the reform process.*

Macroeconomic issues are closely related to those of "rent-creation," for through the creation of macroeconomic distortions (for example, by artificially keeping interest rates low) rents may be created. One striking element of the immediate post-1989 period is the priority that was attached to anti-inflationary policies and the tensions between these policies and the need to subsidize the state sector during the resurgence of inflationary pressures in 1990-91. These distortions reveal much about the political economy of the transition process. One aspect of this problem, however, was the initial macroeconomic weakness of the Vietnamese economy, as an examination of traditional resource "gaps" can demonstrate.

Macroeconomic Performance, 1989-93

As has been argued elsewhere (Fforde 1993), the ending of the two-price system in 1989 was a severe shock to the Vietnamese political economy. Output was remarkably buoyant despite the loss of Soviet aid, and prices stabilized as monetary policy was kept tight. However, although the macro economy was shown to be highly resilient, the political economy was not yet able to accept the loss of high levels of subsidy. The response, in the period 1990-92, was a deliberate destabilization of the economy through the use of heavy interest rate distortions and tax breaks to support the state sector. This policy is of considerable interest. Under the previous system, resources could be, and were, allocated to politically favored state units, and elsewhere, and were then used to create goods that could realize high profits. Much of this allocation had relied upon Soviet commodity aid, but supplies also came from collectivized agriculture and other area, a procedure that demonstrated the ability of the Vietnamese state to impose distributional controls and so obtain goods at low prices. This all changed after 1989. Rent-creation thus played an important role throughout and commanded sufficient importance to override other macroeconomic priorities. This fact supports the argument that rent-creation would be of continuing importance to the Vietnamese political economy through the 1990s.

The high interest rates and opening of the borders contributed to a severe profits squeeze. The party and government's response to this problem was framed in terms of the need to preserve social stability through employment-protecting measures, thus through 1990 large volumes of cheap credit were made available to assist favored units. Tax breaks and credit write-offs were also used. Both acted to increase the fiscal deficit and monetary inflation, making the link clear between macroeconomic deterioration and the creation of economic rents. However, this period only lasted for two years. As mentioned in the previous chapter, by 1992 real interest rates were positive again, and inflation was well on its way to single figures. Macroeconomic rents in the traditional sense had therefore been greatly reduced.

In the short run, the underlying reasons for this performance are related to a number of factors in addition to government and party efforts. For example, crude oil and rice exports boomed through the period, foreign direct investment increased sharply, and there were strong processes of de facto privatization. It is likely that the latter two factors created opportunities for political support to business (and vice versa) that were as useful to preserving such links as were cheap credit, selective tax and credit write-offs, and so on. Levels of corruption rose considerably (but were still at relatively low levels compared with many other Third World countries).

In the next section issues surrounding the resource gaps that faced the Vietnamese economy in the 1990s are examined. It is noteworthy that growth itself helped ease these problems and that the success in attaining macroeconomic stability appears to have been a major means of pointing the economy in the right direction for the 1990s. However, as noted earlier, the rising fiscal and external deficits in 1992-93 were a cause for concern as aid donors and multilateral lenders prepared to contribute major development funidng to Vietnam for its own public investment program.

Resource Gaps and a Path to Rapid Growth?

We will concentrate on the three traditional resource gaps that may threaten any process of economic transition or reform: a low level of savings and investment, a fiscal deficit and excessive monetary expansion, and an external imbalance.

The Crisis of Accumulation, 1989-94

One of the most striking successes of the Vietnamese economy during the period after 1989 was the growth in savings and total investment as compared with total output (see Figure 8.1). This did not happen over-night, however, and until around there were 1994 grave doubts as to whether Vietnam would be able to mobilize sufficient savings to finance rapid GDP growth rates. As argued elsewhere in this study, the exceed-ingly low savings capacity of the Vietnamese economy and the poor effi-ciency in the use of investable funds were basic characteristics of the traditional model, explaining the slow rate of growth exhibited.

According to official data, this was also true during the transition, when the proportion of national income devoted to accumulation was both low and unstable.[1] After rising in the mid-1980s, and reaching a peak of just over 16 per cent of produced national income (PNI) in 1985, it stag-nated in the latter half of the decade as the fiscal situation deteriorated and stabilization efforts demanded restraint on public spending. As is often the case with countries undergoing a process of structural adjustment, it proved politically easier to curtail public investment than current expendi-ture. Between 1987 and 1990, state investment was only around 9 per cent of PNI (for data on accumulation in the transition model see Chapter 3).

After 1989, the savings and investment pattern changed considerably. The traditional source of public investment, Soviet aid, was lost, and investment out of the state budget continued to stagnate, although it picked up in 1993-94. Private investment, however, increased. Since investment data only covered the state sector of the economy (i.e., investments undertaken by central and provincial enterprises and authorities), available statistics increasingly underestimated actual investment. The easily visible boom in real estate and anecdotal evidence about mushrooming private activities in sectors like retail trade, transportation, and services of various kinds clearly indicated that private savings were being used to finance a wide range of small-scale private investment. Unrecorded investment undertaken by district authorities, agricultural cooperatives, and the private sector, including individuals and families, *could have* amounted to 50 percent of all investment, but it is impossible to know. Major investments in the private sector were still hampered by uncertainties about the political, legal, and macroeconomic context and by the virtual lack of access to credit from the state banks.

Survey data suggested that personal savings remained substantial until inflationary expectations shifted sharply upward in 1985-86 (see Figure 3.11). In the early 1980s, state employees appear to have saved around 15 percent of their reported incomes. In the late 1980s, savings fell to nearly zero, and then recovered as the anti-inflationary measures of 1989 helped restore confidence in monetary assets (see Figure 3.11). Savings rates do not seem to have fully returned to earlier levels. However, the amount of private sector investment in housing was, from casual observation, enormous. This showed up in the data on the housing stock but was almost certainly not captured fully by the official investment data. Rural private investment is perhaps the most important area without data.

No official statistics are available for aggregate national savings through the 1980s on a system of national accounts (SNA) basis. In view of the fact that the current account deficit amounted to an average of over 7 percent of GDP during the 1980s, we can, however, conclude that gross national savings as a percentage of GDP were appreciably lower than the already low investment ratio. Between 1986 and 1988--the crisis years--domestic savings in fact appear to have been negative. Public savings declined drastically during the late 1980s and early 1990s.

Table 8.1 presents rough estimates of the savings-investment balance for the period 1985-89. The specific numbers should be taken as "guesstimates" that only serve to indicate, in very broad terms, how Vietnam's investments were financed in the late 1980s.

Despite the likely tendency to underestimate investment and savings in Vietnamese statistics (and in Table 8.1), the savings propensity in Vietnam thus appeared to be extraordinarily low compared with the situation in neighboring countries. National savings in countries like China and Taiwan were well above 30 percent of national income in the 1980s, and all Association of Southeast Asian Nations (ASEAN) countries registered savings ratios appreciably above 20 percent.

If this situation had continued, the low rate of savings and investment would have been, in a medium-term perspective, the most serious impediment to growth. Continued improvements in resource allocation were still possible because slack remained high and growth could thus be expected to continue for some time as the incentive structure improved and market distortions were reduced. But in a medium-term perspective, the Vietnamese economy was doomed to stagnation unless capital accumulation recovered.

The fundamental problem was the poor development of Vietnam's capital market and the still paternalistic behavior of the government in its support to ailing state companies, whose managers made up a strong constituency for the government and the ruling party. This has been discussed in Chapter 7, where the processes involved that helped ease the problem were explained.

In order to mobilize domestic savings and transform the financial system from being a provider of cash to loss-generating state companies to being an efficient intermediary between savers and investors, a wide range of reforms needed to be implemented. Some positive measures had been taken. The Vietnamese authorities had promulgated a number of new laws designed to create the prerequisites for a capital market. What was in question, however, was the political will to put an end to subsidies and the capacity to implement the new legislation already in force and create a macroeconomic environment that would encourage savings and productive investment. Unless this was accomplished, the country's savings would continue to be dissipated in traditional, nonproductive channels.[2] It could be argued that until around 1992-93 political economy considerations dominated those of orthodox macroeconomic management in a way that was inhibiting the emergence of a high savings economy. However, as we have observed, around 1993-94, savings rates started to rise, coincident with the adoption of the state slogan Rule by Law, but also assisted by the spontaneous processes involved in the growth of both domestic and foreign commercial activities.

Investment Requirements: Tentative Projections

In order to support a targeted 5-7 percent rate of economic growth per year during the 1990s, the gross investment ratio would have had to increase from around 10 percent of GDP to 18 percent, assuming an incremental capital-output ratio (ICOR) of 3 (which, in turn, implied a more efficient use of capital than in the past). In dollar terms, this would have represented an increase from around US$1.3 billion to US$2.5 billion per year in new investment (assuming a GDP per capita of US$200).

The loss of Soviet assistance required an even more rapid growth in domestic savings, however. Vietnam's current account deficit with CMEA declined from over 1.3 billion rubles in 1988, over US$500 million, or 4 percent of GDP, if the commonly used conversion factor of 1:2.4 between the dollar and ruble is used--to almost zero in 1991. The savings requirements might then, in a short-term perspective, have looked as they do in Table 8.2 (supposing a gross investment ration of 18 percent, leading to an annual rate of economic growth of 6 percent to be financed without Soviet support).

Given these assumptions, it is clear that Vietnam's domestic savings ratio would have had to increase three times, from 5 to 15 percent of GDP, in order to sustain the envisaged rate of economic growth of 6 percent per year, assuming an ICOR of 3. The lion's share of domestic savings had to come from the private sector, although the huge backlog of public investment and public needs, discussed in Chapter 7, would have required massive state resources *that were not within sight at the time*. In htis regard, the impact of the lack of external assistance in forcing important changes upon the political economy can be observed.

However, domestic savings started to rise dramatically in 1992-94. The lifting of the U.S. embargo and Vietnam's improved access to concessional credit from a number of bilateral and multilateral agencies increased the flow of foreign finance to Vietnam in a manner that might make it possible to sustain even higher growth rates during the rest of the 1990s.

Foreign direct investment would, in the future, also contribute greatly to capital formation. However, in 1990-92 it was still in its infancy, although foreign investors' interest in investing in Vietnam was increasing rapidly. A new law on foreign investment had been promulgated in December 1987 (minor modifications were made in 1991) and offered a wide range of financial and other incentives to foreign investors.

By late 1990, the Vietnamese government had issued licenses to 193 foreign investment projects, the majority being joint ventures. By March 1995, this number had risen to around 1,200 with total disbursements of

FDI to date put at US$ 4 billion. Total capital amounted to approximately US$ 12 billion (World Bank 1995b:33). During the earlier period the foreign capital share was 84 percent on average (Le Van Triet, Luu Bich Ho, and To Xuan Dan 1991:124). However, this outcome had not been certain at the start of the decade. Data about actually invested foreign capital at that time were lacking, and according to informed observers, few of the proposed projects had actually materialized. The uncertainty surrounding the economic and political situation and the authorities' excessive red tape and bureaucracy in dealing with foreign investors were often mentioned as obstacles to more rapid development of direct investment. The U.S. trade and investment embargo and the lack of agreement between Vietnam and the Bretton Woods institutions, the Paris Club, and a number of foreign creditors also acted as deterrents.

There was no certainty about whether foreign aid from the convertible area would increase. During the 1980s, it was negligible; after having averaged over US$300 million during 1976-80, it decreased to approximately US$100 million per year, or less than 1 percent of GDP, and stayed there for the entire decade.[3] On a per capita basis, aid from the non-CMEA area amounted to little more than US$1 per year. A resumption of normal aid, trade, and credit relations with Western countries depended on a number of factors that were predominantly in political character, and largely outside the control of Vietnam.

At the start of the decade, what could be stressed *from a standard macroeconomic standpoint* was Vietnam's large need for foreign economic assistance--to ease the savings-investment gap and other macroeconomic imbalances, to reduce poverty, and to facilitate the continued implementation of economic reform. Vietnam's successful transition with negligible support from Western countries and multilateral financial institutions had received praise from many sources (including a number of observers from the IMF and the World Bank)

However, our analysis suggests the importance of other factors; indeed, *it appears almost certain that the lack of major Western support during the late 1980s facilitated the transition from the DRV model.* Vietnam was, in such an interpretation, simply *forced* to accelerate the process of economic reform and try to "put its house in order"; the reduction of Soviet support was expected by everybody, and there was a clear recognition of the need to prepare for a realignment of foreign economic relations toward the convertible area. Had massive economic assistance been provided during this phase, economic reform might have been postponed, and subsidies and price distortions could have been financed to a larger extent.

There is, of course, no scientific answer to the highly speculative question of whether, say, US$500 million annually from the World Bank,

IMF, and bilateral donors in the late 1980s would have made the transition faster or slower, although we are inclined to believe that the latter would have been the case. By the early 1990s, however, the situation had changed; major reforms had been undertaken, and the continued economic isolation of Vietnam from the Western world would have done harm to both *doi moi* and national economic development in Vietnam.

The Fiscal Deficit

Budgetary Trends. The high rate of inflation throughout the 1980s, which developed into hyperinflation in 1986-88, was fundamentally the result of large fiscal deficits in combination with an accommodating monetary policy. Supply constraints, mainly in the form of inadequate food supplies, also contributed to the creation of shortages and inflationary pressures.

The fiscal deficit averaged 7 percent of GDP between 1984 and 1990. On average, over 50 percent of the deficit was financed by Central Bank credit, with the rest financed mainly by foreign grants and loans, most of which came from the Soviet Union.

The Vietnamese budget traditionally relied heavily on transfers from state enterprises, which accounted for over two-thirds of total revenue between 1984 and 1990, though the level had a pronounced tendency to decline during the last few years of the transition. It should, however, be pointed out that a substantial amount of this revenue was returned to SOEs for capital expenditures; Vietnamese state enterprises normally financed their capital investment over the state budget, whereas credits from the banking system were used to cover needs for working capital (by 1989, new investment was also expected to be financed by bank credit). Net transfers from state enterprises were therefore appreciably lower than shown in the budget, and as the financial situation of many enterprises deteriorated, this source of fiscal revenue was gradually declining.

Table 8.4 provides a summary of the state budget 1987-93. As seen in this table, as argued elsewhere in this study, the public sector in Vietnam was a large dissaver for a number of years. The dissaving--measured as total current expenditures minus total revenue--was around 3 percent of GDP in 1988-90, and revenue collection remained very low.

As stressed earlier, the hidden subsidies to state enterprises through the credit system became very large in the 1989-92 period, as direct subsidies over the state budget were curtailed. In these years, outstanding credit to state enterprises exceeded 10 percent of GDP, and the subsidy element (through the strongly negative real rate of interest) represented several percentage points of GDP. The data presented above therefore seriously underestimates the true size of public dissavings and also underestimates the inflationary pressures that originated with the inability of the public sector, including state enterprises, to cover expenditures.

Stabilization policies in Vietnam during the early 1990s therefore required, as a necessary but far from sufficient condition, an end to inflationary financing of the budget. In order to achieve this, a restructuring of the public sector was necessary, with further cuts in nonessential expenditures and reduced explicit and implicit subsidies. The major source of improvement, however, would have to come from increased revenues. The fact that the role of the state had to change did not imply that the new state would be cheaper; rather, the opposite was true.

Taxation. On the revenue side, the decline in transfers from state enterprises--characteristic of centrally planned economies in the initial stages of a transition to a market economy--had to be compensated for by an increase in taxes, import duties and increased fees for public services. The cutback in assistance from CMEA, in particular from the Soviet Union, also had to be offset. Oil revenues accruing to the central government by the early 1980s amounted to some 3 to 4 percent of GDP, but these were insufficient to close the fiscal gap.

Most of the increase in state revenue had to come from taxes. Tax reforms represented steps in the right direction, and tax revenue increased somewhat. However, the implementation of the new tax laws proved to be far more difficult than their promulgation. Nonpayment of taxes remained endemic, and actual tax rates were still subject to negotiation and outright evasion. Corruption was widespread and by 1992-93 was growing rapidly. Also, taxes collected by provincial and local governments on behalf of the central government were often only partly transferred to higher levels. The weakness of the state in the collection of taxes and import duties was but one symptom of its poor capacity to enforce new legislation and "make its writ run," a trend we can observe in almost all areas analyzed in this study.

Despite a slight increase in 1990-92, tax revenue collected by the Vietnamese government remained extremely low until 1992-93, only 4.6 percent of GDP in 1990. It was imperative to raise tax revenue substantially, otherwise inflationary Central Bank credit would continue to play havoc with the government's attempts at macroeconomic stabilization.

Direct income taxes were virtually non-existent. The largest share of the total tax yield was contributed by taxes on nonagricultural cooperatives and the private sector, which together paid an average 10 percent turnover tax. In 1990, agricultural taxes contributed 15.6 percent of total tax revenue; taxes on trade composed 43.6 percent of the total, with taxes on nonagricultural cooperatives and the private sector making up 40.7 percent of total taxes.

The government introduced new taxes. In June 1989, the National Assembly approved a tax reform proposal that contained the following two key elements:

- Replacement of the current tax regime, based on decrees and regulations by a system with explicit legislation.
- Taxation of state enterprises to be commensurate with taxation of the growing private sector.

At the same time, five new tax laws were promulgated (although implementation was slow): an agricultural tax, a turnover tax, a tax on profits, a special commodity tax, and a personal income tax.

For reasons indicated above, a strengthening of existing tax collection institutions may, however, be as important as the introduction of new taxes. Again, this had important political economy implications.

Foreign Exchange Gap. The balance of trade in both the convertible and nonconvertible area narrowed considerably after 1989. According to preliminary estimates, the drastic decline in imports from the Soviet Union in 1991 actually meant that Vietnam, for the first time, ran a trade surplus with the ruble area in that year. In 1992 and 1993 there was a deterioration in the balance of trade.

Superficially, Vietnam was on the verge of closing its trade gaps. The Vietnamese export market responded positively to the improved incentive structure, showing a healthy threefold increase after 1986. If the competitive real rate of exchange was defensible despite the inflationary domestic environment, there was every reason to believe that exports could continue to register dynamic growth. However, a number of questions surrounded this apparent success.

The first question related to Vietnam's foreign debt. The foreign debt in convertible currency exceeded US$3.5 billion in 1990, with accumulated payments arrears in excess of US$2 billion. The scheduled debt service ratio in hard currency of approximately 25 percent may not appear alarmingly high, in comparison with other heavily indebted Third World countries, but it constituted a heavy drain on the country's resources; arrears continued to accumulate, in the absence of rescheduling and debt-reducing agreements with major creditors. Also, the new nature of economic relations with the CMEA area (discussed further on) may signify that in future years Vietnam will have to incur negative net transfers to the ruble area, thereby weakening further the national payments capacity.

Another area of concern was the weak control over foreign exchange exercised by the central government. This issue has been discussed earlier; it is sufficient to emphasize here that the heavy obligations in foreign exchange confronting the central government--such as debt service payments and a large number of capital goods and inputs for which the state remained responsible--conflicted with the interests at the lower levels of authority, in particular state enterprises and trading companies that were quite successfully struggling to use their hard currency earnings in various speculative and rent-seeking activities. It is illuminating to consider that out of an annual turnover of trade with the convertible area of perhaps US$3-4 billion--smuggling included--the central government was only able to raise US$150 million in customs duties and trade taxes. Indeed, despite having started with an exceedingly closed and introspective economy, Vietnam had (involuntarily, one could say) developed a highly open economy, with actual trade restrictions and tariffs far lower than in most developing countries. In this "spontaneous" way, Vietnam may actually have gone too far, and too fast, in trade liberalization. A controlled, gradual liberalization, with a parallel development of factor markets, public institutions, macroeconomic stabilization, and domestic competitiveness may have been preferable.

We are not, of course, advocating a return to the old, bureaucratic allocation of foreign exchange--we merely want to stress that the Vietnamese economy was in many ways badly prepared for the big-bang that occurred because of the way in which the specific area of foreign trade was liberalized in 1989. This reveals the consequences of the specific path the Vietnamese economy had traveled to arrive at "1989," a transition within which trade with the West had been rather unimportant compared with other processes. However, if the premiums accruing to holders of trade licenses, quotas, and dollars had not been successfully eliminated and replaced by a more transparent market for foreign exchange, severe distortions would have remained, and the struggle for control over export earnings would have continued, with the central government likely to have been the big loser.

CMEA Assistance. In June 1978, Vietnam was admitted as a member of the Council of Mutual Economic Assistance. Until 1989-90, Vietnam's external sector was dominated by its economic relations with the CMEA nations, in particular, with the Soviet Union.

It is next to impossible to make even a tentative attempt to measure the size of CMEA economic assistance to Vietnam. Economic relations between Vietnam and CMEA covered a very wide range of economic relations. In the mid-1980s, CMEA accounted for some 80 percent of Vietnam's foreign trade, which was conducted according to CMEA procedures, using the transferable ruble as a unit of account but with strong barter elements. Since Vietnam consistently ran a large deficit, in particular when trading with the Soviet Union, most of Vietnam's imports were financed with long-term concessional loans. Vietnam's trade deficit with the Soviet Union exceeded 1 billion rubles annually in the early and mid-1980s, which could be used as a very crude measure of the size of Soviet commodity and project assistance. The ratio of Vietnam's imports to exports with the Soviet Union was around 4:1 in the first half of the 1980s, and around 3:1 between 1986-88. After 1989, this ratio declined further. As a result of these trade deficits, Vietnam had accumulated a foreign debt to the Soviet Union of 8-10 billion rubles.

The value of Soviet project assistance in the 1986 to 1990 period is estimated at 1.5 billion rubles, of which around 150 million was in the form of grants. Project aid received encompassed virtually all areas of the Vietnamese economy but was concentrated on capital equipment for the construction of infrastructure, industrial plants, hydroelectric power stations, and the exploitation of natural resources. Other assistance included considerable technical assistance and the training of students in Eastern Europe; more than 170,000 Vietnamese received education or training in the USSR, and several tens of thousands studied in Eastern Europe.

Project aid was concentrated on large-scale, capital-intensive projects. In 1989-90 there was considerable debate about the quality of the assistance, and both sides expressed concern about the mode of cooperation. Delays in the execution of projects were common, and a large number of Soviet-financed projects worked far below capacity.

Apart from the USSR, almost all of the European CMEA countries had provided assistance to Vietnam. The total size of non-Soviet CMEA assistance is estimated to have been between 100 and 200 million rubles annually (UNDP 1990).

As is well known, major reforms were undertaken in CMEA prior to its collapse in 1991. Of particular importance for Vietnam was the abandonment of the transferable ruble in trade with CMEA. As of January 1991, all trade was to be conducted in hard currency, according to world market prices.

As a result of this reform and economic problems in the CMEA countries, particularly in the Soviet Union, which in 1989-91 was often unable to honor existing trade commitments, Vietnam's trade with the CMEA area declined drastically. Since Vietnam had in the past relied heavily on CMEA for imports of a large number of essential commodities such as petroleum products, fertilizers, steel, and raw cotton, an immediate effect of the changes was that a wide range of commodities had to be purchased on the world market and paid for in hard currency. Given the large trade deficit with the nonconvertible area in the past, the shift to world market prices signified a considerable loss for Vietnam, a loss that can be estimated at, perhaps, 2-3 percent of GDP.

The domestic repercussions of the changing relations with the Soviet Union appeared in the form of shortages of key inputs such as fertilizers and cotton. Also, a number of manufacturing firms producing for the CMEA market--generally producing, low-quality products under semi-barter agreements in which the Soviet Union supplied all essential inputs in exchange for the finished products--lost their markets.

To absorb the terms of trade shock, the Vietnamese authorities allowed domestic prices to adjust in order to pass on the increase in CMEA prices. In this respect, the shift to world market prices had a positive effect on the structure of relative prices, since CMEA prices had constituted an important source of distortions and rents in the Vietnamese economy. It might also be argued that the decline in Soviet assistance accelerated the process of economic reform in various other respects; for example, it made clear to the Vietnamese authorities that the foreign exchange regime had to be reformed in order to facilitate a necessary realignment of external economic relations away from the nonconvertible area.

It may be observed, however, that the fiscal implications of the Soviet aid cut were perhaps not as serious as might have been expected. Most of the Soviet commodity aid had been channeled directly to state enterprises, without accruing to the central budget. Indirectly, some of this aid had ended up in the treasury in the form of profits that the beneficiary enterprises partly transferred to the central or local government, but the immediate effect of the discontinuation of subsidized Soviet inputs was to reduce profits, or increase losses, in a significant number of state enterprises. In this way, the change put a heavier burden on the state banks (which were "forced" to bail out ailing SOEs) than on the state budget. It is clear, however, that the near collapse of Soviet commodity assistance had both direct and indirect effects on the inflationary pressures and pattern of rent creation in the economy.

Prices, Inflation and Markets

Distribution and Exchange Systems Before and After 1989

Vietnam's product markets after 1989 tended to be highly competitive. Entry and exit barriers were weak; state trading companies would often use private traders to break attempts by other provinces to protect their own markets. This sometimes had the deleterious effect of exposing farmers to unrestricted pressure from purchasers. Borders were largely open; smuggling was rampant.

Prior to 1989 the Vietnamese economy was, as discussed earlier, segmented by production within and outside the central plan. Under the planning system, central planners allocated resources to locally and centrally run state enterprises at very low prices. Within this sector of the economy, prices mattered little, in comparison with the physical production targets that were established for each enterprise.

Outside the centrally planned system and the official price structure, there was another set of prices determined by supply and demand. This segment of the economy included all private sector production. After the introduction of the Three Plan system in the early 1980s, market prices also applied to the surplus production of state enterprises above the Plan A target. Consumer goods prices were determined both officially and in the free market. Under the state rationing system, essential commodities were sold, at strongly subsidized prices, to civil servants, state enterprise workers, students, and other categories of people with access to ration cards.

In general, free market prices tended to be several times higher than official prices. The official price of rice, for example, was 50 dong per kilo in June 1988, whereas the free market price was 450. The official price of urea, to take another example, was 190 dong per kilo, but the free market price was 500 dong (June 1988). Part of the price differential between the two sets of prices originated in the rate of exchange, which was strongly overvalued until 1989. The free ("black") market price of the dollar was, before 1989, between five and ten times above the official rate of exchange.

Early attempts in the early 1980s to reduce the differences between free market prices and official prices were reinforced again in 1987, when, following the 1986 Sixth Party Congress and the official announcement of *doi moi*, a new system of "official business prices" was introduced. In 1987, the ration system was abolished for a large number of commodities, and official prices of nonessential goods[4] were raised to a level close to free market prices. Administered prices of most consumer goods and of a large number of agricultural and industrial inputs were increased sharply in 1987 and 1988, but despite this effort to realign the price structure, free market prices continued to lie appreciably above the official prices, albeit with lower margins than before. Lacking credibility and coherence, the early attempts at price and currency reform only served to add fuel to inflationary expectations. In particular, differences between official and free market prices continued to be very large in the markets for key agricultural products, such as rice, and for foreign exchange (and, as a consequence of the distorted rate of exchange, in the markets for all imported goods).

In March 1989, the price reform was accelerated, as almost all prices were deregulated, and the distinction between official business prices and free market prices was abolished.[5] With the exception of a few so-called social benefit items (electricity, house rent, medicines, and a few others), all consumer goods sold through the state outlets were sold at prices very close to the free market level and were frequently adjusted to keep pace with free market prices. The price reform was accompanied by a drastic devaluation that brought the official rate of exchange very close to the free market rate.

The anchoring of the new price system in credible "macro prices" was made possible by, among other things, improved producer prices for rice, the establishment of a realistic rate of exchange and--although only during 1989--the establishment of a positive real rate of interest.

Of course, many distortions in the price system remained. But contrary to the earlier distortions created by central planning and the two-price system, the new relative prices suffered from more ordinary market distortions such as monopoly pricing, monopsony power on the part of many local state trading enterprises, entry barriers to many markets that attracted newcomers, supply bottlenecks giving rise to "scarcity rents," and so on. In particular, the Vietnamese price system was marked by the economy's perverse capital structure, inherited from the traditional model, with vast amounts of capital locked into unprofitable activities and a severe scarcity of capital in other areas. This situation gave rise to highly profitable "niches" as the process of marketization and the further development of factor markets proceeded. This was healthy, since it facilitated the necessary restructuring of the economy, but in the absence of well-functioning factor markets, the process was perforce very slow, and in the meantime, relative prices diverged strongly from social costs. Furthermore, this pattern of development tended to concentrate economic power in those areas that already had good political access, especially the state sector and urban areas, leading to the beginning of a vicious circle. This was one clear cause of the pattern of projects approved at the November 1993 Donor's Conference in the wake of the recommencement of IMF, World Bank, and Asian Development Bank lending on the eve of the removal of the U.S. embargo just before Tet 1994.

Inflation

For many years, the Vietnamese economy had been characterized by repressed inflation, typical of centrally planned economies. Officially, the rate of inflation was close to zero during the Second FYP (1976-80), but as shortages became aggravated during the deep crisis of the late 1970s, inflationary pressures came to the surface, and the economy then entered what was to become a decade with a combination of high open inflation and symptoms of repressed inflation, such as rationing and a severe shortage of inputs and consumer goods at official prices.

Developments in the post-1989 period are interesting and revealing. Inflation had decreased drastically in 1989, which surprised many observers. Elimination of the two-price system and the massive devaluations were not accompanied by an acceleration of inflation, as many had feared; instead, a relative stabilization of the price level ensued. The rate of inflation (consumer prices in Hanoi) went down from 300-500 percent per year in 1986-1988 to around 50 percent between March 1989 and March 1990. In May to July 1989, prices actually fell slightly. The development of the monthly rates of inflation is illustrated in Figure 5.7.

One reason why the devaluations of 1988-89 did not cause an acceleration of inflation is that imported goods had already tended to follow the parallel exchange rate on the free market. The primary effect of the devaluations was therefore that profit margins were squeezed for smugglers, holders of import licenses, and other such groups that earned their living on the difference between the official and parallel rates. A liberalization of imports of consumer goods and a massive increase in smuggling, following a relaxation of border controls, also contributed to increased competition.

The major cause of the success of anti-inflationary policies was, however, that the devaluations were accompanied by a series of other measures that served to absorb excess liquidity and also to reduce inflationary expectations. The less accommodating and more disciplined monetary policy was an important ingredient. A credit squeeze in 1989 obliged many enterprises to shed workers and reduce production; however, few bankruptcies were recorded in the state sector.

An important part of the fight against inflation was (as has already been noted) a drastic increase in interest rates. Between March 1989 and late 1990, both borrowers and savers were confronted with a positive real interest rate. The rate of interest was, during this period, linked to the previous month's inflation, plus a few percent. This signified that the real rate of interest had become almost 10 percent per month during the first half of 1989, when inflation decreased dramatically--a clear example of "overshooting." The real rate of interest thereafter declined, becoming zero or slightly negative again, as inflation stabilized around 2 percent per month.

The rise in the rate of interest in 1989, in addition to various psychological factors such as the public's increased confidence in the banking system, meant that the banks increased their deposits considerably. Vietnamese households switched from saving in gold and dollars to saving in bank accounts, and a vast amount of liquidity was thereby absorbed. The velocity of money was greatly reduced. This success in creating confidence in the banking system and in the domestic currency and the concomitant mopping up of excess liquidity was probably the single most important reason for the relative success in fighting inflation in 1989.

Thus, by 1991-92 the picture had changed again. The continued large fiscal deficit and slacker monetary policies threatened the relative success in macroeconomic stabilization in 1989. To these sources of inflationary pressure should be added the effects of the negative real rate of interest and the confidence crisis affecting the secondary credit market discussed earlier. A switch back from savings in banks and credit cooperatives to inflation hedges like gold and dollars had been taking place during most of 1990 and 1991, pushing up the prices of assets that served as a hedge against inflation.

The "confidence effect" is illustrated in Table 8.4 below. This shows the way the money supply (as measured by M1) and the consumer price index follow each other rather closely in the period 1986-92, expect for when periods confidence is growing and the velocity of circulation is reduced (1989) or periods when the opposite takes place (1990).

The 1989 stabilization measures were, in short, largely temporary in character, attacking the symptoms of inflation rather than the causes. The mopping up of excess liquidity cannot be repeated, only reversed, in the presence of a continued large fiscal deficit. By 1992 a determined effort needed to be made to reduce the fiscal deficit by combining of expenditure reduction with an increase in state revenues. In particular, the plethora of explicit and implicit subsidies to the state sector had to be curtailed. This was attained, helped by the shift to profitability of large parts of the state sector, which eased the political economy considerations that underlay the macroeconomic destabilization of 1990-92.

The tax reforms of 1990 were a step in the right direction; around 1992, revenues rose substantially. However, the practice of ex post facto negotiation with individual state enterprises about their tax liabilities continued. The financing of the fiscal deficit was made more difficult in 1990, and even more so in 1991, after the cut in Soviet assistance, which amounted to as much as 4 to 5 percent of Vietnam's GDP. For this reason, domestic noninflationary financing of state expenditure would have had to increase substantially in order to avoid an acceleration of monetary emission via State Bank credits. This was one reason for not putting on the brakes too hard.

With both inflation and unemployment rising rapidly, as in 1991, the trade-off confronting the authorities was classical. What was at stake was more than a choice between inflation and unemployment, however, since an uncontrolled inflationary spiral, accompanied by a credibility crisis within the financial sector, could have jeopardized key ingredients in the process of economic reform, such as the abolition of price controls. A return to the stop-go policies characterizing earlier stabilization attempts in the 1980s would be devastating. Since high inflationary expectations were starting to build up again in 1990-92, it was likely that the longer the government waited before taking measures to break the vicious circle of inflationary pressures and erosion of confidence, the more severe any austerity package aimed at macrostabilization would have to be. There was thus a severe timing problem. This was related to the balance between the rate at which the required subsidy level to the state sector declined and the erosion of popular confidence in macroeconomic stability. Both threatened regime survival.

Vietnam 1994-95: From Systemic Change to Accelerated Development?

The evidence from the early 1990s shows that once again the Vietnamese economy showed its capacity to adapt to new circumstances and to come out of a threatening crisis with new vigor. As will be further discussed in the concluding chapter, macroeconomic developments after 1992 were highly positive in virtually all respects. Economic growth accelerated, and domestic savings grew with FDI to provide an adequate basis for trend rates of GDP growth near 10 percent annually. Therefore, 1993 and 1994 can be said to represent a new phase in the process of socioeconomic development. Or rather, by 1993 or 1994, Vietnam appeared to have managed the final stages of the shift from systemic change to accelerated development.

Notes

1. Data should be read with great caution. For example, a serious bias in Vietnam's investment data from the 1980s can be seen in the undervaluation of imported capital goods arising from the overvalued exchange rate (until 1989). The bias was possibly reinforced by the mechanism for price negotiations between the CMEA members, although the valuation of the increasingly overvalued ruble is another complication, working in the opposite direction.

2. For example, according to some reports and largely as a result of the public's lack of confidence in the financial system and domestic currency, in

the early 1990s US$200 million of Vietnam's scarce hard currency earnings were used annually to finance commercial gold imports.

3. Data on Vietnam's non-CMEA assistance are incomplete. However, a good overview is provided by UNDP (1990).

4. Consumer goods classified as essential are rice, fish sauce, pork, sugar, soap and kerosene.

5. The exceptions were few: electricity, oil, cement, transportation, and a few others. Remaining fringe benefits, or subsidies, to state employees mainly covered subsidized housing, electricity, and social security.

Tables

TABLE 8.1 Saving and Investment 1985 to 1989 as Percent of GDP

	1985	1986	1987	1988	1989
Investment	12.9	8.6	8.0	8.5	10.0
State budget	8.4	4.1	3.5	3.9	6.3
Public enterprises	2.5	2.5	2.5	2.1	0.5
Other domestic	2.0	2.0	2.0	2.0	2.0
Current account deficit	7.3	10.3	9.1	10.5	4.9
National savings	5.6	-1.7	-1.1	-2.0	5.1

Source: IBRD: "Vietnam, Stabilization and Structural Reforms," 30 April, 1990:table 2.2.

TABLE 8.2 Possible Scenario for Vietnam's Financing of Gross Investment in a Short-Term Perspective (as of 1989-90) (in percent)

	1989	1995
Gross investment	10	18
Foreign savings (= current account deficit)	5	3
From convertible area	1	3
From non-convertible area	4	--
Domestic savings	5	15

Source: Authors' own calculations, de Vylder and Fforde, 1991.

TABLE 8.3 Summary of Budgetary Operations (as percent of GDP)

	1986	*1987*	*1988*	*1989*	*1990*
(1) Revenue	13.2	12.2	11.3	11.9	13.1
(2) Current expenditures	13.4	12.8	14.1	12.3	15.1
(3) Government savings [(1) - (2)]	-0.2	-0.6	-2.8	-0.4	-2.0
(4) Capital expenditure	5.6	3.9	4.4	6.4	4.5
(5) Overall deficit [(3) - (4)]ᵃ	-5.8	-4.4	-7.1	-6.8	-6.5
Financing					
(6) Foreign loans and grants	2.2	1.4	2.4	1.5	4.0
(7) Credit from state bank (net)	3.6	2.9	2.9	6.0	2.5

ᵃFigures do not add exactly due to rounding.
Source: Dollar 1992:table 8.2.

TABLE 8.4   Relationship between Money Supply and Inflation: Annual Percentage Changes

	1986	*1987*	*1988*	*1989*	*1990*	*1991*	*1992*
Money Supply (MI)	512	273	400	130	34	72	20
CPI Hanoi	487	317	311	35	67	67	17

Source: State Bank of Vietnam and various IMF reports.

Figures

FIGURE 8.1 Accumulation
(percent of GDP and PNI)

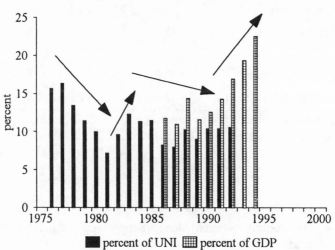

■ percent of UNI ⊞ percent of GDP

Note: UNI is used national income (on NMP basis). 1994 data are estimated from reports in *Thoi bao kinh te Viet nam*. Arrowed lines refer to possible historical stages.
Source: SO 1987, 1988a, 1990a, 1990c, 1993, 1994a.

9

Conclusions: Tiger on a Bicycle?

In this book, we readily admit, we attempt to analyze topics that will inevitably become far clearer as further research is carried out. The main aim of the book has been to outline an analytical approach to the understanding of the Vietnamese transition from plan to market, but as the writing of contemporary history is always risky, much modesty is required. New facts will be presented, and new interpretations will emerge. More multidisciplinary research will be needed in order to grasp the complex interactions between the spontaneous pressure for reform from below and the initiatives (sometimes very bold, but often contradictory, reactive, and reactionary) from above.

We are also fully aware of the fact that the issues of transition from plan to market--and the related problem of structural adjustment programs in the Third World--are controversial topics. They are surrounded by strong emotions and nurtured by deeply entrenched methodological and ideological convictions. Thus, even many economists who would normally agree on a large number of issues are likely to find themselves in deep disagreement over, say, the merits of "shock treatment" versus a gradualist approach in the former Soviet republics, or over the role of the World Bank and the IMF in designing structural adjustment programs in sub-Saharan Africa.

As we leave, in this final chapter, the relative security that the peculiarities of the Vietnamese process have provided us with, we are therefore highly conscious of the controversial nature of some of the more general lessons we would like to discuss here.

However, the main questions we pose are all related to the Vietnamese experience. Can the Vietnamese transition be regarded as successful? Our answer is "Yes, but--." We will therefore attempt to indicate in what respects it has been successful, some of the main reasons for the accomplishments, and finally, some of the clouds on the horizon that may justify our "but--."

Systemic Reform: What Has Been Accomplished?

As has been emphasized repeatedly in this book, Vietnam in 1995 should be regarded as a market economy. Whereas the changes prior to 1989 primarily attempted to attack the inefficiencies of the DRV model, policy and practice after 1989 attacked, then demolished, the very foundations of the old system.

In the mid-1990s, Vietnam still had an emerging market economy, with the development of factor markets lagging behind the explosive development of commodity marketization, and it was certainly not yet an efficient market economy. In view of the still dominant role of the state enterprise sector, it could not yet be called a capitalist market economy, although petty capitalist production dominated completely within the large agricultural sector. However, the inner logic of the economy and its "laws of motion" can only be *analyzed* in terms of a market economy. The primary foreign source of inspiration in Vietnam had not been the development in the former Soviet Union, but rather the spectacular economic development experienced in the newly industrialized countries in the Southeast Asia region.

As in China, the Vietnamese reforms had been more economic than political in character. The Vietnamese leaders' lesson from recent events in Eastern Europe and the former USSR appears to be straightforward: It is imperative to advance further with economic reform, in order to avoid economic chaos. At the same time, political liberalization that might endanger the hegemonic role of the ruling Communist Party should be avoided.

A certain political liberalization had taken place during the 1980s, and the political debate had become far more open than in earlier years. It had not, however, gone far enough to permit the questioning of the legitimacy of the Communist Party, and the glasnost part of Vietnamese reforms had had a pronounced cyclical character, with piecemeal liberalization measures followed by periodic attacks on dissidents.

However, if we limit ourselves to discussion of economic reforms, there is no doubt that Vietnam had advanced very far along, and even beyond, the road of transition from plan to market. Contrary to the situation in

1986-89, when conservative forces could have halted the reform process, had they been strong enough in the Communist Party, by 1995 the changes had to be be characterized as irreversible--the issue was one of speed rather than direction.

When comparing the Vietnamese reform process with the "typical" structural adjustment programs implemented in other low-income countries, in particular in sub-Saharan Africa, there are at least as many differences as similarities. Although certain objectives--macro stabilization, reduction of price distortions, a redefinition of the role of the state, liberalization of the foreign trade and exchange rate regime, and so forth-- are almost identical, it must be stressed that Vietnam started from an highly centralized system in which the private sector played an exceedingly marginal role where relative prices mattered little. State monopoly power in the allocation of resources was far more pervasive than in virtually all other Third World countries, and "structural adjustment" in Vietnam did not merely signify "adjustment," but a virtual revolution in the entire development concept and strategy. In Vietnam, for example, it was not only a question of "getting the prices right"--it was, to begin with, a question of making prices matter. Still, there is no doubt that by 1995 Vietnam, in many important respects, had accomplished more in terms of systemic reform than the majority of sub-Saharan countries, where, with few exceptions, adjustment had been slow, painful, and riddled with policy reversals.

The positive achievements in Vietnam, compared both with other former Eastern Bloc countries and with low-income countries in Latin America and sub-Saharan Africa, are particularly striking when we look at actual achievements in more traditional macroeconomic categories.

According to conventional wisdom, economic development in countries undergoing structural adjustment or systemic change typically exhibits a J-curve, popularly referred to as "short-term pain for long-term gain." In actual practice, however, the J often tends to look more like an L--short-term pain for medium-term stagnation--or can even appear as a symbol (/), denoting the free-fall characteristic of some of the former Soviet republics.

As discussed in earlier chapters and as illustrated in the statistical tables, the development in Vietnam was unusual in this respect. Economic growth was high during most of the reform period, and it actually accelerated when the pace of economic reform accelerated. This was obvious in the very early stages of the process, in 1979-81. The picture was less clear in 1986-88. In this period, official commitment to the transition was clearly pronounced, but the measures actually being undertaken were halfhearted and contradictory, although they did serve the useful purpose of eroding the very foundation of the DRV model, as will be further discussed.

In 1989, however, the death blow to the two-price system and quantitative planning targets had a decisively positive impact; growth accelerated while inflation decelerated. The "slack" in the system was reduced, but it was still too early to create enough confidence and stability to elicit a sustainable supply response from the private sector and to introduce a favorable climate for long-term, private investment. Since 1992, the rate of growth has increased further, and systemic reforms have been consolidated and deepened. Official data outlining economic performance in 1993 and 1994 show growth of around 7-8 percent per annum, inflation at under 10 percent, and fiscal and balance of payments deficits well below crisis levels (SO 1995; World Bank 1995b).

Since official statistics simply do not capture large areas of economic activity, overall growth is likely to have been underrecorded. This is true to an even larger extent regarding data on private savings. The remarkable surge of savings, and the changed composition of savings and investment that appears to have taken place in the early 1990s, deserves a few additional comments. It is particularly important as the transition from stabilization to sustained capital accumulation and investment has turned out to be the Achilles' heel of many attempts at reform and structural adjustment in other parts of the world.

To begin with, experience from other countries suggests that rapid GDP growth rates of near 10 percent per annum would require investment rates almost three times higher, if an incremental capital output ratio of three is assumed (after the early gains of reduced slack in the system have been made). Given that Vietnam in the mid-1990s was growing at around 10% per annum, this calculation implies that the country was likely to be investing at a rate of close to 30 percent of GDP. Of this, perhaps 5 to 7 percent was coming from foreign direct investment and overseas development assistance (ODA) (with substantially more expected to come in the second half of the decade as the international financial institutions (IFIs) flows started to come on stream). Since the official budget indicated that the state was contributing little or nothing to domestic savings, this suggests that the private sector's contributions to domestic savings in Vietnam had grown from almost nothing in 1988-89 to around 25 percent of GDP by 1994.

Such levels are normal, or even modest, for fast-growing East Asian economies (but extremely high by sub-Saharan Africa's standards, where domestic savings rates exceeding 10 to 15 percent of GDP have become uncommon). What is typically Vietnamese, however, is that almost all of the financial intermediation required to shift these flows around the economy was occurring *informally*.

To support such high levels of savings there must already have existed a well-developed informal capital market. The large volume of credit handled by informal intermediaries indicates that transaction costs in these "savings and loan networks" were surprisingly low. This is a valuable asset, that should be allowed to coexist with the banking system for many years to come. However, a better-developed formal financial system would obviously be required in order to enable the Vietnamese investment pattern to move on to more large-scale, technologically sophisticated ventures. Also, as Vietnamese enterprises move from family ventures to joint-stock companies, the informal credit market, based on personal knowledge of each debtor and strict individual liability, will become increasingly obsolete in the modern sector of the economy.

It is worth stressing that these very high rates of savings were the main domestic source of investable funds. Although some resources certainly derived from the plundering of SOEs by their managers, the state was no longer the main source of resources. Instead, the post-1989 Vietnamese market economy showed, like other such economies, that resources are created by the process of expansion of markets and increased business profits. The dramatic increase in personal savings in Vietnam may also partly reflect the erosion of social safety nets that has taken place in recent years. Without collective protection, families seek to build up their own reserves. It is these very high rates of profits and savings and the existence of options in agriculture and services that permitted the labor market to develop in such a relatively harmonious manner. Redundant former SOE workers could return to their home villages and to farming or engage in petty trade, construction, and the like. This put a floor under the level of real wages that had to be paid to keep the workforce; otherwise, workers would simply have quit.[1]

Fortunately, as things worked out, Vietnamese businesses were sufficiently profitable to pay the wages required. One important element of this was the very high levels of investment and reinvestment, and in this respect, the large and well-developed (but informal) Vietnamese capital markets showed capital how to move to profitable opportunities, of which there were many.

Reasons for Success

If we accept that *doi moi* represents a success story, by any international standard, it remains to summarize the reasons for the success.

Being in the Right Place at the Right Time

A superficial, but nevertheless relevant, first explanation is Vietnam's geographic location. Nothing succeeds like success, and Vietnam has today joined in the East Asian regional optimism. However, it has not always been a fortunate thing for a nation to be situated in Asia. In the 1940s and 1950s, for example, the rate of economic growth in Asia was appreciably lower than that in Africa or Latin America, and in the 1960s, Indochina was certainly not an ideal place for economic development. However, as growth has accelerated all over East Asia during the last two decades, *doi moi* can be said to have been in the right place at the right time.

It was not primarily Vietnam's exports that benefited from the country's location in the middle of the world's fastest-growing economic sphere. By 1995, Vietnamese exports remained rather unaffected by regional demand. The rapid increase registered in Vietnam's exports during the first half of the 1990s was largely based on a few products--mainly crude oil, rice, and marine products commodities, which could be exported anywhere. However, in 1994-95 textiles exports started to grow extremely fast, helped by access to the European market, in a classic response to the internationalization of the economy.

In a medium- and long-term perspective, however, the dynamics of the regional markets will have a profound impact on Vietnam's trade composition. And what was already happening by the mid-1990s, and happening fast, was a surge in foreign direct investment from the region into areas such as light industry and certain services (transportation, tourism, and so on). As real wages increased rapidly in neighboring countries, which were constantly upgrading the structure of their manufacturing industry and services sector, the role for Vietnam as a supplier of low-cost goods and services was bound to become important. In the not-too-distant future, Vietnam could also become an important regional hub in areas such as civil aviation, financial services, shipping, and electronic services.

Some foreign explanations of the Asian "miracle" in recent years have put heavy emphasis on religious and cultural factors, for example, on the role of Confucianism. Furthermore, when ordinary econometric regressions fail to capture the astonishing developments in East Asia with ordinary growth equations, a cultural "dummy variable" is occasionally added. While we fully acknowledge, and have tried to understand, how Vietnamese traditions have developed in a historical perspective (see Chapter 2), we would not dare to assess in what way such cultural factors may have contributed to the acceleration of economic growth since 1989. However, in view of the role played by such factors as expectations and psychology in all macroeconomic and development theory, we are not oblivious to the fact that Vietnam's proximity to a number of rapidly growing, self-confident countries greatly facilitated the economic transformation that is taking place in the mid-1990s.

Winners and Losers

A wealth of data, some of which has been presented in this book, supports the view that real living standards for the majority of Vietnamese improved substantially during the period under review. Although statistical pitfalls make comparisons during short periods of time difficult, it also appears as if gains had been greatest during periods of official support to reform (1980-81, 1989 onward), whereas the situation was more mixed when state policy ran contrary to spontaneous forces (1984-85, perhaps 1987-88). This is hardly surprising: The situation improved when people had been given more freedom to do what they wanted to do.

Concerning agriculture, in the mid-1990s the large majority of Vietnamese still lived in rural areas, thus the abolition of producer cooperatives, the work-point system, and obligatory deliveries to the state brought tremendous benefits, as shown by the supply response from the farmers. Agricultural production and incomes rose, and the rural economy diversified. The availability of consumer goods in rural areas improved dramatically (although differences in this respect between urban and rural areas remained large).

The losers were fewer in number and more difficult to identify. Rural cooperative cadres had lost their jobs and their power, as had a number of bureaucrats and party officials at all levels. This does not signify, however, that they were necessarily worse off; many former cadres became successful businessmen.

Large numbers of state workers also lost their jobs, but as new employment opportunities mushroomed, it would be misleading to regard all who had been retrenched as victims. Without denying that unemployment was a problem, the fact that retrenchment met with so little organized opposition from the people concerned can only partly be explained with reference to the still repressive nature of Vietnamese politics and society. Many people simply found a better life outside the state sector.

More significant, however, is the fact that the dismantling of the collective social security system continued at full speed, affecting a large and vulnerable sector of the population. The very poor are likely to have suffered. Data on public expenditure in health and education reveals a mixed picture, but user charges had been introduced, or raised, in health clinics and primary schools. Illiteracy had returned to areas where it had almost been eradicated before. Many young girls, in particular, were being taken out of school; with higher school fees at all levels, families tended to give priority to providing their sons with a proper education. Income differences were increasing rapidly--albeit after starting from a very low level. Negative social effects, such as increased youth criminality, drug use, and prostitution, were visible to all, particularly in urban areas.

However, by and large, poverty in Vietnam had been reduced, at least since 1989, and the quality of life had been greatly improved. People undoubtedly felt freer than they had ten or even five years previously. The constituency behind the reform process had been large from the very beginning; the winners easily outnumbered the losers. A return to the old model would have had little or no political support within (or outside) the country.

In these respects, the Vietnamese reform process appears to be more "Asian" than "East European." The following conclusion from the empirical study "Income Distribution, Poverty and Welfare in Transitional Economies" may serve to emphazize this comparison:

> In conclusion, there appears to be considerable evidence suggesting that, with some exceptions, the massive surge in poverty and loss of welfare observed in Eastern Europe over the last 4 years is, for a good part, due to macroeconomic factors and, in the end, to the choice of an accelerated "Western approach" to the transition . . . Strangely, in the case of China, the conclusions appear somewhat the opposite. The overall "Asian approach" to policy reform has been far more efficient and equitable (in spite of some rises in income and regional inequality) than that followed in Eastern Europe and has contributed to a phenomenal reduction in poverty incidence in only 12 years (Cornia 1994:603).

It is also distinctly more "Asian" than "African," for African structural adjustment programs often led to increased poverty and thus failed to gain widespread popular support and political credibility.

It may be argued (see, for example, David Dollar 1994) that the Vietnamese reform process was relatively "easy" because of the low degree of industrialization. Measures such as strengthening property rights and freeing prices in agriculture were sufficient to satisfy a majority of the population, and a positive supply response could be achieved almost instantaneously. On the other hand, there were--compared to the USSR or even China--few industries connected through a central plan, and the dislocations in the industrial sector following the end of central planning were small, compared to those in many other transitional economies.

Although these observations may explain why the number of direct losers was smaller in Vietnam than in, say, the former Soviet Union, we would not--as should be clear from this book--support the view that the transition from plan to market in Vietnam was a smooth and easy process. Also, although it is true that the Vietnamese economy was underdeveloped compared to the economies of Eastern Europe when the transition started, it was certainly more sophisticated than most economies in sub-Saharan Africa, where attempts at structural adjustment and systemic reform have been far less successful.

One important reason for the relative success of *doi moi* in an international perspective was, in our opinion, the fact that the timing and sequencing of reform--to the extent that one can refer to the process in such terms--clearly deviated from the standard prescription. Orthodox economic advice, as formulated by a number of influential institutions and individual economists, contends that macro stabilization must come at the very first stage of the reform process. This has become the "conventional wisdom," but this sequencing has, in practice, often signified that the programs have started with a highly unpopular austerity package, followed by price and exchange rate reform, accelerating inflation, and policy reversal. We do not deny the need for macro stabilization or price reform in countries with unsustainable deficits and distorted prices, but the Vietnamese case does suggest that unorthodox sequencing may yield both better macroeconomic results and broader political support for the program.

The Role of Inflation: Creative Destruction in the Transitional Model

As analyzed at length in earlier chapters, macroeconomic instability at times played (if our interpretation of events is correct) a positive role during the transitional phase by encouraging the growth of autonomous transactions and relatively autonomous capital accumulation and thereby eroding the DRV model from within. The transitional model, which almost by necessity coexisted with high inflation--witness the many frustrated attempts at macro stabilization in 1981-88--thus helped to reduce the costs of shifting to a market economy. That is, the transitional model and inflationary pressures helped to reduce plan distortions and thus laid the foundations for the removal of the two-price system in 1989.

In a way, the gradualist approach toward price reform and state enterprise autonomy in business transactions also served the same purpose. Quite often, units within the state economy acquired extra inputs through deals with hard currency earners that enabled the import of needed goods, which fetched a high price on the Vietnamese free market. This pattern, more common in the South than in the North, led to the growth of highly profitable state trading companies, often provincially or city-based. But there also remained large areas of the southern economy integrated into the system of state subsidization through the allocation of cheap goods and cheap credit.

In this process of erosion of the DRV model, central government tended to be the loser. The state became increasingly confused in its objectives as line ministries and local authorities became more and more involved, through the state sector, in business activities. The weakness of central authority even in the face of de facto theft was thus part of the traditional model. At its roots were profit-seeking individuals in the state and collective sectors trying to squeeze more subsidized resources out of central government (which meant, in the final analysis, out offoreign donors). A possibly large but unknown share of the subsidies channeled through the system "trickled up" to individuals at higher levels of authority in the form of side payments, as gifts and bribes of various kinds.

The eroding discipline caused shirking, corruption, and secondary occupations to spread throughout the public sector. The appallingly low real wages for public employees encouraged "outside" activities; few public servants were able to make a living during the transitional model without resorting to all kinds of outside activities, which often absorbed the lion's share of state employees' working time.

This process, discussed earlier, greatly undermined the efficiency (and the moral authority and credibility) of central government. In financial terms, it also undermined its solvency. Instead of being able to accumulate capital by absorbing an investable surplus from the rest of the economy--a characteristic of several centrally planned economies in the past--the state became a large dissaver. The virtual elimination of Soviet assistance in 1990-1991 can be seen as the final blow to central government in its old role. The state was no longer able to distribute subsidized resources to the rest of the economy. The shift to an accumulatory role produced public debate that increasingly focused upon market-oriented growth. This gave the state an opportunity to strengthen itself. It was forced to withdraw further from a wide range of expensive activities-- including the bailing out of a number of state enterprises--and in order to become stronger, the range of state activities had to be reduced. Or, rather: the state had to do fewer things than before but do them better. This involved a process of recentralization of political authority in order to support decentralized economic decisionmaking.

These comments should in no way be interpreted as a neoliberal plea for the "withering away of the state" or as a defense of corruption. Thus, whereas inflation, eroding central authority, and even corruption may have been "creatively destructive" during the transitional phase, the same phenomena are today merely destructive.

A strong and competent state is needed; this is one of many lessons to be drawn from the rapidly industrializing neighboring countries and, indeed, from well-established industrialized countries as well. The transitional phase in Vietnam was therefore dangerous: Unable to finance and carry out its old functions, the Vietnamese state might have degenerated into a repressive, predatory, and useless state, stripped of resources to carry out its traditional welfare functions, however minimal, and unable to guarantee macroeconomic stability and other core functions of a state in a market economy. The dual process of a weakening of the state and of markets has been witnessed in many low-income countries and in some of the former Soviet republics, where the erosion of state authority has been accompanied by a takeover of key sectors of the economy by organized crime rather than by textbook entrepreneurs.

Whether by free will or simple necessity, it can, in hindsight, be argued that the Vietnamese leadership opted for a strategic withdrawal of the state from many areas in order to save the state (and themselves) from impending disaster. Had they continued to attempt to defend the old system, this line of thought suggests that there would have been a complete collapse and radical political reformation, perhaps along democratic lines, perhaps not. The preannounced cessation of Soviet economic assistance in 1990-91 almost certainly facilitated this strategic decision. Or, perhaps, the aid cut made it necessary. Another remarkable feature of the Vietnamese reform process (a process however, that is far from unique) is been the fact that policy reforms have been implemented most daringly when unfavorable external events have come to support-- unintentionally--the spontaneous process of reform from below.

The Role of Aid Cuts

As has been shown in preceding chapters, economic reform in Vietnam was initiated after the invasion of Cambodia and the cessation of Chinese and most Western aid in 1979-80. It accelerated in 1989-90, when the Soviet aid cuts were being announced. On both occasions, economic growth also accelerated.

To judge from several indicators, domestic resource mobilization responded quite successfully to these two substantial reductions in foreign aid. According to official data, accumulation as a share of national product increased rapidly in 1979-81 (see Figure 8.1), and private domestic savings have, as previously noted, increased dramatically since 1989, although accurate data are nonexistent.

As for the state budget, similar episodes have been frequent. In 1994, the Vietnamese authorities once again showed their ability to impose the needed discipline upon taxpayers and state expenditure. In a rapid response to a considerable shortfall in expected ODA, the government stopped disbursements to many state capital projects. It also called for across-the-board spending cuts and renewed its efforts to increase tax revenues, which were by now rising in real terms at rates approaching 50 per cent annually.

Events in 1994 and earlier thus reveal the capacity of the central authorities to impose treasury controls when they need to and to keep the fiscal deficit within bounds. This capacity did not exist during the transitional phase in 1986-88, partly as a result of the erosion of state financial control indicated above, but possibly also as a result of the very large volumes of Soviet aid received during this period.

The comments made above should not be interpreted as an argument against foreign aid in general. However, the Vietnamese experience does indicate that the hardening of the external budget constraint--that is, reductions in foreign aid--that has taken place on two major occasions may have had positive effects both on the pace of economic reform and, what is perhaps more surprising, on macroeconomic developments in general. Domestic production actually increased when aid was reduced. Conversely, it appears as if foreign aid to Vietnam in 1976-79 and in 1985-88--although perhaps useful from a humanitarian point of view-- actually served to bail out a number of loss-generating activities, delay economic reform, and reduce domestic resource mobilization and fiscal discipline.

Against this background, the timing of Vietnam's long-overdue resumption of normal relations with the Bretton Woods institutions and with a number of Western donors and creditors in the mid-1990s may actually have been quite fortunate. The Vietnamese economy suffered, of course, from its isolation from Western trading partners. The greatest suffering was, however, imposed upon it by the DRV model itself, which was politically and economically supported by aid from the USSR. As analyzed at length earlier, the economic isolation of Vietnam was more the result of the logic of the DRV model than of unfavorable external factors. It is thus questionable whether large amounts of aid and trade in the mid-1980s would have been able to elicit much productive response or improve the lot of the ordinary Vietnamese.

In our view, the Vietnamese case supports the argument that increased aid to undergird policy reform is most useful when based on past performance rather than on promises of future performance, as is often the case with IFI-sponsored structural adjustment programs (we are not, of course, talking about humanitarian aid or about ordinary project aid, which may, or may not, be highly useful even in countries with inadequate policies). If Vietnam had been granted, say, US$300 million in loans and grants from the IFIs in 1989 and large amounts of balance of payments support from bilateral donors, the subsequent pace of economic reform would probably have suffered. The fact that until recently Vietnam remained ineligible for IFI lending and conditionality has perhaps also contributed to making the reform process more authentically Vietnamese. *Doi moi* is--for very good reasons--perceived by the population at large as a Vietnamese process, a product of the interaction of spontaneous forces from below and decrees and resolutions from above. The reforms have never been regarded as a policy package imposed from the outside.

During a later stage of the reform process, Vietnamese authorities started to benefit from macroeconomic advice and technical assistance from a number of bilateral and multilateral agencies, including the IMF and the World Bank. We know that this advice has been highly appreciated in Vietnam, and we are convinced that it has been useful. However, we are also inclined to believe that the fact that *doi moi* developed in a genuinely Vietnamese context, as an adaptive process based on trial and error rather than on ready-made blueprints, has enhanced both the effectiveness and the domestic credibility of the reforms. Furthermore, we believe that the Vietnamese economy was in a much better position by 1995 than it had been five or ten years before to absorb foreign aid and loans in a useful way.

Given the pattern of growth discussed above, with periods of accelerated growth following upon an acceleration of the reform process, a legitimate question arises: It took the Vietnamese a decade to shift from the DRV model to a market economy, but could this shift have taken, say, only five years, if political circumstances had been different? And could hardship and transitional costs have been reduced, if the reforms has been carried out more rapidly?

We have no good answers to these questions. We have an impression that the answer is yes. Given the long tradition of a market economy that existed in the South before national reunification, we are inclined to believe that the prolonged process of dismantling the DRV model could have been achieved in much less than ten years. In a historical perspective, the DRV model merely represents a short parenthesis--in particular in the South, where it was only implemented for a few years. Certain deregulations--for example, of domestic retail trade--could and should have been undertaken at an earlier stage, in order to accelerate the erosion of central planning.

However, it is also our conviction that regional imbalances and other tensions would have been exacerbated if, perhaps a big-bang set of policy measures had been implemented in 1981 or 1982 instead of 1989. Also, as has been discussed at length in preceding chapters, the prolonged "learning process" had a number of positive effects that, in our view, make it legitimate to argue that in a long-term perspective, the gradualist approach in Vietnam--which was not chosen from a textbook but was simply the outcome of a number of complex social, economic, political, and even international events that took place in the 1980s--was preferable to any attempt at "shock therapy" at an early stage of the reform process.

Concluding Concerns

Our answer to the question whether *doi moi* has been successful is decidedly affirmative. Unless unexpected external events endanger peace and economic cooperation in Southeast Asia, we see no reason why Vietnam should not become a new "Asian tiger"--on a bicycle only for the time being.

In terms of macro stabilization, results by 1995 were truly impressive. Just a few years before, large macroeconomic imbalances appeared to threaten the process of economic reform by eroding the credibility of *doi moi*. The crisis never assumed the proportions of that of today's Russian Republic, but it was serious enough to endanger the continuation of liberalization and decentralization.

By 1995, however, the situation appeared to be under control. All three gaps discussed in earlier chapters--the savings-investment gap, the fiscal deficit, and the external gap--had shown clear signs of improvement. Compared to the situation in a large number of Third World countries implementing a structural reform program, the macroeconomic situation in Vietnam was manageable even in the short run in the sense that no imbalance was serious enough to constitute a binding constraint on continued economic growth. The most remarkable feature was the surge of private savings and investment.

The experience of a large number of countries suggests that the transition from macro stabilization to accumulation and growth is the most difficult part of any reform process, as it requires much more than reduced deficits: The process demands confidence, credible property rights, positive expectations, and a host of other intangible factors that together constitute a good savings and investment climate. "Stability" would be too strong a description of the macroeconomic situation in Vietnam in 1995; in fact, it could perhaps best be characterized by its "dynamic instability." And, again in sharp contrast with, for example, the contemporary Russian Republic, in Vietnam there is no major disequilibrium threatening to become serious enough to endanger the process of economic reform. A concern for the future, however, is that the great achievements of the early 1990s could lead to a certain complacency. To judge from past experience in Vietnam, successful policies often lead to temporary setbacks, whereas crises make the process accelerate.

The most serious issue in the Vietnamese transition was not a conventional macroeconomic imbalance, but rather the skills and institutional gaps. The institutional legacy of the central-planning period was a serious handicap that would take many years to overcome. Thus, most of the "software" needed for a well-functioning market economy was still in exceedingly short supply, with one exception: There was no shortage of entrepreneurial spirit.

The very success of economic developments also created problems. The peasants, one pillar of the early reform process, got the land they wanted but were complaining loudly about the low prices of food and were asking for state intervention, that is, for protection. In a similar way, sectors competing for exports and imports were suffering badly from the achievements registered on the external account, which made the dong appreciate vis-a-vis major Western currencies after 1991. There was an obvious danger that Vietnam, when the international isolation of the country had been broken, would be loved too much by foreign donors, creditors, and investors; the state's budget constraint would be softened, and too much capital inflow would jeopardize the international competitiveness of the Vietnamese economy.

The future exchange rate development was therefore a source of concern. One lesson from the successful Asian countries is that exchange rate policies play a key role in supporting an outward-oriented development strategy; indeed, an almost aggressive policy of currency undervaluation appears to have been pursued by countries such as South Korea and Taiwan during the early phases of export promotion. Too large an inflow of foreign aid and loans in combination with a rapid growth of petrodollars could easily put upward pressure on Vietnam's real rate of exchange, thereby eroding the international competitiveness just when it would be most badly needed.

As for the prospects for a continuation and deepening of the reform process, there were several questions of an essentially political nature in 1995, as some of the major driving forces behind the early reform process found themselves in a state of relative complacency. In the state enterprise sector, both managers and trade unions were comparatively happy with the situation, which gave them both a high degree of autonomy to do business and some state protection if they failed. Although the state enterprise managers and employees had been a powerful constituency behind the process of commercialization of the state sector, they were not as enthusiastic about possible future steps: a further hardening of the budget constraint, more competition, less corruption, the threat of bankruptcy, and privatization.

By the mid 1990s, apparently, the Communist Party leadership was also largely content with the situation as it was. *Doi moi* had met with widespread political support both domestically and internationally. The groups within the state and the Communist Party that had pushed hard for economic reforms during the early years thus appeared to have reached most of their objectives. The fact that the *nomenklatura,* which had enjoyed rents and priveliges of various kinds, had much to lose from an elimination of remaining distortions also weakened the forces pushing for political reform. Thus, while foreign donors and creditors could continue to ask for multiparty elections, accountability, and transparency--to use a few key phrases currently in vogue in the international debate about political conditionality--there was, in Vietnam, a strong domestic coalition that had good reason to fear the loss of its privileges. These groups could be expected to continue to use as their models the examples offered by other East Asian countries, including China, which combined political authoritarianism with rapid economic growth.

Still, social groups in favor of political liberalization were clearly emerging in the mid 1990s. However, any attempt to assess the strength and prospects of such forces goes beyond the scope of this study and, certainly, beyond the competence of its authors.

Notes

1. Compare the view here, in which accumulation is mainly based upon retained earnings, with that of Greenfield (1993) who focuses far more upon the state as a midwife of emerging capitalism in Vietnam. The basic problem with that argument is that the resources available to the state were far too limited, given the other pressures on the regime to ensure its survival, not least of which was the fear of inflation.

References

ADUKI. 1995. Poverty in Vietnam. Report for Swedish International Development Authority. Stockholm.

Allen, Susan. 1990. *Women in Vietnam*. Stockholm: Swedish International Development Authority.

_____. 1993. "Health: The Current Situation and Recent Changes," in Carlyle Thayer and David Marr, eds., *Vietnam and the Rule of Law*. Canberra: Australian National University.

_____. 1994. Supporting the Local Health Provider: Chaos and Change in Vietnam's Primary Health Care System. Unpublished paper.

Amnesty International. 1990. *Vietnam: Renovation (doi moi), the Law and Human Rights in the 1980s*. London: Amnesty International.

Amsden, Alice, et al. 1994. *The Market Meets Its Match*. Harvard: Harvard University Press.

Appleton, Judith. 1985. District Debate in Vietnam 1970-80: Towards Decentralisation. B.A. thesis, University of East Anglia.

Arkadie, Brian Van. 1993. "Managing the Renewal Process: The Case of Vietnam." *Public Administration and Development*, vol. 13, no. 4.

Arkadie, Brian Van, and Vu Tat Boi. 1992. "Managing the Renewal Process: The Case of Vietnam." London: Overseas Development Institute. Mimeo, 4 January 1992.

Asian Development Bank. 1989. "Economic Report on the Socialist Republic of Vietnam." Manila: Asian Development Bank (October).

Aslund, Anders. 1989 and 1991b (updated and expanded). *Gorbachev's Struggle for Economic Reform: The Soviet Reform Process, 1985-88*. Ithaca, N.Y.: Cornell University Press.

Aslund, Anders, ed. 1991a. *The Post-Soviet Economy: Soviet and Western Perspectives*. London: Pinter.

BCNCT 5202 (Ban chu nhiem chuong trinh 5202: The 5202 Committee). 1986. *Viet nam: Nhung van de ve tai nguyen va moi truong* (Vietnam: Problems of natural resources and environment). Hanoi: NXB Nong Nghiep.

Bennet, J., and H. Dixon. 1993. Macroeconomic Equilibrium and Reform in a Transitional Economy. CEPR discussion paper, no. 758, Centre for Economic Policy Research, London.

Beresford, Melanie. 1985. "Household and Collective in Vietnamese Agriculture." *Journal of Contemporary Asia*, no 1.

_____. 1987. "Issues in Economic Reunification: Overcoming the Legacy of Separation. Vietnam: Northernising the South or Southernising the North?" *Contemporary Southeast Asia* vol.8, no.3.

_____. 1988. *Vietnam: Politics, Economics, and Society*. London: Pinter.

_____. 1989. *National Unification and Economic Development in Vietnam*. London: Macmillan.

_____. 1990. The Impact of Economic Reforms on the South. Paper presented at Doi Moi conference, Australian National University, September.

_____. 1994. Impact of Macro-economic Reform on Women in Vietnam. Draft Report for UNIFEM, Hanoi.

Beresford, Melanie, and Bruce McFarlane. 1995. "Regional Inequality and Regionalism in Vietnam and China." *Journal of Contemporary Asia*, vol. 25 no. 1.

Blagov, S., et al. 1988. "Taking Account of Mistakes for the Future." *TASS*, translated in Foreign Broadcast Information Service, 29 March.

Bogatova, Ye., and M. Trigubenko. 1987. "The 6th CPV Congress on the Strategy of Vietnam's Socio-economic Development." *Far Eastern Affairs*, no. 3. Moscow.

Brummitt, William E., and Justin N. Winton. 1993. "Prospects for Growth in Vietnam." *Agricultural and Resources Quarterly* vol. 5, no. 3 (September).

Brundenius, Claus, et al. 1987. "Technology Transfer to Vietnam: Some Issues at Stake, an Interim Report." Research Policy Institute, University of Lund, Sweden.

Carlton, Dennis W. 1990. *Modern Industrial Organization*. Glenview, Ill.: Scott, Foresman.

CACMD (Central Agricultural Cooperative Management Department). 1982. *Khoan san pham trong cac hop tac xa va tap doan san xuat nong nghiep (nhung cau hoi va tra loi)* (Output contracts with cooperatives and agricultural production collectives [questions and answers]). Hanoi: NXB Su That.

Chambers, Robert. 1991. *Phat trien nong thon-hay bat dau tu nhung nguoi cung kho* (translation of Rural development: Putting the last first). Hanoi: NXB Dai Hoc va Giao Duc Chuyen Nghiep.

Chambers, Robert, and Adam Fforde. 1989. "Opportunities and Priorities for Development Cooperation in Vinh Phu, Hoang Lien Son, and Ha Tuyen Provinces." Vietnam: Swedish International Development Authority.

Chanda, Nayan. 1986. *Brother Enemy: The War After the War.* New York: Collier Books/Macmillan Publishing Company.

Chu Van Lam, ed. 1992. *Hop tac hoa nong nghiep Viet Nam: lich su--van de--trien vong* (Vietnamese agricultural cooperation: History--problems--hopes). Hanoi: NXB Su that.

CIEM (Central Institute for Economic Management Research--Vien nghien cuu quan ly kinh te). 1978. *To chuc san xuat va to chuc bo may quan ly xi nghiep cong nghiep quoc doanh* (Organization of production and the management apparatus of industrial state enterprises). Hanoi: NXB Su That.

CM (Council of Ministers). 1976 (3 August 1976), Decree 134. "Ve viec to chuc lai san xuat, tang cuong va cai tien mot buoc quan ly, phat huy hon nua tac dung cua tieu cong nghiep, thu cong nghiep nham phat trien kinh te va phuc vu doi song nhan dan" (On the reorganization of production and the strengthening and improving of management at a step, and the better realization of the capacity of small and artisanal industry in order to develop the economy and serve the people's living standards). Hanoi: *Cong Bao.*

_____. 1980a. "Nhung dieu can biet ve chinh sach khuyen khich san xuat hang xuat khau (Nhung diem chu yeu cua qui dinh cua HDCP)" (What you need to know about policies to stimulate production of exports [Main points of the CM Res]). *Nhan Dan* 26 and 28 February 1980.

_____.1980b (1 October 1980), Decree 312. "Ve tang cuong quan ly thi truong" (On reinforcing management of markets). *Nhan Dan* 27 October 1980.

_____. 1981 (21 January 1981), Decree 25. "Mot so chu truong va bien phap nham tiep tuc phat huy quyen chu dong san xuat--kinh doanh va quyen tu chu ve tai chinh cua cac xi nghiep quoc doanh" (A number of policies aimed at a continuing development of the production and trading rights, as well as the right to financial autonomy, of state enterprises). Hanoi.

_____. 1985 (15 June 1985), Decree 177. "Ve chinh sach, bien phap day manh xuat khau va tang cuong quan ly xuat nhap khau" (On policies and measures to stimulate exports and strengthen the management of foreign trade). Hanoi.

_____. 1986 (26 June 1986), Decree 76. "Viec ban hanh cac ban quy dinh tam thoi ve bao dam quyen tu chu san xuat, kinh doanh cua cac don vi kinh te co so" (On promulgating temporary regulations guaranteeing the autonomy in production and trade of base economic units). Hanoi.

_____. 1987 (14 November 1987). "Ban hanh cac chinh sach doi moi ke hoach hoa va hach toan kinh doanh xa hoi chu nghia doi voi cac xi nghiep quoc doanh" (On promulgating policies for renovating the planning, economic accounting and socialist business of state enterprises). Hanoi.

_____. 1988a (9 March 1988). "Ve chinh sach doi voi kinh te ca the, tu doanh san xuat cong nghiep, dich vu cong nghiep, xay dung, van tai" (On policies toward the individual economy, private industrial production and business, industrial services, construction, and transport). *Nhan Dan*, 22 March 1988, Hanoi.

_____. 1988b (9 March 1988). "Ve chinh sach doi voi kinh te gia dinh trong hoat dong san xuat va dich vu san xuat" (On policies towards the family economy in production activities and activities serving production). *Nhan Dan*, 17 March 1988.

_____. 1988c. "Dieu le xi nghiep cong nghiep quoc doanh" (Statute for state industrial enterprises). Mimeo, 22 March 1988, Hanoi.

_____. 1989a (3 March 1989). Decree 43. "Bo ty gia ket toan noi bo" (Abolishing the internal exchange rate). *Cong Bao*, 15 March 1989.

_____. 1989b (31 May 1989). (150-CT). "Xoa bo viec doi phan lay lua ve thuong mai hoa luong thuc, phan bon" (Abolishing the exchange of fertilizer for rice in order to commercialize staples and fertilizer trade). Unpublished.

_____. 1989c. (2 or 14 December 1989), Decree 195. "Ban hanh nhung quyet dinh bo sung 217 HDBT" (Promulgating resolutions changing Decision 217) (not published in *Cong Bao*). Hanoi, 14 December 1989, or 2 December 1989.

_____. 1989d. (24 April 1989), Decree 44. "Ve viec thu mot phan hoc phi trong nganh giao duc pho thong" (On charging for partial cost recovery in general schools). *Cong Bao*, 15 May 1989.

_____.1989e. (24 April 1989), Decree 45. "Ve viec thu mot phan vien phi y te" (On recovery of a part of medical hospital fees). Hanoi.

_____. 1991. Decree 22. "Quy dinh che do thu ve su dung von ngan sach Nha nuoc" (Regulations for the receipt and use of State budgetary capital). Hanoi.

_____. 1992. (9 March 1992), Decree 84. "Quy che bao ve bi mat nha nuoc" (Promulgating the regulations on protecting national secrets). Mimeo.

Coase, R. H. 1988. *The Firm, the Market, and the Law*. Chicago: University of Chicago Press.

Committee for Rational Utilisation of Natural Resources and Environment Protection with Assistance from the International Union for Conservation of Nature and Natural Resources. 1985. *Vietnam. National Conservation Strategy*. New Delhi: mimeo.

CPV (Communist Party Vietnam). 1978. *Mot so van kien cua Dang va chinh phu ve phat trien tieu cong nghiep va thu cong nghiep* (Some party and government documents on the development of light and artisanal industry). Hanoi: NXB Su That.

_____. 1979a. "Tang cuong xay dung dang trong hop tac xa tieu cong nghiep va thu cong nghiep" (Strengthen party construction in artisanal and light industrial cooperatives). Hanoi: NXB Su That.

_____. 1979b, Decison 6. "Phuong huong, nhiem vu phat trien cong nghiep tieu dung va cong nghiep dia phuong" (Directions, duties in the development of consumer goods industry, and regional industry). *Nhan Dan* 6 October 1979.

_____. 1979c, Decision 6 of the Central Committee (IV). *Ve phuong huong nhiem vu phat trien cong nghiep hang tieu dung va cong nghiep dia phuong* (On the directions and duties of developing consumer and regional industry). Hanoi: NXB Su That.

_____. 1980. *Mot so van kien cua trung uong dang ve phat trien cong nghiep* (Some documents of the party center on industrial development). Hanoi: NXB Su That.

_____. 1981a (13 January 1981), Order no. 100. "Cai tien cong tac khoan, mo rong khoan san pham den nhom nguoi lao dong va nguoi lao dong trong hop tac xa nong nghiep" (Reform contract work, expand the use of output contracts with groups of workers and individual workers in agricultural cooperatives). Pamphlet, Hanoi.

_____. 1981b (13 January 1981), Order no. 100. "Cai tien cong tac khoan, mo rong khoan san pham den nhom nguoi lao dong va nguoi lao dong trong hop tac xa nong nghiep" (Reform contract work, expand the use of output contracts with groups of workers and individual workers in agricultural cooperatives). *Nhan Dan*, 20 January 1981.

_____. 1984 (18 January 1984), Order no. 35. "Ve su can thiet day manh kinh te gia dinh" (On the need to encourage and develop the family economy). Hanoi.

_____. 1986. "Draft Resolution on State Enterprises' Economic Rights, 8/4/86." *Nhan Dan* 25 April 1986

_____. 1987a. *Dai hoi VI--Nhung phuong huong co ban cua chinh sach kinh te* (The Sixth Party Congress--Basic directions in economic policy). Hanoi: NXB Su That.

_____. 1987b. "Thong bao cua Hoi nghi lan thu 4 BCHTW Dang Ve phuong huong, nhiem vu phat trien kinh te--xa hoi trong ba nam 1988-1990 va nam 1988" (Report of the Fourth Plenum of the Central Committee on the direction and duties for socioeconomic development in 1988-80 and 1988). *Nhan Dan*, 20 December 1987.

_____. 1988. "Nghi quyet bo chinh tri ve doi moi quan ly kinh te nong nghiep" (Decision of the Politburo on the Reform of agricultural economic management). *Nhan Dan*, 12 April 1988.

Crosnier, Marie-Agnes, and Edith Lhomel. 1987. "Vietnam: Les mecomptes d'un socialisme asiatique." *Le courier de pays de l'est*, no. 320 (July-August). Paris.

_____. 1990. A first assessment of Vietnam's economic reforms. CEDUCEE: Paris, 1990.

CS (*Communist Studies*). 1988a. "Ve phuong huong, nhiem vu phat trien kinh te--xa hoi trong ba nam 1988-90 va nam 1988" (Report on the Fourth Plenum of the Sixth Central Committee on the direction and tasks of socioeconomic development during the three years 1988-90 and in 1988). *Tap Chi Cong San* (Communist Studies), no. 1. Hanoi.

———. 1988b. "Nhung tu tuong chi dao lon cua ke hoach phat trien kinh te, xa hoi 5 nam 1986-1990 va nam 1988" (Main directions of the Five-Year Socioeconomic Development Plan for 1986-90 and for 1988). *Tap Chi Cong San* (Communist Studies), no. 2. Hanoi.

Dace, Douglas C. 1986. *Foreign Aid, War, and Economic Development South Vietnam, 1955-1975.* Cambridge: Cambridge University Press.

Dam Van Nhue, and Le Si Thiep. 1981. "Ket hop loi ich cua tap the nguoi lao dong trong cong nghiep dia phuong" (Amalgamating the collective interests of the workers in regional industry). *Nghien Cuu Kinh Te (NCKT)* (Economic Research), vol. 5, no. 10.

Dang Nguyen Anh. 1989. *Work and Family Planning in Two Rural Communities in Vietnam.* Hanoi: Institute of Sociology, December.

Dao Cong Hieu. 1987. "Bao dam quyen tu chu san xuat kinh doanh cua cac don vi kinh te co so" (Ensuring the right to autonomy in production and business of economic base units). *Cong Nghiep Nhe* (Light Industry), no. 2.

Dao Duy Tung et al. 1982. *Ban ve cac loi ich kinh te* (Discussion of economic interests). Hanoi: NXB Su That.

Dao Xuan Sam. 1986. "Kinh doanh xa hoi chu nghia va quyen tu chu cua nguoi kinh doanh" (Socialist business and the right to autonomy of economic/business units. *Nhan Dan* 18 March 1986.

———. 1989. *May nhan thuc ve nen kinh te moi o nuoc ta* (Some observations on our new economy). Ho Chi Minh City: NXB T/P Ho Chi Minh.

———. 1982. "Van de loi ich kinh te trong thuc tien quan ly kinh te hien nay" (The problem of economic interests in the reality of economic management today). *Nghien Cuu Kinh Te* (Economic Research), *vol.* 128, no. 8.

Dao Xuan Sam et al. 1986. *Doi moi tu duy kinh te* (Reforming economic thinking). Ho Chi Minh City: NXB T/P Ho Chi Minh.

Dao Van Tap. 1980. "Quan doi nhan dan ve nhiem vu xay dung kinh te" (The People's Army and the task of economic construction). *Nghien Cuu Kinh Te* (Economic Research), *vol.* 6, no. 12.

Dapice, David. "Viet Nam at the starting point : Just another East Asian Economy?," in Borje Ljunggren, ed., 1993b, *The Challenge of Reform in Indochina.* Cambridge: Harvard Institute for International Development.

Davies, R. W. 1980. *The Industrialisation of Soviet Russia.* London: Macmillan.

de Vylder, Stefan. 1984. *Vietnam: A Country Report* (in Swedish). Stockholm: Swedish International Development Authority (SIDA).

_____. 1987. *Import Support to Tanzania: The Macro-economic Framework and Medium-term Prospects.* Stockholm: SIDA.

_____. 1988. "Biases and Distortions in Socialist Economic Polices: Some Lessons from the Third World," in R. Garcia, ed., *Central America: Crisis and Possibilities.* Stockholm: Institute of Latin American Studies.

_____. 1990. "Vietnam - Toward a market economy ? The current state of economic reform in Vietnam." Stockholm School of Economics (November).

_____. 1993. "Vietnam - State and Market." Stockholm School of Economics (July).

de Vylder, Stefan, and Adam Fforde. 1988. *Vietnam: An Economy in Transition.* Stockholm: SIDA.

Desbarats, J. 1987. "Population Redistribution in Vietnam." *Population and Development Review,* March.

Diaz-Alejandro, Carlos. 1986. "Good-bye Financial Repression, Hello Financial Crash." *Journal of Development Economics,* (September).

Diehl, Markus. 1993. "Stabilization Without Crisis: The Case of Vietnam." *Kiel Working Paper,* no. 578. Kiel: Kiel Institute of World Economics, May 1993.

Dinh Thu Cuc. 1977. "Qua trinh tung buoc cung co va hoan thien quan he san xuat xa hoi chu nghia trong cac hop tac xa san xuat nong nghiep o mien bac nuoc ta" (The process of step-by-step reinforcement and improvement of socialist production relations in the agricultural producer cooperatives of the north of our country). *Nghien Cuu Lich Su* (Historical Research), no. 175.

Dollar, David. 1993. "Vietnam: Successes and Failures of Macroeconomic Stabilization," in Borje Ljunggren, ed., 1993b, *The Challenge of Reform in Indochina.* Cambridge: Harvard Institute for International Development.

_____. 1994. "Macroeconomic Management and the Transition to the Market in Vietnam." *Journal of Comparative Economics,* vol. 18, no. 3 (June).

Drabek, Zdenek. 1990. "A Case Study of a Gradual Approach to Economic Reform: The Vietnam Experience of 1985-88." *World Bank Internal DP Asia Regional Series,* IDP, vol. 74 (September).

Ducos, P. et al. 1991. "Une maquette de l'economie vietnamienne de 1980 a 1988." *Revue economique, vol.* 42, no. 1 (January).

Edlund, Lena. 1991. "Market Fragmentation and Rural Industrialisation in China." Stockholm School of Economics. Mimeo.

Ellman, Michael. 1979. *Socialist Planning.* Cambridge: Cambridge University Press.

FAO (Food and Agriculture Organisation). 1990. *Vietnam: Agriculture and Food Production Sector Review.* Rome: FAO.

_____. 1993. "An Agriculture-led Strategy for the Economic Transformation of Vietnam: Policy and Project Priorities." Hanoi: State Planning Committee and Food and Agriculture Organisation of the UN.

Fforde, Adam. 1982. "Problems of Agricultural Development in North Vietnam." PhD. thesis, Faculty of Politics and Economics, Cambridge University.

_____. 1983. "The Historical Background to Agricultural Collectivisation in North Vietnam: the Changing Role of 'Corporate' Economic Power." *Birkbeck College Department of Economics Discussion Paper,* no. 148. London: Birkbeck.

_____. 1985. "Economic Aspects of Soviet-Vietnamese Relations: Their Role and Importance," in Robert Cassen, ed., *Soviet Interests in the Third World.* London: Sage.

_____. 1986. "Unimplementability of Policy and the Notion of Law in Vietnamese Communist Thought." *Southeast Asian Journal of Social Science,* no 1.

_____. 1987a. "Vietnam Fails to Make Reform Programmes Stick." *Far Eastern Economic Review,* 17 September 1987. Hong Kong.

_____. 1987b. "Vietnam: Historical Background and Macro Analysis," in Rita Liljestrom et al., *Forestry Workers In Vietnam, A Study on the Working and Living Conditions.* Stockholm: Swedish International Development Authority.

_____. 1989a. *The Agrarian Question in North Vietnam 1974-79--A Study of Cooperator Resistance to State Policy.* New York: M. E. Sharpe.

_____. 1989b. Papers prepared while at the Bai Bang Forestry Project. Stockholm: InterForest A.B. Mimeo.

_____. 1989c. Paper analysing the activities of the Bai Bang Mill, in Fforde, 1989b.

_____. 1990a. "9 bai hoc doc dao rut ra tu 10 nam cai cach kinh te o Viet nam" (Nine lessons from a decade of economic reform in Vietnam). *International Relations,* Hanoi.

_____. 1990b. "The Successful Commercialisation of a Neo-Stalinist Economic System--Vietnam 1979-89; with a Postscript," in Forbes et al., eds., *Doi Moi: Vietnam's Renovation Policy and Performance.* Canberra: ANU.

_____. 1992. The Institutions of Transition from Central Planning--The Case of Vietnam. Seminar paper, Department of Economics, Research School of Pacific Studies, Australian National University, Canberra.

_____. 1993. "The Political Economy of "Reform" in Vietnam: Some Reflections," in Borje Ljunggren, ed., 1993b, *The Challenge of Reform in Indochina.* Cambridge: Harvard Institute for International Development.

_____. (ongoing). Dragon's Tooth or Curate's Egg? Vietnamese State Industrial Reform.

Fforde, Adam, and Rita Liljestrom. 1987. "Voluntariness and Force in Labour," Part 3 *Forestry Workers in Vietnam, A Study on the Working and Living Conditions.* in Liljestrom, Rita, et al., Stockholm: Swedish International Development Authority.

Fforde, Adam, and Suzanne Paine. 1987. *The Limits of National Liberation: Problems of Economic Management in the Democratic Republic of Vietnam.* London: Croom-Helm.

Fforde, Adam, and Steve Seneque. 1993. The Economy and the Countryside: The Importance of Rural Development Policy. Paper presented at Vietnam Update, ANU Canberra.

_____. 1995. "The Economy and the Countryside," in Benedict Kerkvliet and Doug Porter, eds., *Rural transformation and Economic change in Vietnam,* Boulder: Westview Press and Singapore: ISEAS.

Fischer, Stanley. 1993. "Socialist Economy Reform: Lessons of the First Three Years." *American Economic Review,* May.

Fong, Monica S. 1994. Gender and Poverty in Vietnam. Discussion paper series, World Bank, Washington, November.

Forbes, D., Terence H. Hull, David G. Marr, and Brian Brogan, eds. 1991. *Doi Moi: Vietnam's Renovation Policy and Performance.* Canberra: Department of Political and Social Change, Research School of Pacific Studies, Australian National University.

Franklin, Barbara. 1993. *The Risk of AIDS in Vietnam.* CARE International in Vietnam, Mono Series no. 1. Hanoi.

Freeman, Nick J. 1994. "Vietnam and China: Foreign Direct Investment Parallels." *Communist Economies and Economic Transformation,* vol. 6, no. 1.

Funck, Bernard. 1993. "Laos: Decentralization and Economic Control," in Borje Ljunggren, ed., 1993b, *The Challenge of Reform in Indochina.* Cambridge: Harvard Institute for International Development.

Cornia, Giovanni A. 1994. "Income Distribution, Poverty and Welfare in Transitional Economies: A Comparison between Eastern Europe and China." *Journal of International Development,* vol. 6, No. 5, (September-October).

Gordon, Robert. 1990. "What Is New-Keynesian Economics?" *Journal of Economic Literature,* (September).

Gotz-Kazierkiewwicz, Danuta, and Grzegorz W. Kolodko. 1990. Stabilisation in Vietnam. Warsaw. Mimeo.

Grady, Heather. 1993. *A Glimpse into Poverty in Vietnam.* Vietnam: ActionAid.

_____. 1994. Access to Services by the Poor in Vietnam. Presentation to the UN-NGO Forum meeting with the World Bank, Hanoi. Oxfam UK/I.

Greenfield, Gerard. 1993. "The Emergence of Capitalism in Vietnam." *Socialist Register.*

Grosfeld, Irena. 1990. "Reform Opportunities and Western Economic Theory: Unexploited Opportunities." *Economics of Planning*, vol. 23, no. 1.

Hare, Paul G. 1990. "From Central planning to market Economy : Some Microeconomic issues." *The Economic Journal*, no. 100 (June).

Hiebert, Murray. 1988. "Reforming Pains." *Far Eastern Economic Review*, 17 March. Hong Kong.

_____. 1990a. "Thanh Huong Perfume Co. Scandal." *Far Eastern Economic Review*, 26 April. Hong Kong.

_____. 1990b. "Vietnam Takes Action to End Financial Crisis." *Far Eastern Economic Review*, 1 November. Hong Kong.

Hoang Cam. 1984. "Quyen chu dong cua co so duoc thuc hien nhu the nao?" (How will the base's right to be active be realized?). *Nhan Dan* 2 March 1984

Hoang Lien. 1980. "Khu pho Hoan Kiem (trung tam Ha Noi) dang ky kinh doanh cong, thuong nghiep" (Hoan Kiem (Hanoi center) carries out business registration in trade and commerce). *Nhan Dan*, 6 November 1980.

Hoang Luu. 1980a. "Bao dam cac dieu kien vat chat de phat trien san xuat hang xuat khau" (Guaranteeing material conditions for development of export production). *Nhan Dan*, 5 June 1980.

_____. 1980b. "Gan san xuat trong nuoc voi thi truong nuoc ngoai" (Allying domestic production with the foreign market). *Nhan Dan* 12 June1980.

Hong Ha et al. 1980. *Hoi nghi khoa hoc nghien cuu Nghi quyet hoi nghi lan thu 6 Ban chap hanh trung uong Dang (Khoa IV)* (Scientific conference to research the Sixth Plenum of the Fourth Central Committee). Hanoi: N.p.

Hy Van Luong. 1992. *Revolution in the Village: Tradition and Transformation in North Vietnam, 1925-1988.* Honolulu: University of Hawaii Press.

IEAS (Institute of East Asian Studies). 1987. *Indochina Chronology.* University of California, Berkeley, no. 4.

IMF (International Monetary Fund). 1987. "Vietnam: Recent Economic Developments." Washington D. C. Mimeo.

IPM (Institute of Prices and Markets). 1990. "Cai cach trong nen cong nghiep Viet-nam 1979-89 (Kinh te quoc doanh)" (Reform in Vietnamese industry 1979-89 [state economy]. Hanoi. Mimeo.

Jamieson, Neil L. 1993. *Understanding Vietnam.* Berkeley: University of California.

Jeffries, Ian. 1993. *Socialist economies and the transition to the market: a guide.* New York and London: Routledge.

Kaser, Michael. 1990. "The Technology of Decontrol: Some Macroeconomic Issues." *Economic Journal,* (June).

Kimura, Tetsusaburo. 1986. "Vietnam--Ten Years of Economic Struggle." *Asian Survey.*

_____. 1989. *The Vietnamese Economy 1975-86--Reforms and International Relations.* Tokyo: Institute of Developing Economies.

Kleinen, John. 1982. "Roots of the Sino-Vietnamese conflict." *Monthly Review,* no. 5 (October).

_____. 1994. The Transformation of Rural Social Organization in Northern Vietnam and the Debate on the Asian Village. Paper prepared for the Annual Meeting of the Association for Asian Studies, Boston, 24 March.

Knight, P. T. 1983. "Economic Reform in Socialist Countries--the Experiences of China, Hungary, Romania and Yugoslavia." *World Bank Staff Working Paper,* no. 579, World Bank, Washington D.C.

Kolko, Gabriel. 1995. "Vietnam since 1975 : Winning a War and Losing the Peace." *Journal of Contemporary Asia,* vol. 25, no. 1.

Kolodko, G. 1990. Hyperinflation and Stabilisation in Post-Socialist Economies: The Case of Poland, Vietnam and Yugoslavia. Paper presented at the First Conference of the European Association for Comparative Economic Studies, Verona.

Kolodko, G., D. Gotz-Kozierkiewicz, and E. Skrzeszewska-Paczek. 1992. "Hyperinflation and Stabilisation in Post-Socialist Economies." *International Studies in Economics and Econometrics,* vol. 26. Norwell Mass and Dordrecht: Kluwer Academic.

Kornai, Janos. 1980. *The Economics of Shortage.* North-Holland.

_____. 1982. *Growth, Shortage, and Efficiency.* Oxford: Blackwell.

_____. 1985. "Comments on Papers Prepared in the World Bank about Socialist Countries." *CPD Discussion Paper,* no. 1985-10, World Bank, Washington D.C.

_____. 1992. *The Socialist System--The Political Economy of Communism.* Princeton: Princeton University Press.

Le Duan. 1978. *Mot so van de co ban ve cong nghiep hoa xa hoi chu nghia* (Basic problems of socialist industrialization). Hanoi: NXB Su That.

Le Khac Thanh. 1985. "Cai to phuong thuc hoat dong cua ngan hang--mot yeu cau buc thiet" (Reform of the banking system--a pressing necessity). *Nhan Dan Dien Dan Kinh Te* (People's Economic Forum), 14 November 1985.

Le Kim Que, and Nguyen Le Huong. 1987. *Tim hieu phap luat ve thua ke* (Understanding the law on inheritance). Hanoi: Nha xuat ban phap ly (Legal Publishing House).

Le Thanh Khoi. 1981. *Histoire de Vietnam des origines a 1858.* Paris: Sudestasie

Le Thanh Nghi. 1977a. *Tu tuong chi dao ke hoach 5 nam 1976-80* (The thinking behind the 1976-80 Five Year Plan). Hanoi: NXB Su That.

_____. 1977b. *Thong nhat quan ly va cai tien quan ly kinh te trong ca nuoc, xay dung he thong quan ly kinh te xa hoi chu nghia cua nuoc ta* (United management and improvement of the management of the economy in our country, construction of our country's system of socialist economic management). Hanoi: NXB Su That.

_____. 1977c. *Quan triet va thi hanh dieu le xi nghiep cong nghiep quoc doanh* (Understand and implement the State Industrial Enterprise Statute). Hanoi: NXB Su That.

_____. 1979. *Xay dung huyen thanh don vi kinh te nong cong nghiep* (Building the district into an agricultural-industrial unit). Hanoi: NXB Su That.

_____. 1981. *Cai tien Cong tac khoan mo rong khoan san pham de thuc day san xuat cung co hop tac xa nong nghiep* (Reform contract work, expand the use of output contracts in order to stimulate output and strengthen agricultural cooperatives). Hanoi: NXB Su That.

Le Thi. 1992. *Impact of the Vietnamese state's new socio-economic policies on the life of rural women and their families at present, General report on the results of study of Thai Hoa village.* Hanoi: Center for Women Studies.

Le Trang, and Duong Bach Lien. 1983. *Tim hieu quyet dinh 25 CP va quyet dinh 146 HDBT sua doi, bo sung quyet dinh 25 CP* (Understanding Res. 25 CP and Res. 156 HDBT changing and supplementing 25 CP). Hanoi: NXB Su That.

Le Van Toan et al. 1991. *Nhung van de kinh te va doi song qua ba cuoc dieu tra Nong nghiep, Cong nghiep and Nha o* (Economic and living standards issues as seen through three surveys of agriculture, industry, and housing.) Hanoi: NXB Thong Ke.

Le Van Triet, Luu Bich Ho, and To Xuan Dan. 1991. "A Policy for Expanding Foreign Trade and Attracting Foreign Capital Investment in Vietnam," in Per Ronnas and Orjan Sjoberg, eds., *Socio-economic Development in Vietnam: The Agenda for the 1990s.* Stockholm: SIDA.

Le Xuan Tung. 1985. *Cong nghiep hoa xa hoi chu nghia trong chang duong dau tien cua thoi ky qua do* (Socialist industrialization during the first stage of transition). Hanoi: NXB Su That.

Leipziger, D. M. 1992. *Awakening the Market: Vietnam's Economic Transition.* Washington, D.C.: World Bank.

Lichtenstein, Natalie G. 1994. *A Survey of Vietnam's Legal Framework in Transition.* Policy Research Working Paper, Washington D.C.: World Bank (April).

Liljestrom, Rita et al. 1987. *Forestry Workers in Vietnam, A Study on the Working and Living Conditions.* Stockholm: Swedish International Development Authority.

Lipworth, Gabrielle and Spitaller, Erich. 1993. "Vietnam - Reform and Stabilization 1986-1992." Washington D.C.: International Monetary Fund (May).

Ljunggren, Borje. 1991. "Market Economies Under Communist Regimes: Reform in Vietnam, Laos, and Cambodia." *HIID Development Discussion Paper* no.394, August 1991.

_____. 1993a. "Market Economies Under Communist Regimes: Reform in Vietnam, Laos and Cambodia," in Borje Ljunggren, ed., 1993b, *The Challenge of Reform in Indochina.* Cambridge: Harvard Institute for International Development.

Ljunggren, Borje, ed. 1993b. *The Challenge of Reform in Indochina.* Cambridge: Harvard Institute for International Development.

Lockhart, Greg. 1989. *Nation in Arms: The Origins of the People's Army of Vietnam.* Sydney: Asian Studies Association of Australia.

Mai Huong. 1987. "Khong chi co ca phe" (There is not just coffee), in *Ca phe Viet nam* (Vietnamese Coffee). Hanoi: Union of Vietnamese Coffee Enterprises.

Mai Huu Khue, ed. N.d. *Mot so van de ve to chuc san xuat va quan ly kinh te o huyen* (Some problems in the organization of production and economic management of the district). Hanoi: NXB Khoa Hoc Xa Hoi.

Malinvaud, Edmond. 1972. *Lectures on microeconomic theory.* Trans. by A. Silvey. Amsterdam: North-Holland.

Mallon, Raymond. 1992 (?). N.d.. "Restructuring socialist enterprise : Viet Nam." mimeo.

_____. 1993. "Restructuring Socialist Enterprise: Vietnam" in Heath, John, ed., *Revitalizing Socialist Enterprise: A Race Against Time.* London and New York: Routledge.

Marr, David G. 1971. *Vietnamese Anticolonialism, 1885-1925.* Berkeley: University of California Press.

_____. 1981. *Vietnamese Tradition on Trial 1920-1945.* Berkeley: University of California Press.

McKinnon, Ronald I. 1991. *The Order of Economic Liberalization: Financial Control in the Transition to a Market Economy.* Baltimore: Johns Hopkins.

Milgrom, Paul, and John Roberts. 1992. *Economics, Organization, and Management.* Englewood Cliffs: Prentice-Hall.

Ministry of Agriculture. 1981. "Huong dan viec thuc hien cai tien cong tac khoan trong cac hop tac xa san xuat nong nghiep" (Guiding implementation of the improvement of contract work in agricultural producer cooperatives). Circular Letter, no. 5, Ministry of Agriculture, Hanoi.

Ministry of Defense. 1985. Financial Management of Army Units. From the Third Army conference on this topic organized by the Ministry of National Defense, 20 September 1985. Broadcast, SWB 27 September 1985.

Ministry of Forestry. 1983. *Mot so chinh sach ve Lam nghiep* (A number of policies on forestry). Hanoi: NXB Nong Nghiep.

Ministry of Justice. 1985. *Phap luat ve quan ly thi truong tap I, II* (Laws on market management, vols. 1 and 2.) Hanoi: NXB Phap Ly.

Ministry of Labor. 1981. *Tim hieu chinh sach moi ve kinh te* (Understanding the new economic policy). Hanoi: NXB Lao Dong.

_____. 1990. "Ket qua dieu tra muc song va thu nhap--nhung van de co ban ve cai tien tien luong o Vietnam--luong toi thieu" (Results of a living standards and incomes survey--basic problems of wage reform in Vietnam--minimum wages). Hanoi.

NCKT (*Nghien Cuu Kinh Te*--Economic Research). 1981. "Hoi nghi khoa hoc ve Thi hanh cac quyet dinh 25 va 26 CP cua HDCP trong cac don vi cung ung vat tu" (Scientific Conference on Resolutions 25 and 26 CP of the Council of Ministers in material supply units). *Nghien Cuu Kinh Te*, vol. 4, no.122.

Ngo Ba Thanh. 1985. "Le droit a l'egalite des femmes a la lumiere du droit positif de la Republique Socialiste du Vietnam et dans les faits." *Bulletin de droit*, no. 1.

Nguyen Duc Nhuan. 1988. "Reformes desastreuses au Vietnam." *Le monde diplomatique*, (January).

Nguyen Duc Nhuan, and Vo Nhan Tri. 1987. *Le Viet nam post-revolutionaire--population, economie, societe*. Paris: Harmattan.

Nguyen Duy Trinh. 1980. *Ve hoi nghi 6* (On the Sixth Plenum). *Nhan Dan*, 19 January 1980.

Nguyen Huu Dong.1981. "6e plenum: Adaptations conjoncturelles ou reformes durables?" Essai sur la politique economique du socialisme, *Vietnam*, no. 2.

Nguyen Lam. 1980a. *Phat trien cong nghiep hang tieu dung va cong nghiep dia phuong* (*Develop consumer goods industry and regional industry*). Hanoi: NXB Su That.

_____. 1980b. "May van de ve tu tuong chinh sach kinh te hien nay." (Some current problems in thoughts about economic policy. *Tap Chi Cong San* (Communist Studies), *no*. 3.

Nguyen Manh Hung, and Cao Ngoc Thang. 1990. *Viet nam co mot nam nhu the!* (Vietnam--What a Year!). Hanoi: NXB Su That.

Nguyen Ngoc Truu, ed. 1991. *Kinh te xa hoi nong thon Viet nam ngay nay tap I* (The socio-economy of rural Vietnam today, vol. 1). Hanoi: NXB Su That.

Nguyen Nien. 1974a. "Quyen quan ly nghiep vu cua xi nghiep doi voi tai san nha nuoc trong tinh hinh cai tien quan ly xi nghiep cua ta hien nay" (The management rights of enterprises with regard to state assets during the current situation of enterprise reform). *Luat Hoc* (Legal Studies), no. 7.

_____. 1974b. "Quyen quan ly nghiep vu cua xi nghiep doi voi tai san luu dong va cac quy xi nghiep theo che do quan ly moi hien nay" (The management rights of enterprises with regard to liquid assets and enterprise funds in accordance with the current new system of management). *Luat Hoc* (Legal Studies), no. 8.

_____. 1985. "Xoa bo tap trung quan lieu--bao cap, tu goc nhin phap ly" (Abolishing centralized bureacractism and subsidy, from the legal aspect). *Luat Hoc* (Legal Studies), no. 4.

Nguyen Sinh Cuc. 1991. *Thuc trang nong nghiep, nong thon va nong dan Viet Nam 1976-1990* (The situation of agriculture, the countryside, and the peasantry in Vietnam, 1976-1990). Hanoi: NXB Thong Ke.

Nguyen Thanh Ha. 1987. *Vietnamese Adoption of Western Technology, 1802-1867.* Lund: Research Policy Institute, University of Lund.

Nguyen Thu Sa. 1991. "Ve nhan vat trung tam o nong thon nam bo: nguoi trung nong" (On the central character of the southern countryside: The middle peasant). *Tap Chi Khoa Hoc Xa Hoi So 9, Qui,* March 1991.

Nguyen Tri. 1972. *Ve to chuc san xuat trong cong nghiep mien bac nuoc ta* (On the organization of industrial production in the north of our country). Hanoi: NXB Dai Hoc va Trung Hoc Chuyen Nghiep

Nguyen Van Linh. 1986. Den tham co so "Binh Minh" (Visiting "Binh Minh" factory). 26 October 1986. Photocopy.

_____. 1987. *Bai phat bieu cua D/C Tong B/T Nguyen van Linh khai mac hoi nghi lan thu 4 cua BCHTW Dang* (Speech of Comrade General Secretary Nguyen van Linh at the opening of the Fourth Plenum of the CPV Central Committee). *Nhan Dan* 20 December 1987.

_____. 1988. "Bai phat bieu cua dong chi tong bi thu Nguyen van Linh (tai Hoi nghi lan thu tu BCHTUD (Khoa VI)" (Speech of Comrade General Secretary Nguyen van Linh at the Fourth Plenum of the Sixth Central Committee). *Tap Chi Cong San* (Communist Studies), no. 1. Hanoi.

Nguyen Van Tiem, ed. 1993. *Giau ngheo trong nong thon hien nay* (Rich and poor in the countryside today). Hanoi: NXB Nong Nghiep.

Nguyen Van Van, and Le Chi Mai, eds. N.d. *Kinh doanh xa hoi chu nghia--mot so van de ly luan* (Socialist business--some theoretical problems). Hanoi: NXB Su That (Truth Publishing House).

NhD (Nhan Dan). 1982a. In series, "Nhung su kien Dang ghi nho--25 NQTW 1/4/80." "Ve mot so chu truong, bien phap day manh san xuat, huy dong phan phoi, tieu dung va quan ly luong thuc" (Party events--Res. 25, 1 April 1980 "On a number of policies and measures to stimulate production, mobilize distribution, consumption, and management of staples). *Nhan Dan,* 23 March 1982.

_____. 1988. "Dieu tra (Investigation), Bon nguyen nhan that thu thue cong thuong nghiep" (Four reasons for the loss of revenue from the industry-trade tax). Hanoi.

Norlund, Irene. 1984. "The Role of Industry in Vietnam's Development Strategy," in *Journal of Contemporary Asia,* no. 1.

_____. 1987. "The French Empire, the Colonial State in Vietnam, and the Economic Policy 1885-1940." *Nordic Institute of Asian Studies,* (April).

_____. 1988a. Women in Socialist Reform Policy. Vietnamese Textile Workers. University of Copenhagen, September. Mimeo.

_____. 1988b. "Textile production in Vietnam and the Philippines. The development of the textile sector and woman labour 1970-1985." *Nordic Institute of Asian Studies,* (September).

_____. 1989. "Women in Socialist Reform Policy--Vietnamese Textile Workers" in Mikael Gravers et al, eds., *Southeast Asia Between Autocracy and Democracy.* Copenhagen: Aarhus University Press.

_____. 1994. "Transforming Asian Socialism Enterprise Systems and Factory Life in Northern and Southern Vietnam." *Nordic Institute of Asian Studies,* (October).

NSKDGN (Nhung Su Kien Dang Ghi Nho) (Party events worth noting). 1982. *NQTW* no.26, 23 June 1980 "Ve cai tien cong tac phan phoi, luu thong, gom cac van de tai chinh, tien te, gia ca, tien luong thuong nghiep va quan ly thi truong" (Central Committee Res. no. 26, 23 June 1980: On the reform of distribution and circulation, including problems relating to finance, money, prices, wages, trade, and market management). *Nhan Dan,* 24 March 1982.

Perkins, Dwight. 1993. "Reforming the economic systems of Vietnam and Laos," in Borje Ljunggren, ed., 1993b, *The Challenge of Reform in Indochina.* Cambridge: Harvard Institute for International Development.

Perkins, Dwight, ed. 1994. *Viet Nam Cai Cach Kinh te Theo Huong Rong Bay* (Vietnam--Economic Reform on the Trail of the Dragon). Hanoi: Harvard Institute for International Development and NXB Chinh Tri Quoc Gia.

Persson, Hans. 1987. Appraisal Study: Rehabilitation of the Tablet Production Department of Pharmaceutical Factory No.1 in Hanoi. Helsingborg, Sweden.

Pham Huu Huy, and Nguyen Anh Hoang. N.d. "Nhung dieu bo doi can biet ve kinh te va quan ly kinh te" (What troopers have to know about economics and economic management). Hanoi: NXB Quan Doi Nhan Dan.

Phan Hien. 1987. "Some Views on Renovating Legal Work." *Nhan Dan,* 29 June 1987.

Phan Van Tiem. 1990. *Chang duong 10 nam cai cach gia 1981-1991 quoc doanh* (The ten-year road to state price reform, 1981-1991). Hanoi: NXB Thong Tin.

Pike, Douglas. 1986. *PAVN: People's Army of Vietnam.* London: Brassey's.

Pingali, Prabhu L., and Vo Tong Xuan. 1992. "Vietnam: Decollectivization and Rice Productivity Growth." *Economic Development and Cultural Change*, vol. 40, no. 4 (July).

Polanyi, Karl. 1945. *The Great Transformation*. New York: Rinehart.

Porter, Gareth. 1990. "The politics of 'renovation' in Vietnam." *Problems of Communism*, May-June.

_____. 1993. *The Politics of Bureaucratic Socialism*. Ithaca: Cornell University Press.

'PV'. 1986. "Report on the all-army production and economic building conference." *Quan Doi Nhan Dan* 29 January 1986, in *Summary of World Broadcasts* (BBC) 27 February 1986.

QDND (Quan Doi Nhan Dan). 1987. "Lessons Drawn from the Trial of the Case of Smuggling at the Haiphong Military Command," *QDND* 9 September 1987, in *Foreign Broadcast Information Service* 17 September 1987.

Riedel, James. 1993. "Vietnam : On the Trail of the Tigers." *World Economy*, vol.16, no. 4 (July).

Ronnas, Per. 1992. *Employment Generation Through Private Entrepreneurship in Vietnam*. New Delhi: ILO, Stockholm: SIDA.

Ronnas, Per, and Orjan Sjoberg, eds. 1990a. *Doi moi--Economic Reform and Development Policies in Vietnam*. Stockholm: SIDA.

_____. 1990b. *Economic Reform in Vietnam: Dismantling the Centrally Planned Economy*. Stockholm: SIDA.

_____. 1991. *Socio-economic Development in Vietnam: The Agenda for the 1990s*. Stockholm: SIDA.

Sachs, Jeffrey. 1992. "Building a Market Economy in Poland." *Scientific American,* (March).

Sachs, Jeffrey, and Wing Thye Woo. 1994. "Experiences in the Transition to a Market Economy," *Journal of Comparative Economics*, no. 18.

Scott, James. C. 1976. *The Moral Economy of the Peasant--Rebellion and Subsistence in Southeast Asia*. New Haven/London: Yale University Press.

Skarner, Goran. 1988. Forestry Bibliography Vinh Phu Pulp and Paper Mill Project. Stockholm: Interforest AB.

Smith, R. B. 1968. *Viet-Nam and the West*. London: Heinemann.

_____. 1983. *An International History of the Vietnam War. Vol. 1. Revolution Versus Containment, 1955-61*. London: Macmillan.

_____. 1985. *An International History of the Vietnam War. Vol. 2. The Struggle for South-east Asia, 1961-65*. London: Macmillan

Spoor, Max. 1985. The Economy of North Vietnam--The First Ten Years: 1955-1964 (A Study of Economic Policy and Performance of Socialism in the Third World). M. Phil. thesis, Institute of Social Studies, The Hague.

_____. 1988. "Reforming State Finance in post-1975 Vietnam." *Journal of Development Studies*, vol. 24, no. 4 (July).

State Planning Commission/General Statistical Office. 1993. *Vietnam Living Standards Survey 1992.* Hanoi: General Statistical Office.

SO (Statistical Office) (Tong cuc thong ke). 1978. *Tinh hinh phat trien kinh te va xa hoi mien bac xa hoi chu nghia Viet nam 1960-7* (The economic and cultural development of socialist North Vietnam 1960-75). Hanoi: Nha Xuat Ban Thong Ke (Statistical Publishing House).

_____. 1981. *Nien giam thong ke 1980* (Statistical yearbook 1980). Hanoi: NXB Thong Ke.

_____. 1983a. *Nien giam thong ke 1982* (Statistical yearbook 1982). Hanoi: NXB Thong Ke.

_____. 1983b. *So lieu thong ke 1982* (Statistical materials 1982). Hanoi: NXB Thong Ke.

_____. 1985a. *Nien giam thong ke 1984* (Statistical yearbook 1984). Hanoi: NXB Thong Ke.

_____. 1985b. *So lieu thong ke 1930-1984* (Statistical materials 1930-1984). Hanoi: NXB Thong Ke.

_____. 1985c. *So lieu thong ke 1983* (Statistical materials 1983). Hanoi: NXB Thong Ke.

_____. 1987. *Nien giam thong ke 1985* (Statistical yearbook 1985). Hanoi: Tong Cuc Thong Ke--TCKT (Statistical Office).

_____. 1988a. *Nien giam thong ke 1986* (Statistical yearbook 1986). Hanoi: TCTK.

_____. 1988b. Statistical materials, handwritten.

_____. 1989. *Nien giam thong ke 1987* (Statistical yearbook 1987). Hanoi: TCTK.

_____. 1990a. *Con so va Su kien 1945-1989* (Numbers and dates, 1945-90). Hanoi: NXB Thong Ke.

_____. 1990b. *Tap chi thong ke. Thuc trang kinh te xa hoi Viet nan. Giai doan 1986-1990* (Social and economic conditions in Vietnam during 1986-90). Hanoi: NXB Thong Ke.

_____. 1990c. *Nien giam thong ke 1988* (Statistical yearbook 1988). Hanoi: TCTK.

_____. 1991a. *So lieu thong ke 1976-1990* (Statistical materials 1976-1990). Hanoi: NXB Thong Ke.

_____. 1991b. *Kinh te va Tai chinh Viet nam* (Economy and finance of Vietnam). Hanoi: NXB Thong Ke.

_____. 1991c. *Nien giam thong ke 1989* (Statistical yearbook 1989). Hanoi: TCTK

_____. 1991d. *So lieu thong ke nong nghiep 35 nam* (Agricultural data for thirty-five years). Hanoi: TCTK.

_____. 1992. *Nien giam thong ke 1990* (Statistical yearbook 1990). Hanoi: TCTK

_____. 1993. *Nien giam thong ke 1992* (Statistical yearbook 1992). Hanoi: TCTK.

_____. 1994a. *Nien giam thong ke 1993* (Statistical yearbook 1993). Hanoi: TCTK.

_____. 1994b. *Du Thao--Trich Bao Cao Thong Ke Khao Sat Muc Song Dan Cu Viet Nam 1992- 1993* (Draft--Statistical abstract Vietnam living standards survey 1992-1993). Hanoi: Ke Hoach Nha Nuoc (State Planning Commission)/TCTK.

_____. 1994c. *So lieu thong ke nong, lam ngu nghiep Viet nam* (Statistical data on Vietnamese agriculture, forestry, and fisheries). Hanoi: TCTK.

_____. 1995. *Nien giam thong ke 1994* (Statistical yearbook 1994). Hanoi: TCTK.

Statistical Office Ho Chi Minh City (Cuc thong ke Thanh pho Ho Chi Minh). 1994. *Nien giam thong ke 1994* (Statistical yearbook 1994). Ho Chi Minh City: CTKTPHCM.

SIPRI (Stockholm International Peace Research Institute). 1987-88. Yearboooks. Stockholm: SIPRI.

Tan Leng Lang. 1985. *Economic Debates in Vietnam-Issues and Problems in Reconstruction and Development (1975-84)*. Singapore: ISEAS.

Taylor, Lance. 1994. "The Market Met Its Match: Lessons for the Future from the Transition's Initial Years." *Journal of Comparative Economics*, no. 19.

Thayer, Carlyle. 1984. "Vietnamese Perspectives on International Security: Three Revolutionary Currents," in Donald H. McMillen, ed., *Asian Perspectives on International Security*. London: Macmillan Press.

_____. 1988. "The Regularization of Politics: Continuity and Change in the Party's Central Committee, 1951-1986," in David G. Marr and Christine P. White, eds., *Postwar Vietnam: Dilemmas in Socialist Development*. Ithaca: Southeast Asia Program, Cornell University

_____. 1992. "Political Reform in Vietnam: Doi Moi and the Emergence of Civil Society," in Robert F. Miller, ed., *The Developments of Civil Society in Communist Systems*. Sydney: Allen and Unwin.

_____. 1993a. "Recent Political Developments: Constitutional Change and the 1992 Elections," in Carlyle Thayer and David Marr, eds., *Vietnam and the Rule of Law*. Canberra: Austrlaain National University.

_____. 1993b. "Political Reform in Vietnam," *Current Affairs Bulletin*, June.

_____. 1995. "Mono-Organisational Socialism and The Vietnamese State," in Ben Kerkvliet and Doug Porter, eds., *Rural Transformation and Economic Change in Vietnam*. Boulder: Westview Press and Singapore: Institute of Southeast Asian Studies.

Selden, Mark, and William S. Turley, eds. 1993. *Reinventing Vietnamese Socialism: doi moi in Comparative Perspective*. Boulder: Westview Press.

Thayer, Carlyle, and David Marr, eds. 1993. *Vietnam and the Rule of Law.* Political and Social Change Monograph no. 19, Department of Political and Social Change, Research School of Pacific Studies, Australian National University, Canberra.

The Dat. 1981. *Nen Nong nghiep Viet Nam tu sau Cach mang thang tam nam 1945* (Vietnamese agriculture since the August Revolution). Hanoi: NXB Nong Nghiep.

Thien Nhan. 1983. *Dau tranh chong te quan lieu* (The struggle against bureaucratism). Hanoi: NXB Su That.

To Huu. 1985. *Xoa bo quan lieu bao cap giai quyet mot so van de cap bach ve gia-luong-tien* (Abolishing bureaucracy and subsidy, solving pressing problems in prices-wages-money). Hanoi: NXB Su That.

Tran Duc Nguyen. 1988. *Mot so quan diem kinh te cua Dai hoi VI* (Some economic points of view of the Sixth Congress). Hanoi: NXB Su That.

Tran Phuong (Tran Anh). 1979. *Nong nghiep Bun-ga-ri tu san xuat nho len san xuat lon xa hoi chu nghia* (Bulgarian agriculture shifts from small-scale production to large-scale socialist production). Hanoi: NXB Su That.

_____. 1966-67. "Ban ve buoc di cua cong nghiep hoa" (Discussion of the steps of industrialization). *Nghien Cuu Kinh Te* vols. 36, 37, and 39.

Tran Phuong ed. 1968. *Cach mang ruong dat o Viet-nam* (The land revolution in Vietnam) Hanoi: NXB Khoa Hoc Xa Hoi.

Truong Chinh. 1986. Speech at Handicraft Exhibition, 9/6/86.   *Joint Publications Research Service,* 20 June 1986.

Turley, William S. 1993. "Political renovation in Vietnam: Renewal and Adaptation," in Borje Ljunggren, ed., 1993b, *The Challenge of Reform in Indochina.* Cambridge: Harvard Institute for International Development.

UNDP (United Nations Development Program) Vietnam. 1994. *Vietnam: Technical Assistance in Transition.* Hanoi: UNDP.

UNDP. 1987. "Preparatory Mission on Pharmaceutical Industry in Vietnam." Hanoi.

_____. 1990. *Report on the Economy of Vietnam.* Hanoi: UNDP.

UNDP/SPC. 1994. *Report on Income, Savings, and Credit for 1994 in Vietnam.* Hanoi.

UNFPA (United Nations Fund for Population Activities). N.d. *Programme Review and Strategy Development Report--Viet Nam.* New York: UNFPA.

UNICEF (United Nations International Childrens Emergency Fund). 1987. Outline Strategy for Socialist Republic of Vietnam/UNICEF Programme (1988-1991). Hanoi. Mimeo.

Utting, Peter. 1992. *Economic reform and third-world socialism: a political economy of food policy in post-revolutionary societies.* New York: St.Martin's Press.

Van Brabant, Jozef M. 1990. "Reforming a Socialist Developing Country: The Case of Vietnam." *Economics of Planning* vol. 23 no.3.

Van Dac. 1983. "Nhung quan diem co ban cua mot so chinh sach kinh te lon hien nay--Q 25 CP va 146 HDBT ve cai tien cong tac quan ly xi nghiep quoc doanh" (Basic points of view on a number of major economic policies of the moment--Res. 25 CP and 146 HDBT on the reform of SOE management). *Tuyen Truyen* (Propaganda), vol.8, (September).

Vogel, Ulrich. 1987. The Whole of Vietnam Can Be Considered as One Well-designed Project-- Some Reflections on Primary Health Care Experiences in Vietnam. M.Sc. diss., Swansea, University of Wales.

Vo Nhan Tri, and Anne Booth. 1992. "Recent Economic Developments in Vietnam." *Asian Pacific Economic Literature* vol. 6, no. 1 (May).

Vo Nhan Tri. 1967. *Croissance economique de la Republique Democratique du Vietnam 1945-65.* Hanoi: Foreign Languages Publishing House.

_____. 1985. "Vietnam--The Third Five Year Plan 1981-85--Performance and Limits." *Indochina Report*, no. 4 (October-December). Singapore

_____. 1990. *Vietnamese Economic Policy Since 1975.* Singapore: Institute of Southeast Asian Studies.

Vo Van Kiet. 1987. "Economic Report to National Assembly," in BBC Summary of World Broadcasts, 15 January 1988.

Vu Oanh. 1986. *Mat tran nong nghiep--thanh tuu va kinh nghiem moi* (The agricultural front-- successes and new experiences). Hanoi: NXB Su That.

Vu Tuan Anh. 1974. "Qui mo hop ly cua doi san xuat trong cac hop tac xa trong lua dong bang" (The rational size of production brigades in delta rice-growing cooperatives). *Nghien Cuu Kinh Te* vol. 81.

_____. 1985. "Thu phan tich nen tai san xuat xa hoi ta duoi goc do co cau nganh kinh te" (An attempt at an analysis of social production from the viewpoint of economic structure). *Nghien Cuu Kinh Te,* vol. 2.

Wade, Robert. 1990. *Governing the Market: Economic Theory and the Role of Government in East Asian Industrialization.* Princeton: Princeton University Press.

Wadekin, Karl-Eugene. 1973. *The Private Sector in Soviet Agriculture.* Berkeley: University of California Press.

White, Christine P. 1985. "Agricultural planning, pricing policy and cooperatives in Vietnam." *World Development*, no. 1 (January).

Wiegersma, Nancy. 1988. *Vietnam Peasant Land, Peasant Revolution--Patriarchy and Collectivity in the Rural Economy.* London: Macmillan.

_____. 1991. "Peasant patriarchy and the Subversion of the Collective in Vietnam." *Review of Radical Political Economics* vol. 23, nos. 3-4 (fall-winter).

Wiles, Peter. 1977. *Economic Institutions Compared.* Oxford: Oxford University Press.

Williamson, O. E., and Sydney G. Winter. 1991. *The Nature of the Firm: Origins, Evolution, and Development.* New York: Oxford University Press.

Wood, Adrian. 1989. "Deceleration of Inflation with Acceleration of Price Reform: Vietnam's Remarkable Recent Experience." *Cambridge Journal of Economics* vol. 13 (December).

Woodside, Alexander B. 1971. *Vietnam and the Chinese Model.* Canbridge: Harvard University Press.

_____. 1976. *Community and Revolution in Modern Vietnam.* Boston: Houghton Mifflin.

_____. 1989. "Peasants and the State in the Aftermath of the Vietnamese Revolution." *Journal of Peasant Studies,* Summer.

World Bank. 1987. *World Development Report 1987.* Oxford: Oxford University Press.

_____. 1990. "Vietnam: Agriculture and Food Production Sector Review." Draft report.

_____. 1991. *Vietnam. Transforming a State Owned Financial System. A Financial Sector Review of Vietnam.* Washington, D.C., April.

_____. 1992. "Vietnam: Restructuring Public Finance and Public Enterprises. An economic report." Washington, D.C., no. 10134-VN, April.

_____. 1993a. *The East Asian Miracle: Economic Growth and Public Policy.* New York: Oxford University Press.

_____. 1993b. *Vietnam--Transition to the Market.* Country Department Division, Country Department 1, East Asia and Pacific Region.

_____. 1994a. *Vietnam: Poverty Assessment and Strategy.* World Bank, September.

_____. 1994b. *Vietnam--Financial Sector Review--An Agenda For Financial Sector Development.* Report no. 13135-VN, East Asia and Pacific Region, July 20.

_____. 1994c. "Vietnam: Public Sector Management and Private Sector Incentives." An Economic Report. Washington D.C. no. 13143-VN, June.

_____. 1995a. *Vietnam: Poverty Assessment and Strategy.* World Bank, Country Operations Division.

_____. 1995b. *Viet Nam - Economic Report on Industrialization and Industrial Policy.* Country Operations Division 2.

Yong, Cao. 1992. Chinese Iron and Steel Industry in Transition Toward Market Mechanism and Economic efficiency. Ph.D. thesis, National Centre for Development Studies, Australian National University.

About the Book and Authors

This clear and accessible text explores Vietnam's successful transition from neo-Stalinist central planning to a market economy—"Vietnamese style." After describing the north Vietnamese system prior to 1975 and its colonial and pre-colonial antecedents, the authors uncover the mechanisms of that changeover. They contend that the Vietnamese transition was largely bottom-up in character and that it evolved over a long enough period for the country's political economy to adjust. This explains in part the rapid shift to a high-growth, externally oriented development path in the early 1990s, despite the loss of Soviet aid and the lack of significant Western substitutes until 1992–1993. Based upon extensive in-country experience, a wealth of primary materials, and wide comparative knowledge of development issues, the book challenges many preconceived notions, both about Vietnam and about the general nature of transition processes.

Adam Fforde is a visiting fellow at the Research School of Pacific and Asian Studies, Australian National University, and a chief investigator of the Australian-Vietnam Research Project. **Stefan de Vylder** is an independent consultant and an associate professor at the Stockholm School of Economics. One of Sweden's leading applied development economists, he has acted as a consultant in many developing countries. His recent research has included work on the debt crisis, problems of economic transition, and the macroeconomics of foreign aid.

Index